Self and Community in a Changing World

Self and Community in a Changing World

D. A. Masolo

Indiana University Press
Bloomington and Indianapolis

This book is a publication of
Indiana University Press
601 North Morton Street
Bloomington, Indiana 47404-3797 USA

www.iupress.indiana.edu

Telephone orders: 800-842-6796
Fax orders: 812-855-7931
Orders by e-mail: iuporder@indiana.edu

The paper used in this publication meets the minimum requirements
of the American National Standard for Information
Sciences—Permanence of Paper for Printed Library Materials,
ANSI Z39.48-1992.

Manufactured in the United States of America

Library of Congress Cataloging-in-Publication Data

Masolo, D. A.
Self and community in a changing world / D.A. Masolo.
p. cm.
Includes bibliographical references (p.   ) and index.
ISBN 978-0-253-35481-5 (cloth : alk. paper) — ISBN 978-0-253-22202-2
(pbk. : alk. paper) 1. Philosophical anthropology—Africa, Sub-Saharan.
2. Communitarianism—Africa, Sub-Saharan. I. Title.
B5378.P45M37 2010
126—dc22

2010000088

1 2 3 4 5 15 14 13 12 11 10

To Elisha Stephen Atieno-Odhiambo, that giant of a mind and friend who kept us always on our toes, challenging us to show that we are always relevant to the communities we traverse in our multiple capacities. Thank you for extending those broad wings over me and my family through the years, even during the darkest academic and political times of our country. May your spark, extinguished too soon, forever remain the measure of what we should strive to be.

Nyuol ne okonyo omboga (It is the quantity that makes spinach a vegetable meal)

Ng'eng' ji e teko (Human ability is shown collectively)

—Luo proverbs

Contents

Acknowledgments

My recognition and debts of gratitude go to all those people without whose help I would not have been able to write this book. My loving friend and wife Christine and our children Leiz and Marvin have always been incredibly patient and unfailingly supportive. Never to be forgotten is J.-P., who, despite the fact that she is not here like the rest of us, will always remain a powerful source of strength. The support of these people makes home a comfortable place to live and work. To my dear sister-in-law and friend, Jane Odhiambo, for her friendship and for all the stories and discussions we have shared that have brought to life many things discussed in this book. To my Senior Sponsoring Editor at Indiana University Press, Ms. Dee Mortensen, for her insights and always-on-the-mark advice over the years. She is the reason the book is what it is. To the wonderful anonymous readers whose constructive criticisms and suggestions helped me revise the manuscript into its final form. The shortcomings that remain are entirely my own. Then there is the copyeditor, Ms. Kate Babbitt, the person whose hands on the scalpel, so to speak, have literally molded this book into its current form. I could not be more grateful for her superb job, especially in frequently pulling me back from my excesses and wanderings into unclear or unnecessary realms. To Ms. Korina Stephens in the Department of Classical and Modern Languages at the University of Louisville for her help with the reading and translation from German of Husserl's correspondence. To the University of Louisville, especially to my colleagues and students in the Philosophy Department, for their support, which is always appreciated.

Self and Community
in a Changing World

Introduction

At the beginning of a writing project, every writer faces several questions, including these: What, if anything, would be the significance, both general and specific, of the project—in this case, of writing a book on philosophical themes? And more precisely, what would be the significance of writing a book on themes in African philosophy? And what are such themes? It can be argued that except in some isolated cases, African philosophy has already made its way and claimed its spot on the floor of the trade's open market. Yet like any product whose performance depends on variable factors of specific market conditions, such as the sociopolitical or cultural flexibility and openness of its envisaged consumers, African philosophy has fared differently in different locations, and the specifics of its presentation in those locations have reflected local conditions, including formalistic packaging styles that the peddlers of the product have had to take into account or respond to. There are, for example, noticeable differences in both the style and the preferred subjects of discussion among, say, African, African-American, and Western Africanist philosophers who practice their trade and publish their work in North American or British institutions and their comrades whose works have predominantly been published in continental Europe. As in the divided house of Western philosophy, Mudimbe and Appiah have observed in their essay "The Impact of African Studies on Philosophy," the practice of philosophy by Africans reveals the divide between the analytical brand inherited from the Anglo-American tradition and the one influenced by the tradition of continental European philosophy.[1] In Western philosophy, these two brands of doing philosophy are often regarded as irreconcilable. By contrast, however (and this too was already noted by Mudimbe and Appiah[2]), the African surrogate descendants of the analytical and continental subtraditions have learned to coexist and supplement each other. The collaboration between Mudimbe and Appiah—both African and both acclaimed representatives of the continental and analytical brands of scholarship, respectively—is an act that seeks to reconcile the West with itself through an African

1

manipulation and example. The reconciliation between the analytical and continental brands of scholarship and the co-existence of these two elements of the discipline may already be in place. The growing presence and influence of continental European philosophical thought and movements in the American and British academies (particularly the warm reception of social theory in the humanities) has resulted in the inclusion of African scholars of that intellectual background in the mix of growing continentalists. Among many others, a few examples come to mind. V. Y. Mudimbe's long tenure in positions where he has taught a variety of mixtures of French, Italian, and comparative literature at leading American universities is perhaps the best-known example. But so is Abiola Irele's tenure in comparative literature positions and, more recently, Jean-Godefroy Bidima's chair in French studies at Tulane University in New Orleans. Yet even with this continuous blurring of the divide between the analytical and continental brands and styles of philosophy among African thinkers, some matters still stand out as characterizing the separation of the two sides from each other. For instance, while today's discussions of the nature of mind include the rich legacy of Descartes, African philosophers of Anglophone extraction who address this metaphysical issue plow into the resources preferred by the analytical approach to the relevant issues, especially those offered by empirical research in cognitive science and psychology. Illustrative examples of this are Wiredu's views discussed later in this book and Appiah's positions and contributions to the debate.[3] To be sure, Descartes' texts don't have to lead only to metaphysics, much less to analytical metaphysics, as illustrated in the interests and concerns of today's metaphysicians of the mind. His method generates the equally influential positions and presuppositions in epistemology, logic, and mathematics that tend to dominate commentaries in French-language African philosophy. Recently, in his critical review of the second edition of Houndji's *African Philosophy: Myth and Reality,* Abiola Irele, the Nigerian-born literature scholar and literary critic who is arguably a philosopher in his own right,[4] has suggested that a different look at what has largely but falsely been dismissed in the name of "ethnophilosophy" should in fact include a critique of the Cartesian view of mind by way of taking Léopold S. Senghor's widely noted idea of an African way of knowing more seriously than some African philosophers have done.[5] I will get to that matter at the right time below as I point out its significance in locating Senghor's ideas of mind within the broader context of the critiques of Descartes' reason by French scholars at the time of Senghor's intellectual formation in France. The point is that French and French-speaking African writings and discussions on the nature of the mind are far less driven by the empiricist approaches that are visibly dominant in English (Anglo-American) and English-speaking Africa. Thus, for example, Paul Ricoeur's 1998 dialogue with neuroscientist Jean-Pierre Changeux[6] was a good and welcome discussion, yet it remains largely an isolated rarity. In the same vein, we can point to clearly distinct approaches to talking about mind between, on the one hand, Senghor and Hountondji, and, on the other, Wiredu and Appiah. And by extension, differences of style between the sets lead to separate foci on the nature of thought.

Then there is the factor of cultural integration that is taking place in the context of Western cultural transformation at the popular, professional, and academic levels. In North America especially, the growth in research on and teaching of African and African-American philosophy at institutions of different categorizations and classifications has nearly mainstreamed African and African-American philosophical reflections and writing, leading to their embrace and the dissemination of their texts by prominent publishers there or by their affiliates in northern Europe. This development contrasts sharply with the situation in Southern Europe, where the continued missionary grip on the convert's mind and preference for a European monologue continues to resist infiltration by African and, by extension, African-American philosophical texts into its academic syllabi. There, African philosophy continues to be regarded as an informal discourse that takes place only in undertones or around nighttime bonfires, away from the daytime and formal engagements of the academy. The fact that African philosophy titles have only recently broken through the long-established barriers to publication of African philosophical and related scholarship in France, United Kingdom, and Belgium, for example, indicates the degree of skepticism that continues to greet the idea of African or African-American philosophy in Southern Europe.[7] Two points of note in this list would be the efforts of young Italian philosophers such as Lidia Procesi and Marco Massoni and the interest the work of Fabien Eboussi-Boulaga appears to have initiated. At the same time, a powerful irony hangs over Rome with regard to its role (or lack thereof) in the furtherance of African philosophical knowledge. The ecclesiastical institutions there have played a significant role in enhancing and influencing the emergence of the competing traditions of knowledge of the African world produced by both missionary and missionized intellectuals. Committed to sustaining a relationship with the missionary world (which can only support and make possible the continuation of particular cultural expressions that draw from and remain in consonance with general Christian views and specific Catholic doctrines), Rome has been slow and perhaps unwilling to openly advocate for the growth and autonomy of postcolonial discourse. This ecclesiastical position, which perpetuates the view that African knowledge is dependent, lends a hand, perhaps only unknowingly but also conveniently ideologically, to the secular view in Southern Europe (and in Italy particularly) that Africa continues to lack the mediums of proper philosophical expression and discourse. This lag stands in sharp contrast to the pioneering work of such scholars as Alexis Kagame, Vincent

Mulago, and Fabien Eboussi-Boulaga, among many others, who were educated in Roman ecclesiastical institutions. Yet the scholarly works of these
and other Rome-formed Africans have mostly been produced elsewhere,
mainly in Belgium and more recently in Switzerland. There is no doubt
that in their works, which came at the height of Africa's quest for independence and autonomy, these African intellectuals presented positions
that helped push the Catholic establishment toward what V. Y. Mudimbe
has referred to as the political ambiguities of the missionary Church,
ambiguities that nonetheless are categorical about suppressing the expression of difference in the experience and interpretation of god and other
religious *événements*.[8]

If they are to improve or at least to sustain the presence and performance of African philosophy as a product in the academic marketplace,
those who traffic in it are responsible to display it well, to give it good
exposure, and to make it compare and compete well with other products in the marketplace. In this respect, like all commodities in crowded
markets, it is likely to fare better when the peddlers inject diversity into
what they offer consumers. In addition, it can also be argued that among
ourselves as traders in this (philosophical) or any other intellectual commodity, we are likely bound to think differently about what aspects of
it are most significant or have attracted most of those who have been
drawn to it. Also, as we variously identify and describe such aspects of
the commodity, we are likely to generate debates, hopefully both healthy
and passionate ones, about our respective descriptions of them. Not only
will these engagements make our commodity more visible, they also will
spur better knowledge and clearer understanding of what every trader
carries in her baskets. Participants, whether they merely want to listen
or to take their own positions within the marketplace, will evaluate and
compare not just the makeup of the merchandise but also the nature of
the sales pitches—such as the veracity and other formal features of their
claims—that describe and analyze their object.

If the above commercial metaphor is an apt simile of how knowledge is
produced, disseminated, and treated by and among its handlers, then we
can claim, mutatis mutandis, that the development of African philosophy,
like that of any other philosophical enterprise it shares the market with,
does and will depend on the discourses and disputes that will be generated by the identification, interpretive description, and appraisal or critical consideration of the different specific issues and general themes that
emerge from both the written and experiential text of African experience.
One of the goals of this short text is to identify what I believe to be some
of the key ideas and issues that have guided recent history of African
philosophy. To be sure, however, and as illustrated by two recent publications on the matter—Leonhard Praeg's *African Philosophy and the Quest
for Autonomy* and Sanya Osha's *Kwasi Wiredu and Beyond*—agreement

about what these themes are or should be and how they should be articulated can only be a matter of coincidence or the confluence of opinion, not a norm.[9] In addition, as French philosopher of history Raymond Aron has intimated,[10] philosophers may disagree about what they believe best defines or represents the substance of their trade over time due to the plurality of systems of interpretation and to the fact that the preferences of the historian dictate the choice of what is included or excluded in the representation of a system. The historian's preferences are not random. Rather, every historian's account is an involved (human) narrative, an inquiry to understand what is the historian's take on events and their assumed causal (orderly) connections. In this sense at least, the concept of history is both multiple and complex. For example, in *Histoire de la philosophie africaine,* livre II, *Introduction à la philosophie moderne et contemporaine,* the Gabonese historian Grégoire Biyogo asserts (rather falsely) that whereas modern and contemporary African thought has become a field of research for scholarly work of different categories, none of these research projects have been dedicated to the history of modern and contemporary African philosophy.[11] We know, on the contrary, that although they are thin by comparison to what one would find in the accounts of general African history such as the series sponsored by UNESCO[12] or the Cambridge publication,[13] a reasonable number of publications on the history of African philosophy exist. The works of Claude Sumner on Ethiopian philosophical thought in the seventeenth century, especially on Zär'a Ya'eqob, Wäldä Heywåt, and Skændes,[14] are important sources on the dynamics of African moral thinking beginning with the influences of early Christian expansions in the upper Nile valley in the fourth and fifth centuries, from which seventeenth-century Ethiopian moral thinkers became relatively independent. This list would also include research and publications on the works and thought of Anton Wilhelm Amo, another seventeenth-century African philosopher—from Ghana—and a contemporary of Descartes, whose philosophy of mind he critiqued.[15] Another work that is far less known but is a resourceful collection of texts of historical traditions is Constance B. Hilliard's *Intellectual Traditions of Pre-Colonial Africa.*[16] More recently, historical studies such as Alfons Smet's *Histoire de la philosophie africaine contemporaine: Courants et problèmes* (1980), Maniragaba Balibutsa's *Les Perspectives de la pensée philosophique bantu-rwandaise après Alexis Kagame* (1985), Barry Hallen's *A Short History of African Philosophy* (2002), and, finally, my own *African Philosophy in Search of Identity* (1994) together, if not individually, present quite comprehensive accounts of the developments of African philosophy in the twentieth century and later. And, to cap it all, Kwasi Wiredu's recent *A Companion to African Philosophy* (2004) includes an informative historical section that spans the ancient or classical Egyptian period to the present. What is important, because it drives the trade, is the exchange of ideas or claims and counterclaims that ensues from such differences. To this end, it is indeed my intention in this little text—I hope—to open philosophical discussions and debate by identifying and interpretively commenting on what I believe to be some of the theory-oriented issues that have engaged practitioners in the field of African philosophy.

Obviously, organizing the dynamics of African philosophy around themes is by no means an innovation unique to this project. As a matter of fact, the idea of explicitly organizing philosophical debate around thematic considerations dates back to the early 1970s when the "Philosophical Seminars" were launched at the Lubumbashi campus of the Université Nationale du Zaïre. Given the historical background, both political and theoretical, of the debates in the Zairean institutions of higher learning at the time and in other French-speaking African institutions more broadly, one can say this: almost unintentionally, the English translation in 1983 of Paulin J. Hountondji's acclaimed book *African Philosophy: Myth and Reality* and the publication in 1988 of V. Y. Mudimbe's *The Invention of Africa* brought to the notice of the English-speaking world in Africa and abroad two formidable representatives of the developed reflections whose seeds were originally sown at French and Belgian institutions before they were transplanted and watered briefly at the "Lubumbashi School," the vibrant intellectual community of which both Hountondji and Mudimbe were prominent members. While they localize their projects within those Lubumbashi discursive engagements, both seek to extricate and give autonomy to the African vision from the European vision with which it had become entangled. They do so by trying to identify within the European discourse the exact points of contact from which to develop the possibility for an African perspective that becomes at the same time both local and connected to the broader human scheme. The result is two expositions of masterly acquaintance with the continental European epistemic system, on the one hand, and reflectively courageous suggestions for an African path to autonomy, on the other. One—Mudimbe—exposes the intricate, unequal, and irresolvable relations between the two orders (European and African). Using a Freudian interpretation couched in Sartrean language, he appears to contend that the striving by Africans to free the African order of knowledge from the European system is a useless passion, for the African perspective—at least as it is cast to this point—remains strongly and irrevocably dependent on the European order. In the African order, the paternal odor (*l'odeur du père*) is always detectable in the African text despite the apparent attempts of Africans to shake it off. Connected to the West by the spiritual cord of their gestation in the womb of the European academy, whether in Europe itself or at some extension on the African soil, Mudimbe explains, the thinking of African scholars and leaders are an extension of Europe's own epistemic order, in method and often also its subject matter,[17] occurring, he says, "at the crossroads of Western epistemological filiation and African ethnocentrism."[18] But Mudimbe's twofold project is quite clear: first, to trace and analyze the specific and influential Western texts that over the course of history led to the formation of a nefarious discourse that crafted and fed on a self-serving idea of Africa that justified her conquest by each of the three (administrative, anthropological, and missionary) organs of Western domination; and second, to argue for the necessity of breaking from and replacing the Eurocentric image of Africa with Africa's own self-portrait. Sometimes, it seems, the second part of the project is obscured by the detailed erudition of the first part. Paradoxically, even as an *expositeur,* Mudimbe's own work fails, as Jules-Rosette has observed,[19] to extricate itself from the double methodological mediation that makes a nexus of and bridge between European philosophical debates and African colonial discourse. But while this is a long-beaten path of postcolonial analysis, at least Mudimbe views it (albeit through Freudian lenses) as a problematic one. Hountondji, on the other hand, suggests an unflinching embrace of a European theory of the rules of the mind, namely Husserl's phenomenological structure of consciousness, which, for him, represents the universal conditioning that all processes of cognition are subject to. For this reason, he calls for the rejection of the ethnicization of the mind that underlies Senghor's claim within the negritude project and within ethnophilosophy in general of intuition as specific to Africans.

What, then, are the themes that stand out in the recent history of Africans' philosophical reflections? Identifying these themes is the charge of the chapters of this book. To start with, there is a sense in which the question of reworking and integrating indigenous knowledge into the new philosophical order persists in African philosophical reflections. Although it is given focus in the opening chapter, the issue of the status of indigenous knowledge in contemporary Africa runs through all the matters discussed in this work for the important reason that philosophy is always a specialized type of reflection on different aspects of everyday lives and experiences as well as on the presuppositions that drive them or on which they are built.

The goal in chapter 1 is to drive this rather simple point home or to remind ourselves of it, even when it seems to be redundantly obvious. As the British philosopher Bertrand Russell once said, it takes just a little reflection to realize how problematic our assumptions about the obviousness of everyday beliefs can be.[20] But the idea of the philosopher's birth from and immersion in the indigeneity of everyday experience is equally captured in a statement in 1977 by the Congolese philosophy professor Kabe Mutuza in a dialogue with a colleague during the inaugural deliberations of what came to be famously known as "The Philosophical Week of Kinshasa." (In the decade of the 1970s, the series "Semaine Philosophique de Kinshasa," as it was called in French, was an annual spectacle of interdisciplinary debates among some of the leading French-speaking African intellectuals of the time, who gathered under the formal umbrella of the Department of African Philosophy and Religions in the Faculty of Catholic Theology in Kinshasa.) In that specific exchange, Kabe Mutuza stated that "philosophy, very much like other human sciences, takes shape as directed by the times. Philosophers don't spring from the earth like mushrooms."[21] The question, however, was then (as it still is today) whether the context that produced these Africans and their discourses could be restricted to their apparent total neglect of what they had fed on during their intellectual gestation in the intellectual wombs of the European metropolises. In fact, the political drive in the Zaire of "their times" challenged them to distinguish precisely between what was indigenous and what was imported from Europe.

In their respective and slightly different ways, both Mutuza and Russell, like Descartes long before them, assert the rather obvious point that philosophy begins with a reconsideration of what appears to be routine, the things we take so much for granted in our everyday beliefs that we hardly subject them to careful analytical and critical questioning. Among other methods, then, semantic analysis with the aim of exposing and contrasting the locutional with the conceptual (or the assumed and the known) in our representations or understandings of the world and our experience of it can be a crucial path to exposing the conceptual complexities that shroud our everyday world. As I also attempt later in chapter 5 below, the goal is to identify and isolate mythopoeic metaphors and representations from their intended conceptual implications and entanglements. Russell's statement about capacity of philosophy to uncover or disclose the hidden wonders of everyday experiences, especially the theoretical (logical) problems that we conveniently sweep under the rug of our hurried pragmatic concerns, tells us that our knowledge of the everyday matters is tiered or ordered. In other words, while the general field of our knowledge is integrated, each tier separates itself from the others based upon its object(ive)s. For example, sometimes the findings at one level in the order of knowledge of the nature and content of our sensory experience of the outside world may indeed contradict our assumptions of the same (the nature and content of sensory experience) from a different standpoint or level of knowledge. Some European philosophers have suggested that this structural order of knowledge corresponds to the structure of consciousness itself; I have in mind Edmund Husserl and Gaston Bachelard in particular. As I will show later, these two philosophers have significantly influenced the work of Hountondji. Although he has only recently admitted this phenomenological point explicitly, Hountondji has always been driven by it in his now-well-known critique of ethnophilosophy, arguing as he does in *The Struggle for Meaning: Reflections on Philosophy, Culture, and Democracy*[22] that reflective consciousness occurs not at the lower but at the higher level in the stream of consciousness. Thus philosophy, which is a theoretical consciousness, cannot be identical with (nor should it be confused with) the content of intending at the lower level of consciousness. The premises of theory, which emanate from the higher reflective consciousness, address the content of the lower level of consciousness, which is passive. Reconstituted in this manner, this old question not only spurs further criticism of Hountondji in the eyes of many, it also captures and contributes to current debate by bringing back to scrutiny the idea of mind in the Senghorian brand of negritude literature in light of ongoing philosophical and scientific studies in cognitive psychology and (beyond metaphysics of the mind) its epistemological implications. My aim in returning to this matter is to propose that the old and overbeaten path of ethnophilosophy might be made interesting again by redefining its subject matter in the form of theories of the structure of consciousness and to show thereby the different approaches to this matter in the work of African philosophers. A sharp contrast is easily evident, for example, between Hountondji and Senghor, on the one hand, and Kwasi Wiredu and others, on the other. In other words, the colonial lines are still visible in these approaches. More important, however, I am interested in characterizing the debate on the structural nature of consciousness and on the functional goals of each of its parts, or on the place and nature of mind within the general field of consciousness, as having implications for determining the boundaries between the universal and particular within the physical and mental components of the constitution of selfhood in an African context, not just knowledge as an enterprise. In a way, then, the questions of the nature of philosophy, including its conceptual texture in relation to other mental events, as asked by Hountondji, or in relation to other discourses, as asked by Franz Crahay,[23] are likely to draw fresh or adjusted attention to this old debate about the conceptual elevation (*décollage conceptuel*) of philosophy in relation to everyday beliefs. Even then, the *débat*, at least that between Crahay and Hountondji on the nature of theoretical consciousness and its location in or absence from the claims that constitute African beliefs, already drew significantly from Husserl's phenomenological analysis of the levels of cognition.

Here is the question that I believe to be fruitful: How does any experience, including a philosophical one, regardless of where it occurs, turn us on and lead us into thinking about the world through the lenses of our own heritage? Indeed, philosophical problems arise out of the claims people make, whether explicitly or by implication, and how these claims compare with others with which they may have or only appear to have similarities. Thus, even at the risk of facing accusations of sustaining a Westernization of African thought, the reformulation of previous debates to reveal and embrace issues and considerations that were once hidden but are now arising out of current developments and discourses in other or related fields confirms Professor Mutuza's point that the persistence of philosophical discourse is sustained by the ability to make it relevant to human experience and problems through time. According to him,

> [a] philosopher, an African philosopher above all, if he is careful enough to dedicate his reflection, not on phantoms but on real humans, must make recourse not only to linguistics and philosophy of language, rather he must not ignore other human sciences in so far as they reveal real conditions under which truth is formulated.[24]

In this sense, philosophical discourse bares (because it indeed bears) a formidable capacity for remaining forever young, robust, and regenerative of new insights and debate, and it does this partly by reconsidering the familiar and entrenched beliefs and values in light of their time-bound usefulness. Readers will recall Wiredu's and Appiah's decrying of anachronism in our attachment to aspects of our traditions and customs that are no longer useful.[25]

Chapter 3 of this book takes up this point by indicating how in this age of liberties it is paramount for scholarship in the human sciences and other related fields to focus on and flush out the repressive elements in African cultural and political systems. Indeed, that postindependence chaos and atrocities in the broad African political landscape have generated much debate as well as much suffering for African peoples needs no emphasis. What has lagged behind, in contrast to the scholarship on African political (mis)governance, has been the insistence on requiring of our cultural systems the same demands—such as for the recognition, respect, and enforcement of individual rights and freedoms—we have made of our political establishments. Too many times and for far too long we have either failed to see or deliberately ignored the connection between the standards we expect of our political leaders and those that apply to the practice of culture at the local and household levels. In an indirect way, I argue that the ugliness of this double standard in the consideration of our daily lives is the subject matter of the "Epilogue" of K. Anthony Appiah's widely discussed book *In My Father's House* (among other works). The full range of liberal considerations of our daily lives (or of the debate that Appiah's work has since generated) cannot be accorded fair treatment in just one chapter, so what appears here is only an indication of the springing up of a novel and potent thematic area of philosophical discourse in a field that has yet to be fully exploited.

Chapter 4 is a re-presentation of Kwasi Wiredu's now-familiar yet so diversely read philosophical reflections. I have re-presented his philosophical position with at least two provocative suggestions. First, that Wiredu's philosophical positions in metaphysics, epistemology, and ethics and in the general orientation of philosophical anthropology that informs the axiomatic stances in these subfields are, contrary to some critics' observations (such as Sanya Osha, for example), some of the most systematically Africa-centered to date, connected by a common and (theoretically) robust communalistic underlay.[26] Long before Spivak pointed it out, Wiredu's standpoint assumed, and exercised, a philosopher's reappropriation of his African subjectivity[27] and only occasionally refers to Euro-American alternatives "to see if the magisterial texts [of, say, Kant, Hegel, or Marx] can now be our servants, as the new magisterium constructs itself in the name of the Other."[28] For Wiredu, the African Subject starts with a clearly and radically different axiomatic assumption—he or she is dependent for his or her being on relations with others. Viewed from this standpoint on the subject's standing, a number of philosophical postulations with which one was once familiar through Western texts, such as the nature of truth or the metaphysical grounding of morals, clearly shift perspectives and, at the very minimum, cry out for serious reconsideration. The idea of "standpoint" is to be considered at two different levels here. First, it is the case that people experience the world around them first and foremost as individuals or agents to whom things happen or for whom, on the basis of their organismic constitution and presence in the world of events, things occur. Given the multiple variety of our subjective constitutions, every cognitive experience will be from a "standpoint" or, to use Wiredu's preferred expression, from a "point of view." But human life, as Freud observed about some types of traditions and customs, is lived at the level of directing and regulating the organismic experiences toward results that account for the species' difference. But how exactly do we report to or share with other people our impressions, both descriptive and evaluative, of these experiences? The shift here is from a cognitive stance (the stimulations that are caused in me by external events acting as stimulants on me) to an epistemological one (my claim that "it is the case that . . . occurred"). Because knowledge (a system of claims, whether of the state of the external world or of values) belongs to the second instance, our appraisal of it is subject to *how we appraise every individual's cognitive stance* on the shared (epistemological) stance. This latter appraisal signals another level of "standpoint," one that endows individuals with the means to apply a select variety of values, in the form of regulatory principles, to guide their behavior. The ability to recognize and effectively identify those principles in the conduct of the affairs of persons and institutions makes human beings competent members of specific communities distinguishable by sets of regulatory principles they use to build their institutions and regulate the conduct of persons in public (shared) domains. Inculturation inducts us into these knowledge communities, and sometimes we inhabit them in total oblivion or contempt of other such communities. But also sometimes, happily, when we have the opportunity to know the characteristics of other knowledge communities, we may venture to compare them with our own, meaning that there is little (if anything) that impenetrably closes one knowledge system from another. At the minimum, and barring any unwarranted contempt for or dismissal of the unfamiliar, they can be compared. This kind of "standpoint" will, for example, tell my teacher how and why to consider (with the aim of determining) whether or not it is justifiable to deny me a scholarship because my uncle is wealthy in order that another pupil with no comparably able relative can get financial assistance despite the fact that our respective immediate parents are equally destitute.

Wiredu's work reveals the philosophico-anthropological axioms that underlie African experiences as we reflectively discern them at the core of the principles that govern ideal customary beliefs and practices. He discusses and philosophically defends these axioms as alternative (if not altogether better) assumptions for explaining, understanding, and requiring the adoption of specific concepts that are applicable to different domains of human behavior in living life and in conducting inquiry. In other words, Wiredu seeks to define the axiomatic presuppositions or theoretical conjectures about the nature of humans that allow us to draw implications from those presuppositions on which we proceed to erect other, more specific conjectures about other matters. Kant was right in suggesting that the anthropological question "What is man?" was the most important and foundation of all other questions. The architectonic system that he constructed to analyze the faculties of the mind was aimed at elucidating the transcendental unity that makes human experience possible. If there were to be differences in views regarding the principles on which our beliefs about the world are based, they most probably would be traceable to our beliefs about what the constitutive nature of the person is, which we often trace back to a pool of axiomatic beliefs within the respective systems of our cultural heritages. It is, among other interests, the goal of philosophy to identify (define) what these axiomatic principles are and to critically evaluate them in relation to their role in making possible and validating our experience of and claims about the world. This, I believe, is the intricate and core purpose of Wiredu's philosophy—namely how as a person bred on Akan values, he thinks of the constitution of the person in ways that, by application and implication, make his understanding of such principles of knowledge as truth or the difference between truth and belief and therefore of the world as it is sensed and understood in daily life so different from how they are likely to be understood elsewhere. Another example is his understanding of the basic principle of morals that agrees with the commonly accepted Golden Rule but finds for it a justification— sympathetic impartiality—that is different from Kant's law that guides practical reason, namely the necessary connection of pure reason with moral legislation. I have suggested two things: one, that according to Wiredu, a person is not merely a function of faculties, much less of different substances working in some unity and in conformity to some law so as to make experience possible. As postulated through the Akan lenses Wiredu wears, a person, or the human self, is not exactly what one encounters in the familiar Western descriptions and definitions of the self such as substance loaded with attributes or matter and form or mind and body or ego and so forth. Rather, he or she is a complex biological organism endowed with a specific (as a property of the species or biological type to which he or she belongs) capacity to function with at least some minimal competence in the social world of meanings.[29] To paraphrase Simone de Beauvoir's famous saying about the development women go through from biological femininity to the social category of womanhood, it is Wiredu's view that we are born humans, but we become persons. The implications of this basic sociality of personhood defy the boundaries of metaphysics, epistemology, or even ethics in the restrictive Kantian sense. It proposes far-reaching dimensions for a communalistic view of the world in which the project of becoming a person is always incomplete.

Relying on the idea of the relational basis of personhood that runs through several of the preceding chapters, chapter 5 revisits the unresolved debate over the concept of *juok*[30] in the Luo language of Eastern Africa and argues that the concept, which is rooted in a communalistic ethic, underlines a strategy for containing socially destructive conduct by reminding people of the deviant and stigmatizing nature of antisocial behavior. Because the latter is not a trait to be embraced or to take pride in, the threat of being branded a *jajuok* stands as a perennial reminder that society finally is the function of the positive moral agency of those who constitute it. Thus the concept (of *juok*) is used to draw attention to the imagination and practice of right conduct; it is the moral guiding principle in the interactive intersubjectivity of everyday life. The analysis takes on and significantly corrects the earlier and Tempels-influenced ontological interpretations of *juok* by two prominent Luo-speaking scholars, the eminent Kenyan historian Bethwell Allan Ogot and the late eminent Ugandan poet and anthropologist Okot p'Bitek. As a collateral objective, the analysis also aims at demystifying the idea of *dhum,* the "undecipherable language of the spirits"—what Tempels called "the vital force" (*la force vitale*)[31] in the borrowed lexicon of Henri Bergson's process philosophy. (Ontological) misinterpretations of *juok* (pl. *juogi*) see them as "little beings" capable of autonomous existence either in the bush or by the rivers and in shrines erected for their abode in homesteads or inside human mediums through whom they are believed to "speak." I will try to correct this misinterpretation by resituating the idea of *juok* within the communal strategies for charting and controlling a social order based on a moral code. In this sense, in fact, those who think of *juok* as a metaphysical entity are perfect victims of the human game of teaching morals through an authorized and ritualized use of the past.

Finally, although many points in African philosophy separate themselves from their counterparts in other traditions on account of the communitarian principle, which holds that the individual can flourish as a moral being and as an epistemological and political agent only within the context of a community, community is not defined or experienced in similar ways in Africa and in the Euro-American world. Thus, although indications of communitarianism have emerged in some form in Euro-American intellectual traditions as a significant aspect of moral and social theory (with some historians tracing its origins to Aristotole's moral and political treatises, for example in the *Nicomachean Ethics* and in the *Politics,* respectively, before it reemerged in the nineteenth-century in the works of Hegel and, even more recently, in the work of John Rawls), wide interpretive differences exist, both within each tradition and generally between them as well. The problem, like the one that dogs the conceptual distinction(s) between free will and determinism in metaphysics, is in finding the balance between liberal and collective values in order to make human lives both respectful and rewarding. In other words, to what extent does commitment to the principle of the basic liberties of the individual or to the superordinance of community preclude the incorporation of significant values of the other? In chapter 6, I try to show that despite the parallels between Western and African versions of communitarianism, the former remains rooted in and committed to its methodological strengths as a tool for tempering the periodic sharp rises in liberal individualism to which the Western tradition remains basically committed and is thus significantly different from the robust African communitarianism or communalism (as it is variantly referred to for distinctness). In its recent form, Western communitarianism emerges as a response to both utilitarianism and Kantianism, two major sources of contemporary Western political theory that seek to reinstall the individual and his or her interests and fulfillment as the focus of unhindered rational political and moral goals while also seeking to uphold collective responsibility for sustaining institutions that guarantee those individual liberties. Thus, says Thomas Nagel, "Liberalism involves a division of the moral territory and leaves individuals free to instantiate a great plurality of forms of life, some of them highly self-absorbed, so long as they are compatible with a just basic structure of cooperation."[32] Recent African cultural critiques or philosophies of culture have raised similar questions, ostensibly whether or not and in what senses the claim, pursuit, or augmentation of individual or personal liberties is, was, must be, or has ever been incompatible with the values of community. This final chapter compares more directly what lies in and distinguishes between Western and African brands of communitarianism. I believe that this comparison is an apt way to round up the text.

In sum, then, the aim of this book is to enable the reader to get a handle on the historical origins and broader contexts, in Africa and elsewhere,

from and within which some of the important issues and discussions in
contemporary African philosophy have taken shape and, especially, to get
him and her to participate in and advance the debate. The second aim is
particularly important and pertinent to the philosophical enterprise (or
trade, as I called it earlier). Because one can only interpret rather than
re-present "what there is" in other people's philosophical positions, it is
my aim to provoke and urge the reader to develop a reflection on the
issues for himself or herself in the spirit of seeking to develop standard
interpretations and understanding of the African texts, whether these are
the experiences of African peoples in their daily lives and expressions or
the existing and expanding written texts. Fortunately, we have come to
that point where it is no longer necessary to explain why this is important,
because the discourse is taking place already and this is just a contribution to it.

CHAPTER ONE

Philosophy and Indigenous Knowledge

In a broad sense, the position a culture chooses on the relation between theory and reality or, said another way, between general explanations and observational data, is its center. Grasping what we are taught about what those positions are and how they apply to the immediate world of our experience constitutes learning and general understanding, or, put simply, knowledge. Yet in a world where people travel while carrying their cultural knowledge with them, knowledge wars are likely to ensue, and history tells us there have been such wars, both within and between different cultures. It is no wonder, then, that the degree to which the domains of theory and reality (or explanation and observation) ought to be related has been a special focus of philosophers throughout history, first as an example of the intracultural contentions of knowledge positions, such as most recently (in the Euro-American tradition) the contentions of those whose preoccupation with this matter has been shaped by the interest and debate rekindled by the movement started in Vienna, Austria, in the middle of the twentieth century. Since then, not only philosophers but also natural and social scientists have been drawn to theorizing about the nature of and correspondence between explanations of natural phenomena and "the facts." Sometimes intracultural disagreements about the nature and ideal content of knowledge can spill over into intercultural politics, although sometimes such politics can develop independently, the former case about its protagonists notwithstanding, as we saw with colonialism. At other times a culture's rejection of another culture's knowledge can be quite arbitrary, exposing the sheer bias of the rejecting system.[1] At the center of inquiry in the diverse domains is the role of belief, more broadly put, or collectivistic and conservative tendencies and attitudes more narrowly, about how scientific and other types of explanation get grounded and developed. Critical theorists, in particular, have advanced the view that even entrenched theoretical positions (what Thomas Kuhn called positions of "normal science" compared to the experimental sciences) are often only perspectival, however systematic they might be, because they reflect the dominance of a particular stance in the context of a competition between unequal rivals. Inspired by the claim that knowledge takes place in and reflects the social worlds of its creators in expression and use, formerly suppressed systems liberated themselves from foundationalist claims and monolithic canons and called for different, more rigorous, and comparative approaches to the epistemological enterprise in the latter part of the twentieth century. Thus, culture- and gender-based inquiries acquired a visibility they had never before enjoyed.

The global sociocultural and political liberation movement that accompanied the recession of colonialism made room, quite obviously, for a critique of the colonist epistemological imperialism. While the global debate continues in the different sectors of knowledge, in philosophy (and in the eyes of African disputants more particularly), it has focused on the relations between the forms and claims of indigenous knowledge and different understandings of philosophy, with its Western configuration as the model for evaluation. The outcome, as is now well known, has been a debate firmly grounded on the formal problem once identified by Franz Crahay's famous but relatively much less discussed critique of ethnophilosophy,[2] which was later surpassed in fame and notoriety by Hountondji's unrelenting anti-ethnophilosophy crusade. In retrospect, the central question in the life of the ethnophilosophy debate that ensued and includes what now appears to be a phenomenological discussion of the nature of mind, can be recognized in those two debate-setting critiques of ethnophilosophy: Where in the structure of consciousness does philosophy belong as a specific type of consciousness? For Hountondji, as we will discuss later, the problem was not a lack of abstraction in ethnophilosophical texts, as Crahay then argued—because all representations are already abstract by nature—but one of how to empower indigenous knowledge systems; that is, how to make them inspire and drive change. Thus, in a crucial way for Hountondji, the problem lay in the ability (or, as was the case with the majority of the authors of ethnophilosophical texts) the inability to recognize the crucial point of transition that would make it possible for indigenous knowledge to become a viable tool for transforming the world. Indigeneity was not to be equated with the passive spirit that fed the charges of "primitivism," as was done in twentieth-century European conceptions of African knowledge in different domains (including aesthetic art and, especially, the art of detecting, analyzing, explaining, and predicting the events and processes of physical reality). The disparaging evaluation of African knowledge was already strong in Western anthropological and sociological scholarship and, as was also implied by Crahay in his distinction between philosophy and myth, extended to other domains of non-Western cultures.[3] What must have been utterly unacceptable for Hountondji was the fact that African scholars too were surrendering to and acting to perpetuate the culture of passivity or conformism.

As I said earlier, the problem is not just (and perhaps not at all) about the relevance of philosophy to Africans' conceptual management of the world or to their senses of selfhood but about neglecting or confusing the differences between the structures of thought and of discourse. The problem, which basically is about the relation, or correlation, between the theoretical and the observational ends of the ordinary, reminds me vividly of an incident that took place long ago, when I was in my first year of high school at St. Mary's Kwale, when our young but courageous science teacher swore us to the project of demystifying physics. Father Brian Allen made us take what he called "the oath of the ordinariness of science." While we lifted the relatively voluminous physics textbook high in our right hands in the full fashion of a swearing-in ritual, Father Allen made us repeat after him some statements, largely to the effect that the contents of the book were not mysteries but were some accounts, descriptions, and explanations of the very ordinary material world around us and how we interacted with it: what it was, how it was constituted, how it "behaved," and why it "behaved" the way it did. Our task, he promised, would be to bring the pretentious language of the so-called experts back to the things themselves, thus to enabling us to see the ordinariness of understanding that, he emphasized, was the task or goal of learning. No teacher before him had ever cared to relate formal explanations to the informal world or experience, let alone acknowledge that the English language in which these texts were written was part of the utterly unnecessary colonial burden that doubled the task of learning. What was ordinary and at the root of all processes of thought was, by deliberate acts of obfuscation, made to appear privileged and almost unreachably mysterious. Today, I sometimes muse with friends over the abstractness of the mathematical concept of a "pie chart" when it was first taught to us in my pre-Allen upper middle school classes. Because, from our deep Kaugagi origins, we just had no idea what a "pie" was or could ever be and no one cared to explain or substitute it with another, more familiar culinary analog from our own culture, we often resigned ourselves to memorizing this and other terms from the English and Irish lexicon, often forgetting them, only subsequently to endure severe corporal punishment for untraining our memories. What was an ordinary term suddenly acquired abstractness both in its mathematical definition and in its lack of any clear referent in our practical world. Yet in the village there were many real culinary equivalents of the abstract European "pie," including such familiar staples as chapati. By pointing out that formal explanations and theories were analyses of what the senses delivered for mental organization, Father Allen not only underscored the general contingency of language to the conceptual organization of experience and the contingency of the English language specifically in this case, he also told us that the only thing we had to keep out of the reach of the British colonizers was our minds. He was Irish. Thus, perhaps concerned about finding the space that minimized foreign avenues to knowledge that he believed we deserved against the common circumstances we shared with him and his own folk, he believed that the march had to begin with the position that not only science but also other organized and systematic theories of the world and human experience of it, including philosophy, had twofold aims: first, producing theories or explanations that agreed with experience, and, second, explaining everyday commonsense concepts of or assumptions about nature. I came to learn that this view of knowledge was not limited to the professionals, much less to philosophers. So how could science have looked so strange in the pre-Allen experiences of twelve-year-old rural African children? The answer lay in the nature of colonial education. To be sure, to claim that any organized knowledge, such as philosophy and science, seeks only to explain the ordinary in our everyday experience may sound like an oversimplification of either of these two vastly complex fields of study. To a great degree, both thrive on their abilities to develop sophisticated theoretical accounts not only of the ever-changing range of human encounter with the world and an individual's understanding of it but also of the values best suited for managing and sharing what the world offers as humans adjust to or seek comfort in it. Yet, on the other hand, the claim is not too exaggerated as both, in effect, consist of inquiry into what is not yet well enough understood to constitute a presupposition of everyday experience, which is the reason any serious inquiry is often characterized by deep contentions and rival positions.

One major dispute within African philosophy has been whether disciplines are defined solely internally by the theoretical structures of their contents, such as the abstract and universal character of concepts in philosophy, or whether they are equally influenced by external conditions that account for their acceptability within the schemes they serve. In other words, to what extent are theories driven by the dynamics of the social circumstances and the contexts within which they are produced and to what extent are the disciplines universal rather than ethnodisciplines—such as ethnophilosophy, ethnobiology, ethnomedicine, and so forth? While these questions raged in a slightly different context among African philosophers in the sixties and seventies, a similar discourse was taking place among philosophers in the West in relation to the impact of human interests on the production of scientific theories. Here I will show how these two sets or traditions of discourse complement and breed into each other. On the one hand, African philosophers debating ethnophilosophy contributed to the wider debate, sometimes indirectly, even when their immediate goals and the language they deployed were politically rather than epistemically defined. On the other hand, philosophers who debated the nature of scientific theories have lent their voices to the ethnophilosophy debate, also indirectly, even when their immediate goals and the language of their writings was almost always only epistemically inclined.

The Idea of the Indigenous

Like its cognates (local, native, original, old, or insider) and its antonyms or counterparts (migrant, alien, new, settler, or outsider), the term "indigenous" is used to define the origin of an item or person in relation to how their belonging to a place is to be temporally characterized, especially in comparison to other contenders in claiming belonging. Historians and social scientists constantly analyze and define the known origin and movements of people, ideas, and things between different places over time as one way of identifying and contrasting their characteristics. The term "indigenous" has not always had positive connotations for those to whom it was intended to introduce and create awareness of distant worlds. Perched inside the expeditionary colonial lexicon and later colonial research, the term bore the connotation of geo-temporal remoteness relative to the place and time of the discoverer's own origin. The colonizer's endeavor was partly to mediate and abridge these separations through spreading the "ways" of his or her world.

Implications of diversity persist even as the idea of indigeneity acquires more positive connotations. As pluralism takes center stage in contemporary thought and practical orientations in both the public and private realms, indigenous systems are not only encouraged to remain and show more autonomy, they are also thought to have the capacity to sustain themselves. The study of indigenous systems significantly shifts, therefore, toward "internalist" explanations and theorizations. The idea, which is rather simple and has long been expressed in both political and intellectual circles, is that different communities experience the world differently, including how they experience historical events such as colonialism. Consequently, we need different methods for understanding, defining, and tackling different homegrown problems.[4] To do this successfully, the indigenous realm must be its own primary resource. Indigenous persons must train to know how to systematically explain the "ways" of their world and how it relates to the rest. She who once was only the unrecognized "native informant" must now become the principal investigator. She, not the expatriate, becomes the expert. Similarly, in relation to the practice of African philosophy, the rise of the idea of "indigeneity" has only recently appeared on the academic scene through historical analysis that outlines the mobility of new ideas, schools, and movements of thought that contribute to the practice of philosophy by new generations of Africans as an intellectual movement whose common denominator is to be found in a shared history but whose strengths are to be noted in the diversity of responses to that history.

It is plausible, then, to say that despite such collectivist denominators as "African," "postcolonial," and other terms signaling shared elements of history and culture, African philosophy has schools of thought whose differentiating characteristics warrant analysis and understanding. In intellectual history, the aim of such analysis usually is to determine the historical nature and character of the ideas that make up schools of thought or theories around specific issues. Efforts to distinguish local from migrant, native from alien, or original from settler are often spurred by a political setting in which such separation usually serves other goals, some noble, others not quite so noble, as happens too often in traditional politics. In its historical and formal nature, the debate over the role of indigeneity in African philosophy is part of the larger postcolonial discourse. As part of this global emancipatory voice, debates and views on indigenous values generally and on indigenous knowledges more specifically join the global politics of domination and emancipation. In the rhetoric of this politics, the defense and promotion of the indigenous goes hand in hand with the anti-hegemonic quest for freedom and autonomy, so that whatever is indigenous or locally produced is reinstalled at the head of epistemic regimes of local or regional cultural interests, where it will have greater political and cultural value than what is foreign or imported.

In formal terms, the growth of indigenous methodologies of inquiry and of inquiries about indigenous schemes and modes has occurred concurrently with and has been spurred by an approach that is now widely used or simply assumed by most disciplines, namely the radical philosophical critiques of scientific realism that developed in the late fifties and early sixties. This revolution, popularized by Thomas Kuhn's leading work in theoretical history, *The Structure of Scientific Revolutions* of 1962, gave a new spin to the claims of people who already strongly believed that knowledge generally and scientific theory more specifically is human-centered—meaning that it is a function of social forces in their multidirectional evolution. The central claim of Kuhn's work was that the history of science displays a pattern that may be explained by the institutional structure of science, specifically by the way professional scientists base their research on certain objects of consensus that Kuhn called "paradigms." Because science is thus significantly established by society, the "normalcy" of its theoretical practice and framework is determined by its adherence to the regulations established by and applicable within the "paradigm." Although it is hard (and certainly this is not the place) to fully estimate the impact or direction of Kuhn's influence over the years, he certainly is widely regarded to have undermined a whole philosophical tradition—that of logical positivism or, more broadly, logical empiricism—such that many philosophers no longer regard scientific language to be characteristic of any language used to talk about the world. Importantly, the study of the nature of modern sciences extended to the domains of (usually) comparative social and cultural analyses. For example, according to Sandra Harding,[5] all sciences are local knowledge systems. Internally, she has argued, good scientific knowledge is characterized by strong objectivity, inclusive rationality, and universal validity, but it is still a body of local knowledge claims. Sharing a theme with feminist critiques of science, non-Western perspectives claim that science can make universal claims while remaining locally grounded. Because all sciences are locally grounded, they are ethnosciences. It would seem from these recent developments in the analyses of the sciences that all knowledge, in the Wittgensteinian sense of facts as (propositional) descriptions of the relations of objects in the world to each other, that all knowledge claims are only points of view, some at the individual level (such as those that profess relativist stands) and others (such as those that incorporate stern and open modes of inquiry) more embedded in culture.

Since Kuhn, the study of the nature of scientific theory has progressively blurred the boundaries among science, the humanities, and the social sciences to such an extent as to enhance understanding on all sides, unavoidably placing realism at the heart of the debate. One major characterization made in the course of this scholarship is the distinction between what is independently "there"—what is in the outside world—and what we "construct"; what is the case "in itself" and what is so because of our ways of experiencing, including our participation in structured activities and communities of inquiry.

Carey Francis Onyango, a young Kenyan philosopher of science, formulates his discussion of the relation between realism and antirealism in terms of its impact on the status of African production of knowledge generally and the debate on African philosophy more particularly. In a doctoral dissertation presented to the University of Vienna in 1999,[6] Onyango takes a pragmatic approach to scientific theory and argues that such an approach narrows (or at least disregards) the divide usually regarded as obtaining between realism and antirealism. He argues that those positions usually regarded as antirealist, such as Van Fraasen's constructive empiricism, for example, are only strands of what he calls the "models-semantic conception," which he explains as a combination of the models-theoretic and semantic versions of realism. As such, he states, Van Fraasen's position "can accommodate a variety of interpretations of the claims of theories [such as] realist, empiricist, and constructivist [stands], or any other appropriate interpretation depending on the issue at hand . . . but not antirealism."[7] This view can only hold, as has been shown by the French sociologist of science Bruno Latour,[8] that social context and technical content are both essential to a proper understanding of scientific activity and that science can only be understood through its practice. The Mozambican mathematician Paulus Gerdes[9] has shown that even mathematics, like other technical and abstract knowledge, can best be grasped only in practical terms—that is, as part of everyday practices of coping with, managing, and transforming the world of everyday experience. Such an approach is what would make Onyango's models-semantic conception "essentially pragmatical."[10]

Although African perspectives on the critique of scientific realism are more recent than the ethnophilosophy debate, the works mentioned above, and others, have added significantly and supportively to the anti-Hountondji position and generally to the global debate about the idea that knowledge is socially constructed. The constructivist view, namely that most aspects of knowledge, as we know them through the disciplines, are significantly local and hence partly reflect the communally practical (sociohistorical) contexts of their production not only lends a hand to weak versions of postcolonial theory, it also threatens to slip into relativism, a position vehemently and rightly opposed by Hountondji and Wiredu, to mention just two.

The "African ethnophilosophy" controversy rekindled and contextualized the opposition between local and universal perceptions of knowledge that already was under much discussion in relation to science. As Harding indicates, the idea that science was universal grew alongside European political, military, and economic might, and ideological deployments of universality became a dominant feature of North-South relations in the nineteenth century and its aftermath. Thus the emergence of the social-construction-of-knowledge movement, or the idea that all forms of knowledge are ethnoknowledges, clearly erodes the force of science by questioning its foundational status. To describe or characterize any knowledge or value as "indigenous" is to claim that it bears the desirable qualities of autochthonism, self-representation, and self-preservation, which, by contrast, its "alien," "foreign," or "extraneous" counterparts lack. In Marxist scholarship on Africa, the concept of indigeneity arose as a value concept that is used to identify and separate things that belong to the local political and cultural space from things that are elements of hegemonic intrusion and illegitimate invasion by institutions of global capitalism. It is used prescriptively to change the attitudes of a (politically, culturally, and economically) dominated people by causing them to desire and to seek to reclaim their own schemes of representation from the dominating alien, foreign, or extraneous control. In Western historical and anthropological texts about Africa, Africa was represented as geographically and imaginatively distant, foreign, and alien to the schemes of both the writer and her intended Western audience. The writer seeks to bring it within the margins of familiarity for the Western metropolitan consumer. She is the mediator who must present her product in accessible terms if she is to be successful, meaning that she must present it in the schematic form and categories that are familiar to the consumer. Thus the distant indigenous was the pure object of the metropolitan scholar and its nature, in the scholarly sense, was the object of the distant consumer in the Western metropolis, thanks to the facilitative role of "the native informant," as Spivak calls her,[11] or "the junior collaborator," in Hountondji's words.[12] The perpetuation of this uneven relationship in production generally and in the production of knowledge in particular in which the Western investigator always assumes he or she is superior to the local collaborator, despite the latter's double role as both investigator and subject matter at the same time, is the basis of what has long been known as the forced dependency syndrome, a critical neologue of political economic theory developed long ago (in the seventies) by André Gunder Frank, Samir Amin, and Immanuel Wallerstein, three of the pioneers of the postcolonial political-economic theory. It was their view, as Spivak and Hountondji have each reiterated, that as a result of its disempowerment, the indigenous system is stripped of autonomy and thus could derive its worth only from the interests of its predator, a status of underdevelopment in which the flow of its value always was to the outside, or extraverted, as Hountondji describes it.

Two things result from this relationship. First, the original meaning of the indigenous is lost as it is harvested only as raw material before it is processed through the schemes of the harvester and put out as a finished product for consumption. The circulated knowledge of the indigenous on the open market is therefore always different from, if not at variance altogether with, that at the point of growth. The second result has to do with the engineered psychology of the indigenous consumer, who is made to believe that things processed in and put out as finished products of metropolitan centers in the West are indisputably superior. As once described by the late president Julius Nyerere of Tanzania, the would-be local consumer of the local products is brainwashed into distrusting his or her own artifacts and other products, preferring instead to become a consumer of importations and a producer of exportations. The anomaly pervades many domains of production, prompting Spivak to observe that the really crucial problem for Third World intellectuals is that of being taken seriously. She writes:

> For me, the question "Who should speak?" is less crucial than "Who will listen?" . . . The real demand is that, when I speak from that position, I should be listened to seriously.[13]

Spivak's concern may rightly have been with what she calls "benevolent imperialism," but that case, because it is not altogether surprising, is hardly as bad as the refusal of a local audience to listen to (meaning to take seriously) knowledge produced by their own intellectuals about themselves. They would rather, to use a descriptive term from the eyesore of contemporary global trade, reach out for the easy grab of recycled and tired products from abroad—called *mitumba*[14] in my country—than invest in what has been produced to address their specific conditions.

The reemergence of interest in indigenous knowledge in recent years is due to several factors. First, as industrialization is peaking in the Western sphere or the global North, its effects have become more evident beyond the marketplace. Ozone depletion and environmental poisoning, now increasingly documented and widely accepted effects of the effluvia of industrial processes, for both the earth and the biosphere, have made once-scorned simpler ways of life and controlled scales of industrialization more attractive for their stances toward biodiversity and their general friendliness to the environment, at least at the intellectual level. Second, with the demise of the Cold War, the politics of numbers in the scramble for alliances and geopolitical spheres of influence is a thing of the past, thus making the sustenance of the dependency of distant nations and peoples a far less attractive policy and a sacrifice for regimes and taxpayers in developed nations. There is neither political nor economic gain to show for such sacrifice. Consequently, the current focus of aid agencies, both governmental and independent (or nongovernmental, as they call themselves), is on helping the disadvantaged governments of economically and technologically disadvantaged nations establish self-reliant and internally sustainable programs.

The history of African indigeneity and its impact on different disciplines is long. As Mudimbe has shown, it dates far back to the ancient times of Greek explorations.[15] Critical analyses of how exactly this impact has occurred and grown have been well presented in other works (for example, Evans-Pritchard's[16] critical observations on the implications of Zande witchcraft beliefs for formal logic; the entire "rationality debate" that ensued within the circle of British analytic philosophy when Peter Winch objected in a 1964 essay[17]; Mudimbe[18]; Appiah[19]; and Appiah and Mudimbe[20]). In a general sense, the issue of indigeneity is also well treated in the critical anthropological and other texts of the eighties and nineties. The central question for this generation of writers (in the nineties) hovered around interrogating the pretensions of the metropolitan scholar in relation to the stifling of the indigenous Subject-cum-object whose word about herself could be neither final nor independently authoritative except under the guidance and approval of the investigator from the metropolis.

Ethnophilosophy and the Controversy over Indigenous Knowledge

In the context of the growth of contemporary academic philosophy in sub-Saharan Africa, for a long time much of the controversy over the embattled concept of ethnophilosophy appeared to pit indigenous African knowledge systems against philosophy viewed as a specialized and abstract category of knowledge. The assumption in much of that literature (and in the work of some diehard critics of the idea of African philosophy) is that an idea cannot be both indigenous and philosophical at the same time. Popularized and transformed into a full-fledged topic of debate in the seventies by Hountondji's critique of Placide Tempels's work under the rubric of ethnophilosophy (used in a pejorative sense at the time), the indigenous, exoticized as purely oral, was perceived to stand in a lower position in relation to scribed knowledge. In the wake of the written word, which was believed or perceived to be foreign, the oral, which was indigenous, had slipped into irrelevance. But, as I have tried to argue before, either Hountondji has since recanted his earlier anti-tradition stand or it was never the case that his critique of Tempels amounted to the rejection of the significance of traditional knowledges. A reading of Hountondji's work of the nineties, especially his 1995 essay "Producing Knowledge in Africa Today,"[21] reveals a deep concern for indigenous knowledge systems as the basis of a legitimate concept of development that is both historically relevant, socially meaningful, and responsive to need.

Hountondji's point is that the mastery (that is, active, engaged, and critical understanding) of the forms and specific claims of local knowledge systems should be the starting if not the focal point of development, which he defines as the capacity to harness, manage, and transform natural and other available resources for the improvement of the conditions and quality of life for a community or nation. An expansion of this idea, taking other factors into account, leads to the claim that development, understood in the foregoing way, would be even better if the majority of the people it is meant to benefit can relate to its products. They should first desire it and then be able to sustain it. Yet because it is unlikely that a whole community or nation will desire the same thing or desire any one thing for the same reasons and goals, the notion of development as driven by unanimity about the objects of desire can only be ideal at best. In reality, due to the complexity and diversity of desires and aspirations, development is likely to be the result of a continuous and inclusive dialogical process.

If indeed this is what underlies Hountondji's idea of introverted development (at least in the sense of being the inverse of "extraverted development"), then his embrace of the local as the starting and focal point of development revalorizes the indigenous in a way that avoids the oppositional colonial categories of traditional and modern, or, as it is put in the lexicon of similar literature, the local or indigenous, on the one hand, and the imported or colonial, on the other. Perhaps these categories would not even matter if it were not for the fact that every cultural system of thought and practice exists in time and therefore has a past and a present. The burden of history requires of the inhabitants of any cultural system that the present be critically different from the past at least with regard to some significant aspects. And the role of intellectual habits is to provide the methods and the questions from which the difference between the past and present will emerge. In this regard, the terms "traditional" and "modern," or indigenous and colonial, no longer designate "precolonial African" and "Western," respectively, as they have done in much of the postcolonial literature. I wonder if there is not a broader point here, namely that recognizing the dictates of the present do not necessarily render the modes of expression of the indigenous system (such as the values of collective identity) obsolete, if these are properly defined and appropriately applied to the domains where they remain relevant and potent. At the same time, the point is clear that the validity of those expressions is not to be imposed by symbolic force alone, that is, unquestionably. In other words, transitions have occurred, and we cannot pretend that nothing has happened.

So how do our contemporary engagements, such as academic philosophizing, relate to our indigenous expressive forms, such as the different styles of orality? It hardly requires special effort to notice that philosophy is always about the familiar and the indigenous, whatever its form or epistemic status; it interrogates, deconstructs, analyzes, interprets, and tries to explain it. Philosophy is related to indigenous knowledge as the written word is to the oral. Jacques Derrida reminds us that the discussion of the relation between the two expressive modes is not new and traces it back to Plato in the history of Western philosophy: "Plato says of writing that it was an orphan or a bastard, as opposed to speech, the legitimate and high-born son of the 'father of logos.'"[22] Let us consider two examples that illustrate philosophy's ties with the ordinary and with everyday language, for it was not in vain that the founders of the analytic tradition looked to the clarification of language as key to understanding our knowledge of the world.[23] When discussing his critique of the claim that an analytical statement is one whose truth value depends entirely on the meanings of its terms, the American philosopher W. V. Quine uses as his examples the statement "No unmarried man is married" and its synonym "No bachelor is married" to ask, first, what it is about "meaning" that makes those statements necessarily true (as the proponents of analyticity allege), and, second, what it is that makes them synonyms—that is, interchangeable with each other without altering their truth value. The point is that although Quine criticizes as analyticity the fact that empiricists claim that the statement "No unmarried man is married" is logically true, many of us would hesitate to refute the commonsense impression that such a statement is indeed true on account of the meanings of its words within the English language structure. We assume that the statement is true because it conforms with how we have been taught to use words in the English language to make and convey meaning. But claiming so, according to Quine, implies an assumption about "meaning" that begins to appear funny only after a careful (philosophical) analysis. He says:

> For the theory of meaning a conspicuous question is the nature of its objects: what sort of things are meanings? A felt need for meant entities may derive from an earlier failure to appreciate that meaning and reference are distinct. Once the theory of meaning is sharply separated from the theory of reference, it is a short step to

recognizing as the primary business of the theory of meaning simply the synonymy of linguistic forms and the analyticity of statements; meanings themselves, as obscure intermediary entities, may well be abandoned.[24]

Then there is the question about what it is that makes Quine's two statements "synonymous." In other words, what do we mean when we claim that two statements are synonymous? Again, one possible response may be that it is because the subject in both statements—bachelor and unmarried man—"mean the same thing." According to this example, ordinary commonsense assumptions have suddenly become enormous philosophical problems on account of critical analysis. The problem Quine noticed is not an invention of the empiricists. Rather, it is one embedded in the use of ordinary language, in this case in the English vernacular, which the empiricists use to illustrate what they mean by analytic statements.

Let us consider another example, this time from an African language. The Ghanaian philosopher Kwasi Wiredu uses the Twi phrase *"ete saa"* (which translates as "it is so") to illustrate how the nature of philosophical problems can, at least in some instances, depend on the structural form of the languages we speak. According to Wiredu, the correspondence theory of truth, as we know it in English, for example, would sound cumbersome at best in Twi, so it does not even arise. In his view, in order to render the English formulation of the correspondence theory of truth as "a statement is true means that it corresponds with facts" into Twi, one would have to put it, rather awkwardly, in his opinion, as *"asem no te saa kyerese ene nea ete saa di nsianim"* (the statement is so means that it coincides, corresponds with what is so), which, as Wiredu says, "has the beauty of a tautology, but it teaches little wisdom. It seems to me unlikely that thinking in this language, one could be easily tempted into correspondence formulations of this sort."[25]

Wiredu appears to have at least two problems with the correspondence theory of truth. One, that it is problematic on the grounds of what it assumes to be possible, namely that one can objectively judge the state of affairs in the external world while experiencing them from his or her point of view at the same time. This, he argues, does not make much sense. Two (and this problem may precede the problem with logic), he argues that the claim of the correspondence theory of truth as given in English is not translatable in some languages, which limits its consideration in languages such as Twi. Whereas English speakers may have a greater tolerance for tautologies—which may then lead them to consider seriously as a philosophical problem such a pronouncement as "No unmarried man is married"—Twi speakers, from what Wiredu tells us, are unlikely to give it any consideration beyond recognition of its rhetorical aesthetic. At the everyday level, ordinary speakers of either language either use or avoid

such expressions as a matter of course without having to first take a philosophical stance, meaning that neither one is more or less philosophically
privileged than the other without the problematizing philosopher. The
problems philosophers raise are certainly related to the nature of the rest
of the languages within which they make sense.

The philosopher, aware of these everyday assumptions like most other
good speakers of the language, may often also be able to detect what is
theoretically striking in everyday expressions. Take, for instance, what Hallen and Sodipo say about the Yoruba concept of knowledge and how it contrasts with the so-called "knowledge as justified true belief" in the English
language analytic formulation.[26] When an ordinary Yoruba speaker—one
who is not an *onisegun* —says that she can only *"gbàgbó"* (believe) rather
than *"mó"* (know) that "Masolo lives in Alego Siaya" because Masolo's
brother said so, it is probable (and indeed is often the case) that she says
so only because that is how any Yoruba speaker would be expected to correctly deliver that kind of judgment. She may not be aware of the impact
of her expression on some existing theoretical position in the stricter
world of epistemological theory, and so she implies no critique of the
"knowledge as justified true belief" position. Yet if pressed on why she
only "believes" that "Masolo lives in Alego Siaya" when his own brother,
who probably knows the situation best, asserted so, the Yoruba speaker
may, upon the demands of the Yoruba language alone, correctly respond
that she has no firsthand knowledge of the situation herself and so can
only believe but cannot claim to "know" the state of the matter. A critical
listener—a philosopher, for example—may be drawn to the subtle distinction between "knowing" and "believing" that emerges from the Yoruba
speaker's insistence on only believing that "Masolo lives in Alego Siaya."
Unlike the everyday speaker of the language, any language, the philosopher
pays attention to and scrutinizes any theoretical content in the language
that she otherwise also speaks quite ordinarily at other times.

As Rwandan philosopher and linguist Alexis Kagame illustrated in his
massive work, subject matters for philosophical reflection are contained
in the languages people speak, in the assumptions they convey as well as
in the formal structures of the languages themselves. In Kagame's view,
Kinyarwanda is an embodiment of whole systems of thought (philosophical
thought in his example) as envisioned by its speakers, and Kagame likely
assumed that this was true of most if not all spoken human languages.[27]
He argued that the demonstration of the philosophical content of everyday
(ordinary) language had to be done systematically and comparatively. As
some readers might already know, he did both.[28] In the broader contexts of
their works, both Quine and Wiredu suggest that although it is not impossible to translate certain types of statements from one language to another,
such translation is often loose and indeterminate because a variety of
ontological and other implications accompany language-specific expres-

sions. The difficulty, they must have seen rightly, is due to the elasticity of language that enables it to embrace most concepts we formulate and communicate. These examples suggest that philosophical endeavors begin with the everyday, the familiar, which is part of the indigenous, as embedded in the locutions that bridge our relations with the external world around us, a claim long established in the ordinary language philosophy movement from which both Quine and Wiredu are partially intellectually descended, at least to the extent that they believe that clues can be found to deep philosophical questions through scrutinizing the workaday usage of the words in which philosophical questions are framed.

Hountondji, a student of Derrida himself, was not less aware of this primacy of the everyday, although his route to this position stems from the continental-European rather than the Anglo-American analytic perspective. He therefore could not possibly be casting the practice of everyday life away in order to ground philosophy in the extra-ordinary. The evidence for this may come from one of his most recent works. As he recounts in *The Struggle for Meaning,* his critique of Tempels was driven by a conviction that the underlying premise of his project, the point that became the mainstay of ethnophilosophy, namely that African thought was an enterprise of intuition, could not spur the growth of knowledge that Africa so acutely needed.

The growth of knowledge—and the ability of humans to modify both their understanding of reality as well as the external reality based on that ever-changing understanding—cannot issue out of unmotivated believing. To counter the ethnophilosophical position, Hountondji, probably while conceding to intuition a place in the structure of consciousness, saw in Husserl's phenomenological project (his analysis of the life of consciousness, or the "lifeworld," as Husserl called it) the key to salvaging African thought and the need for its critical orientation from an assumed (that is, not critically proposed or explained) causal relationship with the world and things in it. Probably with Husserl's distinction between *noeses* and *noema* in mind, Hountondji appears to argue that critical thought emerges when individuals think of the world as already *intended* at a lower level, as in the form of common beliefs, meaning that our relationship with the world as an object of intention is grounded in understanding and dialectically seeks to make sense of our senses of it, our *noema,* or meanings of it.

Ethnophilosophers, on the other hand, focus with unnecessary fixation on perceptions of the world (or of things and events in it) as events in the world—that is, as causal occurrences. Here is an example: most normal people (and some animals) experience dreams. They occur to us, we do not create them, and we do not choose which ones to have. In our waking life we may focus on dreams as occurrences to be understood, to be analyzed with respect to how they occur or in terms of what drives them, how long they last, and how they relate to the waking life they mimic. That undertaking, as many psychologists know, can be theoretically exciting as an exercise that seeks to provide meanings to such a complex aspect of our lives as the act and content of dreaming. But we could also choose to dwell on dreams as "in-themselves," as having their own "meanings" as clues to how to live our daily lives. This latter approach to dreams would be taking a causal stand toward them. But while it would also be giving "meaning" to the occurrences we call dreams, this sense of "meaning" would be different from that of the former.

Both approaches, to be sure, take as their object a mental occurrence, a psychological event, and even ask a question that, at least on the surface, sounds the same: What are dreams? Yet one approach takes dreams to have meanings—by so occurring, and by what they so divulge, to be forms of our relation with the world. This approach, which I hereby identify with the ethnophilosophical approach, takes dreams to be prescriptive sources of the principles and objectives of conduct. The other approach, which, I propose, identifies with Hountondji's own position, takes an ascending path, so to speak, to a different level in the idealist structure, one that thereby becomes, in Husserlian terminology, a science of ideas, or "science éidétique."[29] The latter offers descriptions—viewed broadly as theoretical explications—of phenomena as they occur in or offer themselves to intuition, while the former takes the act of intuition as an end to itself. The title Struggle for Meaning may therefore have different connotations of the term "meaning," least of which would be the differences between the regions of meaning in Husserlian terms. Or, as Ricoeur explained of Husserl, "In Husserlian language, the 'region' [of] consciousness is other than the 'region' [of] nature. It is perceived differently, it exists differently, it is certain differently."[30]

The immediate question that arises here is this: How does Husserl's idea of the "lifeworld" bail Hountondji out of the anti-tradition image—a position that grew out of his anti-ethnophilosophy stance—in order to reconnect him with the indigenous world? This is a difficult question, and we shall return to it later below. For now, let us state that for Husserl, phenomenology was a science whose premise was that all differences in theories of things (the world and our feelings, sensations, dreams, imaginations notwithstanding) must be common to all minds—they are public, if you wish, and therefore impersonal. That is why he labored to free phenomenology of the trappings of scientism and psychologism, a project that, as critical disciples such as Jean-Paul Sartre observed, remained trapped within the mechanistic outlook whose destruction had motivated him in the first place. It is important, then, to see Hountondji's attraction to Husserl as pegged on this sense of universality in the scheme, at least with regard to the making of sense. It seems that the goal for both Husserl and Hountondji was, first, to recognize the role of the active structuring of consciousness that enables it to intend its object. Second, Hountondji seeks to show, again (or still) working within the Husserlian scheme, how the world of intentionality is the locus of our everyday experiences. Our consciousness is directed at (intends) this world and forms a relationship with it. Thus consciousness is not passive even at that very rudimentary level, nor can that rudimentary level of intending the world be the constitution of philosophy.

It is instructive here, again, to remember Hountondji's critical response to Franz Crahay[31] in which he reminded Crahay that although myths were forms of first-level awareness, they already were abstract—they were "intentions" insofar as their claims or contents were acts of consciousness. They are more complex because their elements are not identical with those of the objects of the natural attitude. So abstraction was not the problem ethnophilosophy faced. If abstraction is the problem, then consciousness delivers to people a processed or filtered immediate world, not just of objects (through eidetic reduction) but also of beliefs and other ingredients of human experience in a wider sociocultural sense—that is, the ingredients by which consciousness itself is structured. The nature of consciousness is the basis of our accordingly structured knowledge of the world. The variety of interpretations notwithstanding, it is safe to say that Husserl saw a connection rather than a fracture between science and philosophy (or should we say phenomenology?). For him, our knowledge of the external world, when it is presented to us, occurs within the rubric of the preceding content of consciousness that is a combination of both the natural and phenomenological attitudes. The meanings of our statements about the external world are inextricably linked to the lifeworld. Husserl believed that the examination of the lifeworld—the task of phenomenology as a radical retreat from the natural approach to the world—was itself a scientific endeavor, meaning that it is a careful and systematic exercise. For him, phenomenology and science formed a unity; or, put another way, philosophy was part of science.[32] Husserl's now-classic text on phenomenology, published in the *Encyclopaedia Britannica* in 1932, opens thus:

> Phenomenology denotes a new, descriptive, philosophical method, which, since the concluding years of the last century, has established (1) an a priori psychological discipline, able to provide the only secure basis on which a strong empirical psychology can be built, and (2) a universal philosophy, which can supply an organum for the methodical revision of all the sciences.[33]

It is my view that Hountondji's critique of Tempels, even as sharp and nearly as uncompromising as it was at the time of its first articulation, was driven by an eagerness to underscore the realism of Africans' everyday experiences in contrast to what he perceived as ethnophilosophers', especially Tempels's, obsession with staffing Africans' consciousness with only apparent or pseudo-objects, objects that do not exist, such as the so-called vital forces. Such (ethnophilosophers') emphases, he frequently laments, disconnect Africans' consciousness from the real ("scientific") world around them. Clearly, Hountondji, like Aimé Césaire[34] long before him, felt some frustration with a philosophical proposal that sidestepped and almost trivialized African people's everyday concerns with the world of "real" objects and problems in attempt to replace it with one that emphasized magicians' imaginations—even if it was an attempt to claim "reason" for African cultural beliefs and practices, especially those that previously were the most derided. Of course, Africans too, like any normal people anywhere, had beliefs full of superstitions and other unsupportable opinions, justified and otherwise, but these were by no means the only or the most important content of their consciousness. The paradox is that it was Hountondji who, in countercriticism, was then accused of being relentless in pursuit of a nonexistent universal philosophy, an interest that, in the view of his critics, betrayed him as being bourgeois and unmindful of both the local experiences and the knowledge schemes of the masses.

At the heart of the debate about indigeneity around the idea of ethnophilosophy is an old squabble among African—and for that matter also Caribbean—subjects of France: to be or not to be French, or, put differently, what it means and what it takes to be indigenous enough. The challenge for African philosophers and ideologues of indigenous systems is to incorporate Marx's eleventh thesis to Feuerbach into their thinking; namely to cross from mere eloquent but inconsequential definitions to the practice of relying on indigenous resources. Africans will not change Africa if they depend on Western organizations to give them funds even to define what indigenous knowledge and indigenous development are or when they wait for Western organizations to pay them to meet with and tell each other (but also be told by the West) what they should be thinking about. Until Africans discard the attitude of dependency and until they transition to the point of defining their needs and funding their own initiatives, the definitions will remain primarily oriented toward donor boardrooms for the purpose of extracting per diem allowances and the elegant essays will remain little more than tools of personal convenience. A measured application of Marx's eleventh thesis might make the sacrifices of Western taxpayers look worthwhile while the long-decried moral lacuna in the character of our public officials might finally be addressed at the personal level.

Philosophy and the Habitus of Everyday Life

How, then, does one crystallize the indigeneity of everyday life in their thinking? Needless to say, we encounter the everyday not only in the multiple indigenous uses of language as argued by Wittgenstein in the

Philosophical Investigations, we also encounter it as both consumers and agents of the ideological agenda and goals of the social structures and institutions by and through which society itself is defined and objectified. For example, in the workings of the structures of the institutions of society and the semantics of words or syntactical structures of the different human languages are to be found the concepts and theories people use to express and to explain their understanding of the world: their experiences, both in the ordinary and in the Kantian and Husserlian senses of the term. Basic to both is the idea that our consciousness structures what we experience. The task of philosophy, at least according to Husserl, was to analyze the structure of consciousness as a prelude to science.

So what lessons does one learn from Husserl, and how would such lessons apply to an understanding of the relation of philosophy to the indigenous in the African context? There may be several ways of understanding the task here, one of which is to grasp how the basic notion of experience, as found in the works of both Kant and Husserl, opens up to the realm that all along we have been referring to, rather unqualifiedly, as "the indigenous." My response is that the constitution of experience is a function of intersubjectivity, our interaction with others from which we acquire the basic "bricks" of intentionality. The basic axioms—that is, our deep-seated assumptions that we take to be inexplicably obvious in our navigation of truth and falsehood, right and wrong, good and bad, and so on—result from what the cradle (that is, society through the family as its primary agent) gives us through its many mechanisms, including language (words complete with their meanings, understood initially only by their referents in the world).[35] Just as in the process of language acquisition we raise issues and notice problems depending on what society offers us and exposes us to as we inhabit it—which is to say, at least in part, that neither society nor the consciousnesses it births, and which in turn sustains it, can be static. This way, "the indigenous" is the whole sociocultural realm that defines or constitutes certain basic elements of our consciousness. Thus, it does not require that a value or belief first exhibit the characteristics of being fossilized and unchanging, thus good only for the historical space they occupy, in order to be indigenous. Rather, because problems are defined by their sociohistorical contexts, we confront and interrogate cultural inclinations to disregard the wishes and interests of community members as we never did before, because we are driven by demands for liberalism in ways we never openly were fifty years or so ago.

As we shall see in the discussion of the "Epilogue" in Appiah's *In My Father's House,* conflicts between communal demands and individual choices clearly raise issues of the location of moral reason that guides the idea of the moral good. Is the individual as autonomous as some schools of liberalism demand, or should the community be the sole source of moral reason regardless of its authoritarian quest for self-preservation?

And must the embrace of either one of these schemes preclude the other? These are just some of the kind of questions that will spring out of the contexts of social and cultural shifts when the once-assumed homogeneity begins to fizzle out as a result of the surge of demands for greater individual autonomy. In other words, "the indigenous" is constantly being transformed, always negotiating its form. Indeed, a look back might now suggest that at least part of the controversy over ethnophilosophy was about how the indigenous was to be represented. On the one hand was the school that appeared to equate the postcolonial reemergence of the indigenous with isolation from foreign, especially Western, influence. On the other was the view that saw the indigenous in historical light, wishing for it to sustain what was instructive for contemporary times but weary of what would no longer constitute "the indigenous" for younger generations. A number of the exponents of the anti-ethnophilosophy stance adopted this view. And the call for "different approaches" does not and should not always imply importation, nor should importation always entail the demise of the "indigenous." Rather, as Hountondji argues, it is a call for a self-transformation from within first and a reversion to importation only as a last resort, for example where accepting an import not only takes into consideration a careful adaptation, or indigenization, but also may be more expedient and less costly than endogenous transformation. Hountondji is unequivocal about the primary value of the indigenous:

> We should acknowledge achievements and work in progress and seek how to cope with present difficulties and develop new strategies for overcoming dependence. We should promote scientific and technological innovation and self-reliance as means to meet, first and foremost, Africa's own needs.[36]

The Language of the Indigenous

The view that African scholars should revert to indigenous languages as the medium for the expression of their thought has long been popular among many cultural nationalists. Indeed, part of the problem with false representations of African knowledge in non-African texts has been misinterpretation, misrepresentation, or even total misconceptualization of African meanings, indicating lack of mastery of African languages by many scholars of African knowledge systems. (Some anthropologists, in contrast, have done commendable work in their study of African cultures.) The late Ugandan poet Okot p'Bitek illustrated such problems with regard to misinterpretations of local (Acholi and Langi) religious ideas in the hands of missionary translators of catechetical texts into the vernacular. Supposedly, the missionaries reckoned that such translations would help local Catholic converts grasp in their own terms the idea of God as "creator" of the whole universe, including humans.[37] The problems p'Bitek encountered in his studies highlight major problems with the transfer of meanings across languages, and, through language, across different culturally informed conceptual schemes. Careful not to discredit totally the practice of cross-cultural translations—because sometimes the failure of translation is due to the carelessness of the translator rather than to the incongruency or incommensurability of the conceptual fields in question—p'Bitek tried to show the cultural limitations of language and the difficulties often encountered when concepts migrate across linguistic specifics. In his view, the catechetical texts of the missionaries were not adaptations of Acholi cosmology into Christian teachings. Rather, they were part of a project that reinvented the Acholi language in several cases by introducing new terms and concepts from the languages of the sur- rounding communities, including Muslim ones. What is not always clear from such difficulties as they often issue out of cross-cultural translations is whether the limits of language determine the extent of our concepts as well, a theory Wittgenstein subscribed to in the earlier stage of his career (in the *Tractatus*). As p'Bitek argued, largely in inadvertent agree- ment with what Quine was saying elsewhere about the indeterminacy of translation, one needs to be careful to avoid catastrophes such as those the missionaries engendered when they told the Acholi people that God could be both good and creator at the same time. For Christians, the goodness of God is seen in his creation, especially of humans in his own image. Thus, according to this theology, creation was proof of God's goodness. For the Acholi, on the other hand, as for most Luo people generally, divine creation is regarded to be an evil act associated with the forces of pain and death. Artistry occupies a vaguely understood rank in the hierarchy of activities considered necessary for meeting the needs of society and is often shrouded in imageries of marginality, even as the products of that artistry may be important and even evoke aesthetic admiration. The gods of the Basoga and other communities, the ones whose names were given to the Acholi as the "creators" of all things, occupied these marginal spaces in the Acholi conceptual universe.

But perhaps the use of indigenous languages is a matter for which judgments of good or bad become significant only in relation to whether or not such consideration has been an issue, as was the case during and after European colonization of Africa. Otherwise each human language is as good as another, although the same equality cannot be said of the aesthetics that accompany the expressive form of some languages such as Dholuo. Outside these formalistic differences in languages across the world, each language is just as good as another. It is reasonable enough to expect every community to have its own language through which it adequately expresses and transmits its values to its members. Indeed, any- one who takes time to reflect on the beautiful complexity of the language they call their own (or any other language they know well) will notice quickly that the use of language is itself a value, an art in which people's performance is rated, admired, and rewarded in a variety of ways. Poets enjoy this esteem in almost all communities I know of. From an episte-mological point of view too, the importance of the vernacular cannot be emphasized enough. Although it seems rather obvious that the language of any community reflects the structure of its world—that is, how the com-munity understands, defines, and taxonomizes ideas about itself—and its relations, hierarchies, and ecosystem (with all of its values and dangers), it is only recently, with the quest to free colonized peoples and cultures from foreign domination, that this obvious reality has been dwelt on. We know this from the works of the Brazilian Paulo Freire, for example his groundbreaking work in the radical philosophy of education for the oppressed, in which he argues that the objective of education is to help people read their reality and write their own history.[38] Most postcolonial theorists have carried on that quest for a decolonized mind. As one of his radical postcolonial themes, Ngũgĩ wa Thiong'o has popularized the call for using the vernacular, but perhaps for reasons other than those p'Bitek claimed.

P'Bitek's claim that the term "creator" was inconceivable to the Acholi as meaning a supposedly benevolent God (for which they had no specific term either) raises analytical questions that interrogate the relationship between meanings (as concepts) and language and hence call for the analy-sis of the nature of both for purposes of determining their corresponding extensions and connotations. I consider this to be different from what I have perceived to be wa Thiong'o's reasons for preferring the vernacular but I do not claim that his position on language and its use does not have strong philosophical presuppositions. Far from it. In fact, he is opposed to colonial language because he saw it as a strategy for controlling how the colonized people managed their daily lives, their mental universe, their perception of themselves and of their relationship to the world.[39] Thus, while such a position certainly addresses language as the vehicle for ideas, especially in the ideological realm, it raises questions of a different kind, those that address the tools of domination and, conversely, the role of the writer as a medium of the people for whom he or she writes and the goal of writing as being primarily to produce knowledge for the empow-erment of the masses. On the other hand, p'Bitek too was a politically driven intellectual in the broader sense of the word political (as most of us are or need to be), and hence his critique of the missionary and the wider colonial enterprise was first defined by the political reality within which the imposition of Christian ideology and other Western knowledge took place. The questions that p'Bitek raises, which I believe belong at the center of analytic philosophy, may lead us to ask whether we can translate between different languages or whether we can express African meanings in non-African languages such French, English, or any other one, for that matter—languages that, in the course of their adaptations, have taken different local forms.

These questions have been addressed, and I have no intention of claiming originality that does not belong to me when I merely refer to how they help us understand the complexity and evolution of the vernacular. Most of you have seen at least one piece of work that urges the practice of philosophy in African vernaculars. But let us consider for a moment that communication, as Kwasi Wiredu has so lucidly argued,[40] is primarily for conveying concepts between interlocutors. We are then prompted to ask what kind of "things" concepts are, where and how they occur, how we transmit them to others, and, in the end, how we determine whether others have apprehended precisely what we intended. Analysis of these questions reveals that the relationship between language and concepts is often a hit-and-miss affair. Sometimes we hit, as when we use proper names of people or of places (especially when we talk with people that we know to be acquainted with the persons and places whose names we mention), and sometimes we miss, as when I stand in front of my first-year undergraduate class and announce: "Our topic today is phenomenology." I often find that I need more than a semester or, at a more advanced professional level, a whole lifetime to get just a few things right and rightly transmitted to the native speakers of the language I use in the classroom. Concepts are not necessarily made clearer or easier to apprehend because we have expressed them in the native tongue of our interlocutor. Sometimes we may need sentences or even passages to clarify concepts. The reasons for such a difficulty may be multiple, but at least one of them is the fact that meanings are not "objects," so it is harder to be precise in relating words to their meanings (references) than it is with proper names. Sometimes we have no specific words or terms for them, forcing us to strategize, to choose and select words in order to hit as closely as possible to the meanings we intend to pass on to others regardless of the medium we use. I would see no great problem with borrowing a term or phrase from another language to precisely communicate a concept if my interlocutor would have fewer problems of understanding me in that medium. But it is not impossible to express any concept in any language.

Can we, then, use English or French words to transmit African meanings? I believe that the answer to this question is yes. Of course, the point is not one of deciding whether or not we should continue to speak in any of the languages of colonists. At one level, we have dealt with that issue since the rise of our nationalist spirit, which occurred long before the end of colonialism. Responses to this question, while remaining quite pertinent at the political and cultural levels, often include pragmatic factors that need to be considered, just like the persistent questions about the "right" ethnic and linguistic makeup of African nations and their boundaries. Regardless of how the matter is handled at the policy level, it can be expected that any decision will be informed by some consideration that intersects with, if it does not directly spring from, a philosophical worry—namely whether we can preserve the core of our cultural integrity, our conceptual or theoretical representations of the world—when we use other languages.

The problem, I should say immediately, is not limited to the contrast between African and non-African languages, as the debate tends to suggest within the contexts of postcolonial discourse. All languages are beautiful to their native and other well-versed speakers, which is why any good speaker of any given language often believes that there always will be some special features in it that are not replicable in others. There are jokes I know how to tell only in Dholuo, for example, and I believe I would not be able to tell them with the same gusto in any other language, sometimes because of the phonetics of its words or for some other reason with certain other jokes, and so forth. But the same could be said of almost every other language. Indeed, there is little that is more culturally enjoyable and gratifying about the knowledge of a language than the ability to make complex jokes and other language games in it, which goes far beyond the average competence in it. This point brings us to the now-pervasive question, one that I already hinted at when I referred to Okot p'Bitek, namely, Do we lose anything, or, put another way, can we preserve the conceptual and theoretical integrity of indigenous African thought when we use other languages to express it? Although the question arises most often with reference to the contrast between African and Western systems of thought and the languages that convey them, p'Bitek puts an interesting local spin on it, thus broadening the scope of the problem beyond the oppositions between colonial and native. To be sure, for him too, the colonists were primarily responsible for obfuscation and scary confusion, as the Acholi catechumens encountered, because, among themselves, African religions are not used to proselytize others. Chinua Achebe once remarked in an interview that religion is one thing so fundamental to any community's culture that it just cannot be replaced by another. So according to him, Igbo elders, when asked to tell others about their religious beliefs, would retort in a way that can be paraphrased something like this: "You must have your own, the one of your people, which is good enough." According to Appiah,[41] using the conceptual and theoretical idioms of one system to judge another—which is what aspects of African thought have suffered when contrasted to apparently similar views from Western thought[42]—becomes problematic partly because in attempting to judge which one is more true or makes better sense, one runs into difficulties resulting from factors such as the ambiguity of the supposedly shared subject matter between two cultures that is so great that while some may see it as shared, others may perceive that subject matter as so different in the two cultures that the two understandings constitute competing ideas. From that ambiguity other difficulties emerge.

The problem becomes even more complex. Ethnolinguists and historians who use oral traditions to stitch together traces of the movements of humanity across the globe agree that each time a language exits the roll call of linguistic cultures, what is lost is not just a body of words but indeed a whole body of knowledge of the world. Few people understand this better than the Belgian-born historian Jan Vansina, who mainstreamed orality as a dependable source of history.[43] But beyond these obvious peculiarities, proponents of translatability between languages hold that despite the need to use African languages to express indigenous knowledge in Africa, reasonable conceptual translation is still possible. And their premise is not only that concepts are language-free characteristics of the mind, as Wiredu argues, but also that language is an elastic phenomenon that we can bend, twist, weave and stretch in any direction and to any lengths in order to accommodate or to communicate the concepts we have in our minds. It may take a long time and perhaps many class sessions, to effectively communicate a concept, especially if it is complex, for example explaining the idea of "phenomenology" to average first-year college students, or it may take just a short time. It all depends on what kind of knowledge we are talking about and whom we intend to transmit it to.

As may be evident from the example of the term "phenomenology," all languages do not express concepts in equal ways. Many languages have borrowed and continue to borrow from other languages across the globe in order to create new concepts or to simplify the expression of a familiar one with words that have been borrowed and adopted into local usage as either ordinary or technical terms. In the professional disciplines, law, medicine, chemistry, and indeed philosophy itself are notoriously characterized by such conceptual lendings. New concepts can always be introduced into repertoires of local idioms by importing new terms for them from distant languages and cultures. But such practices are selective and don't appear to be able to appease the underlying worry that it may not do justice to local meanings, the main reason being that it is often difficult to determine the exact sense that a term delivers when it is used for a concept or theory from a different system of thought. It must be observed, however, that translating some ideas, for example those of objects, especially common ones, may be far less difficult than translating a more complex idea that may require some explanation even in its native rendering. One example is, say, the idea of *juok* that I discuss in chapter 5 below. Another example, also fairly complex, is the Igbo concept of *chi* that Achebe discusses in *Morning Yet on Creation Day*.[44] Such concepts, like many others from other languages, make the concept of the person, as Appiah says,[45] a particularly difficult idea to translate between different idiomatic cultures or theoretical systems.

One can cite several examples to illustrate what Appiah and others have explained as difficulties in translation. Now imagine two native Dholuo-speaking individuals sitting next to a shared English friend who speaks reasonable Dholuo as well. The two Luo are engrossed in conversation with each other in their tongue when suddenly, in reaction to something the other has said or done, one of them retorts: "*I'jajuok?*" (Are you a *jajuok*?), to which the companion responds with a disapproving remark of his own: "*kik ichak iluonga jajuok, Omera*" (Don't you ever call me a *jajuok* again, my friend!). Later, while narrating this incident to others, the English friend translates the first remark as "He asked him: are you a night-runner?" Many Dholuo speakers would regard the translation of "*jajuok*" into "night-runner" as appropriate or reasonable, but it would be very wrong as a translation of the above. Why? Because although in everyday yet superficial senses, using the term/idea of *juok* in relation to night running is common on the lips of many (and is what many foreign people are likely to be told), "night running" does not mean "*juok*." Rather, it means "*ringo otieno*," and is said to be a form of "*juok*" only when the intentions of those who do so are suspect, because it is not usual for people to run in the night habitually unless they have something to conceal, such as moral waywardness. In these senses, although the translation of the remark "*I'jajuok?*" as "Are you a night-runner?" would be regarded as not out of place or appropriate, it would be wrong.

Or consider this other example, also from Dholuo: to say "*Adwaro chiemo*" means, in English translation, "I want food" ("*dwaro*" means "to want," and "*chiemo*" means "food"). But when you call out to your son to come help you with something quickly and he retorts "*Adwaro chiemo*," the statement, although it uses exactly the same words in the same order, would no longer mean "I want food," because the word "*dwaro*" would no longer mean a state of mind that we associate with "desire," as in the first case. In the second sense it refers to an engagement, not being free to do anything else: "I am about to start (sit down to) dinner." Similarly, we don't attribute special powers over life and death to a gravely ill person who, just before they expire, says to those around them "*koro adwaro tho*," literally "I want to die this moment." Rather, due either to some excruciating pain or to sensing the inability to sustain a vital activity like breathing, a dying person may remark that "I feel like I am about to die," which is what "*koro adwaro tho*" means. Of course, one could well say "*koro adwaro tho*" in the sense of an intention, that is "I want (or I desire) to die" if, when they say so, they refer to intending to deliberately put themselves in a situation from which they know dying would most probably result, like jumping into an industrial carcass grinder or sugar-cane crusher. In the first sense, however, a person uttering those words could in fact be requesting aid instead of asserting the desire or intention to die. Now, if meaning is what appears in the mind when we hear or read words (or encounter some other relevant type of signs), then any competent speaker of Dholuo would not get the same meaning from both meanings of these two statements: *"Adwaro chiemo"* ("I want food" versus "I am about to sit down to dinner") and *"koro adwaro tho"* ("It is my wish to die right now" versus "I feel like I am about to die"). The meanings are different. We don't claim when a dying relative makes such a remark in my language shortly preceding their expiration that "he/she said they wanted—as in being willing—to die, and then they died," to attribute to them special powers. Translation of meaning can be indeterminate, which is not to say that it is impossible but rather that in a minimal sense it can require more than the translation of individual words.

Let us consider for a moment the other side of this issue, keeping in mind that the problem is far broader than that of the opposition between native African idioms and their European translations. Rather, it is one that we face with our colleagues from a neighboring community or country. So imagine that we all wrote in our different native languages and/or dialects spoken in Africa today and that we all understood each other. This would certainly be a wonderful achievement, not only because it would bring the knowledge delivered through these languages to people in other speech communities—again, as in the Acholi case—but also because it would, in pursuit of lexical and auditive (phonetic) specifications for exacting separate ideas, spur such languages and dialects to greater orthographic developments and determination of specific symbols for phonic expressions, as wa Thiong'o has in fact tried to do for Gĩkũyũ sounds. Recently, I sent an e-mail to a good friend to identify by name someone we had both hired to do some work for us separately. His response was: *"Joseph; en or Owino Fred."* It happens that many educated speakers of my language are fond of throwing English words into vernacular sentences. They have tamed and woven English phrases, terms, and other smaller things like connectives into the vernacular with great beauty and elegance. For someone who knows this background, my friend's response could have been terribly ambiguous. In fact, I read his response to be giving me two names, with the "or" in the middle of the sentence appearing to me as a throw-in of the English disjunctive, hence prompting me to read the sentence as "It is [either] Joseph or Owino Fred"; more literally as "Yes, Joseph; it is either him or (it is) Owino Fred." The point here is that the ensuing ambiguity could easily have been prevented if there was a determinate orthographic way of rendering the precise meaning of "or" as it appeared in my friend's response, which could have distinguished it from several other words, especially its English lookalike, which we write the same way using the Roman alphabet. Or should we demand that the speakers of the English language give their disjunctive greater recognizability, especially to distinguish it from "or" in Dholuo, than it currently has? In the sentence in question, my friend intended "or" to mean "brother in-law of." We all can think of such problems within our various languages, some simple, others quite complex. There is no doubt that orthographic undertakings for preserving and improving our different languages should be encouraged as part of our cultural heritage and growth.

The possibility of such orthographic developments aside, there appears to be a problem that makes the beauty of our languages less attractive for practical professional reasons. While I cannot speak for other disciplines, I am often afraid that reading a philosophical text in, say, Lugbara or Kuranko or Twi would present me with an insurmountable task, especially if understanding its content and using the ideas therein in one or another discursive way is what accounts for the furtherance of philosophy as an enterprise. Thus, I wish, for example, to have known at least some of those tongues that make up Akan, such as Twi, well enough to be able to access further and participate in the informative analytical debate that goes on among Akan-speaking philosophers today. Indeed, my quotation of Wiredu above underlines my admiration of the debate as much as it portrays my frustrating limitations in accessing it. It partly means that much knowledge that is available for the philosopher's attention already exists and is constantly produced in the vernacular. The same could be said of the propositions Quine uses. But consider for a moment whether the eighteenth-century Ethiopian philosophical texts would have been known outside the seventeenth- and eighteenth-century Ethiopic-speaking (Amharic or Oromo) world if they had remained untranslated until today or what would have become of the rich Dogon and Bamana (Bambara) texts without such translations and commentaries as were done by Marcel Griaule and Germaine Dieterlen with the help of their notable native speakers? How more limited would they be than they already are for Africans who are so divided along the colonial language lines? Sometimes we don't communicate across different speech communities even within same nations, let alone across them. Hence the practical question about the intellectual benefits of writing in vernacular remains challenging but must be attempted for two reasons: to encourage local debate about the understanding and interpretation of indigenous concepts and theories and to preserve these thought expressions in their original renditions. I wish we could all speak the one thousand seven hundred or so languages and dialects of Africa. My question is: How would that ever be?

Indigenous Thought and Analytical Comparisons: Hallen and Sodipo

If one statement could describe the core of Hallen and Sodipo's joint work, I daresay that it would read somewhat as follows: ingredients of analytical grids are not limited to the Cartesian model of individualist epistemological practice; rather, they are also built into the kind of knowledge that informs general cultural norms and values. The assumptions that ground such contrasting systems and inform how statements produced within them are to be understood make translation difficult, or, as they try to show in Quinean terms, indeterminate. Partly to demonstrate this, in *Knowledge, Belief, and Witchcraft: Analytic Experiments in African Philosophy,* Hallen and Sodipo practice a comparative philosophical analysis across cultural borders.[46] The book raises, from a specific African context, some of the major questions that have also been recently raised by one of the most outstanding American philosophers today. Although with different goals, its methodology shares an affinity with the dialogical engagement with indigenous experts, a practice now widely attributed to the Kenyan philosopher Odera Oruka, namely the professional philosopher's endeavor to tease out philosophically significant and sensitive concepts and theories embedded in local idioms by making cultural experts expound on and elucidate traditional knowledge. Hallen and Sodipo went farther than Oruka in regarding their chosen cultural experts, the *onisegun* of the Yoruba, as their "parallel colleagues" with whom they could and did hold discussions and debates on the philosophical implications of some of the prominent concepts in their teachings and practice as healers. It was then upon Hallen and Sodipo as professional philosophers to compare these with their counterparts in the (analytical) philosophy of the English-speaking world. The authors proclaim the book to be a mix of faithful transcription and a description of those discussions. The most prominent in the ensuing Yoruba-English comparison is the knowledge-belief (*mò-gbàgbó*) distinction. According to the analysis, the Yoruba concept of *mò* (knowledge) exacts stringent conditions under which belief (*gbàgbó*) can qualify as or become knowledge (*mò*). It is not enough, as appears in the Anglo-American rendition of this epistemological problem, that one be justified in believing, for example, that p for one to know that p, even if p were to be true. In Yoruba, Hallen and Sodipo observe:

> *Gbàgbó* that may be verified is *gbàgbó* that may become *mò*. *Gbàgbó* that is not open to verification (testing) and must therefore be evaluated on the basis of justification alone (*àlàyé, papò,* etc.) cannot become *mò* and consequently its *òótó* must remain indeterminate.
>
> The point of difference between the two systems that we find to be of greatest significance is the relative role of testimony or second-hand information. In the Yoruba system any information conveyed on the basis of testimony is, until verified, *igbàgbó*. In the English system [by contrast] a vast amount of information conveyed on the basis of testimony is, without verification, classified as "knowledge that." Much of the latter is information that the individual concerned would not even know *how* to verify. Yet it is still "knowledge that."[47]

The implication is that in the Yoruba system, as distinct from its counterpart in contemporary English-speaking epistemological theory, claim(s) to knowledge require first-person experiential (verifiable) testimony and not mere justification. The Yoruba system draws a much smaller map for knowledge-claims. Furthermore, while in the Anglo-American epistemology it is always assumed that, as stated above, knowledge is always a form of belief under special conditions, in the Yoruba system *mò* does not entail *gbàgbó*. The two are distinct, and any attempt to link the two in Yoruba language creates a contradiction, thus making Yoruba propositional attitudes radically different from their counterparts in the Anglo-American tradition. One cannot say in Yoruba that "I believe that *p*, and I also know that *p*." Either one (only) believes or she knows, but she cannot both believe and know that *p*. This is all a very beautiful analysis and a good use of Quine's doubt about the extent to which determinate translation is possible between, or even within, languages. Within African philosophy in general, such beautiful work may present a material problem for the growth of the debate beyond the speech community in reference, for if one is to sustain the debate on the claims based on the analysis, one must at least be competent in the language being analyzed. In the absence of such broad competence beyond native or adopted speakers of our languages, the doors to a fruitful philosophical enterprise among Africans will remain only thinly and frustratingly open. Yet we must encourage it, and that endeavor must begin with such excellent work as Hallen and Sodipo's.

As I have said before, Hallen and Sodipo's work presents a way of adapting local knowledge to professional philosophical discourse in a way that is very different from raw sagacity. But Godwin Sogolo, another Nigerian philosopher, suggests that there is more to philosophy than the task of exacting comparative meanings across linguistic boundaries. Commenting on the earlier edition of Hallen and Sodipo's work, he says:

> It seems clear [from Hallen and Sodipo's discussion of the meanings of *mò* and *gbàgbó* in Yoruba] that most of what constitutes the subject-matter for African philosophers today, insofar as they use alien languages, belong [*sic*] more to the language analyst than to the philosopher. . . . For, when, after all, all the problems of meaning and translation have been resolved, residual philosophical disputes could still arise. It is possible, for instance, that when it has been sorted out that the concept *ori* in Yoruba conveys the same meaning as "predestination" in English, the philosophical problem still arises as to whether the Yoruba belief in *ori* is compatible with the *babalawo*'s efforts to change the future course of events.[48]

It should be observed that Sogolo's implied critique of the type of philosophy Hallen and Sodipo practiced is indisputably in order. Indeed, it is common among philosophers, as part of their philosophical opinion, to critique or even to totally reject some methodological practices within the discipline as either not adequate or as totally misplaced. Such critiques are frequently related to what is believed to constitute core philosophical issues, and that too is an area that is hardly ever obvious. Indeed, it can be (and it has been in the history of the discipline) a matter of interesting disputation and difference among philosophers. It so happens, however, that analysis of terms with the goal of determining what meanings are or how they fare in translations between languages, as Hallen and Sodipo are concerned with in their work, is quite a household task for a large number of philosophers in the world and rightly so because conceptual analysis is a legitimate philosophical exercise. Its benefits may include a better understanding and appreciation of the beliefs and practices to which the analyzed concepts relate. Hence, it appears to me, the determination of the conceptual relation between the belief in *ori* and in the implications of the role of the *babalawo* could benefit from a thorough analysis of the terms as used in the Yoruba belief system. I also believe that such analysis could help interested people, both Yoruba and aliens, take a peek into the conceptual complexity of the Yoruba world. In whatever minimal sense, the understanding of self and others is part of what philosophers do qua philosophers. From the evidence of the references Sogolo covered in his discussion of this matter, it is obvious that these matters are not unknown to him.

To return to the *mò-gbàgbó* distinction in Yoruba and to the claim that belief and knowledge are incompatible counterparts of consciousness about the world, one would want to ask what the claim entails in respect to the individual-society conditioning of the conditions for knowledge. It should not surprise anyone that Hallen and Sodipo come close to Wiredu's point of view here. According to Hallen and Sodipo's explanation of Yoruba, it appears that a great many of our discourses are both about and made up of belief rather than knowledge—that is, derived from testimonies rather than direct, first-hand experience.[49] Learning from others, which forms the bulk of our source of information, is a provisional medium for acquiring familiarity with the world around us. The only things we know for certain, because we know them directly most of the time, are our own mental experiences (cognitive and emotional processes). Even the idea of the self (*persona mia*), because it is a derivative of other experiences rather than a directly experienced "thing," is only a belief. Now because truth, which is a significant component of knowledge (what I *mò* is *òótó*), is a property of statements—that is, the embodiment of secondary sources—it cannot be possible. In other words, truth is not communicable, it is only directly experienced. Communication can only convey what many who receive the information being communicated will have as belief, not knowledge (where this entails truth-conditions). It would appear, then, that for the Yoruba, as for all people who are aware of the limitations of the human ability to witness everything first-hand, a large majority of our everyday statements are based not on knowledge (*mò*) but on belief (*gbàgbó*).[50]

Finally, Hallen and Sodipo's analysis suggests that the maxims of knowledge in Yoruba language have quite a broad range of degrees of opinion, depending on the nature of the justifications for those opinions. There are strong and weak opinions. For instance, the view that "I believe Okelo went to the market because I saw him walk in the direction of the market" is a stronger opinion than believing that "Okelo went to the market because my uncle (a third party), who saw him walk in that direction, told me so." Both are opinions, but the second one, irrespective of how dependable the uncle's evidence might be, and even when what it reports is true, is one step farther from the maxim of knowledge, namely direct evidence. But even as these two examples show, justified claims, including those based on direct evidence, are not always true, nor do they always amount to knowledge even if and when they are true. Moreover, hardly any ordinary person is concerned with these nuances of truth strongly enough to want or see the need to supply justification for her statements before every enunciation. Furthermore, what Hallen and Sodipo refer to as the "ideal [third party] observer" mediation—for example, the uncle in the foregoing example—is not always available to mediate between disputing claims to knowledge. In Yoruba explanations, however, there is a clear and strong enough indication that truth—matters as they really are or were—is always there, whatever the position of any party to the dispute.[51] Most of the time we cannot verify them for ourselves, so we *gbàgbó* them from other people. If this is so, then for the Yoruba too, truthfulness as a social virtue becomes a more crucial and sufficient requirement for practical everyday life, for it is crucial if we are to stay on track in pursuit of knowledge—and truth—as an ideal. In Hallen and Sodipo's words, "As [this ordinary person] operates on the basis of correspondence, his initial justification should consist of proving that his *account of* his perceptions or that his *knowledge of* is accurate."[52] The stringent Yoruba conditions for knowledge-claims make such claims a rarity in the ordinary person's life. However, what people *gbàgbó* may contain elements of *mò*, such as believing that X can perform action *p* because we have witnessed him do it first-hand before, or when what was originally regarded as *igbàgbó* is confirmed.[53] The *mò-gbàgbó* distinction in Yoruba does not privilege tradition or any other form of received information. In fact, it is so skeptical of untested claims that it even robs science of its predictive strength. Above all, it makes a mockery of the English-language (analytical) definition of knowledge based on mere justification of belief. In other words, although there may be various justifications (in degrees) for why we should be inclined to believe (*gbàgbó*) certain claims, these can never amount to knowledge (*mò*) unless we witness them first-hand. In Hallen and Sodipo's reckoning, the claim of Western critics that the epistemic world of Africans is guided by the proclamation (dubbed "traditional") of custom as the criterion of truth—or, in effect, that any claim is "believed or upheld" by later generations merely on the strength of tradition; that is, "because the forefathers said so" or "because that is how it always has been"—could not be more misguided.[54] According to Hallen and Sodipo, such an accusation ignores the sharp differences between English-language analytical and Yoruba definitions of knowledge. It wrongly assumes that the Yoruba conflate belief and knowledge, as is the case in the English-language analytical definition. Hence the critics assume that what is attributed to tradition is what is held to be "knowledge." But on the contrary, at least for the Yoruba, because oral tradition belongs to the genre of claims heard from others' accounts rather than those that are directly witnessed, it is believed, in the Yoruba sense of the term "believe," only as a corpus of claims that she or he who receives them can hardly claim to make up what she/he "knows"; they could be false.

Philosophy, Method, and the Sages

One aspect of Hallen and Sodipo's text is particularly interesting: it involves the role of indigenous sages in producing and sustaining critical thought. Their text is based on the analysis of quotes from the wise medicine men and teachers of Yoruba community and culture. The conversations with the *onisegun,* the indigenous medicinal experts, would not have been interesting in and of themselves if not for the controversy occasioned by a similar conversation between the Dogon elder Ogotemmêli and the French researcher Marcel Griaule several decades earlier.[55] The latter is still revisited occasionally by scholars who continue to see value in debating, for or against, whether African ancestors were indeed as philosophical as their contemporary and professionally trained descendants. While Hallen and Sodipo recognized the *onisegun* as their "parallel colleagues" (at least in the sense that they were able to have a series of conversations with them regarding the formal structure of knowledge in Yoruba wisdom), they did not regard the *onisegun* as fellow philosophers, unless we loosen this term to include its other and more accommodating senses. Nor was it their primary goal, as was Oruka's, to merely unveil ignored critical thinking among indigenous experts. Rather, driven by a critical consideration of how analytical meanings are determined, theirs was a theoretical goal, to argue that analytical truths appear to be dependent on the languages in which they are framed. Their knowledge of the Yoruba language drove them to this view, which already was the pillar of Quine's skepticism about the so-called necessary truths. Thus, their study extended Quine's view, and they corroborated it by carefully analyzing (and contrasting with the English equivalents of their story of the Yoruba distinction between knowledge and belief) the *onisegun*'s splitting of (the ideas of) knowledge and belief. In this respect alone, Hallen and Sodipo may have separated themselves from Oruka, yet Oruka's text too suggests paths to several matters of theoretical interest or significance. For example, in the text, while explaining the idea of communalism, Paul Mbuya makes many suggestions for understanding the grounding of the principle: he defines it as a common recognition of the kind of needs considered to be basic for living a standard of life that was acceptably commensurate with human dignity. In Mbuya's explanation,[56] communalism lies at the root of human reason, yet it is not a matter of the mind (recognition) only. Rather, it is a norm arrived at for purposes of effecting order in the lives of people by reducing social differences and promoting peace. In other words, communalism is a state of social and moral order, visible in the practices of mutual dependence as indicators of rational concerns for and commitment to (as manifested in practice) the creation or sustenance of a common good. In one aspect of life, the drive toward this common good is manifested in the form of a distributive principle based on an understanding of human rights constructed on communal terms.

To the extent, then, that such texts as those of Hallen and Sodipo, Wiredu, Oruka, Appiah, and Gyekye, and certainly many others too, may be said to have some similarities, such commonality could be described as follows: they suggest that philosophical endeavor, whether by the professionals or by any other person so inclined, does not have to begin with printed compendiums to be analyzed. It can (and should) begin with considerations of the theoretical implications of the belief systems and principles of the everyday practical life in the cultures we inhabit. Their lesson, among other important matters, is that indeed all philosophy, not just African philosophy, is embedded in culture by virtue of the observation that philosophical problems stem from and are part of how philosophers consciously and critically live the cultures of their times. For in contemporary Africa, just like everywhere else, everyday beliefs and practices of ordinary people continue to mingle with the specialized (carefully considered and sifted) beliefs and knowledge of the professionals.

CHAPTER TWO

Philosophy and the Orders of Consciousness

The emphasis on content and methodology in philosophical traditions can be traced to circumstances that identify how different peoples of the world have striven to manage their cultures and their histories. In that sense, such emphases bear the marks of indigeneity, meaning that they are indicators of the ways that people think differently about the world. Yet until recently, assenting to such a view—that different people perceive the world differently, as is evident from different traditions of thought and practice, and that these differences are fine—would have been considered anathema. Today, however, and thanks to those old civilizations whose strong foundations withstood the sweeping challenges of Western influence (for example, those in much of Asia) as well as to those that took advantage of Western fatigue in the post–World War II period to mount a ferocious resurgence of their own (for example, those in much of the rest of the formerly colonized world) the striving is no longer the search for the elusive universal but a search for the integration of diversity—including diversity in knowledge—into the common forum for learning. This novel global attitude not only recognizes what many leading African people of letters and nationalist leaders have long insisted on, it also allows us to re-pose the questions but in a significantly different atmosphere, at least from an intellectual standpoint. The questions, now quite familiar, have included the following: How do African people think differently from other people and what are those differences? What do they stem from? Or do we differ at all?

While there is little likelihood that the statement that these questions lie at the root of our recent intellectual quest will raise controversy, what is likely to raise a cloud of objectional dust is the kind of answers one might give to them. Also likely less controversial is the view that discussing what one sees is more interesting than discussing whether there is even anything to be seen. So, to turn it around a little, there appears to be little disagreement that there is knowledge that is indigenous to Africa—that is, knowledge that is unique, traditional, or local, knowledge that exists within and develops around the specific conditions of the experiences of African peoples. What is generating debate among us, however, is what this knowledge springs from. The passion with which we have pursued this debate can be understood only as the kind of animation that accompanies most debates of people at a crossroads, which is where we are, at least historically and culturally. Should we not ask, for example, what is it we hope for or expect of a person in order for him or her to be admired and be held in high esteem by the community? In other words, is there, and what is, our model of a person? And what, in our value systems, do aspects of such a model point to that are different from other value systems elsewhere? I suggest that it is the search for answers to these and similar questions that has animated recent debate among us. What follows is a way to characterize how that debate has partly taken place.

Although it would be equally valid to characterize recent debates among African philosophers in other ways, I propose to take what I believe now to be a familiar episode: reconciling the indigenous orders of knowledge with the orders of philosophical knowledge, a matter with regard to which Hountondji is one of the most insistent and the most recognized of contemporary African philosophers. He is also perhaps one of the most controversial. The question is not only whether the controversies his writings have generated fairly reflect what he stands for, but also (and perhaps even more importantly) whether his monolithic theme has run out of the steam that gave it currency over three decades ago. We now know that his critique of ethnophilosophy began its explicit existence at a seminar in Copenhagen, but its first published expression, "Remarques sur la philosophie africaine contemporaine," was written in 1969 and published in *Diogene* the following year and reprinted in 1976 as the first chapter of *Sur la 'philosophie africaine'* under the title of "Une littérature aliénée."[1] Ivan Karp and I have argued[2] that three decades later, this critique of ethnophilosophy and the Marxist dressing in which it comes have both run their course. They were preludes. The real act is overdue. This next step, in which scholars debate interpretations of and explanations for the social, psychological, institutional, and cultural values that drive the quests of Africans for specific orders, must be grounded in debates among Africans themselves first, and later with others who are interested in such questions. It is already happening.

The values and beliefs or presuppositions individuals use as the basis for the judgments they make in their daily lives often also show up in the norms that direct how our institutions operate, not just in the formal structures of institutions but also in how they arrive at specific judgments in their operations. For instance, if our cultures teach us from childhood that males are more valuable than females, we are likely to grow up believing that such a statement of gender inequality is a true description of the social order, and if we are male, it may lead us to believe that we are justified in treating women as unequals in the family and in the workplace. This bias is then likely to inform how the relevant laws of the nation are coded and applied to judgments in cases of legal conflict between persons of different genders. It is the case, for instance, that all women are legally disinherited of crucial properties such as land in their families of birth and in the families they marry into. In this age of justice and recognition of rights, does it not fall on us to care about the equal economic security of all our children?

However that goes, it appears that anachronism—like that of making Tempels a lifetime distraction—is sometimes part of this trade. Thus, if there still is any attention left, it is a historical one, and it identifies Houn-tondji as a leading and influential intellectual who was concerned with Africa's performance on the global stage of production and consumption of knowledge and, relatedly, with the role knowledge plays in the material and social transformation of the world. Yet almost no point was made with greater emphasis in postindependence Africa than the question of producing knowledge that is relevant and responsive to Africa's cultural world view and needs. So, one may ask, is there any special significance when philosophers make it? In this chapter we shall take a look at what has happened in the scene of African philosophy since Hountondji's most noted work, *African Philosophy: Myth and Reality,* was first published in English translation in 1983.

Hountondji's work is perhaps best known for his critique of what has gained both notoriety and currency as "ethnophilosophy." Launched by a methodology pioneered by Placide Tempels, ethnophilosophy gained cur-rency among African and Western Africanist intellectuals (mostly theolo-gians) as a handy tool that spoke to the rational diversity and autonomy of African cultural values in a world that was best known for its skepticism about African goodness. Secular anticolonial political awakenings as well as missiological accommodations in response to perceived threats to the mission of the Christian church in Africa made possible expressions of non-Western cultures—using the grids of the same Western frameworks such expressions intended to oppose or separate from. It is from this wider historical context that Tempels's idea of a Bantu philosophy was born. By affirming the indispensability of local cultures to its self-propagation, the Christian church found a passage to both its own self-renewal and its expressive indigenization into local idioms. In the new philosophical and theological movements, there was no substantive change to this formula.[3] In the African context, the notion of merging the universal into the par-ticular became a philosophical project, first noted in the work of Alexis Kagame but growing fast thereafter as the image of the Church acquired local or indigenous appearances with an increasing number of African philosophers and theologians. By the time Hountondji's text came into the scene, skepticism regarding the complementary or grafting relations between the universal and the particular was already clearly under way. While embracing but also radically polishing Tempels's thesis, Kagame identified the local abode of universal philosophy in the structural complexity of local languages, arguing that structure incarnated the categories of being in their entirety as listed in Aristotelian metaphysics.

Hountondji's objection to this view was both scathing and instructive. He argued that what the project produced was only ethnophilosophical at best, driven by the ambition to merge what were otherwise oppositional in relation to each other—the ethnographical and the philosophical. The former is collective and passive and its claims are anonymous. The latter, in contrast, is dialectically located in a radically different kind of rational process. Indeed, the statement that the conceptual categories into which reality (or Being, as its most abstract form) appears in the ordinary language children learn in order to communicate seemed to be an overdone exaggeration of Kagame's ethnophilosophical method. To say the least, critics of ethnophilosophy found this to be too cheap a way to prove any point. On his part, Hountondji insisted that the claim of ethnophilosophy was tantamount to being an insult to philosophy as a discipline which, for him, is a systematic (that is, a deliberately organized) form of discourse, usually with very specific theoretical goals, that is born out of a deliberate reflective practice guided by specific learned rules of the game. It is obvious from the reformulated prescriptive objection of the critics of ethnophilosophy that they regarded the exponents of the new field to be taking advantage of the convoluted character of the idea of philosophy itself to further confuse two related but separable orders of discourse: on the one hand, the general reasons why people believe specific things and practice in certain specific ways and, on the other hand, the very different activity pursued as an academic discipline by people working within or in extended relations with departments of philosophy within institutions of education. Although he was not this restrictive, Hountondji's chief quest at the time appeared nonetheless to be the separation between the norms of a professional practice and the relatively loose beliefs and norms of everyday life. If such separation did not already clearly place the disciplines out of reach of the concern of ordinary folks, he believed that there should be such a gulf.

Hountondji insisted therefore not that there cannot be philosophy in the first order, although it is unlikely that he would grant that there is one so strictly understood (a point that is distinct from his disagreement with Crahay), but that ethnophilosophers were wrongly continuing to blur the separation between the two orders by blunting the divide in their writings, an effort that was evidenced by the volume of publications, doctoral dissertations, and other formal presentations on collective cultural beliefs as philosophy. These texts, he observed, alluded to knowledge scattered everywhere in beliefs, language, and ritual behavior and locutions, all usually meant for very different practical and theoretical purposes in every-day life. Suddenly, the authors of these texts were pulling these pieces of knowledge together and calling them "philosophy."[4] He vehemently argued that philosophy—implying by this, I believe, something similar to what Chinua Achebe, in reference to Igbo cosmology, describes as a "construct [of] a rigid and closely argued system of thought to explain the universe and the place of man in it"[5]—does not reside inside collective beliefs, practices, and other behaviors only waiting to be discovered and re-described for the world. Achebe contends that general communities as such do not produce that kind of knowledge, "preferring [instead] the metaphor of myth and poetry, [thus] anyone seeking an insight into their world must seek it along their own way." This is quite a clear distinction between second-order knowledge in academic construction and useful knowledge of the people. The former are more impressive and the latter are useful or pragmatic.

Hountondji insisted further that the texts that constitute ethnophilosophy had not been aimed at an African audience for reflection and critique, as an endogenous discourse should be. Rather, he argued, African ethnophilosophy was directed at appeasing a Western audience, particularly the less intellectually or completely nonintellectually oriented one. He wrote thus:

> It [ethnophilosophy] was a case, says Eboussi aptly, quoting Jankele-vitch, of "doubly interpreted misinterpretation," in which the victim makes itself the executioner's secret accomplice, in order to commune with him in an artificial world of falsehood.
>
> What does that mean in this context? Simply that contemporary African philosophy, inasmuch as it remains an ethnophilosophy, has been built up essentially *for a European public.* The African ethnophilosopher's discourse is not intended for Africans. It has not been produced for their benefit, and its authors understood that it would be challenged, if at all, not by Africans but by Europe alone. Unless, of course, the West expressed itself through Africans, as it knows so well how to do.[6]

Hountondji's scathing and uncompromising critique of ethnophilosophy soon earned him equally sharp countercritiques and accusations of Occidentalism, idealism, elitism, and aristocratism. In response to such critiques, Hountondji was happy that his primary critique of ethnophilosophy at least had generated a more learned and theoretically informed appropriation of ethnographic data that constituted a real philosophical discourse, in contrast to the formerly naive and disengaged descriptions. As a result, he observed, "ethnophilosophy has moved to another level where it develops *a theoretical defence* by *attempting a grounding* or *conceptual justification* of its claim that what it does is indeed what is appropriate for Africans in the times."[7]

The critiques of Hountondji have been varied, ranging in their tones from populist rhetoric to seemingly serious personal attacks and threats. The former genre was exemplified by the sociologist Abdou Touré and the latter by Koffi Niamkey. Ironically, in these critiques, it was Hountondji himself who was being accused of uncritically adopting (and demanding of Africans) what the critics perceived to be a European idea of philosophy that exists as an elitist idea and practice by virtue of its exclusiveness. This reproach was echoed by Olabiyi B. Yaï[8] and Pathé Diagne,[9] who, ironically, appeared to echo the Marxist view—in his eleventh thesis to Feuerbach—that power should be handed over to the masses as part of the transition from speculative analysis to pragmatic transformation of the world. For example, the title of Yaï's critique of Hountondji ("Théorie et pratique en philosophie africaine: Misère de la philosophie spéculative") is not only clearly permeated by the "spirit" of Marx's eleventh thesis to Feuerbach, it is only a slightly modified reuse of the title of Marx's polemic against Proudhon, *La Misère de la Philosophie* of 1847.[10] Some European intellectuals, too, including such prominent philosophers as Heidegger, eager to protect philosophy in rather familiar ways as the exclusive or essential property of Europeans, followed suit. But while there has been a need, purely intellectual, to respond to the genres of European sophism, such as Hegel's and Heidegger's, that tend to mix the idea of philosophy with a core of European spirit,[11] Hountondji believed that ethnophilosophy in the style of Tempels and his disciples was not the right response. In his view, Occidentalism is not characterized by a demand for conceptual rigor when analyzing crucial issues in one's experience. Rather, it "is the ideological thesis claiming that philosophy should, rightfully and by a mysterious necessity, be of European essence." Such ideology is sheer fantasy and includes among its expressions (in addition to Hegel and Heidegger) Lévy-Bruhl's claims about "primitive mentality" and Husserl's claims about the Papuas. In Hountondji's view, Eurocentrism is character-ized by a discourse parallel to the one that defines itself as Afrocentrism (in North America especially). In Hountondji's view, Occidentalism is not eliminated by finding in Africa modes of intellectual creation that are regarded as the same as those of Europe. Nor will African intellectual productions be given value by merely claiming that they are what they are not or by blowing their importance or worth out of proportion. Their value must come from making of them effective tools for shaping Africa's future rather than from making of them impoverished and simplistic forms of thinking. Hountondji's contention was that vigorous thought makes itself visible in the multiplicity (plurality) and intensity of the dis-cursive currents it spurs, some of which may even be antagonistic among themselves. Contrary to the wishes and abstractions of ethnophilosophers,

Hountondji observed, real African thinking portrays such multiplicity and intensity.

The charge of elitism was more rhetorical than the others. It stated that by refusing to recognize the relation between their own philosophical productions and social positions, African philosophers of Hountondji's school of thought were espousing a hegemonic-elitist posture that was inimical to the aspirations of the masses. By refusing to give ownership of thought to the masses, they were seen to be defending the (foreign) political interests they served or were sympathetic to. Such rhetoric offered populist politicians of the time both the opportunity and convenience of being branded as the "enemies of the people" by academicians who either opposed or chose to remain free of the political demagogy of the time. Suddenly, the political spectrum in sub-Saharan Africa was according ethnophilosophy much higher status than it had originally bargained for. In a general sense, philosophy had suddenly acquired a class-determining value. Spurred by an unfortunate but growing culture of political sycophancy, an individual's views about ethnophilosophy became the criteria for measuring his or her degree of nationalist commitment on a scale known to and controlled solely by the political leaders of the moment. Ironically, it never occurred to any of these "guardians of the masses" that their own critiques were grounded in the norms of European philosophy and ideology. As Kwasi Wiredu observes in his own recent work (which I discuss in chapter 3), "it is not unknown for, say, an African Marxist to chide another African, who betrays a sympathy for some non-Marxist Western conception, with domination by Western thought on the ground that, as Marx showed, the truth was something different. It hardly seems to be an item of vivid remembrance in the consciousness of such an African that, as far as it is known, Marx did not hail from any part of Africa!"[12] Similarly, Hountondji's critics appeared to have forgotten that Gramsci, whose notion of the masses as intellectuals they evoke in criticizing Hountondji's alleged elitist Westernism, was an Italian man whose thought was grounded in the critical analysis of the dynamics of European societies using Marxist methodology. But in addition to this point, Hountondji remarked in his response to critics that "Marx and Engels would also be elitist intellectuals, since such of their work as *The German Ideology* is from beginning to end a declaration of the rupture with what they scornfully call 'ideology.'"[13] Such rhetoric, Hountondji observes in a stinging rejoinder to his African critics, is often a camouflage for empty ideas. Thus, with some irony, it is Hountondji who approximates the Marxian view that knowledge is always grounded in historical ruptures, reflecting the various stages of the holistic progress of the society.

In a new preface to the second edition of *African Philosophy: Myth and Reality,*[14] Hountondji reiterates some of these responses to his critics, but he also provides good and timely clarifications of a number of issues that became the chief targets of criticism of both the original French and the first English editions.[15] In particular, he explains his ambition and vision for the continent's future that led to his strong rejection of ethnophilosophy in the first edition. First, he rejects—now as he did then—the idea and practice of ethnophilosophy because its very characteristics constitute a form of intellectual self-imprisonment. As he states in his critique of the "Témoignages" texts, Hountondji maintains that ethnophilosophy's self-portrait as a form of philosophy that is impersonal, implicit, unanimous, and uncritically descriptive constituted a contradiction.[16] Most of the authors of the testimonies claimed in their respective essays that what Tempels had descriptively exposed as the Bantu mode of thinking about Being was indeed a philosophy. Writing against both Tempels and Tempels's defenders in the "Témoignages," Hountondji claimed that such authors were engaged in self-contradiction since they knew well that what Tempels had presented was not "philosophy" in the (professional or academic) sense in which they themselves knew and practiced it. Writing not long after Hountondji's 1977 text, I explained then that the authors of the "Témoignages" were perhaps not as self-contradicting as they appeared to be since their concern was not so much to affirm the philosophical nature of Bantu thought as it was to celebrate primitivism, which had become a trendy way, especially for European philosophers working out of the phenomenological or existentialist movements, of demonstrating that the (spontaneous) existentialist search for Being was so deeply grounded in raw and unsophisticated human existence that it was close to being the natural human condition.[17] This position did not prevent some of the philosophers in these movements, such as Heidegger, to continue to regard "philosophy proper," the life of reason, as being fused with the European spirit. However one reads the "Témoignages," it appears that to the group of European philosophers who contributed to it, Tempels's book was merely an exposure of this primitive level of human quest that, for some of them (especially those who were Catholic, like Marcel), as it was for Tempels himself, was a yearning for something greater but that was yet to be revealed. The publication of the second edition of *African Philosophy: Myth and Reality* gave Hountondji the opportunity to explain himself unequivocally: "I meant to value discourse and the history of discourse as being the only possible place where philosophy appears."[18]

Since 1976—the year *Sur la 'philosophie africaine'* was first published—the vigor of ethnophilosophy—at least in its original form—has been blunted somewhat, thanks in part to such critiques as appear in Hountondji's work. That decline has led to more discursive and prescriptive approaches to defining and evaluating philosophical positions through African eyes. But the blunting of raw ethnophilosophy was also occasioned in part by the general decline in descriptive or, better, old-fashioned modes of doing the cultural anthropology that provided ethnophilosophy with its initial impetus, thus prompting the appearance and history of the term "ethnophilosophy."[19] But the history of the term itself aside, the critiques of ethnophilosophy, which are traceable to Tempels's own missionary colleagues and run forward through Franz Crahay, Fabien Eboussi-Boulaga, and Hountondji himself, justified a new preface for the second edition of *African Philosophy: Myth and Realty*. Indeed, both the preface to the second edition and his other recent work help clarify that Hountondji is not—and he explains that he never was—an enemy of Africa's indigenous knowledge systems, as was misleadingly assumed by most of those who did not like his critique of ethnophilosophy. Indeed, he has lately become one of the strongest and most visible and audible defenders of indigenous knowledges. His point, as I shall explain shortly, is that in most areas indigenous knowledges are in dire need of critical jump starts.

In Hountondji's view, various claims he makes in the book appear to have solicited numerous misunderstandings and unwarranted critiques, which he has responded to in the new preface. As a successful response to critics, the preface establishes itself and reestablishes the entire text as a new terminus in the discursive process, thus pointing in the very direction that Hountondji's original critique of ethnophilosophy had suggested as the proper nature of philosophical practice—that is, a discursive activity rather than an established body of truths. And so the reality of African philosophy establishes itself beyond a mere possibility; it leaps from myth to reality.

Inadvertently, the controversy over ethnophilosophy gave a new angle to a larger debate that was already raging even as African philosophers and politicians were at war over the philosophical merits of locally produced or indigenous knowledge systems. That controversy, which was rekindled and contextualized by the ethnophilosophy debate, examines the relations between local and universal perceptions of knowledge. Hountondji had emphasized the idea of knowledge as dialectically grounded and the idea of philosophy as a form of "discourse and the history of discourse." According to him, discourse, in both its internal structure and dialectical historicity, is an absolute necessity for the development of critical philosophy and scientific culture as a whole. As I mentioned earlier, the absence of elaboration of this view and the uncompromising nature in which it was stated in the first editions of Hountondji's book prompted the impression that he insisted on a sharp divide between professional practice and the sociological conditions under which professional practitioners lived and worked. Critics saw Hountondji as denigrating indigenous oral traditions as irrelevant to the production of philosophical knowledge. Concurrently with the ethnophilosophy debate, another controversy, initiated by Thomas Kuhn's work on theoretical history, most notably in *The Structure of Scientific Revolutions* (1962), was brewing over whether or not knowledge generally and scientific theory in particular was free of the influence of everyday human aspirations, beliefs, endeavors, and compromises. Supportive reactions to Kuhn's work have since influenced the growth of a tradition in the history and philosophy of science that significantly blunts the dividing line between the natural and social sciences. This tradition, which is shared by people from as far apart as the philosopher Sandra Harding from the United States, the French sociologist Bruno Latour, and the adopted Mozambiquan mathematician Paulus Gerdes, among others in between, holds that despite the fact that good science is characterized by strong objectivity, inclusive rationality, and universal validity, the corpus of scientific knowledge remains an aspect of local knowledge.[20] It is refreshing to note that Hountondji has embraced this line of thought that recognizes the local foundations of theoretical productions. Hence it can now be restated that although writing is comparatively privileged over orature in the promotion and sustenance of a continuous discourse, it does not follow, as some critics misconstrued Hountondji to be claiming, that oral literature generally loses importance or that the oral expression of philosophy—philosophical "orature"—is in particular ipso facto disqualified as an expressive form of philosophy. Yet its appreciation requires qualification. More importantly, Hountondji now explains that the idea of discourse raises pertinent questions in the "sociology of knowledge in the countries of the periphery, entailing an increasing interest in the anthropology of knowledge and issues in the politics of science."[21] It is this idea of philosophy as part of a wider sociological process that provided the threads that linked Hountondji to the Althusserian reformulation of Marxism and clearly accounted for his consciousness "that, whether in France or elsewhere, one definitely cannot overlook the demand that philosophy should, directly or indirectly, enable its practitioners to understand better the issues at stake on the political, economic, and social battlefields, and thereby contribute to changing the world."[22] This is a strong statement, particularly for Africa. The insistence on the theory of science in particular and on the sociology of knowledge generally—understood here as dialectically propelled through critical engagement with problems of life—leads Hountondji to the critique of Africa's intellectual and scientific dependence on the outside world and to the postulation of the value of Africa's own local knowledges. I shall come back to this in the next section of the text.

By using the economic dependency theory inaugurated in the seventies by Immanuel Wallerstein, André Gunder Frank, and Samir Amin in various publications that appeared between the two editions of *African Philosophy: Myth and Reality* (e.g., "Recapturing"),[23] Hountondji has been advocating the termination of the dependency syndrome that defines Africa as a mere laboratory for testing theories developed abroad or as a mere field for collecting raw research data and materials for analysis in the industrial centers in the metropolises of the West. He concludes, in agreement with the pioneers of the theory, that such dependency both engenders global inequalities and stifles the capacity of local knowledges and industrial ventures to grow. His point is that the need to advance a nation's scientific and technological capacities does not dictate dependency. While not opposing fair international trade and transfers of appropriate knowledge and technological tools of various kinds, Hountondji insists that every society is developmentally best served by focusing on the enhancement and improvement of its existing knowledge, skills, and institutions. In Africa, he argues, there already exists a basis for constructing relations between recent advances in scientific research and local knowledge systems. He cautions in particular against the rise of ethnoscience and its different specifications such as ethnobotany, ethnozoology, ethnomedicine, ethnopsychiatry, ethnolinguistics, and so on as hinderances, like ethnophilosophy, to the development of proper knowledges with roots and relevance in Africa.

It is significant for Hountondji's readers, particularly his previous critics, to note that he has reworked the concept of ethnophilosophy along the lines of his emphasis on "local knowledge." But to say that there has been some "reworking" of the former position is to claim some justification for the critiques. The critique of ethnophilosophy had some excesses that appeared to leave no room for a positive engagement with the ordinary or everyday experiences and knowledge articulations of local peoples. It left the impression that philosophy was the opposite of the "ordinary" rather than its clarification, be it analytically or synthetically. Particularly, Hountondji's critique of the "Témoignages" appeared to give the impression that in his view "the philosophical" and "the ordinary" had little, if anything, in common. At the same time, his Marxist position would hardly countenance such a rift. In fact, Hountondji argues that "no philosophy, however new, ever appears *ex nihilo,* that every philosophical doctrine is a reply to foregoing doctrines in the double mode of confirmation and refutation or, better still, as a call for further developments, an appeal for future confirmation or refutation, so that every philosophy looks forward and backward, to the inexhaustible history of the discipline."[24] Hountondji's writings strongly call for the return of the African subject, but a responsible subject who will chart out and take up responsibility for and control of her own intellectual, social, political, scientific, and economic destiny. It is the path toward the definition of African subjectivity that takes Hountondji through the anthropology of knowledge, the sociology of science, and (especially) Marxist theory and its Althusserian articulation.

Hountondji's critics could suggest that this position was not spelled out with univocal clarity in both the previous editions of the book and in some of the earlier critiques of ethnophilosophy (such as the essays of 1970 and 1971).[25] He too admits now that lack of unequivocal clarity and emphasis may have been responsible for the misunderstandings that ensued from that first English edition of the work. Yet, by contrast, it was already a remarkable reworking of the original French original.

Just as there have been multiple African paths to socialism, so there also have been multiple senses and paths to what Africans perceive as a politically meaningful and locally sustainable development. Hountondji's recent focus on local knowledges as the basis for politically meaningful and locally sustainable development is related to what he perceives to be the imbalance in the global politics of production, distribution, and consumption of knowledge. Knowledge, according to him, is the basic capital for sustainable development in any society. But, he argues, for Africa's local knowledges to become legitimate starting points for the production of developmentally relevant knowledge and skills, they must be subjected to critical and constant appraisal and modification. Africa's development must begin with net growth in its knowledge, especially scientific knowledge. According to Hountondji, the fact that today a large number of African peoples inhabit a world built on a "dual language" is enough reason for a renewed effort to integrate and *think together* these two forms of rationality. In other words, because they inhabit and operate within a world that is defined by the coexistence of the "recent" and "older" theoretical and technological approaches to the solutions of everyday problems, African people, especially the professionals, are best placed to pursue the transformation of older indigenous knowledge as a response to new needs and interests.

It is evident, then, that although Hountondji places emphasis on the categories of "scientific" and "modern" as advanced developmental stages in the dialectical transformation of knowledge and technological means and argues that Africans need to transform their world toward these levels, he also makes it clear that the terms "scientific" and "modern" need not mean "foreign," nor does the desire for them imply self-betrayal or self-deprecation or even self-alienation through the desire for what is not African, as several of his critics appeared to misconstrue from the earlier edition of his book.

African scientists need to demonstrate professional ambition or the desire to attain specific theoretical and practical goals. The attending benefits of modern science to African causes hardly need emphasis. But to be beneficial, scientific knowledge must be critically appraised and applied diligently, relevantly, and appropriately in the diagnosis and solution of problems. This by no means implies that African scientists should not aim high in their quest for new knowledge, including new discoveries, or that they should shun the pursuit of such when they arrive at any that would be directly applicable to Africans' needs. Ambition is not in itself a bad thing to have. It can be a positive good for society. In fact, a person is judged to be ambitious when she has quite lofty but apparently well-defined goals. Barring the use of morally or legally inappropriate means to arrive at one's ambitions, positively ambitious persons often demonstrate tremendous amounts of energy and diligence in their work. A nation with good ambitions can be a fertile environment for the growth of scientists and scientific knowledge that will serve and benefit humanity.

However, the past century was rife with pernicious ambitions of various kinds and levels, such as the ambition to develop and manufacture weapons of mass destruction in order to threaten neighbors and the world at large. The aims of some ambitious scientific projects have not been quite clear, so they have generated great amounts of controversy, as in the case of human cloning. Then there have been other types of ambition that are good in their conception but full of folly in their viability and usefulness. The example I have in mind is that of an African nation that invited an assortment of its scientists, especially those in the field of physics and engineering, to develop and manufacture a car. Let us be clear that while there is everything good about developing and manufacturing a car as part of an ambition to industrialize, there is everything wrong with the idea when the nation in question cannot even provide its public hospitals with basic surgical supplies and when nearly 70 percent of the population lives under the conventional poverty line. Needless to say, this nation, my own homeland of Kenya, neither produces steel nor has the critical mass of scientists and engineers that such a venture would require, but its government went ahead to sponsor the enormously expensive exercise of building a vehicle from a scrap yard that did not run fifty meters when it was tested. This is an example of wastefulness that resulted from the absence of critical appraisal of the scientific knowledge that was available in the country. What was available was not applied relevantly or appropriately. Rather, as investigations later revealed, it was an ambitious industrial project that was wrong-headed from the start but was apparently pushed forward by corrupt government officials to financially benefit "friends of the government leaders." Thus, while ambition is a good idea and can be a source of cognitive and organizational drives and diligence out of which great products can result, it needs to be properly harnessed toward appropriate goals. If our example fits Hountondji's argument, then his position on the example I gave would be that the project's flaw began with its inception, that it would appear to have been the result of a desire to imitate someone else's products and the glory that attends to such accomplishments. But neither the product nor the glory had a relevance locally where the imitation was about to be played out. What about putting all the good scientists to work at producing good ideas for durable solutions to the barely existent and badly ailing infrastructure that would serve and help improve the quality of life for poor people who make up close to 70 percent of African nations? The process of responsibly developing beneficial knowledge can be achieved by either developing scientific knowledge from a society's existing resources or by appropriating and adapting beneficial knowledge and skills imported from abroad. And the worth of knowledge is measurable only by its capacity to effectively provide responses and solutions to the questions and problems that led to its presence in the first place. The terms "scientific" and "modern" can then only mean the best-researched and latest of the investigative methods, findings, and products of the day. And in turn, as products of a historically growing process from which they ensue, such methods, findings, and products should be made possible—as the next steps in a pattern of growth—by a past from which they issue and from which, in ideal circumstances, they should be an improvement on or advancement.

Plenty of examples could be cited to illustrate what I believe Hountondji has in mind. I shall mention two. In the field of health, it is undeniable that far too many people lose lives unnecessarily in Africa due, admittedly, to a wide variety of reasons, one of which often results from too much dependence on traditional diagnostic methods. This reliance frequently leads to misdiagnosis of even simple ailments, which then leads to mis-prognosis and even eventual deaths that could be avoided. Respect for the crucial epistemological questions raised in such texts as, for example, Evans-Pritchard's *Witchcraft, Oracles and Magic among the Azande* not-withstanding, it is also true that far too much time and opportunity to save lives is lost through dependency on traditional diagnostic methods alone. I believe that anyone concerned with the catastrophic levels of African casualties from the HIV/AIDS epidemic, malaria, malnutrition, and other diseases and conditions that afflict millions of Africans would urge that greater attention be accorded to enhancing accurate diagnoses of these major killer conditions and diseases. Readers should easily notice that I owe this example to Kwasi Wiredu; I borrow it with gratitude.[26] My second example, also health-related, is from an area where African scientists and researchers have performed commendably well but that could also benefit even more African people if it were given more scientific emphasis. Most of Africa's population is made up of people who depend for their livelihood on farming, fishing, or pastoralism or on some combination of these. The levels of local knowledge of the variables in the conditions under which these are practiced, including diagnostic and prognostic knowledge of dominant veterinary diseases by region, are often high. In recent years African scientists and researchers have made great improvements in the techniques of diagnosis and control of the major threats to African food production. In various areas of Africa's economies, the design and use of these techniques have also led to improvements in farm yields. But greater work needs to be done to disseminate better and more useful knowledge to African farmers so that farm management and productivity at local levels will improve. Primary work will have to begin with changing the attitudes of local people toward an openness and readiness to be critical of the old and familiar knowledge and to adopt, where relevant and needful, new knowledge and techniques, especially where the latter can be proved to work better than the former. For a more specific example, African farmers and ranchers or pastoralists have been accustomed to "borrowing" seeds from friends and relatives both far and near. These loans, in the form of seeds and studs, have produced hybrids of various types, enabling improvements of local products but sometimes also weakening them or failing to produce the results for which they were "borrowed." These experiments were usually "studied" carefully and the results were publicized or discouraged depending on the outcome. These local cross-breeding practices are now largely abandoned, often due to uncaring government restrictions that do not recognize the scientific potential of the practices. With scientific backing such practices could be encouraged in order to modify local agricultural and animal species and brands to enhance productivity and sustenance.

Now it should be pretty easy for anyone to see that a conceptual position that calls for greater adherence to accurate knowledge with its attending benefits hardly lends itself to the accusation of scientism and, perhaps even much less, of elitism, as Hountondji has been accused of. Nonetheless, Hountondji laments that perhaps his manner of expressing these ideas in the first edition gave room to the unfortunate misconstruals. It can only be hoped that the new preface provides effective enough clarifications of the misunderstandings and that such clarifications shall make possible a different and better reading of the text that itself remains intact.

As I noted above, various aspects of Hountondji's position have precedents. The idea of "Third Worldism," also called the dependency theory of peripheral societies, comes from three major sources in the seventies: the works of the Brazilian André Gunder Frank, those of the Egyptian-born Senegalese Samir Amin, and those of the German-born American Immanuel Wallerstein, all political economists who more than three decades ago launched the view that no development had taken place in postcolonial economies of the kind that had been imagined in the post–World War II invention of the concept of non-Western economies as "developing." They contended that this designation was a misnomer because such economies could not attain the characteristics assumed in the idea of "development" in the shadow of the dominant Western economies under which they operated. Third World economies, choked by the strangleholds of imperialism, moved in the opposite direction—toward underdevelopment, viewed as the contradiction of the logic of development. In that relationship, the real benefits of Third World economies remain fatally extroverted or outward-oriented, because Third World countries do not generate self-serving or endogenously capitalizable products. They produce according to the logic of industrial needs of the metropolitan economies and in response to the needs of metropolitan societies. Borrowing this view, Hountondji, like Mudimbe, calls for an endogenous approach to the development of an African order of knowledge.[27]

The idea of a critical reappraisal of the relevance of local theories and methodologies is traceable to Kwasi Wiredu's earlier and well-noted work.[28] Finally, the call to "think together" the "dual language" of Africa's experiences echoes the strategies for a self-sustaining system of intellectual and economic production articulated in the sixties by Julius Nyerere in his now-defunct but once popular ideopolitical theory of *ujamaa*. The view in the notion of *ujamaa*, now differently reiterated by Hountondji, is that the two orders of knowledge, the "traditional" and the "modern," as they are now fashionably distinguished and contrasted, are not mutually exclusive. The former should not be accorded any advantage over the latter only because it is local and familiar if it does not serve as an effective means to adequately understand and respond to the problems of society. Nor does the latter prevail merely because it is different and perhaps imported. Its adoption should depend on its ability to adapt to a local milieu and alongside the growth of its local alternatives.

Hountondji's explanatory responses to the critics of the earlier edition of *African Philosophy* achieve two important goals. Firstly, by explaining the roots of his critique of ethnophilosophy as grounded in Husserl's phenomenology, Hountondji provides a justifying context for such discontent and corrects the earlier misperceptions that he was antagonistic to and unappreciative of local knowledge systems. Such misperception resulted, as pointed out, in the accusation that he espoused scientism, elitism, and Occidentalism, meaning by these that he was disengaged from the values and needs of ordinary Africans.

The second achievement of Hountondji's responses to critics is that they explicitly reassert and reinvigorate the challenge to African intellectuals to critically engage with local knowledge systems in a way that makes them productive contributors to rather than mere dependent consumers in the arena of global economy of knowledge. All those whose interests focus on African or other traditions of philosophy (as well as the general Africanist) shall be most glad that this excellent and widely influential, if controversial, text is available once again. It remains the engaging reading that it always was. In a rather surprising turn, Hountondji's latest book[29] now explains how he arrived at the positions he has been criticized for. The way Hountondji pegs his intellectual itinerary on Edmund Husserl, especially on the latter's *Ideas: General Introduction to Pure Phenomenology* of 1931, will surprise many readers. He narrates in this new book how his intention, following in Husserl's footprints, was to ground the idea of science, which he thought to be crucial to understanding the exigencies of Africans' experiences in the postcolonial period and condition, on the idea and structure of consciousness.[30] By resituating his lifelong concern for an engagement with reality in a manner that reduces science not to a Western paradigm but to a universal human discourse as outlined by Husserl, Hountondji further demonstrates that his critics did not follow the subtlety of his discourse; they misunderstood especially the point that his "ambition was to identify and delimit, within the existing corpus, something like an archeology of science and technology, and apply it critically to Africa."[31] It would appear obvious that by resituating his critique of ethnophilosophy within the context of Husserl's phenomenological project, Hountondji was, in fact, being critical of scientism and psychologism, the twin views that, in the sense of Husserl's critique, presupposed that there was an objective world out there to be revealed if we can discover in the mind the laws that give rise to the meaning of the world. Hountondji's ambition is, then, to explain that even the natural world of matter and its laws are part of our experience, a view that empowers and encourages us all to take our local experiences seriously and to examine the world along the lines of our experience of it. In Hountondji's words:

> This return to the subject does not however imply a retreat into subjectivity—on the contrary! The investigation of experience seeks to confirm the objectivity of essences, by identifying in experience itself an internal element of transcendence that obliges it to recognize its objective correlate.[32]

And a little later:

> It is only subsequently, after having erected safeguards against skepticism, that phenomenological analysis proper, the in-depth exploration of subjective experiences in which the object "is constituted," develops.[33]

What, then, exactly, was Husserl's grounding of the idea of science in phenomenology? To start with, it can be stated in general terms that Husserl saw a connection rather than a division between science and philosophy. For him, knowledge and analysis of the categories of the external world, the object of natural science, had to be preceded by knowledge and analysis of the life-world, without which they could not be adequately apprehended. Similarly, knowledge and analysis of the mind would be incomplete unless they were the foundation for our knowledge of the external world of science as we know it. For Husserl this was not a cosmetic undertaking, for he believed that the examination of the life-world—the task of phenomenology—was to be understood in a scientific sense as a systematic and meticulous elaboration. By these demands, Husserl built a case for his view that philosophy was science. Although analytically, we can distinguish between the life-world that is "pregiven" and accessible only by means of a phenomenological-psychological analysis and the external world of scientific analysis, these two realms are fundamentally connected because (for Husserl at least) the sciences are part of the life-world—in the sense that the mind already intends the external world in its primal mode before grasping it as being scientifically determinable in its specific laws. To be sure, says Husserl, "everyday induction grew into induction according to scientific method, but that changes nothing of the essential meaning of the pregiven world as the horizon of all meaningful induction. It is this world that we find to be the world of all known and unknown realities. To it, the world of actually experiencing intuition, belongs the form of space-time together with all the bodily . . . shapes incorporated in it; it is this world that we ourselves live, in accord with our bodily, personal way of being."[34] Husserl was aware that making this (intuitive) pregiven world the foundation for science was a revolution in a tradition that had drawn a divide between the world of *doxa* and that of *episteme*, but he believed that it was the genuine starting point whose aim should be "not to examine the world's being and being-such, but to consider whatever has been valid for us as being and being-such in respect of *how* it is subjectively valid, how it looks, etc."[35] These sentences suggest that the parallel Husserl drew between the structures of subjective acts (intuition) and the structures of the objects to which these acts refer was his way of showing the phenomenological grounding of the natural sciences, namely that science is to be regarded as constituted or grounded in specific intentional activities of the subject, that the knowledge of the objective world always takes place on the strength of the subjective acts from which it originates. The question, I believe, for Hountondji, as it was for Husserl, is how the objectification of the world by natural science can be comprehended and how science in general can be understood as an achievement of the subject. For instance, any proposition we make about the physical world is related to our perception of that world in simple, everyday, nonscientific ways that are available to all humans. All knowledge of the physical world is structured by the structure of this inner subjective experience. To ask "How?" is to lift consciousness one notch by seeking an explanation of what is already apprehended by or in intuition. The former is the *epistemic act,* while the latter is the *doxic stance.*

Now one may wonder how all this relates to a critique of ethnophilosophy. It is my opinion that Hountondji took seriously the idea that true investigation involves an attempt to establish the relation between this inner subjective experience and its parallel in the outside world. Phenomenological explanation, and perhaps all proper philosophical explanation, should ideally aim at establishing and clarifying the connection between the world of our intuitions and the world of empirical laws. He thought, and I believe he continues to assert, that many of those who wrote the texts that are now classified as ethnophilosophy were satisfied with mere descriptive reporting about the contents of the inner, subjective (intuitive), and passive or implicit realm of Africans' experience, forgetting that this was not in and of itself the complete task of philosophizing. They forgot to make sense of the remaining half in which everyday people strive to bridge the two realms on the basis of their inner (subjective) assumptions, some of which are tested and others not but all of which need clarification and confirmation. In other words, he believed, I think, that the task of the investigator, whether he or she was a philosopher or not, was precisely to conduct analysis to show how the epistemological roots of fundamental scientific concepts connect with or can be traced back to the corresponding concepts formed and used in the nonscientific world of everyday life or, conversely, to show how scientific concepts—meaning empirical concepts of reality—originate in the pregiven realm of intuitive experience. It is possible that Hountondji felt that such a task belonged with philosophy, just as Husserl had thought of it as the main task of his new method, phenomenological inquiry. In their work ethnophilosophers accomplished only half of the task, stopping, in Husserl's terms, at the descriptive phenomenology of the acts of consciousness (which, in the African case, are often expressed in myths) while leaving untouched the constitutive phenomenology of subjectivity. The latter occurs when, while reflecting on the intentional activities of consciousness (transcendental subjectivity), we discover or detect the pillars of belief (doxic positional or thetic components) upon which reality rests in its specific senses.[36]

In Husserl's project, descriptive phenomenology of the acts of consciousness should lead uninterruptedly to the analysis of constitutive phenomenology; that is, proceed from the unity of consciousness to the unities of theory and object in science. Because they are mutually dependent, it is inadequate or of no use entirely to analyze one part, especially only the first one (consciousness), as the writers of ethnophilosophy did, and exclude the other part (the constitution of the empirical world). Philosophy and science appeared to leave little divide between them. Recently Abiola Irele has suggested that Hountondji's celebration of Husserl's phenomenology "as an emancipation from the austere intellectualism of Descartes, with its radical divorce from the immediacies of experience" and Husserl's influence upon his anti-ethnophilosophical stance "begins to look like a form of vitalism, not so different from Nietzsche's or Bergson's."[37]

For now let us stick to Husserl and why and how Hountondji uses him. In *Ideas: General Introduction to Pure Phenomenology*, Husserl analyzes Descartes' "Cogito" to explain "Transcendental Phenomenology."[38] He observes that transcendental philosophy may be said to have originated in Descartes, while phenomenological psychology originated in the three British empiricists (Locke, Berkeley, and Hume) and that the philosophy propounded in the *Meditations* and the Cartesian "Mens" became the "human Mind" that Locke undertook to explore. What Locke provided turned into a psychology of the internal experience. In this analysis Husserl appears to lay out the two realms of reality as viewed through the precepts of his project: on the one side is the "Cogito" as Act, the

cogitatio, while on the other is the world of objects with their qualities, the *cogitatum.* Although an object can be consciously experienced
as a given of, say, perceptual experience, it is, in principle, other than
an experience. The *Ego cogito* is therefore a separate realm, although it
remains a conscious experience removed from the (objective) world and
its property, which, for Husserl, "exists, whether I, or we, happen, or not,
to be conscious of it."

In truth, the separation between these two realms and the manner of
their convergence, or collaboration, in making possible our experiencing of
the world around us can be complex, because in our awareness of the world
there is that grey area of the separation of the two as well as their presence
for each other in concrete experience. Husserl says, for example:

> Under *experiences* in the *widest sense* we understand whatever is to
> be found in the stream of experience, not only therefore intentional
> experiences, *cogitationes,* actual and potential, taken in their full
> concreteness, but all the real *(reellen)* phases to be found in this
> stream and in its concrete sections.
>
> For it is easily seen that *not every real phase* of the concrete
> unity of an intentional experience has itself the *basic character of
> intentionality,* the property of being a "consciousness of something."
> This is the case, for instance, with all *sensory data,* which play so
> great a part in the perceptive intuitions of things. In the experience
> of the perception of this white paper, more closely in those compo-
> nents of it related to the paper's quality of whiteness, we discover
> through properly directed noticing the sensory datum "white. This
> "whiteness" is something that belongs inseparably to the essence of
> the concrete perception, as a *real (reelles)* concrete constitutive por-
> tion of it. As the content which presents the whiteness of the paper
> as it appears to us it is the *bearer* of an intentionality, but not itself
> a consciousness of something.[39]

In this lexicon, there are two modes of "experience." First, there is the
inner experience that occurs in the "Cogito" as it turns to itself in pure
intentionality, a consciousness that is not a consciousness of anything.
This experience is what Husserl describes as the bearer of an intentionality that makes possible or originates the "concrete" experience of objects
outside the "Cogito." Husserl seems to think, like Brentano and unlike
Kant and hence in sympathy with the empiricists such as Locke, that
the "Cogito" merely points to the concrete qualities of the external world
and does not construct them. By its intending act, the "Cogito" makes
apprehension of the world possible, but it does not "create" the external
world, so to speak, for sensory qualities belong *inseparably* to objects.
And if this is the case, then a philosophical endeavor cannot be complete

if it only states or describes the contents of the intentional act of the "Cogito," for although he called this intending an "Act," he believed it was merely a passive disposition of the "Cogito." He called it the "unreflective" consciousness. In this unreflective consciousness, he said, "we are 'directed' upon objects, we 'intend' them, and reflection reveals this to be an immanent process characteristic of all experience, though infinitely varied in form."[40]

The contents of this passive intending are beliefs, *doxa*. If this kind of content of the mind is indeed what Hountondji has in mind when he criticizes the works of ethnophilosophy for describing such and calling it "philosophy," then it becomes clear why, in the essay "Remarques sur la philosophie africaine contemporaine," he distinguishes between the literature whose existence he said was undeniable and what this literature claimed to be merely exposing, or revealing, as "the location of the purported philosophy."[41] He argues in the essay that there would not have been a problem if the authors of the literature had themselves taken responsibility for what they wrote—that is, expounding, like Husserl, the nature and location of beliefs; but they didn't. Instead they claimed that "the philosophy," which can be equated in the nature of its specifics to Husserl's *doxa* above, was in the minds of the people and was revealed in a variety of forms including proverbs, songs, ritual, and so on. In the Husserlian terms we just cited from his "Phenomenology," it is, as Hountondji claims, these texts that "reveal" the contents of the unreflective consciousness that are philosophical because they are "reflective" but not the unreflective consciousness in its mere Act of intending. Husserl himself thought that the major task of philosophy was to ask about the relation between this inner consciousness and the nature of the (external) world. He framed the problem in the following interrogative form:

> This "making its appearance," this "being for us" of the world, which can only gain its significance "subjectively," what is it? We may call the world "internal" because it is related to consciousness, but how can this quite general world whose immanent being is as shadowy as the consciousness wherein it "exists," contrive to appear before us in a variety of "particular" aspects, which experience assures us are the aspects of an independent, self-existent world?[42]

The phenomenological analysis of the intentional act of the "Cogito" is certainly complex, and Husserl included analysis of the nature of other objects of consciousness such as the "ideal" world of pure numbers or the world of pure essences. But it is also useful to note that Husserl gave priority to this method because, he said, "it partly formed a convenient stepping-stone to the philosophy [of the laws of the natural world or of science], and partly because it was nearer to the natural attitude than is the [Cartesian] transcendental."⁴³ By pointing out the importance of the contribution of the empiricists, Husserl appears to have thought that the establishment and elucidation of the nature of the transcendental Ego, or the "transcendental 'Mens,'" as he called it, was not enough without relating it to the external world. He thought that Locke's "psychological exploration of the internal experience," which explains the process of apprehending in the mind the objects of the external world, accomplished the task. This was the second sense of experience in Husserl's *Ideas*. For example, he referred to "the experience of the perception of this white paper."⁴⁴ If this is the case, then it can be conjectured that for a mind at work during the onset of postcolonial liberation, Husserl's analysis and distinctions between the different stages of consciousness provided the tools with which Hountondji excavated his way to the location of the beliefs characterized as "philosophy" by the ethnophilosophers. In this sense, Hountondji found in Husserl's phenomenology of reason the method for estimating the distance in the stream of consciousness between the purported "philosophy" and the real world of everyday experience. He followed Césaire's critique of Tempels (in *Discourse on Colonialism*) in observing that emphasizing the unreflective consciousness as the location of the contemplation of Being was an unnecessary and pernicious distraction from engaging in analysis of praxis.⁴⁵ As propounded in the Tempelsian school, ethnophilosophy disengaged and distanced the thinking of Africans from the real world, their physical world, that so much needed scientific analysis and transformation for the improvement of conditions of life such as through eradicating disease and poverty in their many manifestations.

Concerned that ethnophilosophical knowledge could not be relied on as a basis for formulating scientific analyses of the world, Hountondji proposed, once again following Husserl, that the starting point ought to be the conception of philosophy as a rigorous science. The first question to arise here is, of course, what all this might mean, since, as Quentin Lauer observes in his "Introduction" to Husserl's own *La Philosophie comme Science Rigoureuse,* "after twenty centuries of history one arrives at the modern times which are characterized by a scientific movement that has produced a number of particular sciences in the strict sense of the term but no philosophy worthy of the name."⁴⁶ According to Lauer, philosophy is not just an incomplete and imperfect science, it is not science at all. But Husserl, says Lauer, would not accept the view that philosophy is nonscientific by nature and that thus philosophy ought to abandon the attempt to become a science.⁴⁷ Husserl's reasons for rejecting such a critique would not come until much later: that the design of philosophy to consider the highest human values must have a solid objective foundation and that such a foundation must be realizable. If science is possible in any domain at all, then it must be possible in philosophy as well, since the only guarantee of any science at all is the philosophy of science.[48] In other words, if there is to be anything that could be called a rigorous science, then it ought to have an idea or theory that is similarly and perfectly rigorous like science. And if such an idea has an objective validity, then it ought to be realizable, just as ideas in the Kantian sense are realizable, in a constant asymptotic approach. The issue here, for Husserl, is that of reclaiming an affinity between philosophy and science, which he thought to be attainable through what he established as the phenomenological method, namely that phenomenology is to be understood as a scientific philosophy in the sense that in its scheme, no presuppositions must ever remain unexamined systematically—the sort of thing that the American pragmatist John Dewey was also saying about philosophy. The meaning of "scientific" as related to philosophy, then, must be understood in the continental sense of "systematic" inquiry that leaves no presupposition unexamined in its quest to get to the root of matters, any matters.

It is not clear that Hountondji endorses Husserl's view that only phenomenology rescues traditional philosophy from its inability to make a claim to a scientific character for itself. His doctoral dissertation was on the idea of science in two works of Husserl, namely *The Prolegomena to Pure Logic* and *Logical Investigations*. At least Hountondji demands that philosophy more generally (as was being claimed by the ethnophilosophers) rather than just phenomenology should rid itself of unexamined presuppositions. For him, such a view was aimed primarily at a critique of the methods rather than the consequences of the claimed "philosophy"—the equivalent of what Husserl called the pre-reflective experience of the world—in question. In other words, his fierce critique of ethnophilosophy appeared to make the claim that although we always begin with some presuppositions, whether in science or other forms of inquiry or in the intuitive elements that form the basis of experience, mere descriptions of passive intuitions were a false effort. Hountondji suggested a conception of philosophy that relied heavily on Husserl's idea of rationalization of pre-scientific experience—more precisely, that philosophy is primarily a critique of knowledge and that its goal is to establish the validity or nonvalidity of the judging act itself, not the truth value (truth or falsity) of judgment.[49]

As you can see, the focus is not primarily on the propositions about reality but on the primary consciousness in which the idea of reality first occurs and its relation to the external world it posits. I propose, at the high risk of running into a circular argument, that what Hountondji critiques here refers to his perception of ethnophilosophy as having been fixated on the content of the pre-reflective, namely the beliefs in and of themselves, which ethnophilosophers have described fervently. This fixation on describing collective or shared beliefs is crucially different from what many other African philosophers have done. Ethnophilosophers described the contents of the pre-reflective consciousness while other African philosophers (even if only loosely united by their opposition to ethnophilosophy) have rigorously examined the validity of the propositional nature of those beliefs in their relation to what else is known or is knowable of the external world, such as by the sciences. If indeed Hountondji's critique of ethnophilosophy was based on what (in my view) he believed to be the wrong focus for a form of discourse that proclaimed itself to be philosophical, namely a focus on describing rather than critically analyzing the contents of pre-reflective consciousness, then it saves him from the criticism that he held a disparaging view of the value of orality.[50] Once again, the distinction goes back to the qualifications made in "Remarques sur la philosophie Africaine contemporaine," from which it can be adduced that the problem or disappointment that Hountondji had was neither with the view that oral traditions in their various forms are vehicles for ideas and concepts about reality nor with the analysis of the conceptual content of oral traditions as such but rather with what he perceived to be abdication of responsibility for their own works by those who wrote the ethnophilosophical texts. In other words, he would never have had problems if, starting with Tempels, what was presented as, say, Bamana philosophy, was a presentation of the philosophical doctrines developed by philosophers who were Bamana. My view here is that this position and its counterposition—namely the accusation of elitism—cannot be tackled exhaustively without recourse to the examination of Husserl's idea of the structure of consciousness because it grounds Hountondji's critique of anonymity as a proclaimed characteristic of theorizing.

The Struggle over Mind:
Hountondji and the Postcolonial Currents

Abiola Irele's questioning of Hountondji's reliance on Husserl and "his other European masters" in contrast to a more indigenous position in the understanding of mind (such, in his reckoning, as the one held by Senghor) appears to suggest a shift of focus to an ontological analysis of the nature of mind, or consciousness, as debated more generally in the English-language world today. As we will see later in a discussion of Kwasi Wiredu's reflections on the matter, such an approach is very much in practice already. However, Irele's reference to the warning Albert Memmi once gave (in *The Colonizer and the Colonized*) about the susceptibility of (the mind of) the colonized to the pull toward falsely identifying the colonizer's values with the universal to explain Hountondji's dependency on Husserl points more appropriately to a focus on the social-psychological idea of the mind, more like what one observes or identifies based on the behavior of persons as their mental traits, attitudes, or thoughts that portray them as agents.[51] This is the kind of approach to mind or consciousness that one encounters in Fanon, Césaire, and most other advocates of negritude. These two approaches to the problem of mind, which I will refer to as analytic and existentialist, respectively, for lack of better terms, are related, yet they also are often not discussed on the same plain—which is the reason Irele's call to reinstate Senghor's claims about an African concept of mind is both ambiguous and interestingly challenging at the same time. Why? Because Senghor's stated position, insofar as it remains traceable to the work of someone like Henri Bergson (but also to such backgrounds as Marxism and Sartrean existentialism), straddles both. I will say a little more about that shortly.

The social dimension of Irele's critique of Hountondji, and of which Memmi writes, is captured in this old Luo proverb: *"Ng'a m'oloyi k'onyono kwesi minuu to minuu ema idhawone niya: 'Choke! Un bende ang'o ok ukan giwu maber kar lo keto-gi e yo?'"* (When an intruder you consider stronger than yourself steps on and breaks your mother's pipe, you turn to your mother and rebuke her thus: "Why don't you learn to keep your things tidily so they don't sit in the path of those who are walking?") The Luo must have long been aware of the psychology of domination and alienation. In other words, the Luo proverb indicates the observation that one escapes confrontation with a reality the Luo prejudged as ominous by faulting their own standards, which they then sought to adjust to bring closer to those of the portentous and threatening intruder. It does not matter, according to the proverb, that the intruder may in fact be a clumsy person, may have crooked feet, or is eccentric and uncaring of others. So rather than confront him or her, the weaker subject reverts to self-admonition. In other words, the weaker subject thinks that it's in his or her interest to establish the values of the intruder he or she regards to be superior as the universal norms that provide the standards for a new intentional structure or order in his or her own household. Jürgen Habermas, the German critical social theorist, captures well the kind of strategy that directs the social action of our hypothetical subject mired in a relation of dependency. He contends that discovering such strategies—motives of social action—is a crucial goal of critical social science (one that it shares with philosophy), but he distinguishes social science from the systematic sciences. He argues that rather than seeking to establish nomological knowledge, critical social science may go farther by seeking "to determine when theoretical statements grasp invariant regularities of social action as such and when they express ideologically frozen relations of dependence that can in principle be transformed. . . . The methodological framework that determines the meaning of the validity of critical propositions of this category is established by the concept of *self-reflection*. The latter releases the subject from dependence on hypostatized powers. Self-reflection is determined by an emancipatory cognitive interest."[52] The Luo saying adds significantly to Habermas in claiming that the goals of self-reflection as a strategy can be ambiguous, such that what self-reflection releases a subject from is not always clear. Solemnly implied in the Luo proverb is the idea that in alienation, release from the perceived threats of hypostatized power can, through acts of self-deception, also be a form of submission to its impositions. The subject, in this strategy, transforms the relations of dependency on the hypostatized power by appropriating his or her ways and elevating them to the normative level of virtues.

In the analytic approach, where the problem takes a more general and basic character, the debate on consciousness clearly goes in a different direction, but it is still very Western (Anglo-American). There, it becomes a discourse about the ontological fundamentals of the primary human cognitive encounter with nature, about the stimulations of the neurons and their supporting glial cells in the brain, about the strings of neurochemical streams, and about whether or not we, like Plato in classic Greece, should consider the senses to be pathological chains from which we ought to be freed on the path to knowledge. Or whether, after all, the senses are all there is and that everything is perceivable through them and that mind is either itself another sense or at least not drastically much more than a function of the senses, thus saving ourselves from the doubleness or other forms of pluralism that pervade many philosophies of the Self.[53] Regardless of who he draws on, Hountondji's polemics against ethnophilosophy are not about the politics of the ethnicity of the mind from the viewpoint of the sciences of the spirit—a lesson, I believe, that Hountondji learned well from Husserl's *Ideas* via Paul Ricoeur's interpretation.[54] Inevitably, the problem is also a historical one. Hence, the fundamental point is, first, to lament the lack and then to demand of African knowledge the onset of a new (scientific) spirit that is capable of engendering a new vision of the world, one that directs consciousness toward a new and revisable knowledge of the world of specific things. In this sense, Hountondji brings into play an interesting fusion of Husserl's structuring of consciousness and his idea of science with Gaston Bachelard's historical treatment of philosophic thought that Bachelard thought to be inseparable from the historical emergence of scientific mind or spirit (esprit). It is not surprising that Hountondji's critique of ethnophilosophy as "a body of texts designated by their authors as such"[55] read very similar to the opening page of Bachelard's *The Philosophy of No: A Philosophy of the New Scientific Mind*. That page reads like this:

To use philosophical systems in areas remote from their intellectual origin is an operation which is always delicate and often disappointing. Thus transplanted, philosophical systems become sterile or deceptive, they lose the efficacy of intellectual coherence, an efficacy which is so strongly felt when one relives them, in their real originality, with the scrupulous fidelity of the historian. . . . One might thus conclude that a philosophical system must not be used for ends other than those which it assigns to itself [and not as assigned arbitrarily by the authors of the texts].[56]

Like Bachelard, Hountondji was worried about the impasse that would ensue from imposing closed ways of thinking about situations that required open-ended modes of inquiry as demanded by the character (spirit) of scientific thought. Indeed, it is Bachelard's view that philosophy properly understood is one that brings rationalism and empiricism into a complementary relation with each other, yet he leaves no doubt in *The Philosophy of No* that rationalism is not exactly on a par with empiricism. Although distinct, the former does not merely complement the latter; it serves it. To think scientifically, he says,

is to place oneself in the epistemological terrain which mediates between theory and practice, between mathematics and experiment. To know a natural law scientifically is to know it as a phenomenon and a noumenon at one and the same time. . . . We must add that, in our opinion, one of these two metaphysical directions needs to be given greater stress than the other; this is the one that moves from rationalism to experience.[57]

This combination—of the phenomenological analysis of consciousness with the historicity of the Logos, the latter of which Hountondji partly acquired at the hands of George Canghuilhem and Louis Althusser—was, in its application to the African situation, meant to counter the wind of ahistorical essentialism sweeping through the continent during and soon after his own educational formation.

The Struggle for Meaning reveals many more influences on Hountondji's intellectual development than Husserl and his idea of science. But even if we accept that the latter remains pivotal to understanding Hountondji, the African condition he was so deeply concerned about with regard to proper theorizing is crucially a historical one that required a radically different approach to knowledge. In other words, it is good but not enough to know where theory—like the "how" questioning of reality or the responses it solicits—belongs in the structure of consciousness. Such theories must be directed at nature with the purpose of transforming it; thus, science is crucial. There is a direct and overt appropriation of the Marxist critique of Hegelianism in relating knowledge to praxis, and it leads to the emphasis on the scientific attitude generally and to the sciences more specifically. First, then, there is science, to which philosophy becomes only a legitimate handmaiden by providing "the basis for a chain of reasoning." For Bachelard, "An empiricism without clear, coordinated, deductive laws can be neither thought nor taught; a rationalism without palpable proofs and without application to immediate reality cannot fully convince."[58]

And how does this scheme fit into Africa's historical moment? Or, how does the scientific spirit emerge in the life of a community? Like philosophy, science too can emerge from within Africa itself, if (and perhaps only if) African thinkers generally (and those in the natural sciences specifically) ask the right questions and adopt the right methods that are known to lie at the heart of scientific inquiry. Problems that require this kind of approach are legion. Diseases, both human and of other animals or botanical diseases that affect both agricultural and wild flora, are many and are major issues related to the health and survival of Africans. Thus, scientific knowledge and practice can and (with the move toward indigenization of knowledge) should emerge from within Africa itself. Yet at the same time, in order to explain or justify his view of the suitability of science in the current state of knowledge in Africa, Hountondji makes recourse yet again to Bachelard for a model, because he was also the proponent of the idea of "extraordinary [or] abnormal science," presumably to argue that the emergence and growth of science in Africa does not have to wait. Rather, true to the character of science, knowledge generally and knowledge production in Africa particularly, including philosophical knowledge, must be willing to be corrected and revised. If this is so, then problems remain to be resolved. In other words, because the idea of science as an open-ended enterprise calls for an incessant newness, the onus of explaining the escape path from colonial structures falls on Hountondji himself.

Irele makes two important points in his critical review of *The Struggle for Meaning*. The first, as I have shown above and will return to shortly below, is about Hountondji's reliance "on his French masters." The second, which specifies the position of that reliance—namely that philosophy cannot be thought of apart from the empirical sciences—claims that Hountondji ignores Senghor's position regarding reliance on emotion as a distinctively African epistemological method of processing knowledge as opposed to relying, allegedly, on the processes of reason such as analysis. On the strength of its claim that emotion distinguishes Africans in this respect on an almost biological basis as regards the capacities of the mind, Senghor's position could be seen not only as a theory of mind but, according to Irele, also "a theory of knowledge, indeed an epistemology.[59] Senghor developed the concept of emotion as a form of apprehension of the world and other ideas—such as communalism and reliance on oral expression—as part of the package that he presented as negritude or Africanism, an ideological expression of an African experience. Scholars who have written to defend the cultural nationalism of Africans (and who therefore see Senghor as a cultural theorist, leader, and icon of that movement) are likely to view criticism of Senghor as an affront not only to a leading African scholar but also to African cultural values, especially those that they, like Senghor, regard as being at the heart of Africans' cultural difference. It is in this respect that Irele views Hountondji's criticism of Senghor to amount to a rejection of the oral tradition either directly or indirectly. What is theoretically significant in Irele's critique of Hountondji is what he regards as the sometimes unjustifiable rejection of those values Senghor defended as orality. Irele points out, for example, that "the least that can be said is that Hountondji's citations from the master text of deconstruction [Derrida's *De la grammatologie*] to support a devaluation of orality thus harbors a curious misconception of its constitutive function in language and, most of all, its dominance in the manifold expressive schemes to be encountered within his own African background."[60]

Hountondji's now numerous responses to critics can be summed up as arguing that his discontent has not been with indigenous knowledges just because they are indigenous or with their expressive forms for their own sake. Rather, the discontent was spurred by the worry that much of the work he criticizes,

> instead of developing, of gaining in precision and in vigor through the contact with foreign science, have more of a tendency to turn in upon themselves, subsisting in the best cases *side by side* with the new knowledge in a relationship of simple juxtaposition, and in the worst cases possibly disappearing completely and being erased from the collective memory. The integration into the worldwide process of the production of knowledge thus has the effect of marginalizing the old wisdom, indeed, in the worst cases, of driving them out of the conscious memory of the people who, at a given time, produce them.[61]

The unresolved question between Irele and Hountondji here, but certainly far more general beyond just their exchange, is why African knowledges should need their European counterparts as the means not just to express but also to justify or validate themselves. In Hountondji's view, the drive, which also becomes the result of such projects as Senghor's (namely ethnoknowledges), is to give Africans a leap over real time such that Africans of a century ago can compare themselves with Europeans of the twenty-first century. With regard to philosophy specifically, it sounded like the proclamation of having their own philosophy (ethnophilosophy, that is) would make Africans "properly human." The fact that Hountondji's critique of ethnophilosophy as an ahistorical stance toward knowledge seems to directly address Senghor's concept of negritude is simply a function of the fact that Senghor was one of his generation's best-known proponents of the African essentialist school. Thus, questioning Senghor was not an aberration, nor were the answers Senghor proffered to the general question of his time self-evident or irreproachable.

Also, the relation of orality to the idea of mind would suggest that we re-read Senghor in light of recent currents in psychology and cognitive science and philosophy of mind, which are increasingly viewing mind as just another sense, the sixth one, that responds either to a whole different class of stimuli or to only a segment of the sensations already filtered by or through the other senses. This view, if viable, would call for a reinterpretation of what Senghor called the affective inclinations in the sensation of reality (which he thought of as a factor that separated Africans from at least those he referred to as "hellène[s]").[62] But this position too would have to account for the implications of his position that Africans appear to have a unique biological makeup, if that was indeed what he meant to claim. Or did Senghor, as was absolutely possible, merely make an evaluative choice of which of the multiple theories of mind (and of knowledge by implication) that were available at his time had closer affinity to his understanding of African customary attitudes? The rift between Husserl and Sartre on the idea of whether consciousness is or is not a thing or entity, if it did not directly impinge upon Senghor's choice, was at least a valuable current debate during his time. That too is worthy of consideration. However, without stretching Senghor too far off his course, it is sufficient for now to say that the examination of these matters shed light on how African knowledge (and especially the creation of that knowledge) takes place not in isolation but in integration with other knowledge systems that Africans encounter in the course of their own formation.

Like Hountondji, Senghor is indebted to French philosophy.[63] More directly, Senghor's idea of consciousness can be found to have even closer filiation with Henri Bergson's distinction between two types of knowing, as expounded by the latter in *An Introduction to Metaphysics*.[64] There, Bergson talks of "the discovery that philosophers, in spite of their apparent divergencies, agree in distinguishing two profoundly different ways of knowing a thing. The first implies that we move round the object; the second, that we enter into it."[65] Of the first type, Bergson argues that we stand outside the object and view it in relation to our standpoint, which is inevitably outside or distant from it. In the second type, he says, "What I experience will vary. And what I experience will depend neither on the point of view I may take up in regard to the object, since I am inside the object itself, nor on the symbols by which I may translate the motion, since I have rejected all translations in order to possess the original. In short, I shall no longer grasp the movement from without, remaining where I am, but from where it is, from within, as it is in itself. I shall possess an absolute."[66] Illustrating his point with the example of a character in a novel, Bergson explains how attempts to understand and relate to the character through representations and symbols—the tools of description and analysis—fail to allow him a deep cognitive interaction with the character as an object of knowledge. These representations barely allow him to penetrate into the essence of the character because they focus on what the character has in common with others. In contrast, he explains, "That which is properly [of the character] himself, that which constitutes his essence, cannot be perceived from without, being internal by definition, nor be expressed by symbols, being incommensurable with everything else. Description, history, and analysis leave me here in the relative. Coincidence with the person himself would alone give me the absolute."[67]

But what is this all about? Well, Bergson's goal was to define the parameters of metaphysics, the study of the absolute. Its foundation and possibility, he held, could not lie in enumeration. "It follows from this," he said, "that an absolute could only be given in an *intuition,* whilst everything else falls within the province of *analysis.* By intuition is meant the kind of *intellectual sympathy* by which one places oneself within an object in order to coincide with what is unique in it and consequently inexpressible. . . . *Metaphysics, then, is the science which claims to dispense with symbols.*"[68]

The phenomenological approach is clearly evident in the passages from Bergson. What is more interesting is their similarity with Senghor's now-famous dictum on African knowledge as being "intuitive by participation" and Senghor's view that these similarities already reveal the presence of Africans in the new Europe, not in the sense of the involvement or participation of the African troops that fought alongside European troops but in the sense of the new order of knowledge.[69] This, he says, "is what phenomenological and existential thought reveals."[70] The point, however, is that while these lines of thought undeniably address important aspects of and approaches to knowledge (and by extension important insights on the nature of mind),[71] they are clearly distinct from, say, an approach that seeks to determine what sorts of "things" thoughts or meanings are—one that, while obviously also trying to define "how the mind works," direct its attention toward the calculative identification of the physical (electromagnetic and chemical) flow in the complex network of neurological pathways caused by stimulation. The latter method is not only the opposite of what Bergson stipulated and was reenacted later by people such as Sartre and Senghor, it was indeed what they fiercely criticized as a mathematical and physical objectification of both mind and object. Neither the phenomenological nor the analytic method is unique to Africa; only African philosophers who have found either one to be useful for what they do are unique—like Senghor for the phenomenological approach, or Wiredu for the analytic one.

In its general tone and especially in its earlier, uncompromising stance, Hountondji's rejection of the idea of a communal characteristic of thought left itself vulnerable to accusations of anti-Africanism and anti-oralism. The charge of Occidentalism against Hountondji inadvertently started a theme in African philosophy that was not immediately pursued with the focus it has today. Because of the interests of the time, the charge was aimed specifically at Hountondji's view that academic philosophy was not—

and could not be—the property of the anonymous communities, as the Tempelsian ethnophilosophers had claimed. Philosophy, he contended, was the serious and scientific work of individual thinkers. In phenomenological terms, philosophy has tried to be a rigorous science throughout much of its history, the kind of science that satisfies the most profound theoretical needs and makes possible (from an ethicoreligious standpoint) a life regulated by the norms of reason. Such objectives can be pursued only by means of critical reflection as the guiding method, one that ends up with the establishment of the rigorous sciences of the external world and of the spirit as by-products of critical reflection as practiced in philosophical thought alongside the discipline of pure mathematics. Philosophy is the vocation of a consciousness that starts with the awareness of its own being as made, in Husserlian terms, for intending something other than itself. Hountondji's critics defended the opposing view, namely that the collective has the capacity to produce cognitive, moral, aesthetic, and other values that provide the bases on which individual reason operates. According to this view, the individual is primarily an assenting participant whose identity and interests are submerged under those of the community.[72]

There is something to consider in that view of the collective: the role it plays in producing and sustaining the normative principles of reason by which people make judgments and choices, such as when they determine that a belief is rational, an action is right, or a desire is acceptable. Now several actions, beliefs, and desires, especially at the cultural level, may be in competition with their alternatives that may be just as rational or acceptable within the cultural framework of the group. Take a matter that offers as much diversity of opinion as polygyny, the belief that marriage between one man and several wives is right and is therefore permissible. Although it is widespread throughout the world, this form of plural marriage has never been short of controversy, with strong views on either side. Depending on where anyone stands on the matter, they will be part of a group whose members share some basic beliefs about why this practice is either acceptable or abhorrent. Those beliefs unite those who share them into a cultural group or community, and we say that they share a position of theoretical rationality regarding this matter. Many members of such groups may share the belief without necessarily knowing the arguments that support their belief, although they would accept those reasons if and when they were given or shown to them. In this sense, for example, many people have beliefs (such as about polygyny) because they belong to the Christian faith. Hence, they believe that monogyny is rational because Christian teachings order it as the norm and that anything different from that norm is irrational and therefore ought to be avoided. In this and possibly other examples, one can say that the institution provides the norms by which its members make their judgments and live their lives. Ethnophilosophers must have regarded the institution of communal cultures in a similar manner, and one would not object to a project that aims at identifying the theoretical tenets that define such a community, especially since such a project would likely correct any false perceptions of (African) communal belief systems produced by non-natives. Yet it is a completely different matter to attribute a form of subjectivity to such communities, as ethnophilosophers did. The tenets do not, to use Achebe's words, "construct a rigid and closely argued system of thought to explain the universe and the place of man in it."[73] For this, Hountondji contends, one would have to look for individuals whose rigid and closely argued work is regarded as representative of the system—which should include all the works within the system, including all the agreements and disagreements about explanations or interpretations.

By building his case on the phenomenological analysis of consciousness, Hountondji was emphasizing another point, one that was in defense of a founding ethos upon which certain views of individual selfhood could be built. According to him, it is not enough to single out certain elements in the social structures prevalent in Western and African traditions as the crucial points in defining experience, for more foundational considerations exist that reveal the most basic nature of all humans; namely, that humans are endowed with consciousness. To claim active (reflective) consciousness as the most basic human endowment is partly to claim that thinking lies at the very root of being human, of human nature, and that no one can (nor should) be denied the exercise of that right. Our thoughts are the basic significations and confirmations of our being and of our lives; they are our bridges to the outside world. For Hountondji, as we learn in *The Struggle for Meaning,* humans constitute a plurality of subjects that are not reducible to the anonymous chorus of the crowd that both ethnophilosophy and the totalitarian political discourse of post-independence dictators preferred. Albeit inadvertently (yet conjoined by a common view of the alleged unity of thought and experience in indigenous societies), the discourse and practice of ethnophilosophy and the political persecution of individuals in post-independence Africa formed a dangerous alliance and created a quagmire for Africa's prospects for developing democratic institutions and a viable knowledge base for its social, economic, scientific, and technological advancement. Their shared position was an old European song, now echoed by new and local voices but no less convinced that Africans were incapable of advancing themselves through the production of locally grown knowledge that was capable of transforming the world according to African aspirations.[74] For Hountondji, then, the flagrant political abuse of the right to thought as the basic expression of individuality under the guise of "defending the masses" could not be anything other than part of the move, both anti-developmental and anti-philosophical, to privilege the unanimity of the chorus over the restrained, critical, and self-examining mind of the individual. Irele saw clearly the political implications (or, as I would rather put it, the causes) of this critique; he rejected "the populist tendency of his critics, who equate the cause of the African 'masses' with an undiscriminating defence of the traditional culture in which for the most part they are still bound."[75] Hountondji's need to emphasize the consciousness of the individual became stronger and more urgent than it had been during his sojourn in Europe, partly because (as Irele rightly observed), the need to replace unanimist fervor with argument and debate is not only the heart of philosophy but is also the pinnacle of a democratic ideal grounded in the most basic right of the individual.[76] It is in this respect that Hountondji's critique of the idea of "community as a thinking entity" ushered in a new moral concern, not just with respect to how philosophy ought to be done but also, and more importantly, with regard to the ethical commitment about whether *individualism* or *communalism* should be the fundamental proposition about the value of reason.[77] Although they were ubiquitous and prominent in most African political and literary writings since the early 1960s, discussions of liberalism and communalism in the African academy have been somewhat only indirect and timid, perhaps indicated most significantly in the literature on Africa's cultural characteristics. Developed partly from the negritude movement and partly from the influential moral and political appeals of the Soviet-driven post–World War II socialist ideologies, the embrace and defense of the collectivist ethos became consonant with the popular sense of political correctness, namely the anticolonial stance. The idea of defending "the values and interests of the people"—including attributing to them the ownership of knowledge—popularized the idea and exponents of ethnophilosophy as a philosophy of the people while, inversely, demonizing those who opposed it. As Hountondji explains in *The Struggle for Meaning,* the political expediency of the time had neither the time nor the space for a theoretical justification of the proclaimed communalism or (and especially) of its antonym.[78] Certainly the national mood of the time had little, if any, political or intellectual sympathy for liberalism, even in its most limited form.

Hountondji's critique of Senghor has not been large-scale, but it is by no means any less significant in view of the debate it has produced. His critique of Senghor ranks among the most prominent and best known, not in isolation from but in tandem with the critique of negritude generally. Yet unlike Stanislas Adotevi and Marcien Towa,[79] for example, Hountondji has not addressed the idea and the specific constituting claims of negritude as products of Western imperialist conditioning, as Adotevi and Towa did. Adotevi's criticism of negritude in particular has earned him wide-ranging recognition in the disciplinary fields across which postcolonial theory (as applicable to the understanding of the making of historical agency) is scattered. He (Adotevi) sees negritude, especially Senghor's poetic and essentializing rendition of it, as a crippling embrace of the European (colonial) view of Africans that accepts a self-image built upon a mystified past that will never lead to true independence and progress. In the same vein, Towa saw negritude as a subtle proclamation of Africans' "servitude."

Yet Hountondji's restraint from directly using Marxist critiques to assess what he saw as Africans' passive notions of mind and of philosophical practice does not indicate that he has bourgeois leanings or that he lacks an awareness of the significant issues that the idea of negritude raised through Senghor's elevation of emotion to the status of an epistemological means—that is, to a method of knowing. He considered ethnophilosophy largely to be an extension of the unanimity thesis first sown by Senghor's idea of negritude as indicated in the very definition of the term as an ontology, or the being of blacks in the world, the ensemble of characteristics, of manners of thinking, of feeling, proper to the black race; belonging to the black race. Senghor even thought that negritude had (in the sense of such a definition) a modified element of Heidegger's phenomenological idea of Dasein as a "Neger-sein," or "being-black-in-the-world."

When in *On African Socialism* Senghor describes the affinities between Negro-African modes of engaging with and knowing the external world of things, on the one hand, and the experiences described in what he calls the new European theories of knowledge (such as phenomenology, existentialism, and Teilhardism), on the other, he uses a uniquely Heideggerian vocabulary.[80] He explains that just as it is shown now in these new European theories, ethnographers working in Africa have also shown clearly that Negro-Africans disclose meaning in reality through their unmediated contacts with nature and through their ordinary language. These methods, he argues, are the direct antithesis of the purely rationalist (and therefore abstract) method propounded by Descartes or the method that is predominantly in use in the natural sciences.

It is Irele's view that Hountondji's apparent quick dismissal of Senghor, based on what Irele thinks is Hountondji's truncated or incomplete reading of Husserl, prevents him from developing "greater tolerance, perhaps even sympathy, for Senghor's concept of Negritude than he has displayed in his polemical engagement with the ideas of the great African poet and cultural theorist."[81] But, he says, "To point up the blind spots in Hountondji's assessment of his intellectual antecedents is not to suggest . . . a crippling dependence on the authority of his French masters."[82]

After allowing that Hountondji was introduced to Husserl's works by the French masters and that Husserl was not himself French but was a German of Jewish descent, the question remains this: How universal did Husserl regard his categories of experience to be? If there is an answer, it would probably be contained, at least by indication, in Husserl's letter of March 11, 1935, to Lévy-Bruhl to thank him for the gift of his latest book, *La mythologie primitive. Le monde mythique des Australiens et des Papous*.[83] The letter clearly expresses admiration for Lévy-Bruhl's work, which, Husserl said, had set in motion (influenced) a problematic in him as well as in his entire and long-standing studies on mankind and the environment.[84] For Husserl, Lévy-Bruhl's works pointed to an especially important problem with theoretical anthropology[85] and pure psychology, both of which claimed that humans should be treated not as objects of nature or as psycho-physical entities in a universe of spatio-temporal realities (as in the objective and natural-scientific spatio-temporality) but as persons or as subjects of consciousness who not only realize they are concrete but also call each other by personal pronouns. By saying "I" and "we," they experience themselves as living or relationally connected with others, as members of families, groups, and societies, which are the active and passive means by which they relate to their world—the world, the one that comes out of their intentional life, their experience, their thought, and thus has value, meaning, and importance for them.[86] Naturally, Husserl said, "we had long known that every human has his/her own 'representation of the world', and so does every nation, and every multinational cultural system live in a different world as its environment, so to speak, just like every historical period too lives in its own."[87]

Was this the "naturally" right way to think of diversity among the multiple cultural groups of the world as defined by the plurality of their spatio-temporal locations upon which the "making sense of the world (*Weltvorstellung*)" takes place? This is what Husserl's texts taught us about the analysis of intentionality; namely, that mind, which is a human endowment, posits the world as its Other, as its natural object located outside it. In other words, at least two other things are involved in this process besides the act of intending itself; namely, the structure and unity of the object and the unity and structure of the mind or subjectivity. The subject matter of the letter appears to suggest that Husserl is addressing the contribution of Lévy-Bruhl's works with regard to the nature of the ego, the intending subject, and that as far as this is concerned, Husserl values a scientific study of subjectivity over theoretical ones. So he tells Lévy-Bruhl that "in contrast to this empty generality [of theoretical anthropology and pure psychology], your work and its excellent subject matter have made us realize something stunningly new."[88]

The matter here appears to be about the kind of ego that Lévy-Bruhl has presented—the empirical ego—and how this ego fits into Husserl's scheme. According to Pierre Keller, since the publication of *Ideas* in 1913, Husserl had been inclined to think that "this unity cannot be provided by an empirical ego, for the empirical ego is a kind of spatio-temporal unity from which one abstracts in reflection of the kind involved in the transcendental reduction."[89] For Husserl, Keller further says, "time-consciousness is responsible for the constitutive unity of an individual ego, just as the unity of that ego is presupposed in the individuation of time-streams."[90] If this is correct, then one could read Husserl as deferring to Lévy-Bruhl's scientific authority, thus submitting that since it is he (Lévy-Bruhl) who is the expert on "primitive" tribes, on the strength of his findings, Husserl would agree that the account of the undifferentiating experience of such people, as known to him only through Lévy-Bruhl's work, is evidence that their relationship with the world does not quite constitute a *representation* of the world (Weltvorstellung), because in the account, the "Primitive" people are described as living in unity with their world. This, it appears, prompts Husserl to observe that

> The fact that the Primitive tribes are "without history" prevents us from delving into the stream of their cultural traditions, documents, wars, politics, and so on, and we therefore survey this tangible correlation between the purely spiritual life and the environment as its valid form, and we also do not make it a scientific topic. It goes without saying that similar studies now must be developed for those distant societies to which we may have access. This must happen not only for those human societies whose isolated communal life consists of unhistorical stagnation (as an existence that is only a flowing presence), but also for a truly historical existence that as such has a national future and constantly strives for a future.[91]

Why would this be important for assessing Husserl's stance on the nature of the so-called primitive people's experience in the context of his transcendental phenomenology? Again, according to Keller, "Husserl is committed to the possibility of, and is constantly searching for, that narrow representational content that does not depend essentially on the particular broadly social environment that a person happens to occupy."[92] This would be the absolute being, one that transcends both the strictures of history and the structures of any particular historical organization, and he thought that "history [was] the great fact of that being."[93] In the letter, he says of such historical societies that

> Accordingly, such a human society does not live in a so-called inflexible environment, but lives in a world that consists partly of a realized future (a national "past"), and partly of a future still to be realized and fashioned according to national goals. So this leads us to the common difficulties of history—the psychology of the historic spirit in all its possible shapes and relativities (nation and the internal structure of the nation through separate social communities; and on the other hand the type of the supra-nation as society of nations, and so on). So, for a historic society, just as for the Primitive Tribes, we face the problem of correlation: the unity of a closed-off national life and the world contained therein, tangible, worth living, and real for the nation, with its typical structure. Also, a connection

of nations and the higher entity "supra-nation" (such as Europe, or China, for instance); on top of that the logic and ontology of the respective human societies and environments.[94]

Husserl asserts that he had thought about the problems of the historical relativity of cultural institutions and of the correlation between humans and the environment for a long time—since around 1920, according to Keller—in the course of the development of his lifelong work and found them to be of utmost importance for philosophical inquiry, the "transcendental-phenomenological" one, with regard to the problem of absolute ego. "Because within its circle of awareness," he says, "all societies and their relative environments have created sense and meaning and are continuing to build them in continuous change, I believe I can be sure that, in this way of a thoroughly investigated intentional analysis, historical relativism undoubtedly remains justified—as an anthropological fact—but that anthropology, just like all positive science and their 'Universitas,' may be the first, but [certainly] not the last word of knowledge."[95]

In contrast to the universalist spirit of positive science, one that accounts for its tendency to take for granted the existence of the objective world and of human existence as a real presence in the world, Husserl describes his new approach, transcendental phenomenology, as the radical and systematic science of subjectivity that in the end integrates the world within itself. In other words, he says, "it is the science that exposes the universal truth of 'world and us humans within this world' as incomprehensible and therefore as an enigma, a problem; and it scientifically explains it in the only possible way of radical self-determination. Because of this radicalism, it is a new kind of science that serves as a systematic analysis, which systematically proves the ABC and the basic grammar of the structure of objects as valid units, of the diversity and infinity of objects as valid 'worlds' for the subjects that give them meaning, and with that it ascends and soars from below as a philosophy."[96]

For Husserl, then, the historical relativity of cultural institutions has implications for the very enterprise of philosophical inquiry, meaning that philosophical inquiry itself has a form that cannot easily be detached from the cultural and historical situation in which it has arisen. This position makes Husserl a foreshadowing ally, not an adversary, of the cultural pluralist view advanced by Senghor's theory of negritude. That said, it is also true that (as he illustrated in his "Vienna Lecture") Husserl sees great differences between cultures across the world with regard to how philosophy and science are historically incorporated into their respective intentional relation with their worlds.[97] The leap into the stream of historical progress, he argues, occurs when a radically new sort of attitude of individuals toward their surrounding world arises, such as the one that occurred in the ancient Greek nation in the seventh and sixth centuries BCE and then spread to engulf and effect or give emergence to a "supra-nation" Europe that embodies the "spiritual shape" it inherited from its ancient Greek genesis. In Husserl's view, then, philosophy and science, as "the title for a special class of cultural structures," have not always been there (in Europe), nor is it something that inhabits all persons there, or to be found "fully developed in the personalities of a higher level" there, and much less is it something peculiar to the Greeks that came into the world for the first time with them.[98] Just as the outbreak of the theoretical attitude among the Greeks was the result of factors partly attributable to its contact with the great and already highly cultivated nations of its surrounding world,[99] so

> we must take into account the fact that philosophy, which has grown up out of the universal critical attitude toward anything and every-thing pregiven in the tradition, is not inhibited in its spread by any national boundaries. Only the capacity for a universal critical atti-tude, which, to be sure, presupposes a certain level of prescientific culture, must be present. So the upheaval of national culture can proliferate, first of all when the advancing universal science becomes the common property of nations that were formerly alien to one another and the unity of a scientific community and the community of the educated spreads throughout the multiplicity of nations.[100]

Although Husserl clearly defines philosophy and science and the critical spirit that drives them as historical disciplines, the passage above does not seem to indicate that he regarded Europe's embrace of philosophy and science as an ontological character of Europe. In fact, he regarded Europe's embrace of the disciplines and the emergence of a spiritual culture that facilitated the emergence of "Europe as a supra-nation" as a historical event, one that could have occurred anywhere else. And how does such spread of knowledge take place? His answer, which has striking affinities with Kwasi Wiredu's communicative theory of personhood, again appears to point to the universality of the character of humans and their capacity to transform into persons through the power of communication, precisely because personhood is intersubjectively constituted. He says that although philosophy neither inhabits all persons nor is to be found fully developed in the personalities of a higher level that are constituted by intersubjective acts, still, as part of the broader capacity to form and exchange ideas, it

> has at the same time the significance of an advancing transforma-tion of all humanity through the formations of ideas that become effective in the smallest of circles. Ideas, meaning-structures that are produced in individual persons and have the miraculous new way of containing intentional infinities within themselves, are not like real

things in space; the latter [that is, real things in space, or objects],
although they enter into the field of human experience, do not yet
thereby have any significance for human beings as persons. . . .
This movement [of becoming persons] proceeds from the beginning
in a communicative way, awakens a new style of personal existence
in one's sphere of life, a correspondingly new becoming through
communicative understanding . . . [from which] arises a new type
of communalization . . . a new form of . . community . . . through
the love of ideas, the production of ideas.[101]

This passage suggests that Husserl believes in the universality of the structure of consciousness and that the historical diffusion of philosophy and
science beyond Europe was not only an accidental fact (as opposed to being
a necessary conclusion of predetermination), it also did not eliminate the
crucial differences between the various cultural systems that were known
to and practiced by different nations and supranations. It would therefore
seem, because of these considerations, that although Husserl thought that
philosophy and science had their own universal features—by which they
transformed cultural tasks and accomplishments from the finite to focus
on the open-ended, idealized, and infinite tasks and goals—he appeared
not to dismiss the view that in practical terms (that is, with regard to how
real people actually carry out investigative inquiry), the embrace of philosophy and science by every culture will always have significant bearings
on certain historical and cultural contexts and that such conditionings,
in turn, do not nullify the goal of attaining objectivity.[102] To put it in his
own words to Lévy-Bruhl, he says, "To start with, the tasks are the historically defined ones for the factually known nations and supra-nations,
but then also for the general psychological ones—in the sense of a pure
internal psychology of definitions, for which the methodology first has
to be developed."[103] Even in *The Crisis* he characterizes philosophy and
science, by virtue of their concern with the infinite norms, as the tools
of "consistent idealization [by which] is accomplished . . . a thoroughgo-
ing transformation which finally draws all finite ideas and with them all
spiritual culture and its [concept of] mankind into its sphere."[104]

Clearly, many things in Husserl's letter to Lévy-Bruhl point to significant
aspects of his general theory of experience, and these undoubtedly lie far
beyond my scope here, namely to attempt to pinpoint the source, if there
is indeed one, of what Irele calls Hountondji's problematic dependence
on Husserl. Among these many things is Husserl's critique of speculative anthropology and pure psychology—remember that he calls these
disciplines "empty generalizations"—a berating that appears to stem from
Husserl's rejection, in the *Investigations,* of the Kantian or neo-Kantian
idea of the transcendental Ego as the ultimate grounding of human experience in favor of the empirically based view that the only unity that the

self has is the one that real everyday people exhibit in experience, as he claims Lévy-Bruhl has demonstrated in his scientific research. Pierre Keller observes that Husserl's worry about impersonal consciousness began way back in 1907, long before his correspondence with Lévy-Bruhl, but grew over the span of time that runs through *Ideas* in 1913 to *Crisis* in 1936.[105] Husserl's disagreement with Lévy-Bruhl would therefore appear to stem from the latter's assumption that the "primitive" people's way of relating to the world made them a people with an inferior type of consciousness. Husserl's view appears to be that the most basic stage that defines humanity—at the phenomenological level—is that all humans are "human beings in the world."

To be sure, the proclamation of a universal phenomenological condition of humanity does not preclude the possibility of an anti-African attitude at another level or from a different viewpoint. Hence Husserl's disagreement with Lévy-Bruhl regarding "primitive" people's different way of experiencing the world does not discount the possibility that his attitude was racist. The point, at least only as far as Hountondji's dependence on Husserl as a basis for rejecting ethno-philosophy à la Tempels goes, appears to be a different game than the one that plays into the trap of the possibility that he was racist. As in other instances,[106] Hountondji may selectively have been inspired by "a certain" Husserl—namely by those aspects of Husserl that he deemed applicable to a general understanding of philosophy, African philosophy included, as a second-order (reflective) practice, one that builds on the pregivens of tradition.

But Senghor himself eloquently objects to both the idea of universal consciousness and the idea that the historical diffusion of philosophy and science is innocent. At the Rome Conference of the European Society of Culture and the African Society of Culture in February 1960, he writes, European and African societies of culture disagreed, apparently quite passionately, over the idea of a universal civilization. While their European colleagues endeavored "to maintain that European civilization was identified with the Civilization of the Universal and thus should be adopted as *the* Universal Civilization[,] [African scholars at the conference] had little difficulty in demonstrating that each 'exotic civilization' had also thought in terms of universality, [and] that Europe's only merit in this regard had been to diffuse her civilization throughout the world, thanks to her conquest and techniques."[107] Senghor maintains that there was nothing accidental about the colonization of Africans. He writes, "We have been colonized, to be sure, as underdeveloped, defenseless individuals, but also as *Negroes* or Arab Berbers—in other words, as people of a different race and different culture. This was the basic argument of the colonizer. We were 'primitive' and ugly to boot; it was [therefore] necessary to expose us to progress, to 'the light of civilization.' Naturally, progress and civilization could only be European."[108]

I have no reason to believe that Hountondji was unaware—at least when he attained the age of reason and historical awareness—that the Africa he was born into was under European colonization, or that there were deep cultural differences between Europeans and Africans. And this sounds like quite a trivial matter, so we should look elsewhere for the differences between what Hountondji embraces in Husserl's idea of phenomenology and what Senghor proposes as *the* African cognitive structure.

As I tried to show above, Hountondji adopts Husserl's view of the two stages of consciousness (pre-reflective and reflective) as basic to his understanding of the nature of philosophical practice, which emerges out of the latter stage as a second-order discourse.[109] His claim, then, is that the idea of philosophy that pervades the ethnophilosophical texts bifurcates and fails to recognize this structure of consciousness. Senghor's view, on the other hand, rejects the notion of structured consciousness as universal and with it the idea of "reflective intending," not only because this draws a line between consciousness and its object but also because it is European. Irele aptly summed up Senghor's "emotive" theory of knowledge.[110] Relying on Gaëtan Picon's overview of contemporary European thought, Senghor argues that as a result of new developments in science as well as new approaches in philosophy, contemporary European thought (as evidenced by "the new philosophical revolutions: phenomenology, existentialism, [and] Teilhardism"[111]) appears finally to abandon the method of objectivity, the one that stipulated a distance between subject and object as a requirement for observation.[112] In the place of the method of objectivity, a new elevation of touch is introduced as a valid mode of comprehending the world, one that erases the distance between subject and object: "One must also touch it, penetrate it from the inside—so to speak—and finger it."[113] He continues:

> This is what phenomenological or existential thought reveals, as it follows the path of Marxism and exceeds it while integrating it. In this school of thought, the real coincides with thought, the content of a statement coincides with the form in which it is expressed, philosophy blends with science, as art merges with existence, with *life*. There is more than coincidence here, there is *identity*. In the act of knowledge, one must probe beneath the crystallizations of appearances and education into the primordial chaos unshaped by reason. . . . More specifically, knowledge coincides with the *essence* of a thing in its innate and original reality, in its discontinuous and undetermined reality, in its *life*.[114]

There is no doubt that what we have are two definitions of phenomenology: one (Hountondji's) is Husserlian, and the other (Senghor's) is Bergsonian, and more akin to what is popularly regarded as Sartre's existentialist (largely anti-Husserlian) idea of consciousness, one that lies at the heart of his idea of "Nothingness"—that is, consciousness as not-a-thing or entity. Senghor's path leads him toward a demarcation between what he perceived to be quite distinct ideas of consciousness—one, the Sartrean, he chose to identify as akin to the African, and the other, the Husserlian, he thought of as having remained crucially European. On this point alone, however, Senghor could be proposing a position on the nature of mind that is curiously akin to the one Wiredu proposed within the context of the contemporary analytical debate on the matter (as we shall see later). What does not seem attractive or helpful, however, is the claim that constitution of the object by consciousness, an act that apparently is passive and innate to consciousness as Senghor viewed it—is tantamount to philosophizing. Or, put slightly differently, that philosophizing does not require distance between subject and object. But if that is so, then how does a person know that she knows? And how does a person begin the examination of either their consciousness or its object, the nature of their relation? Finally, whether Senghor's preference for Sartre's brand of the idea of consciousness is less European because of affinities to what he believed was African or Hountondji's preference for Husserl's brand of the idea was bad on account of being anti-Sartrean is a matter that should be interesting as an example of African discourse as a surrogate for a European discourse.

But all is not lost for Senghor's idea of the role of emotion in our attempts to shape the world. There are at least two ways of looking at emotion cognitively. One is the descriptive view, widely held by philosophers and psychologists today, the view that we call emotion any of the mental states that cause largely involuntary physiological reactions, such as blushing, sweating, tearing up, or speaking rapidly as a prelude to shouting when in a state of shock, anger, fear, or attraction, and so on. The mental states and their manifestations can also be caused by the feeling of awe or compassion or by the feeling of embarrassment when we are caught in or associated with a situation or circumstance we do not wish to be publicly identified with. Recent developments in the behavioral sciences, particularly psychology, have opened up ways to "observe," so to speak, the body's network of neurological reactions to different types of stimuli that now enable us to explain most human behaviors in physiological terms. This category of emotions describes processes that "happen" to us because the behaviors involved are caused by the release of chemicals by specific organs and glands in the body that are charged with such functions. When these states explode into behaviors—that is, when they cause us to act in certain ways that are identifiable with those states, we are often said to be emotional, as when we cry because of fear or disappointment or because we feel sorrowful about someone else's misfortune, when we yell when we are disappointed or in a fit of anger, when we caress another person because we are attracted to them, and so on. We also show emotion when we act purely on the basis of sympathy and compassion for people we know or believe to be in adverse conditions, such as when we donate funds to help people who are victims of tragedies. Cultures throughout the world teach their folks about how to manage their emotions, often with differentiations among members of society based on how each society defines and distributes its values. For example, many cultures teach that crying is the antithesis of courage and valor, and because courage is a value expected of people starting from a specific age in their lives, there may be rituals they would be required to go through to mark the attainment of that age and to test if they have trained themselves to show that value. Circumcision is an example; those who go through it are expected to show great courage and endurance as manifestations of adolescence or adulthood. In some societies, it is the males who are expected to embody the values of courage and valor, so they are taught that crying and other feelings that designate weakness are emotions that males should not show, especially in public.

Senghor's idea of emotion is unique in two ways: first, he ascribes to it a special cognitive value, and second, he claims that this type of emotion is unique to black African people and their descendants. As I said a little earlier, there is less controversy today about the concept of ascribing cognitive value to emotions as part of the mechanistic theory of the human organism, although the idea is still widely debatable, especially within the context of the continental tradition that produced Senghor, particularly the Cartesian-driven French tradition. But it is far more problematic to claim that such a theory of cognition is unique to people of black African descent, for if the emotion Senghor was talking about was a function of the structure of consciousness, then it should be part of a general theory, hence subject to analysis and therefore to confirmation or refutation, based on general and well-known criteria of analysis. Alternatively, to account for its uniqueness to only a small group of humans, its basis would have to be proven as either an additional element to the general and already-known features of mind or consciousness or as compensation for something else that black African people lack among such known features of mind or consciousness. In the absence of such additional and racially specific biological attributes that would validate Senghor's theory, one would have to infer that Senghor did not consider black Africans to be exactly normal human beings, either because they lack something other humans have or because they have something additional to everything else that they share with other humans. It has never been clear which of these options serves his purpose.

If the emotion of Africans is to be viewed as an example of the general physio-psychological constitution of all humans, then Husserl already deals with it in his analysis of consciousness, the part of it that he calls "pre-reflective," and Hountondji, in accepting that analysis, views it as a merely passive (that is, physio-psychological) trait and, therefore, pre-philosophical. On the other hand, if by "the physio-psychology of the Negro," Senghor meant a distinctive and essentializing biological constitution of black people that sets them apart as a subspecies of humanity, then this is a matter that requires all the supporting evidence there is. Whatever the case may be, it is Irele's view that the epistemological significance and innovativeness of the theory of emotion as "a manner of thinking" or "way of knowing" (which, in his own words, "perhaps [is] the most significant aspect of Senghor's theory of negritude [because] it contains within it a theory of knowledge, indeed an epistemology . . . [of] *emotion,* which he virtually erects into a function of knowledge and attributes to the African as a cardinal principle of his racial disposition"[115]) is too important a cultural contribution to be dismissed. Irele's position is that of caution. Drawing from his own encounters with European literary and other works of art, Irele worries that such apparently "universal" and neutral works have "the insidious and sometimes terrifying power . . . to obscure with their very brilliance the moral zones they impinge upon." Having this hidden agenda, Irele further argues, is "the fundamental irony of colonial education, whose ideological premises obliged its agents to have recourse to texts, images, and other modes of discourse and representation that devalue the humanity of their dark-skinned wards, as part of the effort to establish the cultural and moral authority of the colonizing race."[116] Hountondji, in Irele's view, may have been a victim of this colonial scheme that camouflages its venom with the overwhelmingly appealing veneer of its aesthetics. But Hountondji has come around, making a significant transition from the uncompromising stance in *African Philosophy: Myth and Reality* to the softened position regarding indigenous knowledges in *The Struggle for Meaning* and other later publications. He now explains in these works that he had all along been an advocate for indigenous knowledges, if only they were placed at the center alongside other knowledge systems of the world instead of being left on the margins. This turnaround is reminiscent of the transition that Albert Memmi described in *The Colonizer and the Colonized* of the colonial subject who abandons the embrace of the colonizer in order to embrace himself.

Irele's reference to Memmi is a powerful criticism of Hountondji who, to use Memmi's words, now appears to distance himself from his previous "assimilation to the standards of the colonizer."[117] According to Memmi, "The middle-class colonized suffers most from bilingualism. . . . The intellectual lives more in cultural anguish, and the illiterate person is simply walled into his language and rechews scraps of oral culture."[118] Two historically possible solutions are open to the colonized for dealing with her condition: one, as analyzed by Fanon in his classic *Black Skin, White Masks,* is for the colonized to attempt to become different by mimicking the colonizer, closely copying many of his values, hoping thus to be accepted, "even if inappropriate," thereby approving of colonization. Or, says Memmi, the colonized can choose "to reconquer all the dimensions which colonization tore away from him."[119] What is ironic about these debates between Hountondji and his critics, especially the one on the validity of the influence of Husserl and Hountondji's reliance on him, is that the struggle against the disparaging colonial classification of the "primitive mentality," as championed by Lévy-Bruhl, for example, was partly aimed at asserting the common features of human nature, including especially the structure of consciousness and cognitive capacity. This is the exact point that Husserl appears to speak to Lévy-Bruhl about in their correspondence. Coincidentally, Husserl wrote that letter only four years before the publication of *Les Carnets,* Lévy-Bruhl's recantation of the pivotal claims central to his earlier work, the claims that had been the subject of Husserl's criticism. But after all, does Husserl's criticism of Levy-Bruhl make his own theory of consciousness free of Eurocentrism? To paraphrase Shakespeare, THAT, indeed, is the question.

In the end, I return to my questions at the beginning of the chapter: What is the model of person in our eyes? What kind of life should a person pursue who is embodying the kind of goods we would encourage in those placed in our care? We probably would teach them to "live a good life," and then they would press us for an elaboration and we would embark on an explanation similar to the following: A good life is the kind of life that, in its manifestation, has those things, call them goods, that are deemed desirable for individuals and groups to possess or to practice in order to be considered happy. A good life, then, is a state of being in which an individual deems him or herself as successful at incorporating into their lives some of the values deemed by society to be worth pursuing as goals. Chinua Achebe gives us a sense of a good life in his classic novel *Things Fall Apart,* where he defines a life of success as one in which a person attains the acceptable measure of the values set by society. A person who grows to be a healthy adult, marries, begets offspring, is a hard worker, is a trustworthy person, is friendly and kind, is a good conversationalist, is a person of measured judgment and restraint, is successful in sports or some other skill, and earns recognition from his or her community for all these qualities that require and build good character is likely to be considered one who lives a good life. Average people achieve these qualities only modestly, and few people achieve outstanding results in all of them. Achieving all these values together was an ideal that constantly eluded Okonkwo. When he succeeded in some, he demonstrated serious flaws in others. As a result, Okonkwo was never happy, for he was always obsessed with the pursuit of the ideals of a happy life, for himself in his specific situations but also for his community of Umofia and Igbo society generally. Despite his failures caused by poor judgment, he strove to be a reflection of what he understood to be Igbo ideals. Moral wisdom should enhance our capacity to live good lives. In other words, it should produce actions that enhance rather than reduce our happiness. Moral wisdom teaches, for example, that no value is worth pursuing whose pursuit causes greater pain than the enjoyment it brings or whose attached pains outlast the good, a point about which there is likely convergence between Achebe and Senghor regarding what most of us need in order to produce good communities: a trust in sense impressions and common sense. As Achebe says, scientific study of social ways has its value, but it is often more impressionistic than useful. We get similar ideas about the requirements of a perfect community, *jumuiya* in Kiswahili, from the works of Shaaban bin Robert, the legendary Swahili poet and writer from Tanganyika. In his works, especially in *Kusadikika* and *Siku ya Watenzi Wote,* righteousness, *adili* in Kiswahili, is both the means and the end on the often arduous road to a society that is governed by respect for others and the practice of equality and justice. A righteous community is one that is made of people who reject pride and eccentricity in favor of working for the welfare of all. And the divide between these two realms is very clearly marked.[120] Shaaban was quite aware of the destructive power of human weaknesses such as narcissism and authoritarianism, yet he was equally aware, like Achebe, that we cannot change the world before us without an effective sense of self-awareness, a view that may provide reasons for moderation. In other words, how is it that these two individuals, removed from each other by geography and intellectual backgrounds, were so fully in agreement on this point?

The answer is captured in the title of Eric J. Hobsbawm's 1994 publication *The Age of Extremes,* by which he refers to the "short" twentieth century, the years 1914 to 1991. In that period, there have been great achievements, such as in science and technology (humans landed on the moon, landed a machine on Mars, made strides in biological and medical sciences, invented and developed sophisticated electronics, and attained supersonic speed in communication). and the attainment of high levels of national and individual wealth. But it was also the period of world wars, increasing poverty, hatred among groups resulting in activities aimed at exterminating or holding some groups in bondage, colonialism, the Holocaust, slavery, racism, apartheid, genocides, discrimination and violence against women, and ethnic cleansing. These extremes reveal something unsettling about the human spirit: the contradictions within it and its frequent failure to see the need for a more equitable distribution of its achievements to other sectors of humanity. The failure is not just one that makes a mockery of the discovery of a treatment for, say, malaria or a type of cancer or heart disease if such treatments cannot be made available to those most afflicted by the diseases, the failure is also an inability to see the correlations between different forms of freedom such as freedom from disease, freedom from ignorance, and freedom from harm or from the threat of war. The failure is equally seen in the disconnect between the nationalist ideologies of liberation movements and the massacres and imprisonment of fellow citizens or silence about the rampant abuses and exploitation of women and children.

What, then, in light of these features of our age, does Shaaban bin Robert mean when he writes that humans everywhere may be quite capable of producing a perfect community "in accordance with the progress of the world and the moral principles of humans"?[121] "How is it possible to establish such a community?" he asks in reflection. His response is interesting. He provides it in this brief dialogue between Sarah, a young lady acting under the pull of the virtue of dialogical reflection, and Adilia, the female embodiment of righteous counsel:

> *"Ebu, Adilia! Nambie jinsi utazamiavyo kuthibitisha ubora wa Jumuiya ya Adili na ibada yake ya umoja wa dini—huoni kuwa ni jambo gumu? . . ."*
>
> *"Sioni kuwa shida. . . .—kwa ajili ya manufaa ya maisha ya kitambo—si ajabu kukosekana umoja wa dini kama ulimwengu wataka kweli kuendesha na kutimiza wajibu wake? Nadhani lazima pawe na namna fulani ya umoja kama huo, ambao utaunga pamoja umoja wa mataifa, umoja wa dola, umoja wa rangi, na umoja wa udugu wa ulimwengu katika kifungo cha mapenzi na amani na furaha. Ulimwengu una njaa na kiu ya miaka mingi ya namna hii ya umoja, ambao hautaamru katika wakati wo wote matendo ya kuuza ahera kwa dunia. Kwa auni ya Mungu yote huwezekana."*

"Tell me, Adilia, what you think about establishing the goodness of a righteous community that is also characterized by a religious unity—don't you see this as a difficult matter? . . ."

"I don't see a problem. . . . Humanity must borrow a lesson from the past to help itself to achieve international, economic, racial, and social unity, while also making room for religious pluralism. There must be a way to attain this kind of unity that alone will bring together the unity of nations, a commonwealth of nations, unity of all races, and a universal brotherhood, all bound together by love, peace, and happiness. Humanity has for a long time starved and thirsted for this kind of unity which should at no time allow conflict and decimation in the world. With God's help, all is possible."[122]

In Shaaban's view, religious unity is not necessary for the establishment of the ideal community or society. In fact, he was weary of the possible eruption of disunity among people based on the pursuit of religious unity. So Adili, or right reason, in Shaaban's figurative language, asserts that *"watu wana uhuru wa kuchagua na kuabudu dini wapendayo, Adilia"* (Adilia, people are free to worship under a faith of their choice).[123] Hence the question: How do we establish a community of moral and sociopolitical ideals? Shaaban's way of dealing with this question reveals not just his own awareness of the hurdles and (sometimes) contradictions involved but indeed also the contradictions in his own suggested resolutions. For example, Mulokozi observes that while in *Siku ya Watenzi Wote,* "Shaaban Robert attempts to come to grips with the challenging reality of Uhuru, the prospects of building a new, just, and prosperous society against a legacy of poverty, urbanization, religious dissentions and class contradictions,"[124] he failed to develop an alternative and enforceable model or system—*namna*—by which to prevent the repetition of the social ills that he associated with capitalist exploitation and the generation of poverty. He failed to question the moral status of the very modes of production that produced the inequalities and poverty that irked him so much. Instead, he relied on tradition, which he believed to have the kind of moral principles—namely love, peace, and brotherhood among humans—that could prevent such conditions and other forms of social malaise.

Mulokozi thinks that Shaaban Robert's moral principles were derived from his Islamic faith, especially what it says about the origin of wealth and how it should be shared. Indeed, Shaaban Robert's emphasis on conscience or righteousness reflects the Islamic teaching on *zaka,* the principle of almsgiving required of a good (practicing) Muslim. Shaaban Robert's reliance on the principle as the basis of distribution of resources illustrates that he saw wealth in basically Islamic terms, meaning that he believed wealth was a gift from God to those individuals that had it. This is the opposite of seeing wealth in secular terms as a product of either group or individual efforts, often in competition over capital and therefore embroiled in the generation of injustices at its very base, in the very modes of its generation. Consequently, because wealth is considered a symbol of divine blessing, it is required of a good and wealthy Muslim and of any Muslim according to his means to recognize his relative advantage over those who are disadvantaged by sharing with them his "God-given" materials. The one significant addition that Shaaban Robert made to this important act as required by Islamic worship is that he generalized it in universalistic terms beyond the Muslim brotherhood as defined by traditional Islamic teachings. Indeed, Shaaban Robert appeared to take note of this when he talked of the failures of both Christianity and Islam—"*Twafikiri kwamba hapo ndipo Kanisa na Msikiti viliposhindwa. Huwapeleka watu katika msalaba na jihadi vikawaacha huko*" (We feel that that's where the Church and Islam went wrong. They lead people to the cross and to the *jihadi* only to abandon them there).[125] In his view, love is not a virtue that is specific to Muslims. Rather, it is a characteristic of all humans in general.[126] After all, oppression of women, the chief complaint confronting today's (Swahili) society, had its genesis in inequality sanctioned by religious representations.

Shaaban Robert's observations that affliction of women—their physical abuse and economic exploitation—had its roots in religious and capitalist systems were indeed surprisingly astute and sophisticated for his time. And his presentations of critical views of religion and colonial economics were even more spectacular. What was not so spectacular was his assumption that in the days of old[127]—presumably in the non-Islamized and precolonial African societies—men were conscientious and respectful toward women, a point that, albeit only implicitly, appears to see traditional society as built on the communitarian principles for which he often sounded nostalgic. In the new times, such men had become few and far between, thus warranting Shaaban bin Robert's evocation of the principles of love, peace, and social cohesion (*undugu*) to replace contemporary culture, which he found to be replete with different types of oppression, especially gender oppression. For reasons different from those of Achebe, Shaaban Robert raises a curious question: How do our old models compare to new ones? Can we identify and apply (any of) them to the solution of today's problems? Although only broadly similar to the problem that brought Hountondji into debate regarding the nature of consciousness—namely whether there are any ways of knowing that are peculiarly our own—the issues Achebe and Shaaban Robert exemplified in their respective works of fiction often seem less controversial because their subject matter—reflections on life, on meaning, and on morality—are accepted as more obviously dependent on sociohistorical and cultural variables than, say, the metaphysical makeup of people and objects are, because we tend to regard the latter as fairly universal (or at least we postulate that they are so). In a way, then, reflection on the form and historical endurance of indigenous knowledge systems affects all fields of experience and different fields and subfields of analysis of experience. The resulting cross-disciplinary approaches of such analyses have made recent work in the philosophy of culture especially interesting, and philosophical studies in African modes of thought have contributed significantly to that work. More broadly, they have shown that the metaphysical question "What is a human being?" does not illustrate the poverty of philosophy. Rather, it should be the basis for tracing the missteps of the past in order to redirect a new and hopefully better human condition today and tomorrow, so long as we don't think disjunctively about metaphysical and moral issues. Doesn't Shaaban Robert himself say that no good comes without discussion (*mazungumzo*)?[128] Without ponderance, he says, we cannot hope to reduce the maddening rift between the haves and have-nots, not just between individuals in society but also among the nations of the world.

Shaaban Robert's exaltation of deliberation needs to be understood in context. Although he built it around the idea of justice guided by the notion of fair distribution, it goes beyond seeking the principles for making claims to material possessions (which he viewed as nonetheless necessary for leading a life devoid of destitution and shame). In addition, a world of righteousness (*jumuiya ya adili*) ought to be one that is devoid of conflict and discrimination of any kind, especially gender-based discrimination as described in *Siku Ya Watenzi Wote*. Inevitably, then, pondering what is a human being ought to include pondering what it takes to be such, and in this, human well-being should be seen as comprised of far more than just transforming the material world. The road to a comprehensive human progress must be lit by an unbending faith in human reason (*akili chuma*) and its capacity to guide us through the self-destructive temptations that are often engendered by narrow-mindedness or by overemphasis on just one or a few aspects of human experience.

CHAPTER THREE

Revaluation of Values and the Demand for Liberties

The world is changing rapidly, and we cannot be left behind. So the question is not whether we in Africa can or will change, but whether we can change fast enough to catch up.

—Kofi Annan, former UN Secretary General

Achebe and Shaaban Robert both exhibit an acute awareness of the ravages of change and of the effects of new institutions on old institutions and values, even though the former is a realist and the latter an idealist. While Achebe announces the tragedies associated with the arrival of the new orders, Shaaban Robert, reflecting historically on the successive sultanic Omani, German, and British colonial empires, recounts and compares their outcomes. Both Achebe and Shaaban Robert unintentionally share a focus on the common humanity of mankind. Like Achebe's *Things Fall Apart* and Shaaban Robert's *Siku ya Watenzi Wote,* the "Epilogue" in Appiah's *In My Father's House* is both a beautiful narrative of a cultural event—the intricate negotiations of practice that accompany the arrangements of the funeral of a prominent member of the matrilineal Ashanti society[1]—and a philosophical statement: a consideration of the changed, and continually changing, terrain of traditional moral wisdom, insofar as it examines liberal values against the backdrop of a system whose propositions of value are embedded in the power of a communal system whose members see it as their fundamental duty to protect its defining customary traditions. As a tale of a cultural event, the story of the "Epilogue" was a phenomenon to be reckoned with and a source of profound concern; for in it there is a strong sense of worry about the consequences for human life and for culture if the realities of change brought about by various historical circumstances are not recognized. As a philosophical development, on the other hand, the event was Appiah's point of departure, from which he calls for a radical reconsideration of the continued impact of tradition upon everything—from life and the world and human existence and knowledge to value and morality. It is an examination of the balance between the roles of public stewardship—in this case the guardianship of a cultural institution—and private virtues, for example being concerned about the rights and liberties of others. Deemphasizing corporate interests, redirecting the focus toward the individual as the pinnacle of values, and reemphasizing universal principles of judgment thus came to be some of Appiah's main tasks in the "Epilogue."

Without evoking the controversy that the term "modern" (and its ideological extensions, "modernism" or "modernity") brings, it is still obvious that at least one of Appiah's concerns is to raise awareness of the transformed consciousness of the world and the self that comes from living "now" rather than "then," poignantly evoking the idea of a "mode" or fashion of viewing and of doing things that is important and inescapable to the person who would live in the present. In this respect, the "Epilogue" is quite a robust and, in a way, also a Hegelian analysis of the condition of the modern man: the character who reflects upon whether he and history are in harmony. In Hegel's own project, the subject was modernity, and in Appiah's, it is a moment characterized in historical consciousness by two forms of "post," postmodernity and postcolonialism—one of which questions the period Hegel stood for, the other of which interrogates one of its specific outcomes. Although the comparison here is one of similarity rather than of replication, both Hegel's and Appiah's analysis contrasts the positive and negative aspects of the respective moments as experienced by the subject. And in either case, there is a demand, although it is always so subtle (at least in the second case), for change not only in the rhetoric but also in the substance of the institutions of the time, namely in political and moral thinking. In other words, every person exists in conscious relation to history. If he or she acts only according to custom and tradition it is in a certain measure from a sense of irony because historical self-consciousness requires him or her to constantly compare the self with his or her history, an idea that contemporizes and makes current the now-famous Socratic saying that *the unexamined life is not worth living*. The contrast between conservatism and (r)evolution is stark, just as the contrast between social realism and idealism is, making conservatism and liberalism the leading philosophico-political concepts driving the moral, political, and social debates of our time.

The adage that "the unexamined life is not worth living" may have originated in classical Greece, but reports on the recent and present practices of Africans have shown that this saying of ancient wisdom holds the key to an exit from traditions and customs of unwarranted misery and suffering for many who are trapped in political and cultural persecutions. Every age in human history is measured by how far it pushes the boundaries of awareness about the world beyond the limits of the preceding age. Thus the twenty-first-century African person is either far more global or only more intensely so than most of her nineteenth- and twentieth-century predecessors. Because of her wider horizons, differences in how she views herself as a subject in that world have come rushing in. Shaaban Robert was right about the correlation between the progress of the world and growth in humans of their moral awareness. In similar terms, by tuning the orders of historical change to those of knowledge, the "Epilogue" to *In My Father's House* ushers in a powerful proposition for a liberal political philosophy: commitment to some rights of the individual. Exposing the traditional system's reluctance to take seriously, recognize, and respect some basic rights and freedoms of the individual—such as the right to be free of the unnecessary physical and social pain that afflicts individuals all their lives or robs them of a life altogether or the freedom of speech and the right to their own opinions—is a strategy for demanding that traditions and customs loosen their unwarranted grip.

Throughout the "Epilogue," the liberal premise that the individual person is what matters for the purposes of social and political evaluation is clearly proposed and defended. This does not mean that there is no warrant for reasonable collective values such as national freedom, freedom of association, and membership in various groups and organizations such as religious or ethnic communities. Nor does it imply that people should not care about each other. Respect for the freedom of others is a crucial principle of the recognition of others' needs so long as they are rationally and legally defendable. In fact, much of the previous portion of *In My Father's House* is dedicated to either the defense of African cultures or attacks on colonialism. But such collective values are still only derivative, although they are not secondary. Still, ultimate value has to do with how things turn out for ordinary individuals, men and women, with respect to their pains, pleasures, preferences and aspirations, their survival, development, and flourishing. Also, because moral thinking takes place at the level of individual minds and wills, individual minds and wills must also be the fundamental objects of moral concern. Thus, when Appiah writes in the "Epilogue" that "the widow and children of a dead man are part of the furniture of an Asante funeral . . . and they do not control it"[2] or that his father had instructed in the codicil of his will that the Church and his "beloved wife, Peggy"—the co-head of his family in his newly acquired order of things—rather than the *abusua,* the matriclan, carry out all his funeral rites, the writing fits well with the objective of setting these liberal values—that individual minds and wills must not only be the fundamental objects of moral concern but also must be the only basis of what is right and good—against the background of the communal or communitarian standard modeled by the *abusua,* whose ethical features require that children be controlled by the corporate group, which they are obligated to obey.

Liberalism lacks a uniform definition, understanding, or application that unifies all its adherents. Yet at least in some form it has always been the visible ally of the trust in reason, although it did not arise as a political force until the twentieth century, especially in the post–World War II period, as a movement around which most opponents of various forms of oppression found a common ground. Because a variety of oppressive practices, beliefs, and organizations exist whose oppressive elements were not always clear to everyone, there have been different shades and types of the opponents of oppression throughout the world. For example, although many right-thinking African leaders and intellectuals may have been vigorously opposed to colonialism, not all of them agreed on the best political model for the newly independent African states and their subjects. Even less clear to many was whether opposition to colonialism was part of a general moral principle against all forms of oppression or just a selective slogan of an ad hoc political convenience. With time, it has become evident that the implication of the anticolonial argument—that political freedom is a necessary condition of a society's collective right to self-determination—has not become obvious to many as having implications for the freedoms and rights of individuals and groups in a politically liberated (postcolonial) state. Instead, the former "liberators" and "protectors" of the masses from the ideological and socioeconomic apparatuses of the colonial systems have become the new class of persecutors and thieves of the public wealth from their own fellow citizens. At the cultural level, village elders continue to subject individuals and groups such as women and children to atrocious acts of violence and human denigration in the name of the practice of tradition. Why can't our hard-won political freedom mean (and be seen to mean) freedom for the still-persecuted women and children of Africa? When one talks of freedom (as we spoke of freedom against colonial control), he or she imagines a new condition in which persons, not phantoms, would regain and enjoy the capacity to attain some goals that were not possible under colonialism. To say the least, while liberation from colonialism offered a well-understood promise, it also hid some of the most nagging challenges: how to apply the much-valued freedom to other, especially traditional, sectors of life.

The storyline in Appiah's narrative reminds all and sundry that the euphoria that came—for right reasons, of course—with the idea of liberation from colonialism drove many people to forget that our own leaders and traditions could be oppressive and a hindrance to the personal and collective growth of the very people who were being delivered. Africa's problems in having and defending practices whose consequences are contrary to anticolonial aspirations are not limited to the conservatism of state authorities, because the authority of custom, for a long time ignored or unnoticed as a source of individual rights violations, can be just as tyrannical and limiting to the ideals of a good life as the oppressive systems that have dotted the African political scene since independence from colonialism have been.[3]

The problem with doing things merely because "tradition says so" is that such reasoning often fails to produce universal principles as a justification for moral action. Instead, it works by means of citing individual cases, especially those involving kinship relations between individuals and groups, as the grounds for treating some people preferentially and others unfavorably. In other words, family ties, rather than the Kantian-like universal maxims, are considered the grounds for the moral value of actions. The dictates of custom or tradition rather than the inner language of conscience and reason direct judgment about what is good or bad and what is right or wrong. Such a method of conducting moral judgments is likely to see each of the cases it considers as having nontransferable principles that are different from all others instead of as derivatives or bearers of general principles. It promotes moral relativism.

Several crucial decisions were made to determine what was being done at the funeral of Mzee Joe Appiah, in almost total disregard of the opinions of his widow and his children. This is frequently indicated in the story as an abuse of the fundamental individual rights (at least to their own minds) of the Appiah family members. The elder Appiah himself, as the philosopher-son tells us, left an unequivocal statement about how he felt about Asante funeral rites: public exhibition of dead bodies was unnecessary and distressing and the trappings of the whole affair were abominable.[4] He asked in his will "that these abominable trappings be avoided at my passing away."[5] What would make the opinions of an educated man and practicing lawyer of international renown subservient to ancestral customs, even after he repudiated them and left a legally binding documentation of his personal views on the matter?[6] Well, the answer is pretty clear from the story: in preliterate societies, to which many members of the *abusua* chronicled in Appiah's story belongs, current social arrangements tend to owe their validity and justification to history—that is, to the generations in the distant past that are assumed to underwrite them and to which the living descendants believe themselves to be obligated. By contrast, the contemporary African lives in circumstances that are built on ideas whose discharge is not premised on the ethical exigencies of kinship and community. Rather, the new codes are based on the rights and needs of the individual as the agent of his or her actions and as the owner of the consequences of his or her labor. The contemporary individual makes contracts that take into consideration only his or her qualities and abilities in total disengagement from the exigencies of the group to which he or she may belong or claim to belong. For example, no employee can base his or her salary negotiations with an employer on the fact that what is offered will be unacceptable to the community. Thus, when the community imposes its old views and principles of ethical judgment on the contemporary individual, demanding that he or she surrender the values of their own times and subserviently replace them with the old, either a practical crisis will occur or the contemporary laborer might be driven to seek morally questionable solutions to the conflict between the demands of the old communal ways and those of his or her new life.

Take the example of a young person who has recently obtained employment in a nearby town. That person now faces demands from the family that he or she do what is expected: help buy school uniforms for several school-age relatives who cannot afford such necessary things. On the other hand, his or her position, which happens to be assistant manager at the school uniform depot, requires that he or she dress professionally and live in a nearby pricey apartment complex. Which of these sets of demands should he or she consider as having priority over the other in terms of what he or she thinks about the meaning and nature of obligation? One mindset would indicate that only the things that will improve his or her quality of life are morally relevant and that he or she should reject the obligation to buy school uniforms for relatives. This value set might suggest that he or she can demonstrate kindness in considering the needs of others, which is the key issue, but that the needs of others do not entail a moral obligation. But perhaps the newly employed person does not share this mindset and instead defines moral obligation in a way that includes family obligations. If that is the case, he or she has a real problem. How can he or she find a solution that responds to both sets of demands satisfactorily? Failure to separate the old, communal way of doing this from the new, individualistic way is frequently cited as the cause of the corrupt practices of many Africans in the workplace or of unnecessary selflessness and the resultant stagnation in the standard of living among many working Africans. Doing what is right from a universal Kantian perspective and doing what is right in conformity with custom appear to be in constant conflict, because the individualism of liberal morality excludes social and collective entities from the realm of ultimate goods.

Put in such oppositional terms, the so-called traditional communalist framework appears to be indelibly distinct from the more recent liberal one, and Appiah eloquently draws attention to these transitional times in Africa's cultural history and theory. Of course, the relation between communalist values and liberal ones is not one of linear historical transition from the former to the latter, a transition prescribed by mutual exclusion. Rather, that relation could also be characterized by exaggeration, the view that wrongly imposes such mutual exclusion between the two when there need not be any such thing. To put it in rhetorical form, the issue is whether communalism has no regard for at least some individual rights and whether, inversely, liberalism is the denial that we can be obligated to some values because they promote community regardless of what they do to us as individuals. Perhaps we don't have to look far beyond our neighborhoods to see the urgent call for a more liberal appreciation of the principles of individual freedom and the right to choose our individual paths in life: the freedom and right to attend school, to choose whether or not to participate in the often painful rituals that leave our children physically and sometimes also emotionally scarred, to enter into marital relations of our choosing and at the times we freely feel are right for us. Liberalism is crucial not just at the political level where it enables us, as members of civil society, to be active participants in the governance of our nations and more broadly to exercise our democratic rights by expressing our opinions and choices in all matters of public interest. It is also needed, equally strongly and perhaps more urgently, in the domain of everyday life to guide us in the practice of those matters that define us as humans. It is urgent at this level because millions of Africa's children are coerced into rituals that disfigure and rob them of adult lives free of pain. One is reminded of the scores of children who, in the name of custom, are not only forced into prearranged child marriages to strangers they have never met but are often also forced into polygamous marriages that perhaps they would not have chosen with their own, free, and well-informed reason.[7] Sometimes it is argued that such individuals *consent* to the cultural practices of their families and communities, yet the reality is that agreeing to a practice on the basis of custom or communal norm—this is the way it is done—is usually quite distinct from *wanting* or *desiring*, of one's own accord, to do the same things the same way. The subtleties of custom—especially when the reason for agreeing to customary ways is given as "not wanting to offend family" or "fear of being ostracized" or "no one will want me for a spouse if I don't"— often succeed in camouflaging the degrees of both coercion and dissent in individual-community relations.

Authorities in customary laws and regulations justify them (and direct their subjects to consent to them) by either citing the superiority of the interests of the community over private interests—for example by stressing the possible disintegration of order and the onset of chaos upon deviation from the common norm—or by threatening them with sanctions if they do not conform. Either way, individuals are made to *consent*—read as "give in"—to practices that privately they would likely not have *wanted* to participate in.[8] Thus, consent to play by the prevailing rules of a group usually camouflages a vicious system of coercion that denies participating individuals the chance to exercise their capacity to make fair and reasoned deliberations and choices. Finally, customary teachings and practices are often based on values that transparently promote various forms of inequity or outright oppression, such as those based on gender or age. Rituals, like the ones called rites of passage, are a good example. In the elaborate moral teachings that accompany the preparations for and the actual performance of rituals of passage, boys are usually taught the virtues of social dominance and control; they are taught that men worthy of the important role of community custodian must be capable of withstanding the tests of ritual passage. Thus, for them, the hurdle is the rite as well as their own ability to withstand its emotional and physical afflictions. The ideal is their own high self-image as a person who will be admired and looked up to by others.

Females are reminded that a good woman is the one who learns to be a good wife and mother; her duty is to take care of her husband, her children, and her husband's kin. Her test and standard is her acceptability to those she is expected to serve. "No husband will accept a woman who is lazy for a wife," or "no husband will marry a woman who is not circumcised," or "you will be chased away by a husband if you cannot cook well for him and his kin" are all very familiar elders' warnings to young women. Proverbs and poems about womanhood are full of references to this service role of the woman: she is the giver of life, the symbol of continuity; her fertility nourishes the earth and gives it history because with each pregnancy she produces the future as much as she articulates the past. But she plays these roles as if she was under contract to give service to someone else, as if she herself was not part of the history she helps create. Thus, she is great in childbearing but derided and humiliated when barren. An apt description of this subservient image of the woman is given by V. Y. Mudimbe in *Parables and Fables*, which he follows with a long and useful quote (from Théodore Theuws) of a Luba master charter given to a new bride. According to Mudimbe, "She might be fourteen or fifteen years old, but with the consent of the two families, she will become automatically an adult and fully responsible for a husband, his home, his tradition, and, the families hope, his children. Nobody invites her to become a subject of a possible history in the making. On the contrary, she has to promote the respectability of her original family by practicing an ordinary life which fits into a discourse of obedience. A master charter is given to her as a bride; it specifies and individualizes her major duties toward her spouse and his family and in so doing maintains the configuration of a patrilineal tradition."[9] The master charter goes like this:

Today is your last day in your father's home, henceforth you will stay in your own.

Now you are an adult, you will have a home of your own; you will meet with all kinds of people.

You will make us known as respectable people to your husband and his people, if you follow the advice we give today.

But you will also cause us to be insulted by your husband and his people if you don't pay heed to what we tell you.

What are we going to tell you? It is this.

There is the work for your husband; there is the work for his brothers; there is the work for your parents-in-law; there is the work for your husband's friends.

And in connection with the work for all these people, some will come together with your husband and some will not.

The fact that your husband came to fetch you means that he left his mother's house, having his own from now on.

In this house he has a right to give what orders he likes; he tells you all he wants, and that is exactly what you must do.

It is becoming for you to serve his brothers in the same way as you serve himself, and to serve his friends as well, whether he is at home or not.

But all this must be done according to his wishes, as he says: that is the way I want it. All these things will show, if you do them properly, that this girl of ours received sound advice from her parents.

Thus, even if your husband treats you badly and you go on doing what he wants you to do, the people of the village will speak for you.

Your husband is like your child. It does not befit you to roast a piece of cassava and eat it all by yourself while your husband looks on.

Whatever you eat you have to share with him; it is not becoming to eat alone by yourself.

It is your duty to know the proper times to prepare his meals.

If there are visitors your husband ought not to have to remind you saying: these visitors, are they going to eat something?

To serve your husband does not mean just to feed him.

In the past your fathers dressed in animal skins. Nowadays your husbands follow European ways and dress in clothes.

A man likes to dress neatly so he may show himself among his fellow men.

He wants the house where he receives his friends properly swept, and the bed where he sleeps well shaken and made.

When your husband says to you: how is it that this thing is in such a state, it is improper for you to answer: haven't you got hands yourself to fix it?

You will run the risk of causing your parents to be reviled, because some husbands are correct; some others, however, are not.

And at the end you will come and tell us: that husband of mine called you names.

But you ought to know that your husband does not start calling us names without reason, and if you do your work properly he will not. If your husband calls us names it is you who made him do so, because you don't work as he wants you to.

It is not befitting for you to come and tell us the disputes you have with your husband.

Now that you are married don't tell your husband: tomorrow your father will come to return the bridewealth. You get married to stay with your husband.

If God grants you his blessing you will bear children and you will raise them as we raised you.

Obedience to your husband is peace and joy in married life; to satisfy his wishes, to do the work your husband wants to be done and to do what he tells you to do is the way to bring joy in your home.

It is not befitting you as a woman belonging to other people, to return every word your husband speaks or to raise your voice continuously against your husband's as if you were a man yourself.

It befits you, woman, when talking to your husband, to speak in a restrained voice. Never say anything which could put him to shame in public.

If you have a word with your husband, even if he puts you in the wrong in public, it becomes you to restrain your tongue from speaking your mind.

Back home, between yourselves, you may ask him questions.

If you have words with your husband it becomes you to talk to his grandparents. If he has none, speak to one of his other relatives.

It is wrong to tell other people the words you have had with your husband, because this is to slander him. Don't you dare!

Your first duties are towards your father-in-law.

After staying in your own place, your own home, for a few days, you will prepare an early meal for your father-in-law.

But this first cassava-porridge you will prepare for your father-in-law, shall not be prepared with greens; this porridge must always be prepared with meat or fish.

While cooking this food for your father-in-law, you must know about his ways: whether he takes his meals in his own fenced-off kitchen or eats in some other place.

If he eats in his own kitchen, you will have to do exactly as your mother-in-law does when she cooks there.

Be it a particular way of dressing during that work, or a special way of calling him when the meat is ready.

When you bring the food, it is proper also to bring some drinking water and a bit of salt, so that he may add some if the food is not to his liking.

When calling your father-in-law, always approach him from the right, kneel down saying: father, I call you. Keep on your knees until he looks at you and says: yes, my child, thank you, or: yes, I am coming.

Then go ahead to the kitchen to wait for him until you see him arriving, then leave.

Don't go too far, by no means. Remain near enough to see him retire.

When he leaves the kitchen, return there to clear away the pots.

Then, after a few days, cook another meal for him exactly as you did the first time.

Thus, if one day your mother-in-law is away, you will be able to cook for your father-in-law, because you will have done it before.

These are your duties toward your mother-in-law.

You daughter of man, it is not befitting for you to sit down with outstretched legs while your mother-in-law tires herself pounding flour.

You daughter, as long as you stay in the house of your mother-in-law, do things in such a way that she always finds the house swept, the jar full of water, the meat cut, and the water for the porridge boiling on the fire, so you can prepare a meal for her as soon as she comes home.

These are your duties toward your husband's other relatives.

A good wife does not wait when her husband's brothers are hungry saying: I will cook food for them only when my husband is here.

Except when your husband himself told you so saying: I don't want my brothers or cousins coming near the house when I am not here.

When strangers call at your house, it is not right for you to wait until your husband reminds you, saying: did I see you preparing food for these people?

You ought to know that, even if they have already eaten before leaving, the food they took was not yours; and you must cook your own food for them so that they may eat it.[10]

According to this charter, the making of a functional family is all about the duties of the woman. Not only does this "Manifesto" lack mention of happiness and how these roles will bring it about, it also does not mention what is owed to the woman or what her rights will be in return for the services she must give to her new, male-dominated family. Even worse, no mention is made of what she must expect or demand of her husband-to-be as his duties to complement her own in the making of the family. Instead, it is her servitude in the form of total obedience toward the world of men that is the prized cause of peace. And should we add that such servitude creates harmony too? Some scholars—anthropologists, to be exact—have argued that despite the strong presence of imbalance of power and influence between the sexes and other demographic categories of traditional communities, mechanisms exist by which even the apparently dominated groups assert their power and authority. They argue that the exercise of power and influence often is the outcome of subtle negotiations. In their view or observation, "what works" is never uniform or standard, as suggested by Pierre Bourdieu's idea of a logic of practice.

Now compare the Luba-Songye "Manifesto" to this one, from far away in Luo Nyanza. It is addressed to a young man who has recently taken in a bride, and it goes like this:

My son, you have taken in someone's daughter to be your wife, whereby you have become a husband. You must therefore know of those matters that make a good husband, lest you become a laughingstock to your age-mates, and to your family.

A grown-up man works hard, both in the farm, and in tending his family's cattle if they have any.

In the farm a man does those things that a man must do so his wife may easily do hers. He clears and burns the bushes, and he may join his wife in tilling the land.

No man should be known for laziness, so do not till the land beside your wife unless you are strong, lest she spread the word in the village and among her folk.

Men congregate and spend time alone away from womenfolk, so you will not spend time needlessly in the company of your wife, lest your age-mates make a laughingstock of you.

You will not at any time do kitchen work. If your wife needs help with kitchen work she will get it from your female siblings, and from your mother before she earns her autonomy. You will therefore not fetch firewood other than split big tree trunks into planks to make work easier for your wife, your mother, or others in the family that may need that help when you are present. You will not fetch water for your wife except as conditions and circumstances will define to be necessary.

You will at no time sweep the house, but a man of respect will demand that his wife keeps the house well swept and orderly.

A man of respect eats his meals with other male members of the family, and if his wife is not given to kindness, he teaches her by these deeds. You must aspire to be such a man.

Also, a man must earn respect from his wife. You must neither quarrel nor rebuke your wife in public, nor do those things that will provoke her to insult and shame you in public. But if she is not given to respect, then you must be a man by disciplining your wife appropriately.

When you have disputes with your wife, you must bring the matter before the elders, beginning with your own parents. Do not rush to your in-laws to settle disputes without first putting the matter to, and seeking the opinion of the elders of your own village. A strong man is he who enjoys the support and pride his own people have for him. And he too must always act to justify that support and pride by projecting his best image to the rest of the world. That pride and respect will be extended to your wife, and then she will take her pride in you to her own people.[11]

The African woman is cast in both charters as the equivalent of Antigone in Greek legend. She has no rights; her place in society is defined by her duties only, her duty to obey and to do according to the pleasures of her male counterparts in society—her father, brothers, husband, father-in-law, and all the male members of any and every group she will live in. How long must it be before the African woman can become Antigone in using right judgment to oppose unjust laws—as Antigone does in defiance of her uncle, Creon, the representative of male-dictated norms—so she can do as her feelings of true love for and connection with others require?

Writing about the Kaguru of mainland Tanzania who, like the Ashanti, are matrilineal, Tom Beidelman tells us that the complex interplay between authority, power, and affection in marital relations reflects different and ultimately unresolvable aims and strengths of men and women.[12] Thus, for example, as Gabriel Omolo, a musician-cum-social commentator from Ugenya in Western Kenya, has observed in a dirge, there always is that time when even the chauvinist wife-beater, the proverbial Mr. Agoya, is reduced to a beggar by his wife, who carefully picks his weakest and most appropriate moments to gain power and control over him. At the end of a day's beer-drinking spree, the abusive husband finally comes home, drunk and hungry, and tries to do what he always does in sobriety: display extreme arrogance, disrespect, and abusiveness to his wife. But the woman, aware that he is drunk and hungry, seizes the moment to force him to beg and show affection before she will give him dinner. But despite the affectionate superlatives and promises to abandon aggression, she denies him dinner all the same. According to Omolo, in his relationship with his wife, Mr. Agoya adopts an attitude and behavior that he believes is sanctioned by the culture whose norms regulate his conjugal life. He doesn't mean to be violent; rather it is the cultural norm which states that a man can go out to drink with his buddies and that his wife has the duty to lay his dinner before him whenever he returns home. According to Mr. Agoya's cultural maxim, it is a woman's duty to cook and serve meals to her man. Also, his culture does not require him to be polite to his wife as it requires her to be obedient to him and his kin, especially the male ones. So it is usual to hear a man hurl insults at his wife but not the other way around. Yet, according to Omolo, a woman can design cunning ways to tone down her man's arrogance, and she is not barred from doing so. So Mrs. Agoya, while not ready to confront her husband with matching violence, "politely" lets him know that she is not ready to be disturbed out of her sleep to honor his arrogance. "You can eat your arrogance," she tells him, which teaches Mr. Agoya that the actual implementation, or the real practice, of the allowances of culture will depend on how each case is negotiated. Although it is expected that men in Mr. Agoya's culture should be dominating in their relationships with their spouses and that a good wife is the one who is unquestioningly obedient to her husband, women who stand up to men's arrogance are also well known and are silently praised and admired. According to Beidelman, "This is not to say that the system is unworkable, but rather that it is propelled along by these countervailing motives. . . . Clever women find ample means to guarantee that their own interests and needs must be considered if their loyalty and affection are to be counted on by such men."[13] And men know it. Thus, whether a man or woman is in a monogamous or polygamous arrangement, such negotiations are a constant dialectic of everyday life. Yet for women to behave in ways not quite expected of them "implies either that they have no confidence in their men or that their men are hen-pecked." Beidelman notes that "Kaguru women and men commented on the weakness of men who allowed their wives to dominate them verbally in public."[14] As an artist and social commentator, Omolo not only celebrates the bravura of Mrs. Agoya, he is equally mocking Mr. Agoya's weakness and unmanliness. Men frequently silence their rival buddies at drinking venues by referring to or (as is probably more frequent) inventing stories about their wives beating them or chasing them out of their homes because they bought beer for friends and came home penniless. It is a form of going one point up above others in *pakruok,* self-praise games. The dirge may not reflect any factual occurrence, but it does offer an awareness of the countervailing motives that drive daily social relations and discourse.

Corinne A. Kratz, an anthropologist working among the Ogiek in southwestern Kenya, makes observations similar to those of Beidelman about the Kaguru, namely, that schemes and regulations are not autonomous processes that regulate themselves in the minds of the people who know and utilize them.[15] Rather, even when actors apply the very generative schemes of perception, action, and appreciation that are learned and reinforced by actions and discourses produced according to the same schemes, there is still room (as is observed in negotiations about how to apply the schemes to specific cases) for a sort of drama in which individuals use personal persuasive and rhetorical skills to improvise arguments to achieve or to counter specific aims or goals. Thus, although the performance takes place within the wider cultural scheme that occasions it in the first place, its real effects or outcomes are the result of the rhetorical manipulations of the individual(s) who perform in the interests of and on behalf of others.

But the liberalist's concern is with the bigger moral issues, those that brought Agoya's wife to her courageous act in the first place. She is courageous largely because Agoya's actions are considered tolerable and expected of a man while hers are out of the ordinary. She only tries to ensure that a bad situation will be the least humiliating and hurtful one. She is considered courageous only because her man is weak, and men strive to be seen as strong and "manly" and they expect unquestioning service from their women, for these gender inequities, according to tradition, are the norms. Thus, Omolo's apparent praise for Mrs. Agoya is in fact a disguised criticism of the man for not being what was expected of him. The challenge, then, is that the attitudes and practices that recognize the agency of individuals, as both Beidelman and Kratz described in their scholarly works or Omolo narrated in his popular cultural performance, are replicated in larger social issues, those about which either hardly any dialogue is allowed or for which there is hardly any time, such as determining who defines the sequence of ceremonial events, who performs what role in ceremonies, and whose word counts in determining the order of such things. For example, although the spokesman at a dowry negotiation brings many personal qualities to the dynamic and rhetoric of the performance of forging new relations, other equally important issues are excluded; perhaps the bride-to-be has had no input in the choice of the groom-to-be or in the fact that she is getting married, either at all or at that particular time and to that particular person. And, as an additional and purely conjectural possibility of freedom, no one bothers to find out what her sexual orientation is or might be. She is expected by the requirements of the cultural tradition only to "consent" to decisions made for her by others, her kin. Yet from a liberalist's view, the interests of these others, namely the kin who do the negotiations, are usually far removed from and should be inconsequential to or at best only marginal to those of the individual whose life the decisions will directly affect. What if my kin should identify for me a person that I regard as ominously ugly or whose character I couldn't stand for half a day? The assumption that tradition has its own criteria for what qualifies as moral right and wrong outside the jurisdiction of basic human rights is one that is likely to make it possible for those who are privileged by a traditional power system to think of and to treat those who are dispossessed of such powers in the same way they treat their cattle and other possessions.

Ngũgĩ wa Thiong'o and Ngũgĩ wa Mĩriĩ have an answer in their play, *I Will Marry When I Want* (*Ngaahika Ndeenda*). When she is rebuking her mother for trying to burden her with traditional expectations for a girl, Gathoni says: "I shall marry when I want. Nobody will force me into it."[16] Similarly, Gabriel Omolo, this time in a different dirge, "Wach Nyombo" (Marriage Issues; 1974), tells of one Apili who, when pressed by his family to find a bride, reminds them that a careful consideration of the economic burdens and social responsibilities associated with marriage require that it be a matter of deep personal conviction and choice.[17] According to Omolo, it is easy for family members to suggest that their son or daughter get married according to customary expectation, but they will not provide assistance with the burdens and responsibilities that go with marriage and raising a family; in those matters, each man or woman faces his or her own burdens. Hence the decision and choice to marry should be entirely one's own as well. It is important that in both of these hypothetical cases, the texts lay down the material independence of the protesters as ground for claiming their right to exercise their respective freedoms, the freedoms to choose.[18] The fears of Omolo's Apili are borne out by Gathoni's discovery that social freedoms are intertwined with economic status.

In the view of the Ngũgĩs, however, the evils of oppression belong overwhelmingly to the new capitalist economy. Thus, despite several suggestions that indigenous cultures can be equally oppressive by not allowing women the liberty to choose if and when to get married—such as Wangeci's several reminders to Gathoni that according to traditional customs women must get married, for "there's no maiden who makes a home in her father's backyard. And there's no maiden worth the name who wants to get grey hairs at her parents' home"—the authors ignore such leads in favor of what they believe to be, and want to emphasize as, the "real" problem for local people, namely the oppressive colonial and neocolonial political economy of the state. Thus, throughout the play, women's views are portrayed as limited in scope or as too local and short-sighted for the grander visions of men, whether they are traitorous visions such as those of Kīoi and his friends Ndugīre and Ikuua or patriotic ones such as those of Kīgūūnda and Gīcaamba. Women live in the shadows of men, where their short-sighted ideas cause them further calamity. This is hardly a call to women to rise up to liberation. Rather, the women's failure to address their fate as a trapped social category becomes part of the widespread practice of avoiding addressing the inequities of indigenous social structures or of sweeping them under the rug of the assumedly grander, masculine-controlled competitions among the players of modern political economy.

African philosophers have pitched the question of individual liberties in African discourse to a new high level. As the examples of Hountondji and Appiah demonstrate, African philosophers and scholars working from other fields have argued strongly that mere conformity to institutional values and rules may lead to (or indeed camouflage) existing suppressions of individual liberties in ways that are not limited to political totalitarianism. The very idea of consent, whether it is found in the political definitions of obligation and fairness or in deference to the authority of custom and tradition, is severely questioned as susceptible to use for sanctioning the tyrannical oppression of individuals by others engaged in cooperative activities—because cooperative ventures always involve unwarranted rule-governed restrictions of the liberties of those who agree to participate in the pursuit of the objectives of the cooperative. Thus, as we are likely to hear from conservative religious thinkers, one cannot be a Christian and be pro-choice or support instrumental prevention of disease and pregnancy.[19] At least we are told that membership in Christianity as a religious organization precludes the kind of freedoms that they condemn. Similarly, many Africans continue to believe that belonging to a cultural community requires submission to the rituals or norms by which the community defines itself and identifies its members. This view treads precariously into the contractual theory of corporate membership, which entails the view that agreeing to join corporate groups or organizations means surrendering freedoms that are precluded as a condition of such membership, a situation that tends to legitimize various forms of suppression (through a variety of retributive actions against those who fall short of their consent to play by the rules of the group) or to limit the freedoms of potential members.

Liberalism defends the liberty of every individual to make rational choices in matters that define a respectable lifestyle that recognizes just laws, including the freedom of the individual to choose whom to associate with and the freedom to demand change in the laws of the corporate body of which already they are members if the existing laws unfairly restrict the freedoms of its individual members. Thus, while liberals defend every individual's freedom to profess the religious faith of their choice, they oppose the moral authority of organized religion or of any individual on the basis of their faith to encroach on the individual liberties of others. They are especially opposed to the religious view that there is "a natural order of conduct," supposedly divinely endowed, to which all humans ought to adhere or, conversely, to the idea that some types of human conduct are bad because they displease a divine figure. The list of behaviors that would occasion such displeasure varies, but abortion and some types of sexual lifestyles are often most discussed, not only because they affect the concept of freedom most directly but also because they stand most prominently at the crossroads between reason and the arbitrariness of cultural variation.

By extension, in the eyes of liberals it becomes questionable to limit the freedoms of individuals and groups on the basis of protecting the values of the majority, usually just another term for indigenous values, whatever they were. The current trend in African philosophy appears to suggest, however, that it can no longer be assumed that indigenous sociocultural systems are free of questionable values and practices that hinder or severely limit the freedoms of individuals. According to the liberal view, we live in a world in which most adults in their right minds are individuals who are fairly rational and capable of making right choices and decisions. Thus, the protection pledged by governments and other institutions of authority is often deemed to be unnecessary unless it is used primarily to protect the rights and lawful freedoms of all, especially the rights and freedoms of those members of society who by virtue of age, status of health, or other social disadvantages have had their freedoms unquestionably violated in the process of or under the pretext of preserving customs and traditions.[20] It is not right, in the liberal view, for example, to prevent people from pursuing their choices in life if such choices do not cause harm to others in any reasonably determinable ways. Liberals often regard the claims of political and cultural leaders that they are protecting the values of others as mere strategies for suppressing the liberties of select groups in an attempt to create monolithic cultural systems. What is necessary, it can be added, is to provide the space in which individuals can enhance and utilize their epistemological capacities and abilities to examine issues in their world critically (and hopefully exhaustively and fairly). This is what Hountondji demanded: a deliberation free of the limiting voices of tradition and custom. It is what Appiah laments is lacking in the way that tradition and custom treat individuals as if they were merely part of the ceremonial furniture on important occasions.[21]

Because liberals place no limit to what can be rationally determined (or at least analyzed and debated), they tend to oppose any attempts by any authority to arbitrarily impose moral regulations on the conduct of individuals and groups. Hence, they are inclined to object to "naturalist" arguments—the claim that there is only one, assumedly "natural," way to define values—as the basis of moral conduct and judgment. It is this position that ultimately leads liberalists to demand separation between state and church in the West, so the state can arbitrate fairly, without taking sides with any particular faith-driven viewpoint, in matters that affect the violation or denial of rights and freedoms. The state's role becomes limited to the equal protection of the civil and lawful rights of the individuals under its jurisdiction. To perform this role fairly and effectively, the state ought to be neutral in its application of the law; it ought to be free especially from the influence of religion, church, or any other belief systems of specific groups. Consequently, religion and church become the domain of private individual choices and ought not to spread their influence in the public domain. Such a position does not preclude the possibility that the church and its leaders can be coincidental allies of those who support and defend liberal causes on purely rational grounds,[22] such as when they defend democratic rights and the protests of citizens against political authoritarianism or when they defend individuals and groups from the oppressive demands of tradition and custom as in cases of child marriages, female circumcision, wife inheritance, or other forms of custom that denigrate categories of people by gender and age by reducing them to instruments of gratification for those who make up dominant groups in society.

Because the defense of liberalism is likely to be perceived as peddling Western ideas and values (or because it may indeed be used to do exactly that), it is worth noting the nature and limitations of the idea of international liberalism. In recent years, the drive toward instituting reason as the sole and universal basis of moral right has led a section of liberals to view various identity claims, such as ethnic and national identities or patriotism, as a hindrance to the full enjoyment of individual liberties. Indeed, this specific school of liberalism, led by the renowned American philosopher Martha Nussbaum of the University of Chicago, argues that ideas that promote our sense of belonging to groups or collective organizations, such as patriotism, nationalism, and various other forms of limited senses of identity (such as ethnocentrism, notions or sentiments of identity by which individuals and groups, give priority to the values of their specific national or cultural group over those that connect them with other people across national and cultural boundaries) are morally irrelevant characteristics of identity that frequently become the basis for the persecution of those who are considered different.[23] Drawing from the ancient Greek classics, Nussbaum argues that attachment to localized identities is inconsistent with the idea of the *kosmou politês* (the world citizen, or cosmopolitan). She argues that "we should not allow differences of national identity or class or ethnic membership or even gender to erect barriers between us and our fellow human beings. We should recognize humanity wherever it occurs, and give its fundamental ingredients, reason and moral capacity, our first allegiance and respect."[24] According to this strain of cosmopolitanism, only the world community qualifies as the source of moral obligation. This school of thought seeks to institute universal reason as the sole relevant moral sovereign above any form of specific identity and to replace nationalism with a new cosmopolitan ethic.

Nussbaum is certainly correct about the need to make moral judgments based on the all-encompassing idea of the fundamental rights of all people rather than on the basis of the limited norms of our local groups. What we hold to be good and right for us should be good and right enough for other people as well. The concept of rights usually reflects this universal positioning, at least in our minds, as something we have historically failed to apply in practice. Thus, while we assume that "all people" is the subject of a proposition that prescribes rights that we like, our discriminative or exclusionary practical applications of such a proposition reminds us that we have a questionable metaphysical idea of people, that we probably do not regard as people those whom we discriminate against or exclude from the distribution of rights. What is questionable in Nussbaum's sense of cosmopolitanism is her idea that because what binds us all in relation to moral judgment of right and good are the fundamental rights that define us as human beings beyond any idea of *paysement* (being rooted in one's country or region) in the form of specific nation or culture, it should follow that any form of identity of self and others below the cosmos or any regard for such forms of identity (such as taking pride in being, say, Kenyan, Zambian, Azanian, or American or a MDuruma, Mkonde, or Wolof) is irrelevant and therefore should matter only in a distinctly secondary way.

Such a call is most unlikely to go down well with anyone who cares seriously about how we love and live our lives. It is likely to be offensive especially for people who have suffered the suppression of their cultures and who have had to wage wars to reclaim their cultural freedom interwoven with their political independence. One is reminded of the twin Kiswahili sayings that *"mila ndio msingi wa utu"* (culture is the foundation of being human); and *"mkosa mila ni mtumwa"* (only a slave, through deprivation, claims no culture of his or her own). These Swahili sayings are not without merit. I remember going to school with descendants of freed victims of the East African slave trade. Offloaded anywhere slave ships were ordered to discard their human cargo at the declaration of the official end of the trade, freed captives settled among strange communities where they neither adapted culturally nor were able to practice their own culture. They just "hung in there," as the American saying goes, but almost literally as far as their cultural predicament went. Freed slaves later adopted new cultures, especially those of the dominant hosting communities. This historical phenomenon not only added to the originary cultural complexity of the people widely known today as "the Swahili," it also served as the source of a great lesson for many locals about the importance of culture in cultivating humanity. Indeed, all humans express their basic human qualities primarily through the fact that they can choose and design the beliefs and practices by which they make their lives orderly, purposeful, meaningful, and fulfilling in the pursuit and attainment of basic human needs. Protecting our cultures is therefore part of the protection that we need from unfair aggression and domination.[25] In these processes—of independently designing and living just lifestyles as free nations and communities—lie the phenomenologically undeniable cultural pluralism that we all live by and that many of us claim to take pride in. The pluralism that emerges from liberalism is a litmus test for the truth or falsity of the promises of freedom, especially when it reminds us that tolerance within our respective cultures is no less urgent than tolerance among them. What the sayings do not take into account is the other side of the matter, namely the capacity of culture to enslave.

Should culture be upheld even when it hurts? And when does it become appropriate to judge that what was once regarded and practiced with pain-suppressing pride no longer warrants such a status? The saying that "time will tell" may be an elegant expression in popular culture, but those who live through moments of cultural transition certainly endure the conflicts in judgment that the appearance in their time of alternative values impose, especially as the old ways may continue to be demanded of them. No aspect of culture, however noble, is an end unto itself.

The major threat for international cosmopolitanism remains the possible fallout from its spread, namely the exportation, for yet another time, of the ethical and sociopolitical values of Europe and America across the globe. While the Greeks thought about the universe, there has never been doubt that they thought of Greece as the center of that world and often judged what their explorers and travelers (for example Herodotus) reported to them about the "character" of peoples overseas against their own character. We don't do much better when we extend visions of ourselves and of our own world when, in metaphysical fantasy spurred by scientific hypotheses, we imagine the possibility of other worlds through an extension of us and our own world. It is easy for one who speaks from a culturally dominant position to define the universe according to his or her own terms and to proclaim universal values when those values are his or her own. It is no surprise that the drive for a cosmopolitan ethic began at the same time as the drive for a globally integrated economy. The removal of significant political and economic competition with and opposition to the West appears to be quite an opportune time to further facilitate the spread of Western interests. This phenomenon is a painful reawakening to the realization that the postcolony is probably permanent, especially in the regions outside the leaping economies of India and China. Because of their immense populations, India and China are markets that Europe and America cannot ignore, thus allowing them to transform their economic significance into a political and cultural advantage that can build on their rich pasts as enclaves of true rival civilizations to the West. The lesson, like the one that opened up Athens, is that other people and cultures don't have to be like us to be good, nor do they have to be distinct from us to be bad. Rather, we will see their ways, and only their ways (because it is only their ways that are at issue), as good or bad based on whether or not they are harmlessly more proficient at achieving results similar to those we too seek or whether they introduce new desirable ends that we will judge on the basis of their capacity to improve our quality of life.

It is important to note that the strain of liberalism that Appiah ascribes to does not go the distance of Nussbaum's own, for not only does Appiah cherish cultural identity, he also believes (contrary to Nussbaum) that cosmopolitanism and patriotism are not mutually exclusive or incompatible ethical stances. His defense of cultural and national identities is strongly indicated in the beautiful wording that he attributes to his late father: he writes that like Gertrude Stein, his father "thought there was no point in [having cultural] roots if you couldn't take them with you."[26] It is thus Appiah's view that for someone to be a liberal cosmopolitan, it is sufficient for him or her to uphold the principles of universal respect for basic human rights because such principles define liberals, or liberalists, as people who value (individual) persons over collectivities, for regardless of where they live, "their rights matter as human rights and thus matter only if the rights of foreign humans matter, too."[27]

What, then, are such rights? Perhaps more by education than by instinct, people tend to believe fairly strongly that nearly everything that exists has a list of things that belong to it by the very nature of what it is if that nature is to be preserved.[28] Largely in response to recent global political and moral developments, philosophical interests, attitudes, and opinions have rekindled focus on the topic of natural rights, or basic human rights. As I mentioned earlier, there is no doubt that as Africans, we too have participated not just in affirming these rights but also in demanding them for ourselves where we perceived them to be unjustly denied. Throughout the continent, many Africans from many walks of life have argued, in their diverse yet almost always very strong ways (and rightly), that colonialism was an unjust system because it denied us what belonged to us as a basic human attribute; we framed colonialism, in all its manifestations, as an inhuman system, meaning that it was a system whose goals and objectives directly denied its victims fundamental (human) rights as individuals and as nations. Colonialism, the policies of Nazi Germany, unjust occupation of other people's lands, racism in many of its forms manifest in America and in various other parts of the world, including the now constitutionally defunct apartheid in South Africa, were all deemed to be violations of the humanity of those at whom they were directed. Such charges against political, social, legal, economic, and cultural oppression were premised on the assumption that certain entitlements belong to humans as individuals and as groups by virtue of the simple fact that they are humans, and we argued that freedom to have our own opinions and the quality of life commensurate with human dignity were among such cardinal entitlements of humans, any humans, regardless of gender, age, or state of mind. It is on the strength of the fundamental nature of these rights, and of their inalienability, that it is assumed that we all owe them to each other without any shade of discrimination. We don't have to ask for them because they are ours without asking anyone. To echo and paraphrase the late African American politician, orator, and civil rights activist Barbara Jordan, human rights are not the exclusive property of the economically and politically privileged; they apply equally to Soviet dissidents; to Chilean, African, or Asian peasants; to prisoners; to the homeless and the sick; to gay people; to handicapped people; to women; to children and the elderly; to believers and nonbelievers everywhere. People in all these socially generated categories are human. We know that their rights have been violated, either by limiting or totally denying them. That is why we need to transform institutions that engender, encourage, or merely support (actively and passively) limitations and denials of human rights. In the view of American philosopher Richard Wasserstrom,

> just because rights are those moral commodities which delineate the areas of entitlement, they have an additional important function: that of defining the respects in which one can reasonably entertain certain kinds of expectation [such that] to live in a society in which there are rights and in which rights are generally respected is to live in a society in which the social environment has been made appreciably more predictable and secure. It is to be able to count on receiving and enjoying objects of value. Rights have, therefore, an obvious psychological, as well as moral, dimension and significance.[29]

But one observes, with great dismay, the frightening degree to which human rights are institutionally flouted in our midst, by commission as much as by failure to protect them from those who violate them.

The religion factor has further helped compromise any gains for African liberalism. Besides the well-documented rise of Islamic conservatism as a cultural way to check the perceived advancement of Westernism, the Christian Church has emerged as an unlikely ally of conservative voices who adhere to African traditional perspectives and of conservative political leaders who oppose liberal sexual practices and identities. Admittedly, the

role of the Church in African history is anything but simple. It spear-
headed the penetration of the African interior in the name of change by
any means, so long as she won African souls on behalf of God conceived
of and represented her way, and to that end she raised no moral questions about the repressive and exploitative activities of the political and
economic forces with which she formed alliances. After all, the Church and
those political and economic forces shared views regarding the underlying
morality of their conquest of Africans: it could only be a divinely benevolent act to give Africans the means for social, material, intellectual, and
spiritual transformation into divinely acceptable beings. And only Africans
who were rescued from the darkness of their traditions and customs could
aspire to the category of divinely acceptable beings.

Over time, as the original mission Church became indigenous, she not
only became an agent for political liberation in the strict sense, she also
began accepting and incorporating into her practices aspects of African
tradition that would help further and deepen her indigenization. This process became prominent in areas of practice, such as liturgical gestures,
that left original and fundamental Christian teachings largely intact. This
separation between outward and core issues has continued to define the
presence of the Church in Africa. Church institutions range from schools to
feeding centers for the poor, shelters for those who have been displaced by
war or other social strife, health clinics, hospitals, and universities across
the continent. The Church was at the forefront of the re-democratization
movements in the 1990s. But the Church was either slow or reluctant to
extend her influence as an important agent of social change to support
some causes that lie at the heart of modern liberal agenda, such as the
freedom to choose one's own sexual orientation. This reluctance is also
applied to issues that touch on or have implications for crucial metaphysical stances preferred by Church teachings, such as believing that ghosts
possess people and that they can be exorcized, as archbishop of Lusaka,
Emmanuel Milingo, claimed in 1973. The backdrop to these attitudes is
the view that there is a "natural path" in the universe that forms the
basis of Christian teaching, one that is willed by God, at least as He is
understood by Christianity.[30]

Several African scholars have been critical of the Church's superficial
and merely cosmetic engagement with the African world. According to
the Cameroonian philosopher and theologian Fabien Eboussi-Boulaga, the
Christianity that the European missionary enterprise produces is a system
of fetishes that needs to be purified of its European cultural, intellectual,
and mythical baggage in order to enable true Christianity to emerge from
what he calls a "Christic model."

In this very brilliant critique of the pitfalls of European missionary
Christianity, Eboussi Boulaga proposes an exposition of the experience of
Christian values in a way that allows room for people grounded in different

Lebenswelts to articulate and experience the ideals envisaged in Christian teachings without the limiting elements of scripture, dogma, and symbolic imagery that these values acquired from European cultures over time. He proposes a Christianity "devoid of content." Here, then, are the questions that Eboussi Boulaga is primarily concerned with:

1. Can the status and functioning of dogmas acculturated in Western Christianity and civilization still be the same when Christianity is transplanted elsewhere, to another universe? Have the "truths to be believed" the same unambiguous weight of credibility everywhere?

2. Can what Christianity *should be,* the identity of Christianity, be conceived and thought, necessarily and sufficiently, from within the same Credo, the same rites, and with reference to one Scripture and one sole Lord?

3. Can tribal human beings, who have known the critique of their certitudes, have lived the death of both their myths and the irrefutable universe of those myths, seriously accept Christianity's pretension to be the foreordained truth and norm of all authentic existence and the solitary matrix of genuine human beings? Further: How is one to think and to live the necessity, supremacy, and universality of Christianity when the latter is imposed as the dominant religion, or the religion of the dominant? How are the truths, commandments, and rites to be inscribed in one's flesh, when they are received from below, in a state of social, political, economic, and cultural subordination and minority of age?

4. Finally, does not the God proposed by Christianity in the exercise of its symbolic domination, as its foundation, suffer in his representation from the taint of a partisanship that makes him necessarily an "other people's god"—the god of the privileged, with which he has struck an alliance [and complicity], the law of one group, the principle of membership in, and therefore of exclusion from, this group? How is it possible to take the metaphors of "Revelation" and "Word of God" literally when they authorize a like human conception, and make of monotheism a political problem?[31]

According to Mudimbe, Boulaga's critique surpasses those of the milder, accommodating, and revisionist tradition of critiques developed in the sixties under the aegis of Vatican II and whose neologisms, such as "stepping stones," "Christian harmonies," "acculturation," "indigenisation," "adaptation," "incarnation," and "inculturation" were merely fashionable currents whose unchanged goal was "to devise and present in a relevant and effective manner the best ways to achieve the christianisation of Africa."[32] Mudimbe laments that such endeavors still persist and are even thriving. In other words, what is wrong with those who insist on imparting to other cultures a Christianity defined and symbolized through European eyes is that they perpetuate, intentionally or otherwise, the schemes by which missionary Christianity seeks to destroy the worldviews of other cultures by ridiculing their views and symbols in order to replace them with its own in which the image of Christ and the rites of its recognition are idolatrously made inextricable from the scripted configurations in which "'Revelation' or 'Good News' are meshed with Western civilisation and myths."[33]

Christianity, like many other religions and other beliefs rooted in how people interpret and account for themselves within the universe, acquires meaning only from a genealogical perspective. Without this genealogy, says Boulaga, the content of an exported religious teaching risks creating "the fantastic, the legendary, the magical, or the allegorical . . . [and] calls either for the sacrifice of the intelligence or for duplicity. Only a genealogical Christianity can avoid both the one and the other, or join them together without contradiction. Apart from such a Christianity, integralism is impossible. . . . [Christianity] thinks it comes off by reducing the number of beliefs or by proposing the *contrary* of what has lately been held, pronouncing the latter passé, transcended, and demonstrating that the opposite of the prevailing obvious sense is the only true one, the one based on Scripture, the Fathers, and the Reformers. One is forced to conclude that the status of beliefs and rites is not the same for us as for those for whom Christianity is the genealogical, cultural religion."[34]

The alliance and complicity that Eboussi-Boulaga refers to have not been limited to Church-state relations but have been forged with agents of traditional institutions as well and made stronger where instruments of state are put to the service of traditional values or agents of the state double as the voices of tradition, as is the case in most instances. Evidence for this is most obvious in cases of sexuality and identity. Gay and lesbian rights, for example, have strongly been dismissed by several African leaders as "abnormal," brutish, ungodly, and against African norms and traditions. President Yoweri Museveni of Uganda is on record as referring to homosexuality as "this unnatural carnality." When Uganda's constitution and penal codes were rewritten in 1990, he directed that homosexuality be punishable with life imprisonment, an increase from the previous fourteen-year jail term for the same. Other leaders, including the former president of my own country Kenya, are known for their comparable intolerance toward this aspect of human rights.[35]

To be sure, intolerance for beliefs and practices different from our own is one of the most subjective traits of human character. The idea of disputation indicates a common antagonistic attitude that describes how we regard many things with which we find ourselves to be in discord. The opposite of this, on the other hand, describes our state of mind when confronted with circumstances that happen to be included on the list of our preferences. Difference and discord or similarity and agreement are therefore representations of a very normal world and of how we direct our mental inclination to cope with and to influence our adjustments to different situations when we encounter other subjects. Disputation is one mechanism for coping and adjusting, namely by striving to find a way that there can be only one point of view shared by all or by a majority. We assess the rationality of another person based on whether we can win them to our point of view by showing that both the point of view and our method of arriving at it are so clear and acceptable that only that point of view would be preferable to anyone.

But why would this type of disputation be better than one that delivers my point of view to everyone faster and without the possibility of any further challenge? There is a saying in Dholuo, *"Teko odago le e thim, rieko to odago dhano"* (While force is the way of beasts in the jungle, reason is the human way). Contractarian philosophers in modern Europe discovered this Luo wisdom too, namely that reason is a better way than violence to settle disputes. Most modern conceptions and theories of political justice and individual morality stem from the assumption that this unwritten agreement between members of a society is the basis of their reciprocal responsibility in their relationships under some form of authority. This type of contract and the principles of obligations and rights that emanated from it had a greater capability of providing and preserving personal and social security than the brutish ways.

Differences among humans and the appeal of the rational means to contain them have been the human way for as long as anyone can remember, which is why anyone should wonder about the recent explosions of violence between peoples on account of difference. In other words, why should any person want another one to be locked up for any amount of time or have their other entitlements unequally given to them, let alone be killed, based only on the fact that they are different? At least in the multicultural setting of Kenya, where I grew up, a great majority of the people already practice such cultural diversity without much fuss wherever they live and whenever they sojourn away from the comforts of their kin-bounded cultural "homes," except for those occasional moments when someone fails to contain biased outbursts. Imagine someone, possibly one who comes from a region in the highlands, whose entire upbringing had never included a fish diet, not even stories about a distant people whose geographical and cultural remoteness was keyed on the strange finding that they fed on funny wriggling creatures they caught from rivers, ponds, and lakes. Then, in his first venture away from sweet home and into the cultural hodgepodge of the city, he finds himself living next door to a stranger. Apart from having to learn a new language in which to communicate with these and other *wandu wa rũgũrũ*[36] next door and beyond, he finds that their diet is intolerably strange, especially to his "serene" sense of smell. He finds that they love fish, which is their traditional delicacy. So one evening while his neighbors are preparing their favorite dinner, he disgustedly walks over to them and tells them to stop their custom of eating such stuff because in the eyes of his own culture, fish should not be part of any human's "normal" diet, at least not for adults. In addition, he swears, it smells.

Well, this highlander's feelings are not altogether strange. We encounter people who think like him every day, not just as neighbors in multicultural cities but also in our classrooms where, in our efforts to promote tolerance across cultures, some of us struggle every day to introduce cultural diversity as part of our curricula and course contents. In our least rational moments, we express fear and react with alarm to most unfamiliar things, people, and events. We reach out by means of these reactions to protect what we have internalized in the depth of our guts as the ideal, which, by this internalization, empirically symbolizes, however falsely, our own identity as the representation of the ideal rational self. That is why the stranger's ways strike us as "wrong," "abnormal," "unnatural," and so on, because our own practices serve us as the normative measure of both reason and nature's course. Such aversion to strange or unfamiliar things and people therefore is no more than an expression of an encounter with values or people that appear to us in ways that we consider to be outside the scheme of values we have been made to feel comfortable with, not by virtue of the inherent superiority of these values to others but due to culturally embedded assumptions about a particular order of things that we are accustomed to and identify with. Xenophobia is no different from the reaction of the fish-eater's neighbor. To this neighbor, eating fish is abominably bad and those who practice such a habit ought either to be stopped or be forced to transport their actions to another world, far away from the world of "normal" people, namely himself and those who think, believe, and behave like he does. In this manner, discriminative thinking is put in place; all that remains is to set those who think and believe like he does against those who are different and to set institutional rules, standards, and requirements that privilege the preferred traits. Astonishingly, international cosmopolitanism risks portraying similar characteristics when it condemns diversity.

It is important to note that oppression doesn't always have to be by a foreigner and that it is neither better nor less hurtful when it is perpetrated by one of your own. Unfortunately, and much in line with the blinding effect of the saying that "the devil you know is better than the one you don't," we sharpen our sensitivity against foreign-bred oppression and other injustices but turn our other cheek to the domestically bred brands. While condemning gay and lesbian rights in harsh terms as imported abnormalities, African leaders have been either slow or unwilling to repeal unjust laws from their own countries' constitutions and penal codes. For example, many African constitutions continue to uphold capital punishment and to give legitimacy to laws that, at least in patrilineal systems, disinherit women, usually by referring cases involving selective inheritance to the already biased system of customary law and authority. At the level of governance, leaders have been conspicuously inconsistent and ineffective in their efforts to enforce laws to protect women from forced levirate marriages (also called wife inheritance), from other forms of domestic abuse, and from institutional biases and discrimination. Such political passiveness and inaction has been even more visible in the failure to protect children from rape, from illegal child marriages, from child labor, and from female circumcision, thereby making such selectiveness in the recognition and protection of human rights a matter of political expediency, ethical relativism, or culture-dependent aspiration.

As important as customary norms and practices must be to most human beings, they can be reevaluated and subsequently modified, replaced, or discarded altogether if it is found that the values they served can be achieved differently or that the costs associated with them (such as the physical pain associated with different customary rituals) are either no longer necessary or cannot be effectively minimized at a (historically later) time when elimination or at least the minimization of pain has become a value. Different people will be able to identify a variety of customs that require such reevaluation, but at least two common practices throughout the continent stand out: circumcision of female babies and children and prearranged or forced marriages for girls. A good place to start in questioning why they persist is to ask, especially in the case of circumcision, about the nature of the good it is assumed to serve and in what ways such a good, if there is any, contributes to the general betterment of life for the person who undergoes it in such a way that their life would be significantly worse without it or how the benefits of attaining such a good are worth the evils associated with the practice. Although similar questions could be asked of the practice of child marriages, changing social circumstances have made the practice less appealing for many, more so than in the case of female circumcision. Arguments against female circumcision suggest that it cannot have been a good at any time and that all reasons offered as its basis by those who practice it are false. Child marriages probably cause no less psychological trauma to the young girls who are married off to men the age of their grandfathers to join women older than their own mothers as co-wives.[37] In the traditional setting, such trauma was compensated by and probably was minimized by the wide social support system from the child-bride's family. These conditions have drastically changed, however.

Why question traditional values and practices now? Ivan Karp and I have said elsewhere[38] that although the phenomenon has been more visible in African intellectual practice in the present time, it is true that philosophy, any philosophy, is a form of cultural inquiry and that because cultures change over time, the history and tradition of inquiry into the conceptual foundations of cultures will reflect these changes as well. The difference is that Africans have needed to restate the nature and content of their cultural values more than other people, including some people whose cultures were subjected to colonial domination just as their own were. By contrast, Western intellectuals take the matter of cultural inquiry for granted; the fact that their philosophy is a form of cultural inquiry does not have to be stated, and nothing has to be stated or defended at the general collective level. Yet like all normal humans who live and think in the contexts of time, they too take account of the way specific theories have changed in relation to changes in knowledge and beliefs. New social, economic, and political circumstances will engender new or different aspirations and new strategies of adjusting to them. It is therefore possible, in this sense, that questions of justice might not have prevailed in the deeply customary contexts of our traditions or that we might not have invoked or demanded them as loudly and as persistently as we do today. For example, some individuals might always have preferred to have the freedom to choose their own partner in marriage or to have a greater voice in the negotiations about their own marriage but that the society they lived in lacked the necessary sociopolitical conditions for them to express such preferences. And if the affected persons indicated preferences contrary to those of family or community, probably no one would have thought of their expressions as demands for justice, because the denial of an individual's preference in such matters was not considered a transgression. Hence the cases where a person was able to marry someone they preferred occurred either by chance or by secret conspiracy, in which case it wouldn't have been an act of real choice. But it is not uncommon for parents to reject marriages of their children to partners they had no hand in choosing. It is also possible that there was sadness in such matters for most individuals but that they accepted their discontent or it disappeared under the power of despair. Generally, then, questions of rights may have been directed at other, different, and more immediate concerns of the time.[39] The implication is not that traditional societies were so righteous that no complaints emerged but rather that perhaps the types of issues that invoke the issue of rights today were either not considered serious enough then or that individual claims to certain entitlements went totally unheeded—that is, they lacked institutional expression and protection or they did not appear in ways that warranted raising alarms about the virtue of rights as a remedy. All of these reasons or any combination of them made it hard for claims to certain rights to enjoy public expression and prominence. Conflicts and other shortcomings were probably resolved by means of several available adjustments, depending on the degree of severity of the discord. Questions of rights, as do questions of respect, kindness, or empathy, gain prominence based on the nature of the circumstances, when changes in society warrant adjustments of the remedial principles of the moral and political order.

Circumstances have changed for many aspects of everyday life in African societies, and there are many indications of our awareness of these changes in our daily utterances, which signal the spirit of disapproval of the consequences of these changes in terms of public behavior. Our disapproval signals dissatisfaction with society's failure to adjust to today's pressures. Previous standards of public behavior are now widely considered things of the past. As an example, let us examine a situation I have been in countless times before, waiting for a public taxi in downtown Mombasa, where I grew up. In the good but long-gone old days, everyone knew that mothers, people of the female gender, children, and the elderly boarded and alighted first and that no one pushed anyone else. These mores were so well known that no one needed to be reminded of them. There was no hurry, as taxi and bus drivers would wait patiently until everyone had peacefully and safely boarded or disembarked, as the case might be. There was what the Swahili call *ustaarabu,* social civility. It made using public means not significantly or rudely different from using private means. There was no push. But recently when I visited this old city of my youth it was unbelievable to hear, almost everywhere, women's cries of distress, *"Haya, jamani! Ustaarabu umepotea wapi? Kwani adabu haipo tena?"* (Oh, my people, where has civility gone? What has happened to respect in today's world?) As people pushed and shoved everywhere, young against old and vice versa, I realized that the good elderly ladies, elegantly clad in the traditional Islamic *bui-bui,* and I and my sisters in my company silently shared a generational memory of a world that was starkly missing from sight. Perhaps the young men and women they were calling never knew that world and so had no memory of it. Matters had changed; respect now was an open question in ways that it never was in the world I shared with these ladies. The majority of younger people no longer respectfully address those older than them as *"Mama"* (Mother), *"Mzee"* (generally translatable as "Sir" but with indication of reverence for elderhood), *"Dada"* (Sister), or *"Ndugu"* (Brother), as those of our age continue to do. Instead, they shout at them with utmost disdain like people do to goats, *"Wee Nani!"* (Heeey, you there!) Interactions have become impersonal and casual. Well, a descriptive comparison of these attitudinal patterns indicates that matters have changed, causing a dramatic shift in behavior, especially in matters of respect for other people. Unlike in the past—where "past" is up to about two or three decades ago—today's individual is less likely to regard the Other in socially bonding terms unless there is established knowledge of a real relationship. Everyone else is increasingly viewed as a competitor and a possible hindrance to the attainment of one's own self-interests. Hence everyone is shoved into a hustle, for a variety of good, bad, real, or only imagined reasons. As the example of the Swahili ladies indicates, the impact of these changes on our mores is astounding. At the private level, the loss of the ideals of personal virtue and their replacement with intolerance, apathy, and violence is rampant, while in the public domain, corruption, political arrogance, and impunity have long been known to propel the rapid social and economic decay throughout the continent.

Other circumstantial changes have contributed to trends of withdrawal from participation in the collective project. An increase in dependency on the modern economy has eroded the guarantees of the traditional social support system, while the onset and growing threat of the HIV/AIDS epidemic has thrown other forms of social support and trust practices into confusion. For example, whereas the relatively strong and viable traditional economy and social support systems made polygamy less intolerable and its tensions much less visible, changes in goals, aspirations, and standards of living are fiercely making polygamy increasingly less desirable as a way of life as old tolerances transform into openly adversarial competitions and rivalries. Relatedly, the view and role of marriage as a means of social bonding and a linkage between larger social units such as families and lineages or clans is visibly yielding ground to a more liberal view of marriage as a pact between the two persons primarily involved. The uncertainties occasioned by changes in the economy and in public health are pushing back and in some cases driving into oblivion the customary participation of the collective in the events that define marriage. The fact that prospective marriage partners often travel or live far from home has decreased the participation of the community, as have the high costs of meeting community marriage norms. In addition, the dangers posed by public health epidemics are increasingly causing families and communities to allow individuals to take responsibility for making their own marriage choices. As my very wise Aunt Akumu would put it, the time of being the *ja-gam* (matchmaker) for one's brother's daughter is over, as one might in fact be the matchmaker for death. Aunt Akumu was referring to the prevalent sense of uncertainty and angst caused by the HIV/AIDS epidemic; no one knows any more what they might be putting their little niece or nephew into.[40] It would therefore sound more plausible as a minimum requirement, she elaborated, that if two young couple were to have a future free of any measure of misery and suffering, no third party should have a role or be held directly or indirectly responsible. Everywhere, customs are suspended or retired when emerging circumstances render them unnecessary or contrary to the needs of survival. Aunt Akumu's sentiments are therefore neither isolated nor exaggerated. They reflect a growing and consistent deference to the individual regarding their right to make rational decisions, especially in matters that relate to their sense of happiness and a good life.

One more value of Nussbaum's call to world citizenship: her call for a return to the classics articulates the value of tradition in philosophical inquiry. Her historical studies on the classics are probably propelled by the assumption that something of value can be realized by the use of the memory of and reflection upon the past. The weight that she selectively places on the idea of the *kosmou* has the value of reminding us that she is committed to the idea that we are all similar in what is important and essential for being human. Kwasi Wiredu similarly reminds us that both the historical unity of our philosophical thought and the cures for today's malaise would benefit tremendously from a careful reconsideration of and inclusion of tradition in today's modes of inquiry and in our search for solutions to both theoretical and practical problems. The stark reality of our history is that our public ethic is built upon the basic metaphysical dependency of the individual upon the collective that provides him or her with the strings to survive and to become human. Hence the demands for the liberties of the individual are not an erasure of the role of the community or of the individual's dependency on community, because the very idea of such liberties is in part strengthened by the social conditioning of the individual. As we shall see in the next chapter, the idea that the metaphysics of individual identity is almost unimaginable without a community to make it possible is a crucial and distinguishing point of contrast between African and other philosophical traditions, especially the Western variety.

CHAPTER FOUR

Understanding Personhood:
An African Philosophical Anthropology

Jadak kende-ni m'unene en ng'a m'oyuma miwuoro. (The isolated
and autonomous individual is like a proverb, for he/she develops no
sense of rules or obligations.)

— Gabriel Omolo, Kenyan musician, poet,
and social commentator

No human society or community is possible without communication,
for a community is not just an aggregation of individuals existing
as windowless monads but of individuals as interacting persons. . . .
Without communication there is not even a human person.

— Kwasi Wiredu

Africans' notions of the person are scattered over different forms of cultural expression, and so their analyses are correspondingly scattered in
the different disciplinary fields as they focus on the different aspects of
culture—in studies of religion and ritual, in creative and analytical literature, in the study of social institutions, in gender studies, and in the study
of myth and cosmology, besides philosophy. As the German philosopher
Immanuel Kant suggested, the notion of the person, the ultimate question of anthropology, underlies and is assumed by all other questions,
suggesting also thereby that the ubiquity of the idea of the person in
cultural expressive forms is hardly an African peculiarity. But the foundational nature of the notion in African thought has never been given more
interesting and philosophically savvy treatment than in the work of Kwasi
Wiredu. He makes it the pinnacle of an African difference in philosophical
theory. Its exposition will be the subject matter of this chapter.

Recent studies have gone a long way in shedding light on our understanding of the nature of the mind and the nature of the person more
generally, which play significant roles, as mentioned in the allusion to
Kant. The reasons for the recent scientific and philosophical hype about

135

the mind are easy to appreciate if not to understand: it remains one of the most enigmatic aspects of human nature, full of wonders as much in its achievements as when it simply stalls. Thus, new information or ideas about the mind may be enlightening or scary to us, depending on the presuppositions we have acquired from our upbringing. The wonders of the mind have led to many hypotheses, all well intended, I believe, yet all also restricted to explanations tied to analogies that are far from perfect— such as comparisons with the function of the computer under the broader rubric of artificial intelligence. The empiricist advances that inform this analogy in the study of mind are balanced by the strong skepticism about the physicalist stance, thus perpetuating the old dualist stance or spurring a new debate over the matter. The field remains fairly evenly divided, as I discovered recently in some informal discussions with high school teachers in rural France. This discussion reminded me of the unresolved issue in French literature, dating back to Descartes, of the relation of mind to the body as reenacted in the 1998 debate between Jean-Pierre Changeux, a neuroscientist of repute, and Paul Ricoeur.[1] The matters they touched on, namely the correlations between cognition, brain, and behavior, occupy a special place in recent studies in brain sciences and psychology, but they also extend and give a new spark to the traditional metaphysical, moral, and legal problem of freedom and determinism.[2]

Farther afield, the rise of debates about liberalism and its limitations or about its rival frameworks is not tied solely to recent crises of authoritarianism in the present century. At the same time, however, the collapse of centers of social and political authority in its various facets at the end of the twentieth century certainly enhanced and accelerated the maturation of philosophical anthropology that began, for Western philosophical traditions, with the modern age and flourished especially in the philosophy of Immanuel Kant. Since Kant, the anthropological focus has remained the starting point from which and around which the ever-polarized philosophical discourse revolves, seeking, as Kant did, to understand and resolve the many theoretical problems of philosophy by means, first, of understanding human nature. Critical inquiry launched by Descartes became the necessary starting point for any philosophizing whose goal was to make humans its primary object. In *Ethics,* Spinoza's objective was to scientifically establish the purpose or goal of human life and the means to attain it. In the *Treatise on Human Nature,* Hume sought to offer a framework that would define man as basically an individual while Comte and Marx tried to demonstrate the opposite—that man is a social being. Freud proposed man as primarily a complex of instincts, while Heidegger and Bloch saw him as a mine of possibilities. Yet this modern European quest for a philosophical anthropology remained closely indebted to its Platonic grounding in metaphysics, as is clearly visible in the contributions of Descartes, Pascal, Spinoza, Leibniz, and others. The new approach began only after Kant's critique of the absurdities of metaphysical pretensions, as it was his view that the human mind cannot attain absolute knowledge of the world or of man or of God. He or she can only attain knowledge of a practical kind, namely moral knowledge. Armed with these convictions, Kant embarked on a path to elaborate a practical brand of anthropology, according to which humans differ from other beings in their value, dignity, and condition of persona. In correspondence to this, Kant said, there must be appropriate conduct, as epitomized in the Golden Rule. In the introduction to *Logic,* Kant captured the position of anthropology in the philosophical disciplines. He wrote:

> The field of philosophy . . . may be summed up in the following questions:
>
> 1. What can I know?
>
> 2. What ought I do?
>
> 3. What can I hope for?
>
> 4. What is man [*Was ist der Mensch*]?
>
> The first question is answered by *metaphysics,* the second by *morality,* the third by *religion,* and the fourth by *anthropology.* At bottom all this could be reckoned to be anthropology, because the first three questions are related to the last.[3]

In articulating answers to these questions, Kant's philosophy was critically different from the preceding systems and grounded subsequent philosophical inquiry decisively in a new anthropological orientation. It turns out, however, that this new orientation remained deeply tied to metaphysics because of its emphasis on structure (of humans in their physio-psychological constitution) and function as the basis for a transcendental philosophy of experience. And while his system offered a formidable basis both for toning down the expectations for the possibility of metaphysics and for objectifying the moral maxim of conduct, it appeared to leave unanswered questions regarding the primal bases of his principles, namely how the physio-psychological constitution comes to be in the first place, which is how Wiredu's philosophy comes in. The question "What is man?" (*Was ist der Mensch?*) cannot be answered satisfactorily merely by describing the structural givens or the a priori categories as the bases of human powers of understanding and other (natural) human characteristics, but must be answered by showing the origin and bases of the a priori categories themselves. In other words, although Kant's theory identifies the categories as the very foundation on which understanding becomes possible at both the first- and second-order levels, it merely posits, without a further explanatory account, the mere fact, existence, or sheer presence (phenomenally being there) of the categories as the building blocks upon which the powers of understanding rest. This is quite a formidable task and achievement in itself, but Kant saw this anthropology as only a stepping-stone, a prolegomenon, to further inquiry into the nature of external world from the viewpoint of the constitutive nature of the Subject. His project thereby (or therefore) became an anthropology of philosophy, which he analyzed in varying degrees of penetration and complexity: from general descriptions of human nature, as he does in the *Anthropology from a Pragmatic Point of View,* to the technical analyses of the faculties of under-standing, as executed in the *Critiques.*

Because Kant's objective was geared toward identifying and describing (in amazingly complex and detailed ways) rather than theorizing the ori-gins of the characteristics of being human, his philosophy was, ipso facto, a phenomenological account of different types of perception, of understand-ing or knowledge in general, and of our attitudes toward form, establish-ing thereby the norms that govern these perceptions, understanding, and attitudes. As a theory of experience—that is, of the encounter between the (knowing) Subject and the (knowable) outside world—his philosophy logically focused on identifying and analyzing the elements, the categories on both sides of this epistemic enterprise that were the enabling compo-nents or ingredients of the response to the metaphysical questions "What sort of thing is mind or understanding?" on the one hand, and "What is the essence of anything?" on the other. While in the first instance the categories became the "texture" and filters of understanding, so to speak, in the second they became the veneer over the objects of experience. As he argues in *Logic,* everything has its structural order, that which makes it work according to its nature, whether or not we are aware of such order of all things in the world, and philosophy's task is to unravel the nature of this structure in every instance of human experience.

A different view of anthropology is suggested by Wiredu's statement that "a *human being* deprived of the socializing influence of communication will remain human biologically, but mentally is bound to be subhuman."[4] As I will explain a little later, this position digs even deeper below the a priori categories, for it seeks to establish the very basic conditions from which the categories emerge. While Kant starts with human nature as phenomenologically complete in its (metaphysical) constitution at least in the domain of understanding,[5] Wiredu seeks to establish the view that such defining characteristics of being human are not endowed in humans by a force that exists outside an already existing environment of the deliberate actions of other humans, namely the socializing processes out of which the actualization of human capacities emerges. Thus, Wiredu argues, in an Aristotelian fashion,[6] what makes humans humans cannot be their psychology, for this is an already-constituted aspect of them. For the sake of clarity and distinction, it is not very helpful, however, that Wiredu calls his view "philosophical psychology" while Kant referred to his own as "anthropology." Reversing the designations clarifies the distinctions between the two positions.

The Roots of Universal Categories

Over the years, many African thinkers, including professional philosophers, have had a view of the individual that is quite in contrast to the one represented by Kant, arguing in their different ways that humans are such deeply social beings that they would not be able to develop their full capacities as persons outside their relations with others; that they would not, for example, be able to develop communicative capacities, which include mind, or the capacity to develop language and form concepts. They have argued that because personhood is socially generated, interaction or intersubjective penetration, not aggregation, is the formative foundation of human nature and the conduit through which humans develop their sense and basis of the moral and cognitive values. This position takes us to the anthropological conditions, the human-making or pre-metaphysical processes by which personhood is gradually actualized in practice. One can therefore estimate that when Wiredu says that "no human society or community is possible without communication, for a community is not just an aggregation of individuals existing as windowless monads,"[7] he is, at least in part, expressing a critique both of Kant's atomistic perception of the person and of his mechanistic perception of the mind, views that remained unshaken even by the moral principle of the categorical imperative.[8] In an essay on African metaphysics, Wiredu asserts unequivocally that although "the concerns of traditional African metaphysics are, perhaps, best characterized, in the phrase of KANT as God, freedom, and immortality . . . one has not advanced one step towards understanding African thought unless one understands the radically un-Kantian connotations of these concepts."[9] In other words, contrary to the Kantian monadological framework, traditional African philosophy, which is essentially a philosophy of the person, "is extremely sensitive to the complexity of the human psyche and the social dimensions of individual consciousness."[10] On this view, what Wiredu lays down is a groundwork for the metaphysics of mind, namely the processes that make mind a dispositional rather than a substantive reality.

The pertinent question for African philosophy is, then, whether moral and political obligations, the pillars of Kant's doctrine of the Kingdom of Ends, are rooted in the nature of reason itself or in the community of rationally competent and interacting agents. By articulating the pre-metaphysical social genesis of the individual and his or her dependence on others for self-actualization, African philosophers have contributed significantly to the establishment of an alternative normative standpoint for viewing the world from a communalist rather than the individualist perspective, and no one accomplishes this task nearly as well as Kwasi Wiredu does. Although the articulation of his view on the complexity of the human psyche and of the social dimensions of individual consciousness can be accessed most directly and with some sense of unity in his two collections of essays, *Philosophy and an African Culture* (1980) and *Cultural Universals and Particulars* (1996), they are spread out over most of his works in ethics, metaphysics, and epistemology.

The earlier collection, *Philosophy and an African Culture,*[11] has long been the centerpiece of the growing philosophical deliberation among philosophers in Africa and beyond. It set the tone for the pursuit and use of African categories for dealing with a wide range of philosophical issues. Of particular interest in the collection is Wiredu's attempt to subvert the way of defining and dealing with the concept of truth as it was traditionally familiar to the history of Western philosophy. In his now widely debated position, Wiredu suggests that truth is an unattainable ideal, both in the sense that it is something worth aiming for and in the sense that it is something we are ultimately incapable of realizing. He argues that the solipsistic approach to the problem of truth as suggested in the significantly dominant aspect of the Western tradition, such as is encountered in the correspondence theory, makes it fundamentally indistinguishable from opinion. Truth, he asserts, "is opinion or a point of view," for someone always knows something from some point of view, regardless of the number of people who might find themselves sharing one point of view. *Cultural Universals and Particulars: An African Perspective,*[12] also a collection of essays, provides new aspects of Wiredu's thought that offer a useful background for understanding some of the longer and more complex arguments contained in the first collection. Taking advantage of linguistic and other cultural resources that many Western philosophers often lack, Wiredu expands the analytic field of the references and meanings of terms and concepts in ways that both reveal conceptual contrasts between intellectual traditions that emerged from diverse cultures and suggest fresh cross-cultural ways of reconsidering both old and new philosophical problems that have remained unresolvable within their limited (Western) traditional linguistic frameworks.[13] In so doing, Wiredu reveals the view that although the framing and discussion of philosophical issues take place within linguistic particularisms that may limit the variety of possible solutions, the problems themselves are always universal. Therefore he urges philosophers to think comparatively about the universal character of philosophical issues without giving up philosophy's dependence on the specificity of local knowledges and frameworks. What this approach does regarding the general nature of philosophy is that it strongly advocates pluralism, namely the view that there are competing evaluative points of view with compelling merits of their own that ideally all people can and should recognize. In other words, multiculturalism, of which the variety of the human languages across the world are an indicator, endows us with multiple avenues to work with and therefore is anything but a luxury in the pursuit of that philosophical quest we call understanding. From the comparative standpoint, linguistic multiculturalism enables us to see conceptual limitations when they are produced by means of limited linguistic models.[14] Although much less visible in contemporary Anglo-American philosophical practice, the exegesis that Wiredu calls for was once a thriving philosophical practice both in and of itself and as a method lies at the base of the transitions from texts in the classical philosophical languages such as Greek, Latin, and Persian to those in modern-day European languages. Such exegetical expositions (used to) allow for cross-cultural conceptual comparisons and contrasts in a manner that advanced and expanded conceptual fields. This sort of work, now much less done, illustrated the migration of concepts through translations by showing different ways in which precise meanings of terms and their uses in theories differ from one linguistic rendition to another. It is important to give an example.

The Becoming of Personhood

What, then, are the distinguishing marks that set the African philosophy of self apart from, say, dominant Western views of the same? To make a workable comparison, let us take two examples, one from either side, as representative samples, namely Wiredu's and Kant's respective ideas of self as the Subject of understanding. As explicated by Wiredu, Akan thought proposes a theory of self that radically alters the way we have understood many philosophical matters according to the Western tradition, although we found, as mentioned earlier, a curious statement by Husserl about the communicative making of personhood.[15] Not only is the proposed African idea of self or the person different and interesting, it also subverts familiar notions in epistemology and metaphysics such as the nature of truth, mind, abstract ideas, God, spirit, life after death, and so on. Furthermore, it also leads us to a different understanding of the basis of moral universals.

Wiredu's view begins with a quasi-physicalist understanding of reality. In a view that sharply subverts the popularly believed African dualism, Wiredu contends that the physical world with its capacities is all there is as the primary basis of all nature; everything else either springs from physical reality as its mode of behavior or is metaphorically imagined on the basis of similarities with or differences from the physical world. Although Wiredu's thought focuses almost solely on the nature of humans, it would not be unreasonable to infer from what he says about humans that all inhabitants of reality, especially those of the animate world, are endowed—each according to the place and vocation of the species to which they belong—with a variety of responsive capacities on which their survival rests.

Human nature can be understood fairly well by understanding the capacities or endowments specific to the biological type to which it belongs. Observation teaches us that human nature crucially depends on the intra-species interaction and mutual dependency of its members. Almost all human capacities, including those that are vital to sheer physical survival, require some form of input from other members of the species. Even capacities that spring almost completely from the biological development and maturation of the body, such as the ability to use our limbs, require the guidance and support of others to develop properly. Generally, the human body has the ability to respond in different ways to a variety of stimuli, and different limbs and organs are charged with these roles as the agents that fulfill the needs of a complete person. Chief among these abilities, because it is based on mutual dependency among humans, is the ability or capacity to receive those things for which we interactively depend on others: their ideas. Even in the most basic sense of imitation, humans are constantly in communication with each other. By means of communicative interaction we become more than just human beings: we *become* persons.

Communication is basically a system by which humans emit and receive noises, and the capacity to organize these noises when they are received is a basic event in the chain of stimulus-response behavior among members of the species. A successful communication involves, then, the organiza-tion of noises (or other symbols that substitute for them) to determine the nature and exact aim of the stimuli and then give them the appropri-ate response, a process that is generally referred to as comprehension or understanding. This capacity is within, is part of, the human bodily nature. It is specific to human nature as an endowment of its organism, and it is borne into action by the communicative stimuli of others.

The capacity to process and respond to communicative stimuli is what is called mind, and although it is closely related to the brain as the organ that makes it possible as an activity, we cannot say that "our brains think," just like we don't say "our legs walk or "our mouths eat." The mind is not a separate, embodied substance. It is not a once-and-for-all fixed and thoroughly knowable "thing." Rather, it is a *disposition* or capacity of the whole person, making it hard to think, except through sheer and meaningless imagination, of the mind as an "entity" that is independent of other things that make up personhood.[16] It is the person who thinks, although the specific agent of personhood charged with the duty is called mind. According to this view, our only contact with the world is through the body, making empiricism the basic origin of most of our knowledge. Through the laws of its (organizational) operation, the mind forms ideas and concepts out of the various stimuli or sense data of experience. We have no access to knowledge or any types of existence other than those that are part of the realm where we are located, which suggests that many concepts about the nonphysical world are only metaphors derived from how we think of the concrete physical world.

How, then, do concepts compare to observation or direct sensory experience? Are concepts far less important than direct sensory experience? I almost chuckle as I ask these questions, lest I promote a gross misunderstanding of Wiredu. Consider, say, the idea of life after death. We know life by what we grasp of living things here in this world. Suspicions of and continued research into past but now-withered life in other parts of our solar system notwithstanding, no one has proven to us that there is life elsewhere, and if they did, our basis of comprehending such a claim would largely be by analogy and comparison to what we know about life here. In fact that is what guides research into the historical and present state of things on other planets. The mind is not incapable, based on what we know here, of imagining the possibility of a continuance of a mode of existence similar to or modeled after what prevails here. We can imagine such possible situations by mentally putting together the bad or the good, respectively, from what we know of our own world, which boasts an admixture of both sides. But imaginations of such models are usually not mere duplications of what pertains here. Hence people imagine (and the more gullible indeed believe) that there are kinds of existence that spread beyond existence in this world that are complete with their own types of space: one a combination of the worst we can imagine from our world; another a combination of the best of our desires and imaginations; and a third, an in-between world that is usually imagined to be temporary or a transitional space for one of the first two. But now consider another, different case—that of the concept of the chair. Modeled on our experience of specific individual chairs, the concept of a chair is stripped of all the specific qualities that we actually associate with any individual chair that we ever saw, yet (or perhaps because of that) the concept contains only the elements that we believe could fit any actual chair, even with its peculiar individual details. When we talk to others to explain things, these concepts are what we draw on, because explanations are usually general in nature and the mind is always manufacturing concepts, so to speak. Although they belong to two distinct conceptual domains, both of these examples describe the different ways we organize experience to create mental images as part of our reasoning, communication, and experience. They are both metaphors, because concepts are metaphors.

The Social Origin of Mind:
An African Quasi-Physicalism

Recent philosophy of mind seeks to understand the nature of ideas (or concepts) as a functional aspect of the body rather than as something distinct from it. In these terms, contemporary philosophy of mind has influenced and incorporated new thinking about the nature of ideas, thus pushing the classic Cartesian problem to new horizons. As African philosophers embrace and participate in these contemporary debates, views on the nature of mind will inevitably force a rethinking of the nature of personhood, thus refocusing on new interpretations of indigenous beliefs on the matter and reigniting a new debate between pluralists and those whose views on mind lead to a different metaphysical map of the constitution and moral agency of personhood.

Descartes popularized the mind-body problem through his dualist view of the person—called substance dualism—by arguing that the thinking mind and the physical body were irreducibly distinct substances because they were bearers respectively of two incommensurable orders of being, namely that the mind is an active thinking thing while the body is a passive unthinking matter. By contrast, physicalists, or materialists, as they are sometimes called, consider the mind only in physical terms, so they view ideas as aspects of the physical state of the brain under certain conditions. This position has been strengthened in recent years thanks to the technological advances that have made possible sophisticated empirical studies of the brain, mainly by psychologists. In the 1970s, this led to the emergence of cognitive science as a new, separate, and highly influential discipline. The physicalist thesis about the nature of mind, called *the mind/ brain identity theory,* or simply *the identity theory,* is part of the general materialist view that everything in a certain sphere, normally the sphere of our experience and what we can discern from it, is made of matter, that only matter exists, and things like mind and spirit are either illusory or mere metaphorical ways of speaking or can be reduced to (that is, explained as aspects of) matter. In other words, physicalists make up a subschool among monists. But because I have called Wiredu a monist, it is crucial that I examine to what degree, or if at all, his position shares anything with this (physicalist) brand of monism. To that end, I should state quickly that given the observations I have made to this point, it should be obvious that Wiredu is neither a substance dualist nor a vitalist. The latter hold that living things contain a nonphysical substance, an élan vital, that is unique to them and accounts for mind and for all those things and capacities that, over the ages, have been attributed to it or to the soul. Many students of African philosophy will remember the widely debated concept of "the vital force" that was introduced by Placide Tempels.[17]

Recently, two American scholars, George Lakoff, a linguist, and Mark Johnson, a philosopher, have grounded their philosophical analysis of the human mind and its enterprises on the materialist or physicalist approach,[18] and other scholars have seen an African overlap.[19] According to Lakoff and Johnson, metaphors are not just names for the familiar that are used to identify things that belong to another realm. They are not a characteristic of language alone. Rather, in their view, "metaphor is pervasive in everyday life, not just in language but in thought and action."[20] Many aspects of our lives, they argue, are organized on the basis of metaphorical representations. As in my first example above, many people live their lives based on contrasts between two metaphorically imagined worlds that follow this earthly one. One of them, constituted of the worst of all sufferings that we can imagine on the basis of what we have seen here, also called Hell, is to be avoided by living morally agreeable lives here; this will guarantee entry into "the land" of joyful rewards, Heaven, which is a metaphorical rendition of a combination of the best of experiences, based on what we have known or desired of the values here. This is how, as we are told in the mythical stories of the Bible, the Israelites were able to imagine a world flowing with milk and honey for which they were ready to fight even unto death. Nietzsche has observed how metaphors are embedded into our strategies for ordering the social world. He observes in the *Genealogy of Morals* that people have developed a variety of methods for coping with problems of good and evil. He thinks of "good and evil" as categories of the slaves—all the low, low-minded, common, and plebeian who, out of feeling that they were distant from the position of those who legislated their own actions as values, not only created values and coined names for those values but also regarded their masters as evil and defined "good" by what was unlike themselves. By contrast, the original nobles, the masters, first defined themselves as "good" and then defined as "bad" whatever lacks their own qualities.

But while the incidence of metaphorical representation appears to be more obvious in the domain of morals, in the view of Lakoff and Johnson, the entire conceptual system by which we organize our experiences into intelligible orders is deeply metaphorical in nature as well. In other words, they argue, we use terminologies that are germane to one domain of experience to describe actions or experiences in other domains. They give as an example the common terminologies used to describe war situations and in logical arguments.[21] This example has problems, because it gives the false impression that one of these activities is more natural than the other, such that the terminologies are viewed to belong "more appropriately" to the one than they do to the other. But this is hardly the case, since the common factor in both war and logical arguments is the nature of the relations between the sides involved, namely disputation or competition, which usually occurs when there are conflicting claims over an object of common interest and each side is seeking victory in the form of sole recognition and dominance over those with whom it is in competition. Hence, although there are different kinds of disputes as well as different ways of conducting them, such as physical or argumentative, sportive or litigious, entertaining or belligerent, the concepts that describe the general nature and dynamics of disputes are likely to be similar. Due to the dynamics involved, competitions also bear elements of dispute. In the war-argument example cited by Lakoff and Johnson, the general features of the dispute may include such elements as the claims and counterclaims of adversarial parties, the strengths and weaknesses of positions or tools in the dispute, attacks and counterattacks, hitting or missing points or targets, and so on. These features would remain the same and would guide the process and performance of participants in any competitive interaction, provided that the performance is deemed not only an entertainment but also a competitive act, making this evidently different from a case of conflictual competition. The idea implied in their argument that human actions are simple and monolithic in their goals fails to recognize the multilayered complexity of human performance in the social world. The reason their idea of metaphors fails in the examples they cite is that there is no real transfer of terms from "war" to "argument" since both are subspecies of real conflictual competitions.[22]

On a recent visit to my neurosurgeon, I noticed a beautifully and expensively framed wall hanging in the examination room entitled "Neurons and Astrocytes," with the following statement below the title:

> Neurons, or nerve cells, are the basic functioning components of the brain. Scientists study neurons to understand how they organize, connect to one another and ultimately transfer information from one area of the brain (and body) to another. Chemical and electrical activity between neurons allows us to perform all our actions and shape our thoughts, affects our dreams and lets us imagine. . . . [Previously, it was thought that] neurons were held together by glial cells, originally thought to be passive. Today, researchers are finding evidence that a category of glial cells, termed astrocytes, plays an active role in brain function by promoting the activity of neurons.

The physicalist tone of this writing is evident, even though my neurosurgeon, an undergraduate philosophy major prior to choosing the medical path, quickly points out that he personally does not identify with the ultra-materialist brand of brain scholarship. Yet to many scholars and professionals in that subfield, physicalism is gaining a strong and growing influence. To this school, matter and its complex activity is all there is. What allows people such as Lakoff and Johnson to regard terminologies used to describe mental—that is, nonphysical—situations as merely metaphorical is their view that the physical realm is what is primary, both in existence and in our experience of it. The sensorimotor structuring of subjective experience is what primarily defines our relationship with the outside world, so our basic language refers directly and only to this primary reality. Everything else, including the conceptual or judgmental, is frameable only by expanding the meaning of the terms that emerge from the basic structure of physical reality. Hence, they say, for example, that "In More Is Up, a subjective judgment of quantity is conceptualized in terms of the sensorimotor experience of verticality."[23] Admittedly, the effects of verticality, or height and depth, can be experienced directly through the senses because changes in them affect the effects of atmospheric pressure on our body fluids and their flow through our organs. But "verticality" itself is not experienceable as a phenomenon. The sensations of light-headedness or compression as effects of variations in verticality are what we experience, because they affect the distribution and flow of fluids in the veins of the brain. The ideas of up, down, vertical, lateral, or whatever are all linguistic conventions for making those sensations or experiences intelligible. In themselves, the terms are neutral regarding the sensations or events for which they are used, making them no more "appropriate" for those events, as if they were ontologically inalienable from them, than they are for others. In other words, neural experiences are simply that: sensations and events, and to that extent they are not different from those that happen to bodies other than our own, for example a tree leaf shaken by the wind.

Despite its opposition to the Western idea of mind or reason as an autonomous cognitive instrument in both its metaphysical and functional senses and generally to the idea of the person through the Enlightenment period and its aftermath, from Descartes to the present,[24] Lakoff and Johnson's variety of physicalism continues to uphold the monadological view of the person, albeit a thoroughly mechanistic one, since it argues that we can experience the world only as it is presented to the neural sensorimotor system of the bodily organism. According to this view, each person is a complete and autonomous cognitive system that functions as a complex and detailed cognitive machine. According to Lakoff and Johnson, "Reason is not disembodied . . . but arises from the nature of our brains, bodies, and bodily experience . . . [for] the very structure of reason itself comes from the details of our embodiment. The same neural and cognitive mechanisms that allow us to perceive and move around also create our conceptual systems and modes of reason . . . [which are] shaped crucially by the peculiarities of our human bodies, by the remarkable details of the neural structure of our brains, and by the specifics of our everyday functioning in the world."[25]

What, then, would be the difference between the position adopted by Lakoff and Johnson, on the one hand, and that held by Wiredu, on the other? Such a difference must be sought in their respective views of the mind and of the person. Lakoff and Johnson's long list of rejections of the different characterizations of mind and of personhood by Western philosophers suggests that they subscribe to eliminativism, the hardest type of physicalism. The other brands are reductionism and parallelism.

In opposition to the latter two, eliminativism claims that there are no raw feelings such as desires, no intentionality, and, in general, no mental or conscious states whose contents are distinctly different in their nature from the physical processes or events with which they are correlated or from which they arise. To those who subscribe to eliminativism, the idea of mind and of all its contents as separate entities, are part of an outdated science that recent developments in cognitive science, particularly in behaviorism, now see as false. It is this position that allows Lakoff and Johnson to claim that our thoughts and beliefs do not belong to a separate physical or metaphysical category and thus lack a vocabulary of their own. Rather, our thoughts and beliefs are mere speculations that benefit from metaphorically transferring the terminology of purely subjective (neurophysiological) experience to descriptions of such experiences as if they had a separate existence.

As we saw in the passage above, Lakoff and Johnson regard persons as detailed or complex physical machines. When physicalists refer to "specifics of our everyday functioning in the world," as do Lakoff and Johnson in the passage above, they claim that mental states are responses to external stimuli. The essence of mind is not, therefore, something that is private to the subject, but something that is public and observable because it is produced by the stimulus-response occurrences in the neurological pathways of the brain. "Since reason is shaped by the body," say Lakoff and Johnson, "it is not radically free. . . . Once we have learned a conceptual system, it is neurally instantiated in our brains and we are not free to think just anything. Hence, we have no absolute freedom in Kant's sense, no full autonomy."[26] Most of our thoughts, physicalists claim, are unconscious in the sense that they are part of a system of stimulus-response activity in the brain, so most of the time they take place without our conscious awareness of them. Because they all take place as electromagnetic transmissions and receptions in different parts of the brain, what the writing on my neurosurgeon's office wall called "chemical and electrical activity between neurons," and between the brain and stimuli in the external world, most of our thoughts take place far too rapidly for us to develop conscious awareness of them. But cognitive scientists claim that technological developments now enable them to identify and study precisely these mental operations in response to a variety of stimuli, thus enabling them to understand the structural nature of, say, emotions or language as different kinds of stimuli. This cognitive unconscious is, to use Lakoff and Johnson's expression, "the hidden hand that shapes conscious thought."[27]

How does all this compare with considerations of the same in African thought and with Wiredu's position in particular? In some general sense, Kathryn Geurts endorses Lakoff and Johnson's view that much of what we believe as the axiomatic assumptions by which we judge our experiences can be traced back to the basic sensorimotor structures that connect us to the world, thus, like Lakoff and Johnson, erasing the dichotomies between mind and body, mental and physical states, or mind and the external world that dot the history of this discussion in Western philosophy.[28] She argues that the ways we frame our experiences and build evaluative methods of dealing with theoretical issues related to sensory experience involve cultural variations in the content of sets of sensoria (a Latinized form of "sensoriums," the plural of what she calls the "sensorium," or sensory order) around the world. Because the senses are ways of embodying cultural categories, she says, "a cultural community's sensory order reflects aspects of the world that are so precious to the members of that community that . . . they are the things that children growing up in this culture developmentally come to carry in their very bodies."[29] Geurts observes that despite recent fascinations with the idea of "the sixth sense" in Euro-American cultures and frequent allusions to it when the causes of certain feelings cannot be precisely determined, the idea that experience is overwhelmingly dependent on the five senses has been central to Euro-Americans' definition of experience (until recently). In contrast, for the Anlo-Ewe people of southeastern Ghana, she argues, the idea of balance as a sixth sense is central to the sensory orientation with which they experience and make sense of the world.

Geurts's study is different from that of Lakoff and Johnson in at least one significant way: she does not openly subscribe to physicalism, although she borrows from Lakoff and Johnson's materialist ontology and even endorses their idea of the primacy of the sensorial relatedness to the world as the door to understanding the structure and categories of knowledge. Yet like them, she seems to reduce all conceptual schemes to inner physical processes, assuming thereby not only that matter itself is a simple and unproblematic thing to understand but also that the primacy of neural processes in relation to how we form concepts and make judgments is itself an obvious and unproblematic "fact." Eliminativism, it should be remembered, rejects the distinction between observation and theory. Thus, eliminativists do not consider the realm of judgment to be one that operates on the basis of its own (logical) laws, for, they contend, the "mental" cannot occur without the "physical." In other words, they argue that based solely on empirical investigation, the reason for any brain state (at least in principle) can be explained solely by other physical states.

Wiredu's opposition to dualism could not be more unequivocal; he rejects any attempt to bifurcate reality into irreducible mental and physical substances. Thus, his position contrasts significantly not only with the dominant view in the Western tradition but also with the African views of personhood that take any form of pluralism. But while Wiredu's position must therefore to be located among those of the monists, it is not identical with the type of contemporary behaviorist materialism that pervades the work of Lakoff and Johnson. In the first place, his position casts doubt on the plausibility of what many scholars have embraced as constitutive of dualism in African traditional thought systems, arguing that what appears to be indicative of separate constituents of personhood, for example, might, upon sufficiently serious consideration, be no more than different functions or activities of only one bodily substance. Of these one might mention in particular the example of Yoruba concept of ènìyàn, the person who, at the everyday folkloristic or popular level, is thought of as a living pantheon of sorts, because in the Yoruba conceptual scheme a person is viewed as an amalgam of different divine elements supplied and controlled by the originating divinities.[30] But within the dominant expressive modes in African thought systems, especially the way of expressing abstract ideas, it is likely that the metaphysical problematic resulting from Yoruba expressions is only an apparent one, one that partly results from the failure to understand abstract meanings in the context of the figurative and mythological representations in which they have been expressed. Barry Hallen has provided an analytical explanation and understanding of Yoruba thought about the nature of the person in a way that not only puts the religious metaphors into perspective but also clearly sifts conceptual content convincingly out of its folkloristic sheaths. Needless to say, then, it appears that the difficulty of determining what exactly in conceptual terms the many allegorical terms mean would have to be tackled analytically case by case.[31]

The second issue is whether or not, again as Wiredu argues,[32] the variations of beliefs and practices that constitute human cultures are really only superficial elements of the underlying unity of the species. In his view, "the dualistic conception of body and mind, which is often attributed to Africans, in fact, presupposes a mode of conceptualization that ill-coheres with African traditional thought habits which are frequently empirical, as distinct from empiricist."[33] In another text, Wiredu notes that "this [mind and body problem] and other issues [such as the soul, immortality, or life after death] in the interpretation and evaluation of the Akan concept of a person, remain matters of controversy among Akan philosophers."[34] These two statements are significantly indicative of Wiredu's position regarding the mind-body problem and, generally, the nature of the person, namely that one cannot talk of mind as a thing or entity without explaining *where* such a thing would be located.

First, however, let us see an example of the pluralist interpretation of the African concept of the person, one of the species that Wiredu rejects as incorrect. Anthony Ephirim-Donkor's recent work[35] on the Akan conception of a person points to a pluralist conception of personhood in Akan thought. According to Ephirim-Donkor's Christian-driven analysis, the constituents of personhood in the Akan system of thought can be classified within two distinct categories: capacities that are passed through the genetic processes of biology and capacities that point to the divine (spiritual) nature in humans. The goal of leading a virtuous worldly life, he explains, is to earn admittance to "the immortal community of ancestors called *Nananom Nsamanfo*. This model is predicated on a theory of the personality that has its ontological basis in God (*Nana Nyame*), and the archetypal woman and her children who constituted the ideal *abusua* or matrikin."[36] It is Wiredu's view that Africans' dualist descriptions of the nature of the person have been influenced by the teachings of Christian dualism, which many African scholars at the turn of the century were uncritically eager to embrace. Ephirim-Donkor's work is a good example of Wiredu's point regarding the Christian origin of the dualist view in contemporary African thought, but long before it, in the decade after Vatican Council II, scholarship in African ethnotheology was a vibrant practice as African scholars endeavored to make Africanity and Christianity penetrate each other in what thrived as a dynamic yet precarious relationship. Coming as it did when cultural reaffirmation constituted part of the broader political reawakening and the dismantling of the colonial structures, ethnotheology sought to define and adapt African belief systems to the Christian metaphysical and religious frameworks, thus establishing what Aylward Shorter has called the process of "social and pastoral anthropology."[37] Writing from an evangelical backdrop and with the goal of illustrating how the Akan concept of the person related to the Akan sense of the ideal life as "predicated upon the God-given existential purpose called *nkrabea* [destiny],"[38] Ephirim-Donkor claims that Akan beliefs fit into the wider Christian scheme of the religious world view. Given this objective, Ephirim-Donkor is careful to confine himself to only references that lend support to his dualist exposition while totally avoiding texts, including those by noted Akan scholars, that point to different conclusions.

By putting the mind back into the body, Wiredu's analysis of the African conception of the person solves several moral and epistemological problems that are germane to the dualist conception of the person as they have been articulated throughout much of the history of Western philosophy from the pre-Socratics to the present day. Whether it is cast in the idealistic mode of Plato or in the Aristotelian idioms of the collaboration of the different substances of being, dualism has, until recently, represented the pinnacle of Western metaphysics, epistemology, ethics, and psychology, frequently only modifying the nature of the collaboration between matter and nonmaterial substances, or force. African thought, on the other hand, especially in Wiredu's interpretation, sees nature primarily in its physical sense and fundamentally recognizes the various capacities or dispositions of the body according to its various specifications (species). Human nature in particular is accorded great attention in African thought. In Wiredu's view, every substance either is or is wholly made up of physical particles because everything that is is thought of in physical terms, such as its capacity to occupy space. In Wiredu's account, the Cartesian idea of a nonphysical substance does not make much sense in the Akan mode of thought, because in the Akan scheme of things, the idea of a "spiritual substance," that is, a substance that does not occupy physical space, does not make much sense. It is plausible to believe, however, that the well-functioning brain is the material seat of the capacity that produces mental experiences. As we shall see shortly, these mental experiences are enabled by but are themselves not reducible to the physical functions of the brain, which leads to the question How do mental experiences emerge from the physical properties and functions of the (physical) brain?[39] Wiredu contends that mind, or *adwene* in Akan, is not a constitutive element of personhood, for it is not a substance.[40] Mental predicates and concepts are governed by principles of rationality that do not apply to physical phenomena, objects, or entities.[41] Concepts, which is what meanings ultimately are, are not entities of any sort; they are only significations, the constituents of mind. It is no wonder, then, that, as Wiredu reports, "in the Akan language the word for 'thought' is the same as the word for 'mind'; it is *adwene* in both cases. . . . Mind . . . is the function of thought."[42]

What exactly, then, is thought, and how would it, as a nonphysical *whatever*,[43] arise from the physical state of the brain? Wiredu answers this question rather briefly,[44] but let us assume that the brevity of the treatment of this rather complex issue does not necessarily obfuscate the point. We can summarize it thus: he says that "no reason has been given for supposing that every aspect of every state of a physical entity should be physical. Nor are there any immediate indications of intelligibility in the notion that an aspect of an entity must be supposed itself to be an entity."[45] These statements are a critique of the physicalist view that because cognitive processes from which thought stems are physical (electromagnetic neural processes), thought cannot be anything but an aspect or a state of those processes (what Lakoff and Johnson call the "cognitive unconscious"), meaning, as I understand it, that thought has no ontological difference from the processes that produce it; it too, in the physicalist view, ought to be physical. According to Wiredu's objection, there might be some aspects of some states of some physical entities that are not subject to empirical reduction—that is, not reducible to a state of physical properties. In other words, Wiredu finds unintelligible the claim that only physical properties can be assumed from brain-state theory.

Let us assume that humans are that type of species of animals whose physical makeup includes among other attributes a special physical aspect—the brain—whose functional aspects include, in addition to the physical states such as those described on the framed writing on my neurosurgeon's examination room wall (neurons firing electric charges to each other), also an aspect that is nonphysical. The latter is what we know as thought, the process by which we form (or the state of having) concepts. Thought is complex in that although its existence is rooted in the material (that is, in the specific type of and functioning of the physical brain), neither the physical processes of the brain nor the physical domain are sufficient in themselves to produce it. Imagine a baby who is several days old, for example. Although the baby can perceive objects around him or her as different as he or she lies in the crib (as evidenced by the movements of his or her eyes to follow moving objects or by his or her reflex reactions when touched), babies normally would not be able to *tell* the differences between the objects of his or her perception. But I can imagine a quick objection to this position, namely that if the said infant was standing before my desk now, he or she would not need an additional training to *see* that many different objects are sitting on it; he or she would be able to identify as distinct from each other any two objects on this overly crowded desk. One of the reasons for this perceptual competence is that, apart from the required normalcy of that part of our physical constitution that controls visual perception, we easily perceive the different qualities of objects—whether they are rough or smooth, hard or soft, large or small, hot or cold. But to assume that one would learn nothing by, say, hearing from others what specific objects are called would be tantamount to claiming that one does not learn anything of the objects they have seen and touched since birth when they are told that "this is a computer," and "this is a book, and the other a pen, and so on." This is not likely, simply because "knowing that this is a pen" is neither identical with nor reducible to the electrochemical magnetic states that seeing or touching a pen triggers in the brain. Furthermore, as Wiredu himself argues, some concepts, such as nonexistence, addition, sameness, nothingness, necessity, and so on, have no empirical origins. Although conceptualization occurs on the basis of the law-like capabilities of the specific type of brain that human beings have, we need to acquire and master the concepts that come with the package of language acquisition if we are to have the ability to recognize and apply concepts. Communication, then, complements and completes the potentialities of the physical (biological) structures that we have, or are, as human beings. In other words, communication is an inevitable circumstance of the occurrence of thought and therefore an essential means by which we become persons, not just human beings.

The contrasts between Wiredu's view and the views expressed in the examples from Western thought (or some African versions of these views) support the conclusion that Wiredu's monism differs remarkably from hard materialism or robust physicalism. Let us call his position "moderate physicalism," because by attributing thought to a disposition or capacity characteristic of the specific type of brain humans have, it occupies a narrow but significantly unique space between dualism and hard materialism, thus escaping the rift that characterizes the history of the philosophy of mind in Western philosophy. The capacity to conceptualize in the manner characteristic of humans is part of the law-like response to stimulus that enables humans to achieve their specific difference from other organisms. Mind, on this account, Wiredu says, "is the function of thought."[46]

Persons as Products of Community

Being a person and being a human being are not the same thing. We are human beings by virtue of the particular biological organism that we are. Our biological type defines us as a species among other living things, and it involves, among other things, having the kind of brain that we possess and all the activities that this kind of brain is naturally endowed to perform. Many conscious and unconscious experiences belong to this state. The systemic functions of our bodies, including both sensory experiences and the psychological acts of memory and imagination, belong here too. Being a person, on the other hand, involves other capacities in addition to those I have mentioned. As persons we are not only able to perform or do what our organism enables us to or what our organism inclines us to do by virtue of its *specifically* (species-specific) natural or mechanistic ends but also to organize, vary, and order these functions in the service of socioculturally imposed ends. For example, the sensations that we associate with the idea of pain or of pleasure belong to the body, as do our reflex responses to them. But as members of specific communities, we learn to control some reflex reactions to specific sensations because of what our culture tells us is the value of such control—for example, being able to hide the behavior associated with the feeling of pain when we are undergoing a ritualistic circumcision or the extraction of teeth. So we harden our nerves during those procedures because our culture has told us that bravery (or the public show of it) is a virtue and that those who fail the test of bravery are publicly ridiculed. In other words, pride and shame become socially generated norms on the basis of which we control the physical processes of our bodies. And because these ideals and defects are modeled by others within the sociocultural contexts to which they apply, we often associate them either with heroes we wish to imitate or with weak individuals whose pusillanimity we strive to differ from—just as Okonkwo of Chinua Achebe's *Things Fall Apart* strove to prove he was different from his father, who was perceived to be unindustrious. Because they relate to the realm of valuation, some of these normative principles vary from place to place among different groups of human beings, thus revealing the unlimited variety of ways of manifesting or acting out our common human-beingness, or humanity. Learning to participate in any one or more of these specific ways of being human takes place as a process and grows by the degrees of our competence. The Luo saying that "age nurtures wisdom" (*luor lwar*) is not a claim that all elderly people will be counted as wise people by virtue of their age alone. Rather, it expresses a maxim, an expectation or desire that people should strive to improve their knowledge of the world to the best possible level that long life may give them the opportunity to do. This process of depending on others for the tools that enable us to associate with them on a growing scale of competence is the process that makes us into persons. In other words, we become persons through acquiring and participating in the socially generated knowledge of norms and actions that we learn to live by in order to impose humaneness upon our humanness.

But how, then, does Wiredu's functional theory of mind stem from what I have claimed to be his brand of philosophical anthropology? According to Wiredu, mind would not be possible without communication. Communication, he says, "makes the mind."[47] We have seen that he rejects dualism. Also, we have seen that although his position is built upon the empirical evidence of how humans develop into fully functional persons through their full and appropriate biological growth and development, especially the development of their brains, his monism does not embrace the reductive physicalism of contemporary cognitive or psychological sciences. He maintains, in contrast to hard materialism, that there is a radical ontological difference between mind or concepts as the function of thought and matters of the physical realm. In general terms, then, he maintains that through the empirical evidence that is available, we produce concepts (or thoughts and beliefs) in and about our world only as products stimulated by other people's communication. As some philosophically minded anthropologists observe in their discussion of African concepts of personhood and agency, "by locating thought within the body, the [African] model avoids the Cartesian split which beggars so much ethnographical description and leads to false antinomies between the rational mind and the disorderly life of the body and the emotions. . . . [It] seem[s] to escape the everyday appearance of things with metaphors, images and actions which dramatically transform our experience."[48] Indeed, according to this view, neither a substantialist view of the person (such as the views of Western philosophers such as Aristotle, Descartes, and Locke) nor a view of the person as a stream of sensations (as found in Hume's associationist view) are independently tenable, since human experience includes both modalities. Actual thought formation, the end of the reaction to communicative stimulation, epitomizes and completes the particular functional capacity that is attributable to being a person.[49]

Being as a Relational Category

Wiredu does not consider relationality to be an isolated foundation of personhood; in a system where empirical experience is basic, and in a world that is thought of as primarily constituted of its physical conditions, relationality is the condition or context of all existence. His philosophical anthropology recognizes the biological constitution of humans as a necessary but not sufficient basis of personhood, because human beings require gradual sociogenic development to become persons. This relational condition circumstantiates not only the physical existence of things and our development into persons but also our cognitive and moral experience of the world. Wiredu defends the view that "there is no equivalent, in Akan, of the existential 'to be' or 'is' of English, and that there is no way of pretending in that medium to be speaking of the existence of something which is not in space." This is because, he says, "in the Akan language to exist is to *wo ho,* which, in literal translation, means 'to be at some place.'"[50] In the Akan expression, existence is always locative, in relation to something else. In other words, existence is an attribute of things in their relation to other objects or to place. The notion of the transcendental self in the philosophies of Descartes and Kant as absolutely autonomous is hard for the Akan to comprehend and to express in their language. Expressing in Akan the notions of abstract existence, or of creation ex nihilo,[51] becomes cumbersome and calls for further examination of the basis of such metaphysical notions as are found in Western philosophical and religious traditions and of the epistemological theories and concepts that derive from them. The Akan think of god in quite naturalistic terms; they see god as someone like a "cosmic architect [and] fashioner of the world order, who occupies the apex of the same hierarchy of being which accommodates, in its intermediate ranges, the ancestors and living mortals, and, in its lower reaches, animals, plants, and inanimate objects."[52] According to this metaphysical edifice, all beings exist in nearly the same plane—empirically. God and ancestors alike are thought of as existing and acting in time and in space, although they are not constrained in their actions by speed and geographical limits and are subject to at least most of the mores that guide humans. They are held in respect, and their friendship and favors are courted and sustained through a variety of symbolic acts such as those that constitute ritual and sacrifice.[53] In their standard forms, these acts indicate respect and inspire friendship and favors from those we associate with in our human-social domain. Thus, while the acts are a means of affirming the existence of such spirits as god and ancestors and indicate human respect toward them as well as the belief that the favors asked of them will be granted, the offerings to them are merely symbolic because there is no belief that either god or the ancestors will actually take or consume the offerings made to them in ritual as living humans would do.

I just referred to the concept of "truth." It is reasonable to assume that because of the central role truth plays in cognition, when we make the claim that we know something, the proposition that expresses knowledge must be true in order for us to have knowledge. Truth appears to be a more integral part of the definition of knowledge than other elements of that definition. But Wiredu argues that assuming that our propositions are true, especially in the correspondence sense, amounts to assuming too much about what they are capable of delivering. In English-language philosophy, knowledge has been understood to be a special type of belief—that which is true and also that which we are justified in believing. Great discussions may (and in fact do) arise regarding the type, nature, and degree of justification (or about what needs to count as necessary and sufficient justification) that is required for belief to constitute knowledge.[54] But to the extent that knowledge is some sort of content of the mind or consciousness, it is melded or identified with belief but is separated from other types of belief by its truth and its justification for being believed. In other words, as distinct from other types of belief, knowledge has a truth conditional. But as we shall see a little later, at least some versions of African thought object to the idea that knowledge can be a species (a particular type) of belief, as the two do not conceptually belong together. Hallen and Sodipo demonstrate that the Yoruba language does not separate truth and belief by the thin veil of justification alone, as English-speaking philosophers have tended to do. Yoruba language further separates knowledge from belief by virtue of the origin of each or, more precisely, by how they are acquired. In Yoruba, knowledge, *mò*, must be acquired first hand; anyone claiming knowledge must be a first-person witness to his or her claims. Everything else, even with the best and most trustable justification, is only belief, *gbàgbó*, not knowledge, *mò*. ("The one you use your own eyes to see and which your *okòn* witnesses you that it is [the case, or true,] *òótó*—this is the best.")[55] If anyone were to learn their respective languages well and seek in them contrasting views of how they affect our understanding of the theoretical issues aligned with their uses, they would discover a variety of understandings of those issues. It is important, however, to note that the type of pluralism Wiredu recommends is not one that endorses a coexistence of incompatible views. Wiredu's position is, rather, that the human species is universally bonded in all those things that matter for the species (such as norms of thought and communication) and are uniformly common among and between all humans cross-culturally, cross-nationally, and intersubjectively. It seems, then, that the type of pluralism he endorses is one that opens doors to a comparative approach to philosophy by textually and pedagogically integrating diverse perspectives into the philosophical discussion of a wide range of issues; it sees traditions of thought on a par with each other at the center of a universal philosophical discourse without drawing demarcations. Without conceding anything to relativism, this scheme, because it is built on a universal approach of a philosophical-anthropological analysis, should work equally well at both the interpersonal and intercultural levels.

Wiredu's notion of cultural universalism is based on a pan-psychological position—namely on the form of the mind rather than on its content—and suggests the view that the enabling conditions of mind, or the cognitive structure and process(es) through which knowledge and other forms of consciousness are formulated and expressed and that are the very basis of the idea of mind and of personhood as a whole, are the same in all members of the human species by virtue of the fact that they are the same biological type. The basic characteristics of the biological type that all humans share are many, but in the epistemic domain they include, in concurrence with Kant, the *conditio sine qua non* of thought, the formal rules of thought that, according to Wiredu, give humans their "biologico-cultural identity as *homines sapientes*. At the very minimum this status implies that we are organisms that go beyond instinct in the drive for equilibrium and self-preservation in specific ways [by which he means ways peculiar to the species], namely, by means of reflective perception, abstraction, deduction, and induction,"[56] just as grammar provides the formal rules of language. Thus, from an epistemic perspective, these rules of thought are the basis of the operational similarity among all members of the human species in matters that are essential to the practice or conduct of human life.

In view of the nonmonadological view of human nature, Wiredu's *Cultural Universals and Particulars* provides a defining and grounding framework for African modes of thought. It poses the fundamental question that could be re-framed as follows: What would the philosophical theories as we have been made to know them look like if one were to change the basic underlying sociological assumption—the category of the subject—upon which they are built? The backdrop of this question is what Wiredu refers to as the "radically un-Kantian concept of the person" in African thought.

As I described briefly earlier, Kant's concept of the person exemplifies a long-standing and dominant tradition in Western philosophy that views the person as a metaphysically complete unit of faculties that make him or her a transcendentally autonomous moral and cognitive agent. As epitomized in Kant's three *Critiques,* such a view extends to an understanding of human intellect as a self-sufficient tool because the individual person is regarded as autonomously related to the world through the functioning of the faculties in the three major areas of that relationship to the world (although its unencumbered freedom exists only in the moral domain, while in metaphysics and epistemology its encounter with the a priori structural conditions of the outside world exists only in its comprehension of the phenomenological reality). The individual, then, as an integral agent and not just in terms of the functioning of his or her faculties, is regarded as the most basic and primary fact, and his or her status of autonomy becomes the measure of all things: correspondence of his or her intellect to reality becomes the measure of truth and his or her happiness becomes the goal of moral and political ends. The individual reigns supreme as the unquestionable and axiomatic point of all inquiry, making that famous Protagorean saying (that humans are the measure of all things; of things that are, that they are, and of things that are not, that they are not) more than a merely rhetorical reference to the emerging world of cultural change that followed the Peloponnesian wars and the realization, as recorded by Thucydides, that historical process was determined, not by the gods, as Herodotus had falsely thought, but by natural causes. Some aspects of the wisdom of the Sophists, such as the view that no perception or judgment is more true than another except that some are more useful and that the more useful should be followed, may make better sense today than they did to people in the subsequent history who relied on Plato's characterization of their teaching. At the same time, however, the Protagorean dictum (that "humans are the measure . . .") may, by a different interpretation, have been precisely what led to epistemological objectivism: the view that there is a reality out there that can be known as it is by the mind. Despite its later Kantian modification, the view of the person as an autonomous individual endowed with an engine for truth has lingered as an a priori truth with few exceptions until recently.[57] Consequently, it became customary to assume that propositions or claims about the external world can be assessed by determining the relation between objects and the individual's rendition of them. Whether it is thought of as an entity or simply as the ability to reason or understand, the (individual) mind is thought of in Western philosophy as a self-sufficient and independent agent and, excepting cases of defect or illness, every individual mind should be regarded to be as good as any other because they all function on the basis of a constitutive (that is, metaphysical), nonpersonal (disinterested) relationship with the world.[58] Such a view is likely to develop a theorization of the world that sets values, whether they be cognitive (what is true), moral (what is good), or aesthetic (what is beautiful), as if they themselves were pre-specified and independently true descriptions that human reason can and should be able independently to find or discover, provided that specific rules of procedure are followed and the functional purity of the mind is present and preserved.[59] It is clear that if one assumes such a primal view of the individual as subject, not only will their understanding of the nature of knowledge be aligned to such an assumption but also their definitions of values, such as what the nature of moral and political goals are, who the chief beneficiary such goals is, how these goals should be pursued and protected, will similarly be aligned to such a view of the person.

It can be assumed, then, that when Wiredu says of African metaphysical conceptions that they are radically un-Kantian and stand in striking contrast to much of Western thought, such differences can be extended to include, at least in part (and a significant part, for that matter), a difference in the conception of the nature of the person.[60] In Wiredu's view, then, subtle cultural differences and similarities, both at the ordinary practical level of everyday life and at the level of theoretical idealizations of the ends of human endeavor, are to be found precisely in how the category of the individual or person is laid out.[61]

Body, Mind, and Meanings: The Discernment

In Wiredu's rendition of African thought, persons are members of that biological species of organisms—humans—whose nature (specific difference) is the capacity of their organism to develop thought, also called the formulation of concepts. This capacity is set off into actual manifestation by communication, first from others. Later, as the individual matures, she learns to actively and critically process such communication, which is the basis of that special tool called mind, in which concepts reside and with which, by use of concepts developed by and within the mind, she determines various principles for relating to the world around her and to other people. According to this conception, it is difficult to think of persons outside the social circumstantiation of their development and function. Every individual person has this special relationship to the world as an individual, on the one hand, and an essential relationship to others as the source of meaning-making, on the other. What we "know" of the world does not and cannot emerge from only one of these two sides of our relation to the world. Rather, what we "know" of the world is a constant striving to reconcile both sides of our relation to the world, namely, reconciling what we (empirically) experience as a stream of physical stimuli with "what" we have learned these stimuli to "be" or to mean. This, as I understand it, is the philosophical-anthropological condition of personhood that grounds the epistemological theory of "truth as opinion." Imagine, for example, walking down a city street or in a rural neighborhood when something catches your attention: you have a visual perception of a glare coming uniquely and in isolation from a source around the corner. The uniqueness and distinctness is due to the fact that everything you turn to look at triggers a separate stream of sensations that constitute your empirical experience. As I noted earlier, we are exposed to many different experiences each time we look around us. From a purely physical point of view, our experiences are mute: they do not *mean* anything by their sheer and primitive physical occurrence along except for the different sensations they create in us. But because one of the things we were taught while growing up was how to identify the different streams of sensations by attaching conventional codes to them—such as color codes (red, blue, etc.) to visual sensations—you now relate this particular experience with what you learned was called "light" in terms of the type of thing and "red" in terms of color. So you determine or conclude that what you just saw *was* "red light." Your individual (or basically biological) constitution enabled you to perceive the sensation in the way you did. Besides that, what your biological circumstance allowed you to perceive may also have been subject to other factors, for example, if the light you saw was far away on a rainy night. But your judgment that "what" you have perceived "is a red light" is your association of your sensations with what you have learned such sensations are to be identified as. This particular experience is just one among many that you have learned to make sense of. In addition, there may be other meanings (such as "it is a traffic light," and "it means that I must not drive through the intersection") associated with the primary one ("this is a red light") that are not always or necessarily related to the primary experience. But whether or not what you perceived was indeed "a red light" is not only a whole new matter (regarding truth), it also depends on how we reconcile our private perception with the public meaning we have learned is associated with what this kind of perception "means" or is about. Wiredu explains that in Akan, because of the multiple intervening conditions under which perception regularly takes place, emphasis is shifted from the idea that there should be correspondence between our perception and the perceived object (*adaeguatio rei et intellectus*) and toward the truthfulness of reporting what we believe we are perceiving. Thus, in the Akan scheme of things, although the statement "I see a red light" describes what it is that I believe I am perceiving, it is only my opinion. To say that something is so means just that, namely "as I see it." It is our responsibility to report correctly or truthfully because genuine and useful inquiry can emerge and progress only from such truthful reporting. In other words, according to African modes of thought, at least as exposed by Wiredu, the nature of mind and the thoughts that reside in it are conscious states and are therefore subjective: what they convey about the external world can only be a point of view. This position favors a dialogical sense of truth over the objectivist one.

Wiredu argues that if the fundamental goal of communication is to share meanings or significations with other people (which it is), then, at least by assumption, meanings or significations must be the kind of "things" that are universally accessible to all people who engage in communication as a basic and species-defining human practice. Meanings surpass the finiteness of either their referents or the forms of their culturally specific (that is, linguistic) expressions. Meanings are objective, not in the sense suggested by the conceptual realists or as implied in negations by their conceptualist adversaries but in the sense that they can be accessed by anyone who, by virtue of having a sound brain, is capable of formulating and subsequently using them competently to participate in communication. Yet, Wiredu observes, the history of Western philosophy is fraught with mistakes regarding what is meant by the idea that "meanings are objective." While Platonists defended the view that because meanings are objective, they must be "entities" of some sort, thus envisaged as existing separately and independently of human minds, conceptualists, in an exaggerated opposition to the Platonists, argued that if meanings were not entities, they either were not real or they did not exist. Clearly, the two positions pulled away from each other on account of the "thingness" of ideas or meanings: either they are "things" or they are nothing (empty names). In Wiredu's view, both sides are making the same mistake. He contends that if meanings were entities, they could not be explained, as doing so would regressively require recourse to a third entity, ad infinitum. More important, however, is his question about whether it is the case that for anything to be real it has to be an entity. To answer this question in the negative sends us, as it has sent many philosophers since Plato first broached his theory of Forms, to search further for the exact nature of meanings and their role in clarifying the (social) conditioning of human mind and knowing.[62]

There is no doubt that philosophical concern with the idea of meaning as the object of determinate understanding or definition has occupied a central place in analytic metaphysics since the inception of analytic philosophy as a movement in the latter part of the last century. But preoccupation with what kind of "things" the contents of mind are is by no means only recent, nor is it linked solely to the influence of the Vienna School. As a matter of fact, there are thinkers, such as the Tanganyikan (or Tanzanian, as he would have been referred to in the post-Union era) Swahili poet and essayist Shaaban Robert, who have deliberated on such matters from outside the confines of Western philosophy completely. Two of his books, *Kusadikika* (*The Nature of Belief,* in rough English translation), and *Kufikirika* (*The Nature of Ideas,* in similarly rough English translation) are particularly significant. However that may be, analytical considerations of meaning as the conventional, common, or standard sense of an expression, construction, or sentence in a given language, including nonverbal signals or symbols, reveals a rich view of categories and subcategories of what meanings are. What is particularly interesting about meaning in our current discussion is its association with the concept of mind that we have identified to be African or, more precisely, Akan, using Wiredu's interpretation.

So far, we have seen that the Akan think of mind as real but not as an entity. Its realism is functional and describes a special capacity of the type of biological organism human beings are. Such realism of the mind is manifested in how we participate in communication as a special stimulus-reaction process among members of the species. Meaning is, then, at least in this view, the core of communication;[63] it is among communicants what one person intends to communicate and another to apprehend by a particular utterance, bearing in mind different aspects or "types" of meaning that may come into play even in just one communicative act.[64] Meanings are what the mind is designed to handle, and handling meanings is a mental activity called thinking. This is why Wiredu asserts that "mind is the function of thought," an assertion that appears to save the accompanying saying—namely that "meanings exist in the mind"—from being merely rhetorical, although these assertions should give anyone some difficulty with setting the logical sequence (which comes first?) between mind and meanings or concepts. The solution, I believe, should come from considering the developmental process by which humans spring from the physical state to one that is significantly human—namely, one that springs from the pure perception of the different objects on my desk to one that adds meanings to the physical experiences such as happens when we are told that "this is a pen" and "that other object over there is a computer," and "the other one is a book," and so on. They are the nonphysical aspects or accompaniments of perception in its physical or sensory sense. This accompaniment involves social dependency but is not a physical necessity. In other words, meanings are not necessarily entailed by our sensory experiences like the sensation of a sharp feeling of pain is entailed by the piercing of our bare skin by the tip of a sharp pin (unless the nerve endings in that part of our body are dead).

However, we are members of a species whose older members have a duty to the species to embrace new members and teach them the "meanings" of what they perceive physically or through their senses. This process of accommodation, in which the new members learn the "meanings" and the older members teach that content, is necessary for the survival of the species. In addition to this physical benefit, dependence on others furnishes us with what we need to become competent functioning members of the species. Through communication, older folk enable us to become mentally functional in ways that characterize our species. We first become capable, then we actually begin to form and organize thoughts, concepts, and beliefs by which we make sense of the world around us. We learn to develop and organize these in order to improve the quality of our lives by developing moral principles and ethical standards to regulate our conduct. The intervention of society is, in this sense, a necessary requirement for our growth and development into what our physical makeup is prepared for but is unable to attain by itself. It is in this sense of a specifically human life that meanings are necessary, but they have no necessary relationship with anything in the external world whose sense they are designed to convey. In their various forms, meanings derive from established locutionary or symbolic senses that make communication possible. Put in other words, meanings are the assigned property of locutions by virtue of which any two or more communicants actually do or assume they can share the contents of their minds.[65]

From a pragmatic point of view, communication, with all the meanings it has, comes by means of specific linguistic (or other compensatory symbolic) expressions as one of the instruments of our human enculturation. But as a capacity of humans, the mind is not restricted by the pragmatic particularisms of our communication. Rather, its universal character as a special capacity of the species so endowed is what enables it to form meanings as, in most cases, the universal aspects of objects and contents of real languages. Thus the close relationship between mind and language makes the study of language an extension of the study of mind. The human phenomenon of language use stimulates the functions of the mind, and it is through this process that the mind develops.[66] Language and mind and the relations between them do not have to be entities to be real and are defined by their anthropological role of enabling humans to become competent members of their species. On the basis of these ideas of mind and, by implication, ideas of meanings or thought and language, we can say that the Akan view humans as mutually dependent rational animals.

For Wiredu, communication is made possible by the universal character of meanings. When other people's utterances are not immediately accessible to us by virtue of the unfamiliar specificity of tongue, still the meanings they convey can successfully be sifted and recovered through translation. To say, then, that meanings are superior to the culturally specific and limited communicative mediums by which they are transmitted and received implies that they are more general than the culturally multiple and idiosyncratic human languages by which we communicate within the groups to which we belong. Irrespective of the specific primary languages they have been trained to speak, all human beings who are properly biologically developed and healthy are thereby capacitated, or "wired," so to speak, to process meaning. This capacity is initially passive from a physical standpoint and therefore would be of no significant consequence, in the social-human or communicative sense, if the relational *practicum* of communication did not activate it.[67] It is dependent on society. In other words, although our biological nature enables us to be "physically conscious" of thought (that is, to process the stimuli coming from the world around us by means of the system of sensors composed of cells and neurons), the type of consciousness that is specific to humans is realized only in the company of and by learning from other humans by means of communication. Biology provides us with the grounding of the universal capacity, including the laws on the basis of which meaning is constructed, but society provides the condition under which we functionally complete this biological order as persons by stimulating the brain into forming thoughts and, thereupon, the appearance of mind.

What, finally, do we learn from Wiredu's rich and complicated rendition of an African concept of meanings? In general analytical terms, Wiredu views meanings as mental contents of consciousness. They are real and natural and therefore are, in this respect, not dependent on us in the sense of being arbitrary or relative. Rather, they are ingrained in the communicative nature of mind and thus are the very basis of what makes us persons. They arise, "live (in the mind, of course)," and fulfill their role by means of special laws.[68] Meanings can be transferred from one person or speaker to another not only by virtue of their abstract nature in relation to their referents but also because they can be translated from the characteristics of the specific tongues in our culturally and empirically diverse world. It is on the strength of this position that relativism dissipates rather quickly from Wiredu's philosophy. In his view, communication would be unimaginably difficult (if not outright impossible) in a relativistic world. Without meanings and without the universal character of meanings, we wouldn't comprehend and communicate to others (about) the world around us.

It is important, however, to keep in mind that the world of meanings that Wiredu describes is not set a priori. Such a world was possible only to Plato and his followers. A carefully considered philosophical anthropology quickly pokes holes in that view, for we do not simply "find" such a world. Comprehension is established through inquiry.[69]

Humans who are deprived—by impairment, for example—of the ability to communicate are deprived of something fundamental to their nature, namely full participation in the world of persons. It is not uncommon that the realization of the severity of such deprivation in individuals tends to lead family members to seek a variety of remedies to lessen the degree to which communicatively incapacitated persons can or will miss out on this basic human function. Both social (symbolic) and technological conventions and inventions (such as sign language or hearing and speech aids) for enhancing the reception and transmission of meaning for persons who are communicatively challenged biologically are compensatory means aimed at making it possible for such persons to gain and experience some reasonable and appreciable degree of the expectations of a "normal" human life. But if a person were to be born with a total lack of capacity for communication, including the absence of the capacity to use or benefit from such mediative interventions, we would likely engage in debates about the humanness of such a person's condition.[70] With high probability, such debates partly would revolve around such questions as whether people so severely incapacitated had enough brain function to develop mind, which is the basis for participating in the world of meanings. Indeed, the severity of such incapacitation would be deemed to be commensurate with such a person's inability to perceive, recognize, understand, and appropriately respond to the world around them.

Akan and Other Theories of Mind: More Comparisons

In Wiredu's reading of Akan philosophical anthropology as it relates to psychology, mind originates in society as a reaction to communicative stimuli, which is part of what the human brain does in the complex manner that is specific to that species. Clearly, Wiredu adopts a quasi-physicalist brand of monism according to which the existence of mind is not denied but is defined as an integral and essential or inalienable aspect of the ways that the normal (fully developed and healthy) human organism functions. Just as the bright light emitted by a light bulb is neither identical to nor exists independently of the wires on which it depends for its "existence," so the mind is neither identical with nor exists independently of the materiality of the brain that makes it possible, and it would be unsatisfactory to conclude only that it is physical like those things on which it necessarily depends or it must be an entity of a completely different, opposed (i.e., nonphysical) nature. Rather, the mind is the natural function of the relations between the parts of the brain that respond to certain stimuli whenever certain conditions obtain. According to Wiredu, because the unique characteristic of the specifically human organism is the communication of meanings, the defining uniqueness is made possible by a process that necessitates the development of the capacity, which itself is completely dependent for its existence on the organic (biological) capacity of humans to both encode and transmit meanings and to receive and decode the same from other persons, animals, and objects, just as the glow of light is dependent for its existence on the material nature of heat-conducting wire.

Wiredu's view on the nature of communication and on the related idea of the nature of mind is both novel and familiar. It is new because it avoids the double dualism[71] that characterizes the history of the subject in Western philosophy, as it is neither hard materialist nor spiritualist. Because of its dependence on the biological nature of the species, (the existence of) mind is not thinkable outside the biological nature of humans, yet it is neither matter itself nor is it (in my reading of Wiredu) reducible to a material reaction (such as an electrochemical reaction). At the same time, it is not a spiritual entity; it is not immediately evident outside the biological nature of humans because it is dependent upon empirical experience. Finally, according to the Akan language, as Wiredu reports, existence is locative, so anything asserted to exist would have to occupy space, whether real or metaphorical, and, according to him, the Akan do not talk of the mind in such locative terms.

Mind, then, is not thought of independently of the body but as a status enjoyed by one part of it, the brain. It is in this sense that mind can be said to be quasi-material. In the American tradition, Richard Taylor,[72] among others, is a well-known contemporary exponent of the metaphysical view that reality consists of matter and that this includes what we call mind. Another well-known American philosopher whose work in the philosophy of mind and cognitive science supports the materialist conception of the mind is Daniel Dennett, who has written widely on mind in terms of "content" and "consciousness," two themes that he believes to be basic to the philosophy of mind.[73] Dennett is known for arguing that a creature (or, more generally, as Wiredu's position appears to regard it, a system), say S, possesses states of mind if and only if the ascription of such states to S facilitates explanation and prediction of S's behavior. When put that way, it quickly becomes clear that Dennett's S could be anything from a human being to a monkey or a computer. According to him, we could explain such behaviors according to different "stances" or approaches. If we claimed the explanatory or predictive nature of such systems by ascribing beliefs and desires to S, we would be taking what he calls the *intentional stance*—in other words, we claim that S has mind because we argue that S seems to have intentions. Or we could take a *design stance* if we regarded S to be some kind of engineered system or even a *physical stance* if we regarded S as a purely physical system. We find, however, that although intentions, thoughts, opinions, ideas, and designs are not entities, they are not dispositions either.

Wiredu would say that they consist of ideas or concepts. It follows, then, that although Wiredu shares with Dennett the nonsubstance view of mind, he still distinguishes clearly between his dispositional and Dennett's ideational sense of "mind." He says that "these two senses, unlike the substance and non-substance pair, are not contradictories. A disposition is a potentiality, and its actual exercise may take the form of a concep-tualization. Therefore, far from being contradictories, the disposition and its ideational actualization may be thought of as complementary phases of mind. Nevertheless, it is important to distinguish them clearly."[74] Wiredu's view that "mind" is a disposition is made even clearer on the strength of the difference between how he defines mind and how he defines "spirit," or whatever it is that is believed to survive the physical death of humans. He says that it is hard to characterize the latter, because "it is not of identically the same type as the material body, and yet it is not of a dia-metrically opposed category; it is, as the phrase goes, a cross between the two."[75] Spirits, it would appear, are the metaphorical analogues of humans; they are metaphorical beings that occupy (exist in) metaphorical space. He says: "In Akan thinking there is, in my opinion, nothing analogous to the soul, which appears to be conceived as an entity that is responsible for animation and also forethought. . . . It seems to me to be a distinct advantage not to identify the mind with any sort of entity. Thereby one avoids the category mistake of hypostatizing what is arguably a capacity into a substance."[76] Spirits, in his view, are considered to be "entities" only in a metaphorical sense because they are described as occupying or moving in metaphorical spaces. In the Western tradition generally, a mix of materialist and ideational conceptions of mind can be traced backward in history through people such as Hume, Locke, Hobbes, Leibniz, and Spinoza to the classical times of Democritus. Most recently, in Britain, the list of adherents to the ideational variety has included people such as the famous Gilbert Ryle, whose position, as articulated in his *The Concept of Mind,* is so close to that of Wiredu. Ryle's position, expressed in his famous objection to dualism (the view, famously attributed to Descartes, that there must be something separate from the body that does the thinking, a position now ascribed, as a result of Ryle's critique of Descartes, to the mistake popularly known as "the category mistake"), states that we make such a mistake when we assume that new concepts resulting from consideration of the function of an entity indicate the existence of a new entity separate from that which performs the function. Ryle observed that this mistake, notably made by Descartes, led to the view that the concept mind, which is a functional concept, indicated the existence of something—to be called mind—that is a separate substance from the body. This mentalism, he contended, introduces a "ghost in the machine" view of mind in relation to the body. There appears to be an element of this "Rylean view" in Wiredu's position, because, like Wiredu's, Ryle's view is also of the nonsubstance variety. Ryle's position, however, does not account for the mind as a capacity or disposition of the "person" (*onipa* in Akan) to produce the nonmaterial ideas or concepts. Ryle, for example, argues that mind is the functional component of self, which is to be understood as made of both body and mind. When one sees a self, they have seen mind as well because, like a military battalion, the self is made up of different "functional divisions" that have sense and existence only to the extent that they are the inextricable part of what the self-"battalion" is.

The view that it is *onipa*, the person, who thinks is especially significant because it points to the typically African relational nature of personhood as the basis of this quasi-material theory of mind. According to this perspective, the person is not only the physical entity we encounter every day. His or her makeup is also such that the person has different instruments with which he or she performs different functions. Legs are the instruments for walking; they are not agents in their own independent right. The brain is the instrument of thought, that part or aspect of the person with the status for producing thought.

Finally, there is one similarity between Wiredu's position and one once suggested by John Locke that is both important and particularly interesting. The seventeenth-century British philosopher is credited with suggesting that there is no contradiction in the notion that God might have added to matter the power of thought. It must be quickly added, however, that while many Western materialist theories of the mind, such as that of Richard Taylor or Daniel Dennett, are based on the identity theory that claims that mind and body (brain) are one and the same thing, Wiredu's theory, as I have tried to show, separates the two (because the mind is not reducible to an "entity") without accepting dualism.

Wiredu's position, based on the method of philosophical anthropology, expresses the view that humans are relationally interdependent for both survival and self-realization. Later I will compare Wiredu's view of mind as based on the analysis of Twi with one extracted from Dholuo. Obviously, as Wiredu himself urges, it would be interesting to compare this view with analyses of various other African conceptions of the person to determine whether various categories implied in such conceptions indicate or refer to body, mind, and possible other elements as separate substances or only as capacities produced by the organically specific type of the (human) body.

Mind and Immortality in Akan Thought

Apart from the pluralist-monist problem that Wiredu's theory of the person raises in African metaphysics, its implications for the equally hitherto widely accepted views on immortality require serious debate. Immortality is a false consequence of the view that posits mind, and whatever else is thought to accompany mind, to be "entities" that heave off from the body at death because mind and body are not only separate substances, they are of such opposed natures that according to Leibniz's law, they must be different if their qualities are not just different but are distinct and stand in contrast to each other. In ancient Greece, Aristotle thought, unlike Plato, that although it is matter that individuates things, no form can exist apart from the particular substance in which it is instantiated. So, he says, "the soul is inseparable from its body."[77] Earlier, he says that "there seems to be no case in which the soul can act or be acted upon without involving the body. . . . Thinking seems the most probable exception; but if this too proves to be a form of imagination or to be impossible without imagination, it too requires a body as a condition of its existence. If there is any way of acting or acted upon proper to soul, soul will be capable of separate existence; if there is none, its separate existence is impossible."[78] This Aristotelian position was hardly clear with respect to immortality of the soul since Aristotle thought of forms as universals instantiated by the body to give each person his or her individual identity. Not so for later philosophers, especially those who considered this issue with eyes raised toward the Christian faith and its teachings on resurrection. Aquinas, for example, taught that the soul does not need the body for thinking. In his view, the soul, which is made to unite with the body, is what makes it possible for a human person to perform human operations—such as thought, desire, and so on—of which the body is not capable. Moreover, he argues, since all corruption occurs through the separation of form from matter, there cannot be a corruption of the intellectual substance, the light of the soul, because, "where there is no composition of matter and form, there can be no separation of them; neither, then, can there be corruption."[79] Aquinas spends much time demonstrating that even by virtue of its function—namely that it is the agent for apprehending universal and incorruptible objects as such—the human soul, which is an intellectual substance, is not corrupted by being separated from the body.[80] We see from these accounts, therefore, that whatever it is that survives death and however it must be in that later state, belief in immortality is grounded in the claim of substance dualism as the nature of humans, a claim made popular by Descartes in his *Meditations*.

So far we have seen that Wiredu denies that mind is an entity distinguishable from the biological makeup of personhood. Hence, from his point of view, the conception of mind as an entity, as occurs in the Cartesian *Meditation II*, must be due to the invalid assumption that for anything to be objective it must exist independently of thought or of the mind. For Wiredu, mind is little more than a function of the complex *process* that occurs in the course of and as the result of the formation of ideas or meanings during communication. In that regard, then, mind is the *state* that is simultaneously formed or made in the course of participating in communication, namely in the course of formulating ideas as meanings or mental pictures in different stages of formation or degrees of clarity. Communication—the exchange of meanings between interlocutors—triggers special stimuli that the brain receives as communicated meanings, thus creating a *condition of meaning formation*—that is, the act of deciphering the complex body of symbols from other persons. (The ability to do this is already provided, if all is "normal," in the biological "wiring" of the body.) It is this *condition of meaning-formation* that we call mind: a systemic (biological) disposition to react, in the way that is specific to members of the human species, to the sounds that reach us. Humans are defined functionally in reference to this prototypical characteristic that identifies them as "made communicatively for each other." To quote Wiredu again, "mind is a function of thought," and its physical seat is the brain, the physical organ whose job it is to react to a variety of stimuli, including communicative stimuli.

Given the foregoing Akan theory of personhood generally and the Akan theory of mind in particular, we may now pose the ontological question regarding the dissolution or disintegration of *onipa,* the person: What happens to the person at death? What happens to the mind at the corruption of the body? Clearly, it should be apparent from all the above considerations on the nature of mind that immortality, as defined under the substance dualism claim, is not possible. At the same time, there appears to be a clear indication from the many descriptive variations of African thought at the cultural level that mind does not relate to the body without a principle that gives personhood its unity and the individual her or his unique identity, character, and destiny. As we will see in chapter 5, this principle is conceived of in Luo thought as one's *chuny,* the seat of the biological and mental activities of the person and the basis of his or her moral capacity or agency, his or her *juok.* It is said, according to the Luo scheme of things, that the real difference between people emerges from their deeds, meaning their public character, a differentiation that in turn indicates that differences between people are measured by what their *chuny* has enabled them to do in the course of their lives. When a person is remembered after his or her death, it is the images of their persona that emerge; thus, they are said to occupy individualized "places" in the memories of others, even when they are dead.

In his metaphysics of immortality, which is closely intertwined with his more widely debated concept of time (because, he says, "death is a process which removes a person gradually from the Sasa period to the Zamani"), Kenyan theologian John Mbiti argues that the African concept of personal immortality is based on memory, the privately executed but collectively expressed act of the living through which the dead either continue to live (in the Sasa period) or cease to do so when the ritualized memorization of the dead dies off and they are left to slip into the Zamani period as their places are taken by others who are more recently departed. According to Mbiti, in the Sasa period the dead are considered to be living-dead. He says: "While the departed person is remembered by name, he is not really dead: he is alive, and such a person I would call the *living-dead.* The living-dead is a person who is physically dead but alive in the memory of those who knew him [or her] in his [or her] life. . . . So long as the living-dead is thus remembered, he [or she] is in the state of *personal immortality.*"[81] Hence, the idea of immortality does not produce separate nonphysical substances.

Similarly, whether they are of the superhuman category or derivatives of living persons' memories of the dead, spirits are only mental projections or analogies from the world of real people. These projections either reproduce images or idealize human capacities into humanized forms, sometimes positively and sometimes negatively. When we think of and project the moral idea of "the best a person could possibly be," we are likely to come up with, say, the image of a grand elder, male or female, who is ancestor to countless descendants, superhumanly wise and gray-haired, limitlessly generous, loving and caring, and so on. The opposite of such a positive image might produce a mean-looking elder who seems to be so mean that he or she could not possibly be the head of a family; perhaps he or she is a witch, a *jajuok* (the Luo term for a morally evil or perverted person) by virtue of having the attributes of socially undesirable or antisocial character.[82]

Mbiti's concept of the living-dead thus should help us understand the wider African sense of community that includes those who have physically died but continue to be regarded as members of their respective families or clans due to the influence they continue to have upon the living. This influence is particularly dominant in the attitudes people adopt toward specific cases within naming traditions due to the expectation that when one is named after a departed relative, they might well live to be like that relative in character, partly as a result of the many stories they are told about the departed ancestor. Society not only produces the present and influences the future, it also reproduces the past by sustaining discourses and practices that keep the idioms of the past in the present.

The Relational Basis of Morals

In addition to the metaphysics of personhood, the relational nature of the person sheds a new light on how we understand the foundations of morals. This enables us to see the origin of moral principles as emanating not from the idea of an autonomous and transcendent mind that is endowed with the capability of "discovering" correspondingly transcendental and objective laws and truths of conduct stacked away in the "objective world of norms" but rather as emanating from the socially conditioned and located persons whose minds are the capacities of their bodily lives and experiences. In this relational understanding of persons, moral principles are the standards of conduct that press themselves on the mind as reasonable criteria for survival and well-being; they emerge when people understand the needs and interests of others at the same level as their own and when they understand the founding and reciprocal nature of the idea of freedom itself. Moral principles are viewed as reasonable because they are neither self-evident nor instinctive. We learn or become aware of their worth as part of the course that takes us from the false sense of autonomy and fixation on self to the realization of mutual dependency with others.

Suggestively, this moral view of the person and of the nature of moral principles takes a critical stance toward the Kantian atomic view of mind and of moral agency. Wiredu argues in *Cultural Universals and Particulars*[83] that the problem of morals arises out of the fact that not all people are naturally inclined to be as concerned about the interests of others at all times as they may be about their own, hence the principle that at all times in our conduct we ought to manifest concern for the interests of others. According to Wiredu, it should not be difficult to see the justification or basis for that principle, since even the concern for our own interests cannot be considered fully without the thought of how other people's interests may affect it. Thus, in a manner reminiscent of the Golden Rule, he suggests a principle that allows a person to see what their own interests might be by imaginatively positioning him or herself in the place of others. Thus, he writes, by definition, "a person may be said to manifest due concern for the interests of others if in contemplating the impact of his actions on their interests, she puts herself imaginatively in their position, and having done so, is able to welcome that impact."[84] Wiredu further suggests that when expressed in the form of a categorical imperative, this principle could be called "the principle of sympathetic impartiality." By placing the origin of moral awareness within the social order, Wiredu provides the pre-metaphysical condition of personhood from which the principles of morals emerge. In other words, it is difficult to think of the functional capacity of the person as not grounded in the relational circumstances that make his or her metaphysical peculiarities possible and concrete. Because of this, Kant's own categorical imperative is in need of an "injection of a dose of compassion [that] would convert it into a principle of *sympathetic impartiality*." According to Wiredu, it is not difficult to see the practical strength of such a principle, since "it takes little imagination to foresee that life in any society in which everyone openly avowed the contrary of this principle and acted accordingly would inevitably be 'solitary, poor, nasty, *brutish*,' and probably short."[85] In Wiredu's view, Kant's categorical imperative would thus have made more sense if it had been built on this human biological principle, which "is a human universal transcending cultures viewed as social forms and customary beliefs and practices. In being common to all human practice of morality, it is a universal of any non-brutish form of human life."[86] Here, as he does with the materialist theories of mind in Western philosophy, Wiredu builds on what is particularly underdeveloped in Kant's enterprise; namely that despite his focus on the mind's discovery, within itself, of its own unity, of the unity of the world, and of the unity of world and mind in experience, it still seems as though Kant's moral project was built on an unexplained jump from personal experience to a supposed universality of principles without adequate ontological grounds for transcending the individual psyche. Thus, although the categorical imperative is a compelling principle, it lacks, in Kant's formulation, an adequate account of how it transfers to others from a purely intuitive and therefore private experience. Wiredu closes that gap by suggesting that the moral connection between the individual and other people by means of universal principles is not intuitive (as directly and necessarily grasped by the mind). Rather, it is the function of experience, of relations with others, and is grounded in the biological needs (relational interdependence) of the species, fine-tuned through a mix of education and trial-and-error experiences. Indeed, if morality arises out of the need to manifest due concern for the welfare of others, it would be difficult to imagine it arising in the thinking of someone who from birth lived by him or herself in absolute isolation. Even with the best instinct, self-interest would barely suffice for that person's survival, and if it did, then only at the most basic levels, levels not usually considered sufficient for the human condition. For Wiredu, both the cognitive and moral capacities of humans are based purely on their biologically specific type of existence, but they require community in order to become activated. This imaginary nonsocialized human being would therefore not develop these capacities, hence failing to become a person. Both the appearance and workings of the mind, on one hand, and the development of moral principles for survival and a humane type of life through both negative (restraint) and positive (doing what is good) principles of behavior, on the other, are part of the biological type that is proper to humans, and their emergence and development are conditional upon the social nature of human life. If a person were to be isolated from any form of human contact from birth but could develop fully biologically, their defining human capacities would not develop, let alone be used, and it would not make sense to assume that such a person would have a human mind or be moral. In other words, that individual would not be a person.[87] Human beings are born, but persons are socially cultivated. For Kant, the moral life is a continuing struggle between the call of duty and the lure of inclination, both of which he thought to be intuitive or instinctive drives. For Wiredu, inclinations are the fodder for continuing discourse, out of which the best guiding principles of conduct are agreed upon.

One should add rather quickly here that Wiredu's theory of personhood does not go so far as to claim that the nature of a person is socially constructed. A social constructivist theory of personhood claims that ideas about the nature of persons are formed in the course of society's value choices and practices that cohere with their other views and interpretations of the general nature of the universe. In this general sense, the social constructivist theory of personhood would share the basic thesis of other varieties of constructivism in claiming that personhood, like other aspects of the world, is constituted by the theories, practices, and institutions that a society may deem meaningful to its peculiar experiences. This would make the nature of every person different from every other person depending on the constructive cultural discourses and choices that have made them. Wiredu, on the contrary, views personhood as grounded in the empirical fragility of human biology, which requires of the person a great degree of dependency on the specific and deliberate actions of other members of the species in order to grow, develop, and flourish. This dependency is a real and universal characteristic of all human beings, not a matter of choice. In other words, although human value is intrinsic in that it does not depend on the active roles that one performs as a member of society, the realization of that intrinsically valuable status does not occur outside of an existing society; it depends on it for its realization.

Truth

The concept of truth is not just another of the many interesting themes Wiredu examines as an aspect of the relational underpinning of his philosophical anthropology, or psychology. On the contrary, truth is perhaps the most widely discussed theory in the entire corpus of his work.[88] Despite the controversy over Wiredu's theory of truth, it constitutes a tightly coherent and integral part of his general theory of personhood. It is, perhaps, one instance where Wiredu's contrast of selected issues in African and Western philosophical traditions is the sharpest and the most strongly stated. It points to deeper and more general differences between these two traditions and highlights the contrasting basic assumptions or tenets about personhood in the two systems. In Western philosophy, the correspondence theory of truth assumes such a privileged status for the individual that correspondence of his or her propositions or assertions to reality is considered to be an adequate condition of truth. This view points to an objectivist notion of truth by implying that there are independent and timeless states of affairs out there that are knowable equally by all who care about them. For Wiredu, the cognitive agent would have to be disturbingly abstract for this definition of truth to obtain. In the real world, however, whatever is called the truth is always only someone's truth. In other words, for a statement to be qualified as "true," it must be discovered by, known by, or defended by human beings somewhere, sometime. Thus, he refutes the objectivist view of truth (according to which what is considered to be true of the propositions or assertions of any one person should be regarded as binding to anyone and everyone else) and replaces it with the view that truth is and can only be an opinion. Truth is a function of the human endeavor in both its individual and social dimensions.

This view appears to add, like the moral one we saw earlier, a social dimension to the structural (call it mentalist) view of mind that was so well developed by Kant. Wiredu identifies, examines, and tries to distinguish the nature of the physical and private cognitive activity of individuals—call it pure perception—from the social and public or shared dimensions of knowledge that we call meanings. This approach rejects the autonomous view of mind in both the cognitive and moral domains. Mind is not a windowless monad. At the individual, private, and purely cognitive or physico-functional level, we perceive objects according to the universal physical laws of our biological constitution. Thus, perception, as a purely physical-cognitive event or process is a fairly private and individual affair that is carried out by each brain independently, yet it is intrinsically crucial to the concept of truth itself. Due to their individual qualities, every object of perception stimulates the brain uniquely, regulated, as Kant explained, by the spatio-temporal conditions of perception. Thus, even objects that are very similar are perceived separately. Also intrinsic to cognition, from a purely biological endowment specific to humans, are the formal laws by which we organize beliefs. "At the very minimum," Wiredu says, "this status [as *hominus sapientes*] implies that we are organisms that go beyond instinct in the drive for equilibrium and self-preservation in specific ways, namely, by means of reflective perception, abstraction, deduction, and induction."[89] These laws allow us to formulate and process conceptual relations in such a manner as is required for our very survival. They are intrinsic to or are ingrained in the nature of mind and organize the structure of thought—what we communicatively transmit to or receive from others. The drive to truth—matching thought with the contents of our perceptions—is part of this crucial human endeavor. We are always striving for truth. In this fact, though, lies the implication that truth, as a basic drive in all human organization and communication of thought, has a fairly significant private aspect, that it derives from our experience.

What is not a wholly private matter is the sense of the content of cognition, or meaning—that is, the seat of what counts as knowledge. As agents who are physically (that is, biocognitively) constituted, our knowledge of the world can only be from our perspective, our point of view. This is what each of us brings to the collective and dialogical enterprise: our opinions. Knowledge claims (such as "this object O is green") are a form of relating our private perceptions to public meanings (such as what kind of sensations are called green) that we have already learned. There is here a recourse to the methods of philosophical anthropology or psychology again, attempting to examine and to illustrate with an additional example from epistemology the relational or social spring of human nature. The example helps explain the complexity of the human psyche and the social dimension of human consciousness.

In communication we transmit our points of view to others. And unless we are insincere with ourselves and want to be insincere with those with whom we are in communication, we will be expected to transmit to them truthfully that what we say—that is, our point of view—is an exact rendition of how we have perceived and thus describe the world. Thus, to say of anything that it is so is to say that I believe that it is so or that I believe that it is just as I say it is—I am being completely truthful about what I perceive or have perceived. This position retains the drive to objectivity while also emphasizing that objectivity independent of opinions is only an ideal at best. The locutor reports truthfully what he or she experiences from his or her point of view, or, according to Wiredu, what he or she reports is his or her truthful point of view. Truth, then, is nothing but a point of view, an opinion, or a belief.

How does this work? And does just any opinion count as truth? What about when the facts are not as claimed by my proclaimed opinion? Well, I have spoken of Wiredu's theory of truth as opinion before, but many will remember the rich debate this topic has generated in the past, the best-sustained one being that between him and my late compatriot Odera Oruka, who raised questions similar to the conjectural ones I have raised above.[90] Although I am clearly no longer inclined to interpret this theory as embracing elements of relativism, I do not intend to revisit that debate here or to correct aspects of my own earlier misunderstandings of it.[91] My aim is to point out another feature of it that I previously skipped but that now appears appropriate to bring out, especially in light of a recent focus emerging from African as well as from other traditions or quarters of the discipline: namely that Wiredu's theory of truth as opinion springs from and supports a communalistic stance.

For every assertion of knowledge, there are two aspects, one that describes an attitude (belief) of the asserter and the other that describes the state of things in the world. Thus, in a belief-statement such as "I believe that Omolo is in Siaya," one is actually making two assertions: one, that it is a fact that she believes that Omolo is in Siaya; and two, that that which she believes—that Omolo is in Siaya—is actually so. How do these two realms of knowledge assertions relate to each other? Critics, both real—as in Oruka's objections to the theory—and imagined—as the "critic" in Wiredu's Socratic format of the debate[92]—have raised concern that the theory makes it possible for someone to entertain beliefs contrary to facts. An example would be "I believe that p but p is false" (I believe that Omolo is in Siaya but it is false that Omolo is in Siaya). According to Wiredu, by committing herself to the content of her belief, the utterer also commits herself to the segment of her utterance that describes reality. Thus, the utterer commits herself to the description of reality only as an extension of her belief, which means that an utterer cannot commit herself to believing p and to believing $-p$. In other words, there can be situations when one could say "I believe that p" when, as a matter of fact but one that is unknown to the utterer at the time of believing that p, p is false (I believe that Omolo is in Siaya, but, unknown to me at this very time, it is a matter of fact that Omolo is in Kadem, not in Siaya). According to Wiredu, "There is here the idea of two distinct points of view, namely, the point of view of [the utterer] at one time and a possible antithetic point of view of [herself] at a later time."[93] Such situations when one could believe that p when p is actually false arise either when the same subject utters a second point of view or when the subject presupposes a corresponding third-person point of view (Adhiambo believes that Omolo is in Siaya, but Omolo is actually not in Siaya). Adhiambo herself could not say "I believe Omolo is in Siaya but Omolo is not in Siaya," for that would be contradictory. But there is no contradiction when there are two statements that are made distinctly from each other, even if they are uttered by the same person.

But does the truth of a statement depend solely on the role of the third-person intervention? What about the relation of the belief itself to facts or objective state of things "out there"? Well, it must be noted clearly that Wiredu's thesis is not that the truth or falsity of a proposition depends on its being believed, for that, he says, "would amount to relativism, which, in [his] opinion, is an absurd doctrine." Relativism makes truth arbitrary, whimsical, and ungrounded in serious gnostic endeavor. On the contrary, whether a proposition is true or false should depend on a thorough appraisal of the ideas expressed therein and of the situations it describes. He says: "It is the insistence on the need for belief to be in accordance with the canons of rational investigation which distinguishes my view from relativism. Truth is not relative to point of view. It is, in one sense, a point of view . . . born out of rational inquiry, and the canons of rational inquiry have a universal human application."[94] But this should not be extended to the point of claiming that the truth of a proposition depends on its correspondence to a state of affairs, thus making the proposition "a manifestation of reality," as Tarski's theory of truth[95] and objectivist

theories of truth state. Wiredu has been adamantly opposed to the correspondence theory of truth regardless of the formulation in which it may
come.[96] It is clear, Wiredu says, "that in his schema (T) Tarski intends
the sentences that replace p to be regarded in that position as disclosing
states of affairs, reality."[97] According to Wiredu, the best way to understand
Tarski's replacements, their logical status notwithstanding, is to view p as
a declarative sentence constructed from an antecedent point of view and X
as its corroboration. In other words, p confirms X. But this, says Wiredu,
is still an ordinary sentence, which means it is a human assertion, a belief,
an opinion, or a point of view. Thus Wiredu rejects the relativist theory
of truth and is cautious about the objectivist one as well. In his view, "a
truth always comes, and can only come, in the shape of a truth claim,
and a truth claim is a point of view."[98] But lest this be misunderstood to
imply that truth depends on a point of view, Wiredu clarifies that a truth
carries an attitude that a mere truth claim lacks, namely a commitment
on the part of the utterer or speaker.

It looks like Wiredu's idea of truth has more than just a logical relation to propositions. He appears to suggest that the law of the excluded
middle—the principle that in a two-value context (also called bivalence, as
in "either p or $-p$"), as is commonly presupposed by the law, a proposition
can only be either true or false—appears to assign truth value to propositions before inquiry. Instead, he says, truth values should be "properties"
that we assign to ideational contents in inquiry—that is, when we confirm
(or negate) claims upon investigation (rational inquiry) or observations of
reality. The idea "Omolo is in Siaya" is the (ideational) content that we
confirm when we say "yes" or negate when we say "no" in response to the
question that occasions or prompts such a truth value assignment, namely,
"Is Omolo in Siaya?" According to Wiredu, the claim of the principle of
the excluded middle implies that problems such as "Is Omolo in Siaya?"
are already solved before the inquiry, since the possible answer can be only
either true or false, decided beforehand as a matter of principle. However,
the principle works only with regard to solvable problems and does not
take into consideration the variety of other problems, yet unknown, that
may not be so easily resolvable, which amounts to this: "To say that your
logic is a two-valued logic is [to say] that you are dealing with solvable
problems,"[99] which is a point of view.

Points of view, beliefs, or opinions, in Wiredu's sense, are not to be
taken at their face value, but neither should they be regarded as arbitrary or whimsical. All points of view need to be sorted out and their
rational acceptability determined. In other words, not all points of view
are rational. In fact, whether a belief is rationally supportable or not,
Wiredu argues, is determinable through argumentation or, in empirical
cases, by experimentation as part of a careful examination of the rational
justification for beliefs that do not agree with the justification, an act that

in turn presupposes the possibility of an opinion that is commonly shared with others, which usually is the goal of argumentation. The ideal aim of argumentation—and of rational inquiry generally—is to arrive at one rationally warranted opinion. Put in yet another way, the rational (what Dewey called assertible) warranty of opinions, according to Wiredu, is assigned to inquiry, not a priori by analytical relation, as Dewey's definition requires. And Wiredu states that "the canons of rational inquiry have a universal human application."[100] They are part of the laws of thought. As he spells out in *Cultural Universals and Particulars,* this commonality enables all humans to communicate by use of language governed by the laws of thought. Truth, then, lies not just in the equivalence between propositions and reality (or whatever "name" we may replace either with) but also at the base of what it means to be human at all. The difference between Wiredu's idea of truth and John Dewey's idea of truth as "warranted assertibility"[101] may be small, but it is certainly important. Wiredu points out that while Dewey defines truth as analytically identical with warranted assertibility, he, on the other hand, defines truth as a continuous quest that (metaphysically) underlies the human epistemic endeavor. Truth is the result of inquiry, which usually is a dialogical practice that engages and compares different points of view. Truth, then, does not reside in the formal structure of propositions that can be dismantled analytically—as in what it *means* for any statement to be considered true, although this is an important part of the meaning of truth—but with the metaphysical significance it has to the whole constitutive ends of being human. And this, Wiredu reckons, is to be found intertwined with the basic sociobiological finitude and fallibility of humans. He provides an interesting summary of the idea of truth at the end of *Philosophy and an African Culture:*

> The question "what is truth?" looks simple, but it is now obvious that its answer, even when given in one word: "opinion," is by no means simple. In such matters there is no excuse for dogmatism, and I too will continue to reflect on them. . . . A relativist who believes in the existence of inter-personal criteria of rationality among the human species, who grants that disagreements are, in principle, resolvable by rational argument, is a relativist only by name. Historically, that is the opposite of what the relativist has maintained.[102]

By placing both individual and collective truth at the center of human endeavor,[103] Wiredu rescues knowledge from mechanism and returns it to the (pre-metaphysical) roots of being human in a strongly relational context. As further indulgence into *Cultural Universals and Particulars* will quickly reveal to any reader, this social location of knowledge not only charts the character of human fallibility that is the basis of knowledge, it also becomes the foundation for the appreciation of and respect for human rights and democratic institutions. It is communalism in a robust sense.

Knowledge, taken in its most general sense to include its significance, methods of acquisition, and formal characteristics such as structure and truth value, is a crucially important social endeavor that, in Wiredu's view, is a constant social pursuit that requires the best available and sincerely applied tools, both intellectual and instrumental or technological. It is a social endeavor that is, or at least is supposed to be, accomplished in the most objective manner possible.

Once more, it is important that Wiredu's position here, this time an epistemological one, not be confused with the claims that are widely attributed to social constructionism. The latter can be framed as the claim that "there is no such thing as objective truth. What we call 'true' is simply what we agree with. So-called truths or facts are merely negotiated beliefs, the products of social construction, not 'objective' features of the world."[104] Wiredu's position neither denies objectivity nor repudiates truth. It is therefore also quite distinct from deflationism—the view that the pursuit of truth is worthless and futile because it either does not exist or it is impossible to attain. In fact Wiredu's position adores, pursues, and is passionate about truth. It argues, however, that claims to objectivity need to take into account the relation between (or the transition from) the cognitive or psychical constitution of humans as epistemic agents, which is a private state, and the epistemological domain (that is, the stage of knowledge claims), which is a social enterprise. It is based on the view of the limitations of the subject rather than on the denial of the object. Given how these two (individual and social) aspects of human nature are related to each other and how they relate to the enterprise of epistemological inquiry, objectivity as a state of the world independently of how it is perceived and known (or truth as the property of an establishable nonpersonal statement about the assumed objective state of the world) is graspable only as an ideal at best that is not attainable by humans. There may be confluences of opinion, and that may be good for theoretical as well as for practical reasons or ends, but they should not be mistaken for proof or grounds for claiming an objectivist view of truth. Indeed, Wiredu writes, "any claim to know something *as it is in itself* would be a contradiction in as much as it would amount to a claim to know something *as it cannot be known.*"[105] It seems clear, then, that Wiredu's position rejects relativism in its known and commonly discussed variants, including the view that what counts as true is variously determined by cultural institutions. On the contrary, it is his view (and a strong one at that) that truth is and must remain a central concern of all cultures, including African ones. He introduces the idea that the social dimension grounds human nature so strongly that all human endeavors, including epistemic phenomena, are crucially entangled with this social dependency of our being.

The enterprise of knowledge is about comparing, contrasting, reevaluating, and testing points of view, which is why inquiry, especially of the scientific variety, remains critical to Wiredu's view. Knowledge, then, requires both the private cognitive and the public social dimensions of its pursuit. He argues that truth is not just a matter of whims, be they subjective or collective, for a false statement remains false regardless of how many ascribe to or believe it. Instead, truth is the fundamental goal of rational inquiry. Unless we are just kidding around, when we make statements we believe them to be true; that is, our statements are considered opinions. The practical significance of this belief can be easy enough to test by trying to run through what we believed to be a wall but suddenly wish to doubt is in fact a wall. But the theory of truth as opinion suggests that truthfulness be considered to be crucial virtue upon which many moral, social, and cognitive human endeavors should focus, as the Akan do in their modes of thought.

Wiredu argues that although the concepts of truth and truthfulness clearly have some overlap between them—that is, that truth has something to do with agreement and that truthfulness involves the concept of truth—the Akan distinction of the two meanings is clear-cut in contrast to the ambiguity that results from the English-language use of the single term "truth." Wiredu's "Truth: A Dialogue" is an earlier and shorter version of a later essay[106] in which he explores more fully his contention that the Twi word *nokware* (of one mouth) means truthfulness in the moral sense, while the phrase *nea ete saa* or *asem a ete saa* (a statement that is so) conveys truth in the cognitive sense. He says in the earlier essay that the differentiation has the advantage of reducing, if not eliminating altogether, the ambiguity that may occur when only one term is used for both the moral and cognitive senses of truth.

Wiredu's theory of truth gives the phrase "truth and reconciliation," now central as a strategy and process for healing broken trusts and healing from political conflicts, an important epistemological grounding. Reconciling our different and often conflicting aims and aspirations is the path to a collectively acceptable and workable world.

CHAPTER FIVE

Juok as the Moral Foundation
of Personhood

Indigenous concepts of personhood are often unhelpfully shrouded in mythical, allegorical, or proverbial terminologies that conceal the direct and clear meanings that were intended for them. Much of oral literature uses these allegorical modes of presentation to convey teachings about and explanations for intricate meanings of things and values; the implication is that the concealed conceptual intentions can be teased out only by careful analysis and interpretation. Anthropological texts are frequent vehicles for the persistence of these obscurities. Until recently, ethnographical explanations of some of these concepts did little to unpack these concepts from the original modes in which they were presented, thus leaving the core of the teachings largely inaccessible to the uninitiated. And some who were well versed in these narratives often learn to recount rather than expose or explain them in simple and clear terms. Those in the past who were (or are, where they can still be found) capable of such analyses were often protective of these ambiguities in the name of secrecy and protecting the domain of initiated experts. It is therefore not unusual for people to experience a great deal of frustration when they try but fail to find explanations to accompany the grand metaphorical and allegorical tales. It was partly due to these dead ends that ethnophilosophy acquired the infamous characteristics of unhelpful repetitiveness and anonymity. For example, imagine yourself inquiring of a grand priest of Ifá what *ènìyàn* (a person) is and getting as an answer a long story, directly from the rich Yoruba lexicon, about Ògún's skeleton, Obàtálá's fleshy clay, Èmí the daughter of Olódùmaré (also called Olódùmaré's breath), Òrì from Àjàlá's pottery warehouse, and so on. As fascinating as this narrative often is, there is no doubt that if you are a foreigner or a local who is uninitiated in the Yoruba language and knowledge system, you will become terribly frustrated by the apparent literalness of the story because none of these terms becomes conceptually accessible until the concepts they convey are shaken out of their cultural pods. The reason is this: the terms for the *composantes* of personhood appear to be used so interchangeably with

182

those for deities that it sounds reasonable to demand that some separation be made to separate analogies from synonymities as they are used
for the inhabitants of different ontological categories. Fortunately, much
philosophical exposition of Yoruba concepts has been and continues to be
done that makes these concepts partially easier to access and understand.[1]
Marcel Griaule's well-known and now-classic recordings of his conversations with Ogotemmêli constitute another metaphorically shrouded and
impenetrable text. Other examples, both recorded and in their original oral
forms, can be identified by African scholars from across the continent.
One common feature of these texts is the impression that emerges from
them that personhood is plurally constituted, a view that easily flows from
the indigenous methods of presenting concepts in the form of nouns.
One hears, for example, some Yoruba scholars speak of the person as a
"pantheon," because in him or her reside (or he or she is indeed a meeting point of) some of the multiple deities of Yoruba religion. Whether this
really is what is intended in the many mythical and proverbial accounts
of the nature of the person in many cultural systems across the continent
awaits formal analyses in many instances, including analysis by the Dogon
themselves. In the vast complexity of language, we often fumble around
to find expressions that we believe (and sometimes trust) will adequately
express the concept we have in our mind. We may do one (or more) of
several things: we might find an already familiar and close enough term
from current usage and apply it to a new idea we have, usually by taking
pains to point out the subtle differences, or we might invent a new term
by either borrowing from another language or by stitching terms together
from our own familiar language. Or we might try to find a term that can
simulate—be analogous to—the different idea we intend to express. By any
of these stylistic variables, we reach out to the flexible nature of words in
the hope that we can convey intended meanings but also remain clearly
aware of the otherwise separate references the terms may ordinarily have
in the short but extendable list of our respective lexicons. Proverbs are a
good example of this ingenuity with language.

Grialule's conversations with Ogotemmêli narrate myths that tell of
the plural constitution of personal identity out of a collection of spiritual forces or spirits of ancestors.[2] We are told that every individual
self or person (*ine,* pl. *ineũ* in Dogon) is, in addition to his/her somatic
(*gódu*) individuality and particularism, also constituted of four bodily
principles that, according to Dieterlen, have been called *âmes* by scholars interpreting Dogon (for lack of a better term); a set of twin *âmes,*
called *kikinu say* (a commonly used contraction of *kindu kindu say*),
which are "*âmes intelligentes*"; another set of twins that is the opposing counterpart of the *âmes* (*kikinu bumone,* or *kindu kindu bumone*),
namely "*âmes rampantes*"; four "*âmes de sexe*" classified like the preceding two sets of twin principles; a principle of basic nourishment that

is symbolically believed to be located in the collarbones and is comparable to two granaries containing four grains each; and a composite
vital force, *nyàma,* usually thought of as a kind of energy that is mixed
with blood and circulates through the joints and internal organs of the
body.³ The repetition of terms in Dogon implies their double nature,
because the Dogon think of many aspects of reality as doubly composed
of opposing principles. *Kindu kindu say* (or *kikinu say*) designates the
male-female composition of the principles that direct personhood in its
active manifestation. Because *"say"* means intelligence or consciousness,
kindu kindu say means self-awareness and implies in the full sense of
the expression that self-knowledge, including knowledge of one's body,
differs based on one's sex or gender. The term *"say"* is interpolated from
another one, *"soy,"* which means the number seven (7), the total of two
other numbers—three (3), which means masculinity, and four (4), which
is femininity. Gender, which is an essential concrete part of and way of
thinking of selfhood, is comprised of elements of both masculinity and
femininity, but the external identity is determined by the domination of
one over the other. This is why the Dogon further externally symbolize
this dominance, already determined by the inner reality of the body, by
circumcision and excision.⁴ The Dogon say that Nommo, the deified principle of organization, is the origin of and is responsible for the sustenance
of this human and external reality based on the complementariness of
opposites. According to Dogon beliefs and teachings, these elements not
only define humans as members of their species, they also identify them
as individuals who are members of specific clans and families. *Kikinu
say* is the seat of a person's capacity to exercise will and use his or
her intelligence. It works in unity with another element, *nani,* a part
of *nyàma,* which is passed down from ancestors through generations
but is placed under the control of *kikinu say. Nani* is the individuating
principle that makes each individual person uniquely different from every
other person. In other words, the uniqueness of individuals is manifested
in and through their moral and intellectual qualities, which they reveal
through their public behavior. Every person's uniqueness is judged on
their moral character as well as on their intellectual abilities, the qualities
of their *nani* and *kikinu say,* respectively. This Dogon idea of the person, like many other similar African ideas, simultaneously distinguishes
between two separate processes and integrates them: the process of ego
development as the integration of the inner nature into the structures
of language, thought, and action and the process of identity formation
as the capacity to produce a continuity in life history. In the expansive
anthropological literature on African concepts of personhood, the role of
character and character formation has been downplayed, sprouting only
recently in selective scholarship that utilizes the critical social theory
that was inaugurated by Maurice Mauss.⁵

The Concept of *Juok* Reconsidered

Bethwell A. Ogot and Okot p'Bitek are the major scholars who have analytically debated the idea of *juok,* an ambiguous term used variantly among Lwoo-speaking peoples to refer to a number of things ranging from vaguely defined nonphysical entities to moral behavior.[6] Given both the term's social significance and its location at the heart of the controversy about the identity of persons and things, such ambiguity and the scholarly discords around it should hardly be surprising. Both Ogot and p'Bitek claim that *juok* is a metaphysical concept that refers to quality of nature or to something that nature possesses. In what follows I reexamine and refute some aspects of these claims and argue that linguistic evidence suggests that *juok* is a moral concept that seeks to idealize social virtues rather than a metaphysical concept that describes the nature of entities—that in its denotation of character, *juok* is a descriptive term used to order the everyday reality of social and moral behavior of individuals and groups.

A careful reading of Ogot's and p'Bitek's analyses of the concept of *juok* suggests that in pioneering local scholarship on the belief systems of the Luo people, these eminent scholars were influenced and driven by the then-popular missionary search for African cosmological entities to imitate the cosmological order of the dominant Christian culture. This domination reordered indigenous patterns of thought by denying them the status of independent apprehensions and conceptualizations. Thus, although Ogot and p'Bitek surrender to this Christian transculturation in radically different ways, their definitions of *juok* as soul or spirit reveals the impact of colonial and religious influence on our modes of thinking about the world. African philosophers have taken note and rightly warn against the failure to critically clean African thought of colonial superimpositions. Among the noted advocates of mental decolonization is Kwasi Wiredu, who decries the colonial legacy evident in representations of African thought as the function of "the historical imposition of foreign categories of thought on African thought systems . . . through . . . the avenue of language . . . religion and politics."[7] In his now-classic text *The Invention of Africa,* V. Y. Mudimbe clearly also charted the historical drama of European construction of the idea of Africa through discursive enterprises in anthropology, mission work, and political domination. Outside these philosophical rungs the call for the decolonization of the mind has been popularized, of course, by my compatriot Ngũgĩwa Thiong'o. The early works of the first generation of postcolonial African intellectuals reflected this legacy in their use of categories of European thought to explain and analyze African thought. It is to this mold of African thought, constructed under the shadow of the Christian paradigm, that Okot p'Bitek and Bethwell Ogot's debate on the concept of *juok* clearly belongs.

Okot p'Bitek is not the typical disciple of Western thought. He is not like Mbiti or Idowu or even any of the younger African scholars of African religious thought writing at the peak of African ethnotheological scholarship in the seventies. Much of his scholarship was dedicated to drawing sharp oppositions between African and Western thought and value systems. By many measures he was an uncompromising cultural nationalist, a characterization both his scholarly and creative works attest to. His famous satirical poems, *Song of Lawino* and *Song of Ocol,* are a scathing derision of Western cultures and of Africans who have been blinded by those cultures into rejecting their own heritage. But there is an irony in the significance of the intervention of such critics as Okot p'Bitek: they are simultaneously insiders and rebels in the practice of postcolonial theory and critique. That is the nature of the dialectic in the history of colonialism and its negating aftermath.

It is within this paradoxical standing of postcolonial theory that one finds elements of Western thought firmly anchoring many ideas in Okot p'Bitek's works, even as p'Bitek viciously critiques the imposition of Western categories on African thought systems. P'Bitek's critique focuses especially on the study of African religions and, by extension, on the entire discipline of social and cultural anthropology. In *African Religions in Western Scholarship,* p'Bitek criticizes social anthropology as a typical colonial discipline that was created as an appendage of and justification for European expansionism, one that specialized in the study of the "problems related to the culture and welfare of the less advanced peoples of [the] Empire."[8] Throughout imperial Europe, programs to study colonized peoples were hosted in the royal institutes, either of anthropology, as in Britain, or of overseas studies, as in Belgium. P'Bitek contends, then, that because of the background and raison d'être of the discipline itself, anthropology was a colonial discipline, the weapon of the colonizer, and that both its language and conceptual framework became the representational tools of the colonizer. The colonial disciplines thus were completely irrelevant in independent African institutions. According to p'Bitek, "Western scholars have never been genuinely interested in African religions per se. Their works have all been part and parcel of some controversy or debate in the Western world."[9] Similar sentiments have recently been expressed by a new generation of Western anthropologists, those who view the old anthropological tradition as largely a European self-projection that represented the Other as that which the European self was not. The works of Clifford Geertz, James Clifford, George Marcus and James Clifford, Marcus and Michael M. J. Fischer, and Johannes Fabian echo p'Bitek's contempt for colonial social and cultural anthropology.[10] In the context of postcolonial theory, p'Bitek's critique, which begins with his long satirical poems, aptly foreshadowed both the idea of the European invention of Africa[11] and the calls for the decolonization of the mind that one finds in the work of Wiredu and the novelist Ngũgĩ wa Thiong'o.[12] Along with this general project, adds Rosalind Shaw, the concept of "African traditional religions" was invented as the more "primitive" genre of religion as perceived through Judeo-Christian categories of the West. According to Shaw, "'Invention' critiques such as Mudimbe's would seem to apply with particular force to the study of religion, given that the term 'religion' itself is absent from the languages of many of the peoples whose practices and understandings I describe as their 'religion.'"[13] Shaw's argument is not so much that terminologies cannot be adapted across cultures to stand in for ideas similar to those that a term may refer to in its linguistic origin. Her point is about the inadvertent "invention" of previously nonexistent realities through the uncritical transfer of terms to sets of categories of thought and practice that might not be related. In other words, the taxonomic archive of anthropology by which we know and identify various aspects of non-Western cultures acquires its significance only from its comparative and derivative status vis-à-vis its Western springs. Thus, Shaw argues, "if we examine those traditions usually selected as 'world religions,' we find that even if they have little else in common, they have written texts, explicit doctrines and a centre or centres of authority, all of which have characterized those religious forms which have been dominant in the West."[14] Similarly, the so-called African traditional religions were created with the collaboration of Christian-trained African theologians by translating Christian concepts and doctrines into indigenous African languages.[15] That this practice took place and continues is evidenced by the controversies frequently precipitated by African clerics such as the former Zambian bishop Emmanuel Milingo, who are considered wayward when they propose that "rejected" African concepts and practices (such as the acceptance of the idea of the existence of ghosts and the practice of their exorcism or the rejection of Catholic celibacy) be incorporated into mainstream Christian liturgy.

The Status of Dualism in Luo Conceptual Scheme

P'Bitek is one of the sharpest critics of Western anthropology in Africa, especially of the Christian missionaries' use of the conceptual grids of that discipline to categorize African thought. In this critique of Western conceptual grids p'Bitek sharply differs from B. A. Ogot, who appeared to have been enamored of Tempels's idea of an "African philosophy." Like Tempels, Ogot sought to study "*jok*" as a key theoretical (conceptual) linkage between "African customary practices and institutions" and the "African ideas of the universe, of existence, and of destiny [that are] particularly important if world religions such as Christianity and Islam are to have their roots in the African soil."[16] According to Ogot, African beliefs and practices came in "old" and "new" forms. The former are "pagan" while the latter owe their (superior) nature to the process of Christianization and Islamization. That Ogot embraced "pagan" as a useful category for characterizing African indigenous thought and values as rationally and morally inferior is betrayed by his admission that he had confided in the Western anthropologists in order to show "us [Africans] what can be done with some of these concepts," just as "Evans-Pritchard has recently shown . . . in his analysis of the [Nuer] term *kwoth* . . . which, as I hope to show, is similar to *jok* in many respects."[17]

Both Ogot and p'Bitek concur that the concept of *jok* or *juok* could not simply be wished away since it occupied a central place in the Nilotic people's languages and conceptions of the universe. But the two differ fundamentally in the meaning or conceptual nature of the term. Ogot first. In his view, which concurs with that of the anthropologists who have studied the concept as it occurs in the languages, beliefs, and practices of several other Nilotic groups, "The term *jok* or *juok* . . . usually means God, spirit, witchcraft, ghost or some form of spiritual power."[18] It is quite apparent from Ogot's discussion of Lienhardt's and Howell and Thompson's studies of the Shilluk and of Evans-Pritchard's own study of the Nuer that the translations of *juok* (as god, spirit, ghost, or spiritual power) were significantly influenced by Christian categories.[19] The characterization of the Shilluk's sense of *juok* as two levels of spirit (*wei*) and body (*del*) into their version of the "trinity" imposes an interesting but non-useful foreign category on the term and imparts new meanings to it. Lienhardt must have relied on the frequent uses of the term in Shilluk language to infer that "*juok*" was in everything and so must have been for the Shilluk the first principle, the ultimate explanation for everything.[20] Lienhardt indicates further that the Shilluk distinguish between the *jok mal* (the "*jok* up high," allegedly the heavenly *jok* or spirits) as deities and the *jok piny* (the "*jok* below," or worldly spirits), which they attribute to Nyikang, the founder of the Shilluk nation according to local legend, their first ancestor. According to Lienhardt, this distinction indicates quite clearly that the Shilluk hierarchize the *jok* powers into divine and worldly categories, with the latter as derivatives of the former. Thus, he infers, the *jok mal* refer to the creative powers of god while the *jok piny* refer to the orderliness of the Shilluk world, especially their sociopolitical organization, which Nyikang oversees on behalf of the divine.

The distinction between heaven and earth that Lienhardt and other anthropologists saw cannot, in the Luo conceptual distinction, be taken in the literal spatio-physical sense it appears to denote, much less in the Christian implications it has acquired over time. Nor does Dholuo have such distinctions as indications of high versus low in the moral order. A crucial difference between the Shilluk and the Luo is that the Shilluk posit a deity at the beginning or highest point in their conception of order but the Luo are godless. The Luo speak of *mal* or *malo* in purely spatio-physical senses. *Polo malo* is where the clouds gather and birds fly. It is the "location" of the stars, the most prominent among which is the sun, *chieng'*. Because of their tiny sizes relative to the human position, other spatial bodies only twinkle (*mil*) like fireflies in the night. They are twinklers, *otide* (plural for *otit*), but the sun, *chieng'*, glares or is disproportionately bright compared to the twinklers (*chieng' rieny*). Although the Luo attach great importance to the sun, they don't think of it as a deity or of its position as the abode of supernatural entities.[21] *Polo malo* merely means "up in the air" as opposed to "on the ground," or *piny*. The sense Lienhardt "identified" (that is, *mal* or *malo* as being hierarchically superior as in "upper," if that makes any obvious sense) appears to be newly introduced into Luo reference to indicate something close to the Christian "heaven" as the assumed abode of all perfections, in opposition to "earth" in the Christian sense of "worldliness" as the location of perversion and good that is only relative and imitative. Thus, rather than "identifying" in the Luo languages the Luo use of the term *mal*, Lienhardt and his fellow European anthropologists were in fact imposing on Dholuo a new use of the term. This imposition had some fundamental conceptual problems, as the analysis of p'Bitek's notion of *jok* below will show. The Luo think of entities in physical or quasi-physical terms as occupying space from where they can be summoned or related to in several other ways, indicating their proximity in nature to the physical reality of the living who communicate with them or the reality of the world in which such communication occurs. Because of this understanding of the nature of reality, the Luo speak of *piny* in ways that demand some explanation, however brief.

The term *piny* encompasses both physical and quasi-physical senses. In purely physical senses, *piny* means earth, the ground, or territory, all signifying occupied or occupiable space. At other times the idea of time is conjoined to the physical idea of *piny* to refer to the spatio-temporal category where existence takes place. *Ru piny*, for example, refers to duration or, rather literally, to the sequence of days in which the reality of objects is determined. The Luo speak of "*ru piny*" as real time because *piny*, viewed as reality in general rather than as merely physical space, is regarded as greater than the possible cumulative life span of all humans. For them, that greater reality is unthinkable except in terms of its own duration, which must be greater than the duration of the possible cumulative life of all humans. This is why the Luo speak of *ru piny* as wearing down even the slow-maturing *apindi* (of the family Rubiaceae) until its fruit ripens (*aming'a piny ne ochiego apindi e thim*). It is also said of *piny* that it is *piny nang'o*, that it outlasts (licks, swallows) everything. Because "*ru*" indicates time, as one can infer from the alternation of day and night (the visibility and invisibility of the sun and the twinklers), it appears that when used in this spatio-temporal (*ru piny*) sense the term *piny* refers to the entire universe and not just the earth or world. Everything that exists does so in time. *Ru piny* is therefore an abstract expression that depicts the category of space and time, which is almost always conceived of as one thing rather than two.[22] Also, the saying *"piny nang'o"* is used to indicate that the dead go to *piny*, not to *polo* or *malo*, "above," as in the Christian sense of "heaven above." Rather, for the Luo, the dead become *jo-piny* (*jok-piny* in central and northern Luo variations). To talk with the dead is to talk with those from *piny*, an act that the Luo regard as symptomatic of mental troubles or episodes of hallucination. Indeed, curiously, missionaries referred to nonconverts as *jo-piny*, those who remained traditional. So according to African missiology, there are *piny* names, such as Masolo, Omolo, Onyango, Athieno, Adongo, Okelo, and so on, all of which they saw as being in opposition to Christian ones such as George, Thomas and others that are "heavenly" (because they belonged to saints) that converts acquired when they were renamed at Christian baptism. The invention of this dualistic separation of indigenous worldliness ("of *piny*") from missionary godliness indicated the meeting of two irreconcilable oppositions in a space where only one could survive or dominate. In this case, Christianity sought to obliterate and replace African names with those of European and Jewish ancestry. As Mudimbe writes, "The indigenous traditions seemed like a sort of old alliance waiting for its conversion and transmutation into a new one."[23] As a result, *piny* came to signify evil for the missionaries, who quickly assigned it an opposition in the form of "up" or "heaven," the firmament, for which they used the term *polo*. With time, a new and parallel meaning of *piny* developed from these Christian twists.

The Concept of *Jok* in p'Bitek's Work

What, then, is or are *jok*? In tackling this question, Okot p'Bitek arrived at answers slightly different from those of Ogot and the missionaries and anthropologists. Inadvertently, however, p'Bitek began by unquestioningly accepting the category of religion as a helpful tool for analyzing and organizing Acholi thought, even though he disagreed with the earlier missionary and anthropological positions of Driberg, Lienhardt, and Hayley.[24] The English term "religion" is sometimes extended to refer to a variety of beliefs and practices that have not been found in many Western cultures since the dawn of Christianity and Islam. But this extension, as Shaw argues in "The Invention of 'African Traditional Religion,'" happens alongside the translation of elements of non-Western cultures into Western categories that continue to serve as the measuring standard. Hence, she concludes, "African religions" are the creation of, not just the victim of, Western scholarship. So how does the concept of *jok* fare in this new world? p'Bitek himself appears to be aware of the varying Christian attitudes toward non-

Western concepts of the inhabitants of the spiritual world.[25] Depending on how conservative a Christian scholar was, non-Christian deities were classified as "ghosts," "devils," or "pagan deities." The latter characterization, p'Bitek notes, was first introduced by a German missionary Max F. Müller and came to permeate the work and efforts of anthropologists and missionaries, including those who did not share in Müller's evolutionist view of "paganism." Quite arbitrarily, missionaries selected the local term they thought was closest to their Christian idea of god. In some cases, for example missionaries who lived among the Acholi, they experimented with different terms before settling on one, "Rubanga," which they borrowed from the Nyoro language.[26] In others, they introduced new words from their own vernaculars or from Kiswahili, both of which were equally foreign to the host community. Committed to proving the universality of the experience of the one supreme god, which p'Bitek denies ever was part of the Acholi world view, the missionaries not only reverted to awkward methods for their task, they often also chose quite wrong local terms for conceptualizing the Christian god. P'Bitek remarks that while the missionaries were eager to overlook the roots of the local words lest they frustrate their goals, "the original etymological sense of the word matters a great deal to someone who is primarily interested in the conception of gods as Africans see them, rather than in the *christianized* conceptions of these deities, the result of many years of preaching and teaching."[27] Guided by a strong sense of the autonomy of cultures, p'Bitek views conversion as highly doubtful, especially to an extent that would transform Christianity into a local experience. Many of his works reveal an understanding of culture as an arbitrary formulation of statements about origin, history, conduct, and social relations by which people define and make sense of themselves and their worlds of experience. To that extent, in p'Bitek's view, no culture is better than another, but each one becomes a source of deep pride for those who ascribe to and call it their own. Colonialism and cultural imperialism more generally were based on the misguided view that some cultures, particularly European ones, were better than most others in the rest of the world and needed to run them over. At the same time, cultures develop over such a long time that their conceptual ingredients become so standardized that they appear to be objective to the exclusion of other possibilities. For p'Bitek, relations between different cultures are guided by differences in political and military power, the ability of one cultural community to invade another and impose its own ways on it, rather than by the rational grounding of the constitutional beliefs of the respective cultures. In his *Song of Lawino,* the young cultural nationalist Lawino challenges her "westernized" husband Ocol to provide even one rational justification for his superficial aping of Western cultural characteristics (dress, speech, and other forms of comportment). P'Bitek also felt that African scholars became disciples in the project of Christianizing African religious conceptions through their work to counter Western scholars' and missionaries' disparaging assertions about African beliefs.

After an eloquent critique of Western misinterpretations of African ideas and concepts in the service of Christianity and other aspects of Western cultures, p'Bitek settles down to his own rendition of the concept of *jok*.[28] To put a critical question to p'Bitek: How does one escape the Christian influence with regard to the notion of *jok* without rejecting the dualist Christian influence of the two realms of reality, viz., the physical and the spiritual, the *piny* and *malo*? As I argued above, the dualism of the separation between the world and heaven was introduced rather arbitrarily by zealous missionaries intent on splitting Africans' worldviews into two separate, mutually independent, and unequal spheres in order to locate and provide an abode for a new deity in one of them.

According to p'Bitek, missionaries invented the idea of a high god for the Acholi and Lango and gave him the name Lubanga, which they borrowed from Bunyoro, where they had earlier worked, because they believed that the word *jok* did not have a precise referent or a definitely religious significance in Acholi language. The idea of a high god among the central Luo, p'Bitek writes, "was a creation of the missionaries."[29] The local (Acholi) idea of *jok* stands for "things" in Acholi conceptions of reality that can only vaguely be described as "spirits." They are not completely nonphysical, since the Acholi do not believe in spiritual entities (à la Descartes) that are independent and separable from their physical counterparts, as mind, or soul, for example, are thought of in Western modes of thought as separate and separable from the body. *Jok* are "members" of society (the clan, family, lineage, community, and so forth). Shrines (*abila*) are erected for them at different social (chiefdom, family, and individual) levels. Some *jok* originate from within the clan. Others are encountered in new settlements once inhabited by other Acholi clans or non-Acholi communities, and they are usually recognized by and can interact with their new neighbors. Such foreign *jok* speak their own tongues, hence those whom they possess imitate their tongues in gibberish utterances during ritual interactions with them. The Luo, including the Acholi and the Lango, distinguish foreign *jok* from their own familiar ones. The former tend to be violent and more demanding. Owuor Anyumba, writing as a young undergraduate researcher at Makerere University in 1954, made what remains the clearest analysis of the concept of *juok/juogi* yet.[30] He argued, correctly, that analysis of the concept reveals the reasonable belief that once people inhabit a place long enough to have called it home and to have buried their dead there they leave a sense of their influence on the environment. They give it a sense of their identity, especially by referring to the place by the names of some of their most prominent ancestors and leaders who may have helped conquer the territory or who died and were buried in it. Similarly, with time, the Luo regarded some places as theirs by identifying the ancestors (*juogi*) who had given these places their identity just as much as they recognized the *juogi* of groups who earlier had occupied the places they settled. Hence the appearance of the ferocious *juogi* of Lango (*juogi mag Lango,* also called *sewe*), by which name the Luo meant not their Ugandan kin the Langi but some groups of the Kalenjin and Maasai peoples. The *juogi* of these latter groups are called "Lango" because of their "wild" war cries and their behavior as if they are of control of their minds. The migratory Luo had seen these behaviors since the time of their arrival on the shores of Lake Lolwe (Lake Victoria to the British) and in the ensuing battles for territory. Historians tell us that probably this place once was inhabited by the Nandi, the Kipsigis, the Maasai and/or other Nilo-Hamitic groups, either contemporaneously in different parts or successively prior to the arrival of the Luo around 1750.[31]

If Anyumba is right, then p'Bitek's categories of *jok*[32] are understandable as part of the sociohistorical topography of the Acholi landscape and history. The various chiefdom *jok* name the various ancestors with whom members of some chiefly lineages identify. Their *jok* status is associated with mass deaths that were the result of war or other large-scale calamities, such as epidemics. To these one can add the *jok nam* (the *jok* of the river or lake), the *jok kulo* (the *jok* of the pond), the *jok thim* (the *jok* of the wilderness), and so on. These refer to the lingering identities of those who may have met their deaths in these places, some by accident, others as a result of war or suicide. Their bodies were not recovered for proper rituals and burial. The Luo believe that people who take their lives in anger or who die as victims of mistreatment by family "conceal" their remains from recovery but can be heard singing their lamentations when people visit or pass by the places where they died. They become *jok* (or *juogi*) of those locations. When they avenge their unfair deaths they become *chien* and torment the conscience of the culprits. In these senses, *jok* is a category of the mind—that is, it refers to mental content, a memory (as in historical knowledge) that people carry with them for generations and from which they infer a variety of moral and emotional awarenesses.

The categories of *jok* suggest that all *jok* were *jok piny,* as *piny* is the only place where they could abide. Also, it appears from the categories that the *jok* were not deities and were not worshiped, as was suggested by the old studies of the Shilluk, Acholi, and other Luo groups (by Driberg, Hayley, and Lienhardt). As p'Bitek remarks, European scholars of "African religions" were eager to find a pagan construct on which to build the conversion of natives to Christianity. Where there was none, they readily invented one. Missionaries appear to have introduced *malo* (up above, or heaven) to pave way for the construction of a dualist worldview that would facilitate the teaching of the heavenly Christian god whose abode was "up there."

According to p'Bitek, the *jok* are always particular; they are referred to by both their "proper" names and the specific category to which they belong.[33] "When the Nilotes encounter *jok*," he writes, "it is [always] with a specific and named or easily definable *jok*, and not some vague 'power' that they communicate with."[34] The *jogi* are individualized and are concrete; "they can also be, as it were, known [apprehended] through the senses."[35]

It would appear, therefore, that although p'Bitek asserts that the *jogi* are identifiable in their individuality, they actually are not entities in the sense of independently existing substances. Rather, they are part of the wider social world extended to the departed through the ritualization of memory. When people claim a historical identity, they cite their ancestors and the places they believe they came from. They align with them in claiming places because of known or believed relations with them. Hence the saying "this is the American way, or spirit" exhorts in those who utter it or in those at whom it is aimed a sense of aligning with those who relate similarly to the utterance. As we would say in my mother tongue, it is a sort of *gweyo*, a declaration of a social identity. In broader political terms, it is a patriotic call that separates us from Others. For the purposes of personal identity and for identifying places as once occupied by foregoing ancestors, the Luo place their claim to land, to history, and to a place within their social organization. Personal narratives are composed around clan biographies that tell of one's clan and its territory and history, which are crucial elements in the composition of personhood. For one to claim to be a Ja-Kaugagi (sing.), for example, implies the ability of the claimant to identify with leading ancestral figures of the Kaugagi clan, to narrate the history of that clan's achievements, and to describe and identify with well-known symbols of that clan's claimed territory. By doing this the claimant reveals their personhood, they lay claim to moral ideals that they perceive to make such a community, and they give to others their social identity (the stuff with which they are made). He or she becomes part of the wider social world of Jo-Kaugagi (pl.), which determines how he or she plays his or her part in relation to others in the expanding social landscape.

Piny as the Center of the Universe

There are other senses of *piny*. In the political sense, one can speak of "*piny*" as ultimate authority, especially when or where the idea of political authority is implied. *Jo-piny* is usually regarded as the ultimate source of current and long-established laws. In the former sense of juridical source, authority is referred to simply as *piny*, "the land," and is usually to be understood to refer to the regulations of civil society, a system of laws as enforced by a recognized and orderly chain of command. "*Piny owacho*" (literally, "the land has spoken"), used in the present tense and without the prefix *jo-*, refers to directives from a higher office of government or civil society. But when it is used with the prefix and in the past tense, as in *"jo-piny nene owacho"* (literally, as it was said by those who now have gone into the earth [ancestors]), a second and different source and type of law is implied. In this second sense, the phrase refers to the authority of tradition as long set by the dictates of the wise. *Jo-piny*, as opposed to *jo-dak* (resident aliens, usually a few families from a different clan, one or more of whom may be related to the locals by marriage), are the indigenous local people whose customary laws rule supreme and define the traditional regime over the conduct of those who consider themselves to be members of the group. The customary laws provide the grounds by which members identify themselves; they provide the threads for the cohesion of the group. Hence, to attribute a required action or behavior to the dictum of *jo-piny* is to appeal to a genealogy of a principle in the search for guidance about the rectitude of conduct. That genealogy is the key to reconstructing the informing reason in people's moral preferences, as is well said by the Cameroonian philosopher-theologian Eboussi-Boulaga:

> The living person will bring into play all the resources of hermeneutics, that art of demonstrating one's participation in the same moral, intellectual, and aesthetic community with those of the past in spite of distance and differences . . . the value of the acknowledgment of the historicity of one's own particularity.[36]

While the civil or legal *piny owacho* carries a tone of surrender to and frustration with the apparent unquestionability of the dictum as an order, the customary or moral *jo-piny nene owacho* lends itself to a possible reexamination and interpretation for particular application. It is often called *jo-ma riek*, those versed in the understanding of appropriate application (i.e., interpretation or rationalization, if you wish) of such matters. The history of the juridical sense of *piny* in *piny owacho* suggests that it is usually used in jest, a sort of critique of sources of principles of conduct that do not allow for discourse about their legitimacy because they present themselves as if they were authoritative by nature or as unstoppable as the earth's natural revolution around the sun. It was coined as a critical reference to the absolutist image of colonial authority.[37]

It is clear from these accounts of the meanings of the concept *piny* (as world, earth, authority, or universe) that it is not always thought of as being lower or less than anything else. Rather, in a human-centered consideration of the complexity of life and its travails, there might not be another place to look for an ideal prototype. Humans can only refer to their genealogies to recover lessons that sustain social stability. Thus, inferring worldly matters from the dualism the anthropologists and missionaries spoke of, which Ogot sought to defend and legitimate as supposedly lesser values compared to the values of *mal* or *malo,* is invalidated by this analysis of the concept *piny* because it cannot be inferred from the Luo world view.

The Tempels Factor

Ogot's analysis of the concept of *jok* (or *juok*) as the vital force has its origin in historical circumstances. Writing in 1961, only two or so years after the English translation of Tempels's *Bantu Philosophy,* Ogot was an understandable victim of the sweeping influence that the missionary's work had on a wide range of readers in his challenge to the primitivist view of Africans that the colonial archive (of administrators, missionaries, and anthropologists) advanced. His endorsement of Tempels's idea that the vital force was present in all things explains his accord with Lienhardt's invented distinction between *jok mal* and *jok piny* as "higher" and "lower" *jok,* respectively.[38] But these too are probably overzealous interpretations of the term *jok. Jok* (or *juok*) has several shades of interrelated meanings, although all of them lie at the center of social and moral thought. First among these is the use of the term for the ancestral name(s) (sing. *juok,* pl. *juogi*) given to individuals as their "official" or ritual family names, often from the maternal or paternal sides of one's ancestry. When a child is named after such an ancestor, the child's name becomes a special point for regrounding the memory of the ancestor among kin, and members of her/his family relate to the name with respect and fondness befitting the social status of the ancestor the child is named for. The Luo believe that the dead continue to linger "somewhere" after death and continue to interact with family. But because this "lingering somewhere" is not meant literally, if someone were to claim that they "saw" an ancestor, however well regarded he or she might have been in life, the claim would quickly be taken as a sign of a mental degradation on the part of the claimant. In other words, things of the mind are not subject to claims of direct sensory experience unless one is out of his or her mind. It is believed that the ancestors "demand," through the mediation of diviners, to be named, and several descendants can be named for the same ancestor. This is the way the Luo keep track of their social world and its network and history. That is, it is a system of nomen conservandum, or *nono* (as in Nyaugagi, which indicates Ja-Kaugagi, or Nyaruoth, which indicates Ja-Ka Ruoth, etc.). This must have been a socially and morally useful practice because it made the ancestry of individuals evident through their names, thus helping to prevent inbreeding by incest: people are not allowed to marry or have sexual relations with anyone known or suspected to share with them even the faintest shade of ancestry. And, as I mentioned earlier, it provides individuals with the means for articulating their personhood. Christian missionaries classified these *jougi* as *piny*-names and condemned them as signs of pagan ancestor worship. Ironically, on the other hand, names of European and Jewish ancestry were regarded as godly and were imposed on African converts to replace their own indigenous ones because, the missionaries explained, the owners of those names were in *polo malo* (heaven above). Even today African converts are encouraged, even by their fellow African churchmen and churchwomen, to pray to the European and Jewish dead whose names they bear to intercede for them when they want favors from god. But praying to one's own clan ancestors amounted to ancestor worship and was therefore prohibited. A few Africans have been added to this overwhelmingly European and Palestinian heavenly population, most notably the Christian Martyrs of Uganda in the 1880s, but such additions are first and foremost grounded in a person's renunciation of African ways and authorities. Kenyan theologian John Mbiti wrote eloquently about Africans' idea of community as one that includes not only the living but also the "living dead," as he called them.[39] Perhaps the idea of the living carrying the names of their ancestors as their *juogi* is a good example of Mbiti's point that ancestors are seen as continuing to live for a long time until they are no longer remembered by the living, meaning when their genealogical position is too far back for active and useful memory. The best-known Kenyan case of rebellion against the missionaries' war against African names is what the late Kenyan politician Oginga Odinga recorded in his political autobiography, *Not Yet Uhuru*. Although it was fashionable for converts to adopt new foreign names, Odinga was indifferent to the usefulness of baptism generally and to the significance of adopting non-African names particularly. Despite his opposition, he accepted the imposition of the names Obadiah Adonijah as a condition of attending school. He never used them. For a while Odinga appeared to like the white man's religion, until, he says, "it dawned on me that I had listened to many preachers and they seemed, all of them, to preach one thing in common—the suppression of African customs. . . . They tried to use the word of God to judge African traditions."[40] In later years Odinga raised much controversy when he insisted on having his children baptized with African names in missionary churches. Ironically, it was a European missionary, not the African padres, who agreed to baptize Odinga's children with African names, a practice that became fashionable thereafter for both its elegance and political significance. Says Odinga: "I was delighted: I had lived up to one of my strongest convictions. But the stories went about that I was abnormal, and strange."[41] The charges of abnormality and strangeness stem from the position, shared by missionary and indigenous cultural theories alike (albeit for different reasons), that the two were contrary to each other; one could not be both a follower of indigenous ways and a Christian. In one sense, Odinga's narrative seeks to undermine the separation the missionaries created between the "old" and "new" in their quest to overrun indigenous customs and traditions with Christian ones. His narrative is even more interesting than usual since he describes the "old" Luo traditions as that of a cultural "Other" whose deep significance appeared to be totally unknown to the agents of Christianity. According to him, "religion" is the real sign of difference between his people and Europeans, and his description of being Luo takes the form of an account of the customs and manners of the people. These accounts show the strangeness of Luo traditions in all kinds of detail, but especially in the practice of naming and giving identity to people.

In another sense, Odinga's accounts of Luo customs and manners and his defiance of Christian views of him as a pagan fiercely reject the practice of publicly branding people by totally overlooking how the affected persons privately view themselves. The account thus reveals the tensions between public-objectivist and private-subjectivist theories of identity; that is, opposing how people view themselves to how sets of collective beliefs, especially those that define membership in institutions and movements, standardize how, who, and what the members should be. Yet contrary to this demand, identities are not totally public spaces that are freely accessible from the outside.

Few Africans have actually reinstated the dignity of African ancestral names within Christian discourse as Odinga did. This fact gives the impression that conversion to Christianity is possible only when one negates one's African identity. This schism, obviously, reflects the oppositional dichotomy that scholars such as Lienhardt and Driberg created. Odinga sought to break this dichotomy by demanding that his children's *juogi* (Ng'ong'a, Molo, Oburu, Rayila, Amolo, and Odinga) be assimilated into an African Christian ancestry, thus paving the way for what Eboussi-Boulaga offers as an example of a Christic model.

P'Bitek's analysis of *jok* reveals that there is more than one way to understand the term. He maintains that *jok* are perceived as physical or quasi-physical in nature and that they act as good or bad moral agents, by which he aims to show that the Luo-speaking Acholi do not think of reality in dualist terms that include the idea of spiritual entities or substances. Some *jok* can prevent personal or collective misfortune such as illness, plague, or crop failure, while others are blamed for delivering misfortune. But the Acholi do not think of such outcomes as the result of visitations by spiritual entities from another world. There are morally good and bad *jok*, an idea that seems to be part of the idea of the possessive *juogi* among the southern Luo, as Anyumba discusses.[42] In p'Bitek's view, the good *juogi* are usually a source of medicinal knowledge that they are believed to reveal to those they possess. The bad *juogi*, on the other hand, torment their mediums and demand sacrifice from them more often than they are helpful. In Anyumba's view, the *juogi* of Lango (more precisely, of the Nandi, the Kipsigis, and the Maasai), or *sewe*, are usually identified with the latter type.[43] They are generally regarded as hostile. This is only figurative language, as the *juogi* (Southern Luo; *jogi* in Acholi) are not physical beings. The noun is a conceptual indicator of how a community that is moving to a new territorial space for the first time represents and deals with its awareness that other people have preceded it there. This awareness, which sometimes includes memories of conflicts, may involve getting rid of foreign values connected to uses of space and replacing them with new ones. The process is often complex, as some of the values of preceding settlers may be good and fit to retain while others must be discarded or avoided. The *juogi* (*jogi*), then, are "real" only to the extent that they are ideas and images of other people, especially in historical terms of their perceived influence on the social and psychological adjustments of later generations or communities.

It is in these figurative respects of dealing with historical memories and representations, that, according to p'Bitek, the bad *jok* can be hunted down, captured, and killed, suggesting that *juok* is a mode of being that merely conceals the *referent,* which are the real (physical and historical) people, but does not transform or transubstantiate from the physical mode.[44] These analyses of the indigenous uses of the term show that *jok* does not even once come close to referring to a substance or to a metaphysical quality or attribute of a substance.

Juok as the Moral Quality of Practice

In the social and moral senses, *juok* means an anti-social attitude and character. A behavior is branded as *juok* if it is intentionally aimed at harming others or if it is intentionally weird and out of line with expectations of reasonableness toward other people and/or things (such as other people's property) or when it is determined to have been well calculated to cause some form of harm or unpleasant experience (such as fear, anxiety, or shock) to other persons. *Juok* is usually carried out covertly, even when it involves some form of violence. In this sense, the harm that is caused through *juok* is quite different from the harm caused by acts that are generally classified as criminal. Thus, killing another person in a physical fight does not qualify as *juok* if the protagonists openly engage in a conflict from which they are aware that physical harm can ensue. A *jajuok,* as the agent of *juok* is called, waylays his or her victim at conveniently isolated or bushy places or stalks them to such isolated spots before making moves and/throwing objects to frighten them. Usually a *jajuok* does not kill and does not throw objects to hit his or her victim in order to cause physical harm; such harm can occur only by accident. Thus a *jajuok* is not a murderer, unless the habit of *juok* of this kind becomes for them a convenient cover for committing a premeditated crime. Sometimes, and indeed most frequently, they simply terrify others, causing fear in them by frightening them under cover of night or frightening them by sneaking into their homestead and throwing objects on the roofs of their houses as they sleep. Also, they simply run up and down inside or around other people's compounds in the night, frightening the owners and their animals. This act is called *yido,* and the habitual practice of it, which becomes part of a person's character, is known as *juog yido.* It is said that the "power" of this *juok,* actually an intense urge similar to the drive of an obsessive compulsion, can overwhelm its practitioner so much that he or she may feel like "running" even in daylight or it can drive them to want to play "*juok* games" (usually dirty tricks) on others. But, unlike the obsession of Freud's theory in which the individual is actually a victim of the drive of which they may not be aware or have an explanation for, *juog yido* is acquired. It is learned, and a person can decide of his or her own free will whether to take part in the practice or not. When one is called *jajuok,* moral blame is implied. It is assumed that the person has freely chosen to behave in that manner and that he or she continues to freely decide to do so.

Acts of *juok* are recognized as radically different from those of mentally ill or spirit-possessed persons. Unlike the latter, acts characterized to be of *juok* are considered to be intentional; they express the moral intention of the doer. Despite occasional similarities in the behavior of a mentally ill person and a person who is *jajuok,* a person who is mentally sick (*wiye rach, otuo,* has a bad mind, is sick) exhibits a consistent pattern of unwanted conduct; they consistently behave in ways that are considered deviant regardless of place, time, or social circumstance. They lack the capacity to understand the consequences of their actions and fail to deliberately vary the timing of their behavior to match goals with appropriateness, a fault that reveals their lack of awareness of self-esteem and moral self-preservation. Thus they may, for example, urinate or behave in other indecent ways in full view of an in-law or the general public or say taboo things in awkward circumstances. Like mentally sick people, those possessed by spirits are also generally regarded to be free of moral blame for their behavior. Because their condition follows a public and ritualized pattern, the public symbols they carry (objects associated with spirit possession such as rowing paddles) exonerate them from public judgment and sanctioning. The implication is that there appear to be clear criteria for the classification of public behavior that make these behavioral distinctions possible.

Juok is acquired or learned by both instruction and imitation, perhaps interspersed and alternated according to age of the learner. It is practiced within families and can be brought to a man and his future children by a wife who was born into and brought up by a practicing family. Similarly, a woman from an innocent family can learn *juok* after marrying a husband who already practices it with his own family of birth. But due to its social stigma, *juok* is not publicly admitted, and a dissenting initiate or an unrelenting importer could be killed for fear that they would reveal the family secret or spread the unwanted behavior to a nonpracticing family or clan. It is said that a *jajuok* lacks moral restraint (*wang'e tek*) and shame—that is, he or she is not restrained by the presence of others. At opportune times, a *jajuok* boldly suspends her conscience in pursuit of her individualistic motive. The saying "*Wang'i tek ka wang' jajuok*" (You are bold or lack moral restraint like a *jajuok*) is a strong rebuke of persons prone to unflinching public misconduct. Such persons lack compassion for others, except perhaps for members of their own immediate family, with whom they share habits and therefore mutual sympathy. The idea and practice of calling a night-runner *jajuok* derives from the more general moral connotation of the term.

Because of these habits, this type of *juok* is practiced strictly in the night, which makes a *jajuok* a master of the nocturnal world. Both legend and scanty evidence suggest that people who practice this type of *juok* tame nocturnal and other wild animals (such as leopards or snakes) as pets, which they take with them on their rendezvous. If true, such company would certainly greatly enhance their capacity to terrify their victims. Yet they would also need to handle them with care so their unusual companions would not cause any physical harm to people. The best-known account of this type of *juok* is Onyango-Abuje's novel *Fire and Vengeance,* a curiously detailed description of the demeanor and mental state of a *jajuok* during the act. According to Abuje, a *jajuok* does not venture into unfamiliar territories lest they fall into traps or trip over unknown obstacles. Like soldiers of the night, their dominance over victims is based on the element of surprise and knowledge of escape routes. Should their victims turn against and try to attack them, their safety would depend on speed and thorough familiarity with the terrain of the neighborhood.

Another form of behavioral *juok* is believed to be practiced by individuals who use a variety of means, all of which are classifiable under the general category of "magic and witchcraft," to cause real harm to their victims. The *jajuok* of this category can be a *janawi*, a *jandagla*, a *jasihoho*, a *jabilo*, or a *jatung'*. It is believed that the "medicine" of the first three kills instantly or after only a short illness. It is believed that the "medicine" of *janawi* and *jandagla* is usually materially symbolized and that it can be sent or shipped to the victim. It must contact the victim to work, yet it is not poison in chemical terms. A *jasihoho*, on the other hand, has her "power" "inside" her and is said to strike her victims by merely looking at them. A *jatung*'s "medicine" is believed to kill its victim slowly, after a prolonged and often emaciating illness. The *jabilo*, whose practice does not quite fit with the others in this category, is believed to cause harm by frustrating the efforts of his or her victims, especially by turning them into failures even where success has been routine or a genuine reward. Thus, the *jabilo* is driven by jealousy, either his own jealousy or the jealousy of those who hire their services against an envied third party with whom a person is competing. He overpowers and puts in check the performative capacities of a real or perceived rival for the benefit of himself or his client.

Juok Is Not a Metaphysical Property

Contrary to older interpretations, especially those influenced by Tempels, such as Ogot's, there are different senses of the term *juok* that are not reductively reconcilable under one concept. To claim that *juok* is a kind of "force" in Tempels's sense is tantamount to claiming that all the senses of the term (as ancestral names, as the mischievous actions of the night-runner or *juog yido,* and as the magical powers of the *janawi, jandagla, jabilo, jasihoho,* and *jatung'*) listed above share a single basic or root meaning. Such a position claims, for example, that *juok* is a "power" that enables people who act in those capacities to do so. Two problems arise from this claim. First is the universal extension of the attribute to everything, à la Tempels. Second, if *juok* was a metaphysical attribute, then calling someone a *jajuok* would not amount to an accusation, and anyone who was called that would not take offense. It would be an amoral description similar to describing him or her as having two legs and arms. But, ordinarily people do take offense when they are described as being *jajuok* because the description is understood to imply culpability for conduct associated with the trait. I have shown that the extension of the meaning of *juok* to everything that is, as a metaphysical attribute, is attributable to the influence of Tempels's idea of the "vital force" but that it is hardly supportable by an analysis of the various meanings and uses of the term within the languages or dialects to which it belongs. According to Ogot's theory, all existents—that is, humans, spirits, animals, plants, inanimate objects, and ideas—share the common property called *juok.* But if indeed it was the case that *juok* was a general property that humans shared with the inanimate world, objects would, at least at times, be referred to in Dholuo as *jajuok,* as is done for humans, to impute to them some sort of agency. But this is incorrect Dholuo, both grammatically and categorically. Things (inanimate objects) cannot be referred to with the prefix *"ja"* because, as in relation to *juok,* for example, it implies attribution of agency—that is, the capacity to deliberate about or perform actions and hence responsibility for actions that can be either praiseworthy or blameworthy. For these reasons, only humans are truly *ja*-something, for example, *jakuo* (thief), *ja-mriambo* (liar), *ja-mrima* (ill tempered), and so on. The exclusion of the nonhuman world from such agentive noun formations is based on the classification of (nonhuman) things outside the category of moral agents because they do not deliberate. Another noun-forming prefix is *ra-,* as in *rakido* (multicolored or, in moral terms, of unfixed and hence unpredictable temperament), *ranyiego* (prone to jealousy), *raneko* (mad), *rasihingwa* (incompletely developed mentally, as in schizophrenics and people with a debilitating degree of autism), and *rariwa* (closely akin to *rasihingwa*). In all these cases, the names apply only to humans because of the agency of those to whom the names refer. The prefix *ra-* is used commonly for both humans and nonhuman things only in cases that refer to physical attributes, as in *rateng'* (black), *rabet* (big one), and so on. One cannot refer to (nonhuman) things simply as *juok* (without the prefix), because *juok* is pure character or quality of action. One does not refer to a stone in Dholuo as *juok,* but in appropriate circumstances one can refer to it as *gir juok* (an object or tool of *juok*). To say of something (or sometimes of an animal) that it is *gir juok* is to claim that it is an object that belongs to someone who uses it in their practice of some kind of *juok*. It may be a chip of rock or stone or a collection of a variety of different objects. Sometimes it is the strange nature of the location of such object(s) or the unusual nature of the collection that bring to mind suspicion of a deliberate action behind the object(s). In such circumstances the mind behind the object(s) is probed and may be regarded as either functionally twisted, as in the case of someone out of their mind; functionally immature and playful, as in the case of children; or morally twisted, or calculatively or deliberately up to some dirty trick, language that means that malice is intended, as in the case of a *janawi,* a *jatung',* a *jandagla,* and so forth. If one of the former two possibilities is established, that is, that the objects were the work of someone rationally incapacitated or out of their mind or that they were the work of children at play, then the charge of *juok* is usually invalidated. In other words, when a charge of *juok* is made, it must be assumed that the perpetrator has a moral motive and that the behavior is indeed the act of a well-reasoning but evil-bent agent. But the object(s), in and of itself or themselves, qualify(ies) only as *gir juok* (pl. *gik juok*), the artifacts of someone with *juok* (morally evil) intentions. It is clear that in such a case *juok* is not being attributed to the objects but to the moral intentions of the human agent suspected to be behind the objects. The tamed leopard that the night-runner takes on the nocturnal rendezvous is his or her "*juok* thing" (*gir juok*), and so is the potted fire he or she carries to flash around as he or she dashes through the dark night. The only time *juok* is attributed to a thing is in regard to earth, *lowo,* when it is said, usually in mourning, that *lowo jajuok,* meaning that it (mother earth) is so evil it takes the beloved ones at their prime. The attribution of *juok* to the earth is a symbolic reference to the earth's value as a caretaker, like a mother who should be kind and caring. Instead she takes away beloved ones. Thus, even in this context, the attribution of *juok,* always to a deed, requires at least the figurative senses of person and moral capacity. So a mourner remembering their departed beloved one can sometimes be heard to say "*Lowo wang'e tek n'okawo Julie-na*" (The earth is so bold it took my Julie).

In these behavior-related senses, the term *juok* is understood to indicate moral judgement on the conduct of persons. Hence, not everyone can be referred to as a *jajuok*, but anyone can be referred to as such if they behave in ways that suggest ill intentions in their conduct. A person can be called *jajuok* if, for example, when swimming with others, he or she tries to play games that mimic or are perceived as betraying intentions of drowning a companion. A person is also said to behave in a *juok*-like manner if he or she intentionally misleads others into misconduct that will likely cause harm to themselves or a third party. A *jajuok* is, by and large, a person who is publicly regarded as having a propensity to behave in morally unacceptable ways. Thus, *juok* is not a characterization people attribute to themselves. Rather, it is imposed on them by the judgment of others. *Juok* is the daring and unrestrained moral capacity to commit evil.

Public and Private Identity

The second problem with the interpretation of *juok* as a metaphysical attribute is the claim that it can be extended to humans and objects alike. Let us assume now that *juok* does indeed stand for something in the identity of people and objects. In that case it would be so commonplace that it probably would matter little to them that people had it at all, except in the degree of its quality, just as people care not about why they are made of matter like lizards or like wood but about whether or not others regard their bodies as beautiful or admirable. Hence they take care of their bodies so they don't look scaly like lizards or dry like the bark on wood. If *juok* was this kind of attribute—that is, if humans had or were *juok* in their natural constitution, just as they are material or corporeal, they probably would take it for granted as an integral part of existence. People would talk about or refer to this specific attribute in ways that indicate that they reconcile their private sense of identity with what is publicly attributed to or said of them by others, because it would be a commonly and universally possessed thing. It would not be a problem for anyone to accept being referred to as having *juok*, just as no one objects to having *del* (a body), an appropriate amount of *teko* (physical strength), and *paro* (thoughts, ideas). People generally possess these attributes in varying degrees (such as having good or bad physical health; much, just enough, or very little strength or energy; good or bad ideas, and so on), but they do not object to having the attributes themselves. Together these attributes make up what everyone refers to as their *ringruok* (self). We accept and feel proud when we are told that we have greater degrees of those qualities or attributes but we do not react this way when we are told we have *juok* in any form. When someone accepts being called *jajuok* it is usually either in jest (as when they are aware that *juok* is being attributed to them as a friendly joke) or because they are not in the right mental state to comprehend the moral significance of the attribute for their public standing. The average person who is aware of their moral self-worth will be very disappointed and angry when they realize that they are being accused of such a grave matter.

The fact that people will usually not accept the attribute of *juok* for themselves may indicate that it is either not an attribute that people share or one that is not a constitutive part of selfhood and so cannot be taken for granted as we regard having a body, being strong, or having ideas. Indeed, the reason people reject the attribute is that it does not describe one's social standing or relations with others in a positive light. Rather, it is a negative reference to possible behavior. Morally conscious people tend to easily accept praise and strongly protest blame or the imputation of wrongdoing.[45]

The question, then, is whether *juogi* really are metaphysical entities or whether they are a strategy for exerting social and moral control over others. The discourse around the idea of *juogi* points to the practical social and moral implications of the idea rather than to its metaphysical status. In genealogical terms, *jok/juok* (pl. *jogi/juogi*) is a noun or concept by which the one indicates or describes the social history of a group such as a family, clan, or lineage, which may be their own or that of another ethnic community with which they may have interacted.[46] That way, a family's collective memory and its collection of complex social origins are publicly manifested and immortalized in the knowledge of the names individuals carry. Thus when a family is identifiable as Jok-someone, as in Joka-Masolo or *jok'*Ajienga, for example, they will, by virtue of the history of the name, be in turn identifiable as related to Joka-Ugagi and Joka-Nyinek. This knowledge usually is not solely for the consumption of people outside the family that is portraying itself thusly. For the members themselves, the symbolism of names is a reminder of the social and moral obligations across generations of individuals and the groups they belong to. It facilitates the transcendence and isolation of the self by exposing individuals to the binding moral relations they have with others. Elsewhere I have described the social and moral importance of this network as follows:

> Knowledge of the larger social system of which one was part, and of one's exact location within it, was crucial for determining rights and duties as well as general comportment (from and) toward others. Individual and community were related in a constant mutual dependency: the specific behavior of individuals in various contexts gave the community its cultural boundaries and identity just as much as the normative standards of the community regulated the practices of individuals and groups within it. . . . They provided the ultimate reference for social and moral control. . . . By constantly evaluating

and adjusting one's conduct in accordance with known or assumed expectations of other members within any relational circuit, one shifts the focus of their conduct from self to the group where the maintenance of shared values takes precedence.[47]

In moral terms, this social situation indicates strongly that while determining whether an action is right and wrong takes place partly as a process of judgment and inference at the cognitive level that is itself explicable in terms of physio-psychological events, the grounds for and the significance of making such judgments and inferences stem from the fact that our moral agency is propelled by our basic reality as relational beings whose specifically human abilities are grounded in communication. This social foundation of morals is what Kwasi Wiredu called the "principle of sympathetic impartiality."[48] According to Eboussi-Boulaga, the social system, in its historical and present forms, is the genealogical basis of the religious and moral construction of the world in which "the logic of membership, confronted with the problem of temporal continuity and discontinuity, does not proceed according to the binary logic of true or false. A living community's past cannot be contradistinguished from its present as 'true' or 'false.'"[49]

The voices of *juogi* are equated to those of ancestors that are considered a source of authority and guidance in the setting of order (*jopiny owacho*), especially when the voice can allegedly be heard "directly" by a chosen one such as a medium. By mediating the ancestral voices (authority), the diviner and the medium become semi-autonomous sources of power: they exercise the capacity to exclude, repress, subjugate, and censor knowledge and information in order to prescribe what they alone will determine becomes public knowledge and behavior. It is not surprising that rulers usually hired the services of *jobilo* as symbols and legitimators of their claims to extraordinary authority, which is exactly what chiefs and priests have done with the coming of colonialism and Christianity. The colonial authority became the *piny owacho,* the unquestionable authority and ultimate source of law. Under the protection of the claim that he or she performs on behalf of society, the diviner produces and reproduces "objects" and "truth." An *ajuoga,* as the diviner is called, is one who determines and allocates what people should know about both their historical and present social worlds, the character of those they interact with in their daily lives, and how they are to respond to those individuals. An *ajuoga* acts with, on behalf of, and assumedly for the people, as do his or her *jabilo* colleagues. In these terms, then, *jajuok* is the linguistic antonym and social and moral antithesis of *ajuoga.* Unlike the latter, a person who is *jajuok* acts alone, against the majority, and for selfish interests.[50] That is why a person who is *jajuok* is said to be antisocial; usually he or she is a loner, which evokes suspicion that he or she must be mischievous, ill-willed, evil, and so on. The "must be" is not a logical inference from their characteristic reclusivity. Rather, it is an expression of disapproval of their deviance from communal norms and expectations. It is a rhetorical rebuke. *Jatung', janawi, jandagla,* and *jajuok* are all considered to be adversaries of the communal good. They are the unwilling wielders of much power in their communities. They are unwilling because none of them ever does or would ever accept any such label; it is the *ajuoga* who claims the ability to reveal them. Even the much less harmful *jajuog-otieno* (night-runner) will do anything to conceal his or her identity. They act in dead silence and will not make a sound by crying out or pleading for mercy even under the severe physical punishment to which they are often subjected when they are caught in the act. Nor will they plead guilty to charges branding them as *jajuok*. Instead they will offer alibis or tell make-believe stories that portray their conduct as ordinary, reasonable, and harmless. In other words, *juok* is an attribute and characterization that no one accepts publicly because of the negative moral connotations it entails. One is only suspected of being or believed to be a *jajuok*, but one is never known for certain to be one. Those who claim they actually have caught or seen and identified a *jajuok* in the act are always vague about the identity of the culprit. They will cite another commonly held belief—that a *jajuok* is likely to cause physical harm to those who reveal them—as justification for such vagueness.[51] Thus, while the identity of who exactly in a community is a *jajuok* remains a mystery, the attributes that befit the designation are openly discussed, and people enjoy telling tales about how a *jajuok*'s behavior outside their houses kept them awake all night or how a *jajuok* menaced them as they walked home from or away to some other village at night. The majority of rural Luo have at least one story of an encounter with these mysterious masters of the nocturnal world.

The accusations and denials of having *juok* reveal an interesting competition between public-objective and private-subjective perceptions of the identities of persons. On the objective side, society endows a person with distinctive qualities, capacities, and roles that, as Meyer Fortes writes, "enable the person to be known to be, and also to show himself to be the person he is supposed to be."[52] But this is so only when the allocated qualities, capacities, and roles and the social image they create place the individual in a positive enough public or social standing for them to want to identify with such attributes. Thus, in *pakruok* (public boasting about one's virtue), people do not object to the names and other forms of characterizations friends heap on them, even when they are inaccurate, grossly exaggerated, or totally false, so long as they are positive. But protest is never in short supply when such names and characterizations are deemed to cast a negative image on a person. Schizophrenic persons usually believe and act as if it is everyone else who is sick, not themselves. So, according to Fortes, "Looked at from the subjective side, it is a question of how the individual, as [an] actor, knows himself to be—or not to be—the person he is expected [and is said] to be in a given situation and status. The individual is not a passive bearer of personhood."[53] Because *juok* exposes the objective-subjective dialectic in the cultivation of personhood as observed by Fortes, it is an important tool for tracing and identifying the connections and separations between public (external) and private (internal) knowledge and expressions of personhood.

Philosophers have only recently come to appreciate this classic thesis of cultural anthropologists—namely that individuals and society are interconnected in mutual regulation—which they formulated after observing and analyzing how social organization and culture shape the expression of personhood.[54] Reflecting on the possible ramifications of the qualitative theory of action, Charles Taylor, who is perhaps the best-known contemporary Western theoretician of the action-based concept of selfhood, puts it thus:

> The notion is that we are capable of grasping our own action in a way that we cannot come to know external objects and events. In other words, there is a knowledge we are capable of concerning our own action which we can attain as the doers of this action; and this is different from the knowledge we may gain of objects we observe or scrutinize. . . . Action is distinct in that it is directed, aimed to encompass ends or purposes. And this notion of directedness is part of our conception of agency: the agent is the being responsible for the direction of action, the being for whom and through whom action is directed as it is. The notion of action is normally correlative to that of an agent.[55]

In his massive work dedicated to the study of the changing understandings of what it means to be a person in the history of Western history and thought,[56] Taylor believes the self to be an inherently moral entity, an agent of his actions, always situated in moral space. Tom Beidelman's discussion of the Kaguru idea of witches captures the notion of the social basis of the idea of evil and reveals similarities with the idea of *juok* as a concept for imagining the character of individuals in relation to a society's moral ideals. These ideals include decent self-presentation, openness, and mutual sympathy in relations with others, virtues that stand in direct opposition to the character of a *jajuok,* who runs naked at night, is secretive, and derives pleasure from causing fear in others and watching it engulf them. As I said earlier, a *jajuok*'s strategy lies in his or her ability to grab control of a situation by surprising the victim and overwhelming him or her with fear, especially under conditions where or when they are likely to develop a sense of helplessness, thus reducing the victim to such extreme levels of fear that they become almost totally senseless. This is why it is said that the power of the *jajuok* makes victims become so overpowered by the fear of the unknown that they surrender to fate, especially when a *jajuok* frightens them in dark and isolated places. A *jajuok* will choose a victim carefully, always avoiding people known in their villages for their courage and combativeness. The power of a *jajuok* is not absolute; it can be countered and even be conquered by an ordinary yet stronger will. According to Beidelman, "Belief in witchcraft is a mode of imagining evil, judged harmful, bad, and beyond any moral justification."[57] In other words, *juok* or evil is a means by which society marks the boundaries of social order by identifying behavior, real and imagined, that threatens its sustenance. The aim is to check the behavior of wayward individuals by labeling them with dispositions they are unlikely to accept as accurate descriptions of who they know themselves to be. And the accusations are made to help place the suspect individual's behavior under public scrutiny and disapproval, thus—at least it is hoped—influencing the individual toward self-examination and possible conformity.

The Double Role of *Ajuoga* as a Moral Guardian and Agitator

Related to the moral connotations of *juok* is its derivative sense, *ajuoga*, usually used for the diviner. He or she is the person who reveals the complicity of a *janawi*, a *jatung'*, a *jandagla*, or even a *jajuog otieno* in the misfortune of others. He or she is also the "medicine person" who gives the curative antidotes against the *juok* of the aforementioned individuals. Sometimes an *ajuoga* can double as a *jachieth*, usually an herbalist whose expertise is purely pharmacological, but he or she will mainly be known for divining work as the basis of their practice. Also, sometimes an *ajuoga* can double in one of the morally negative roles because they have the diagnostic knowledge of the powers of a *janawi*, a *jatung'* or a *jandagla*.

I submit that given the many incompatible senses of the term, it would be hard to back up the view that *juok* has just one common meaning for everything in nature. If it were so, the term would have to be understood as signifying some property, such as mass, that is shared by all things of which it is an attribute. This would further imply that all the members of at least one category of material things, such as stones, for example, would have it in the same proportion. We have just seen that people do not speak of the *juok* of stones, grass, trees, or beasts. Nor do they refer to all living humans as *juok,* much less to nonhuman nature. We have also seen that among humans, some individuals are said to have *juok* (bad moral character) while others do not. Furthermore, the *juok* of the night-runner (*juog otieno*) and of the *janawi*, the *jandagla*, and the *jatung'* is a behavioral attribute and refers to the moral nature of acquired behavior and not to some material quality intrinsically present in them.

In the next section I will try in another way to disprove dualism in the nature of personhood by explaining that apart from their moral capacity, humans are otherwise perceived in fairly mechanical terms; that humans are ontologically constituted in an organistic form and perform functions commensurate with their biological type, thus further isolating morals as the basis of selfhood.

Juok and the (English Idea of) "Soul"

The analysis of *juok* reveals that the concept includes neither nonphysical substances that operate independently of physical reality in the general sense nor a nonphysical constituting substance that complements the physical nature of humans. Like "evil," *juok* is not an independent substance or a substantive quality such as mass or shape, color, or smell but is rather a moral quality of action that is predicated on people's actions when they are discordant with, undermine, or decrease the quality of life for other people in the community. *Juok* creates fear, anxiety, distrust, and suspicion in ways that are incompatible with the ideals of peacefulness and happiness. Thus, contrary to what Hayley says of the Lango idea of *juok*,[58] it is neither "power" nor "soul," unless the latter terms are used strictly in the context of moral agency or capacity for action. The saying that "there is *juok* in the world" can be translated rather roughly as "there is evil in the world," which does not indicate a substantive meaning for the term "evil" as a substance or entity that exists either by itself or in dependence on or inside some other entity. The term "*juok*" (or its English version, "evil") is a nonsubstantive noun and implies only that from a moral perspective, we recognize and classify some experiences to be qualitatively bad or unpleasant. But they are not objects or any other form of substance.[59] Luo-speaking people say that unpleasant experiences are caused by people, either by oneself or others, through foul speech and deed.[60] *Juok*, they say, is a behavioral tendency that anyone is susceptible to if they are not steadfast in their pursuit of moral uprightness. The tendency is sometimes manifested in explicit (observable) behavior, but at other times it is hidden in the attitudinal state of one's will. He or she who wills ill of others is a *jajuok*, whether they express such an attitude in speech or deed or merely "intend" it.

In terms of the ontological constitution of personhood, Dholuo provides all the indications of materialism and none of dualism. The Luo attribute the sustenance of life to *chuny*, the kernel of biological life. Every organic thing has *chuny*. It makes plants germinate and grow, and it is responsible for the organic functioning of animals, including humans. *Chuny* is just as responsible for the pulse as it is for the growth and use of limbs and other biological organs. Thus a living cockroach has no less *chuny* than a living dog or living human, and no more than a living plant. Living organisms wither when their *chuny* begins to wane, and they die when their *chuny* "gets disconnected (*chot*)." A person, plant, or beast is pronounced dead when their *chuny* is said to be "gone"—that is, to be "disconnected" or to be no more—*chunye o-a* (there is no more life in it, him, or her). It is said of a plant, dog, or human that *chunye ool* (their *chuny* is weak, he or she is critical, or he or she is in a sad or somber mood) when they show signs of biological fading and frailty. In these senses, *chuny* has a purely material or organic meaning as the principle of biological life. *Chuny* is thus separate from but is what enables the *adundo* (heart) to beat (*gudo*), although one says "*chunye gudo,*" rather than "*adundo-ne gudo,*" meaning that it is the presence of life or organic wholeness that enables the heart to beat. Or it is said simply that *chunye yueyo* (it, he, or she is still breathing).

Chuny as the sustainer of organic life is also different from the liver, for which the same word is used. In other functional senses, *chuny* also means emotional and cognitive capacities: the emotional attitudes of liking, desiring, and willing as well as the cognitive acts of believing, doubting, and conviction. Thus, one says "*chunya dwaro*" or "*chunya gombo*" (I would like to . . . I desire . . . I wish I could . . .), "*chunya nitie*" (I have it in mind, I desire it), *chunya onge* (I don't feel like . . . I have no desire to . . . or for . . .), or "*chunya o-aye*" (I have given up, I have taken my mind away from it, I will shift my focus, I don't like it anymore, I have lost the desire for it), which is radically different from "*chunya o-a*" (I am in shock or in mental disarray or I have lost consciousness, there is no sign of the flow of life in me). The former is an emotional or attitudinal statement while the latter is physical in its first sense but metaphysical because it distinguishes animate existing beings from inanimate ones (that do not possess *chuny*). These uses of the term indicate clearly that *chuny* is neither a substance nor an attribute of all things but is rather a complex term that describes a variety of physical and psychological states in living organisms when their ability to respond to stimuli are manifest.

Again, also in emotional terms, one says of another that *chunye ber* (she or he is pleasant, or kind) or that *chunye ler* (she or he does not get revolted by nasty situations or likes people indiscriminately) or that *chunye rach* (she or he is angry, nasty, unpleasant, in a foul mood, or ill-tempered) to express a person's various emotional attitudes toward other people and things. In cognitive terms, one says *chunya oyie* (I am convinced, I am in agreement, I accept, or I believe) or *chunya ok-oyie* (I am not convinced, I don't believe) or simply *ayie* (I agree, I accept, I believe [it]).

Finally, *chuny* also means "center," "key," or some other indicator of the core of something such that other aspects of the thing can be identified only as peripheral. Thus, *chuny wach* (the center or main point of an issue) pinpoints the key or essential idea or issue in a complex discourse or disputation. This is the formal analogy of the physical meaning conveyed in biological terms too, as in *chuny yath* ("the core of the tree" that sustains its livelihood), because it refers to "that which holds everything else together," the essence of a formal or material object that is not separable from other parts that may be connected to or with it. In organic or animate things, then, *chuny* is the driving biological principle that occasions the organization and performance of different living organisms according to their species.

After the arrival of the missionaries, however, *chuny* was given a new meaning. They restricted its meaning to something called "soul," which had hitherto not been part of the metaphysical or psychological vocabulary in Dholuo. It is quite understandable that missionaries, in a fruitless search for a dualist structure in the conceptual and linguistic repertoire of the Luo to accompany their new teachings, settled on the term *chuny* and redefined it for their converts, who were not analytically sensitive. Indeed, it does not seem odd to contemporary Luo-speaking people, as it surely should, that they now almost blindly claim that the *chuny* of humans leave the body at death in order to ascend to some other place, *polo* (sky or heaven), an idea that is also new to their thinking scheme, while the *chuny* of a cockroach or of a millet stalk simply vanishes at some point in their respective lives. So it is common to hear someone say in Dholuo of a dying cockroach or of a withering crop of beans in the field that *chunye onge* (its *chuny* is no more, is departed, is gone, or is severed). The matter used to be left at that, because the fate of *chuny* was common in all organic things. Today, however, converts will add, upon probing, that the *chuny* of the dead human for which they are praying "has gone to the skies" (*polo*), an utterance that simply sounds like gibberish in Dholuo. On the other hand, no one attributes this "heavenly journey" to *jok* (*juok*). But let us imagine that a convert claimed that his or her *jok* (*juok*) would "go to the skies" (*jok-na* or *jok mara, juoka n'odhi ei polo*). It just wouldn't make any syntactical sense and would not convey any meaningful information. It turns out, therefore, that this kind of analysis does not reveal the term *juok* to be the central idea in Luo conception of reality, as claimed by Ogot and p'Bitek.

Personhood and Immortality

Related to the concepts discussed above is the lingering problem of what happens to personhood when one dies. In a general way, the Luo appear to believe that something in the nature of persons survives the death of the body. Whatever it is that survives, the Luo appear not to have a term for it that might betray what they think to be its nature. I spoke above about how the name of an ancestor becomes the *juok* for a living descendant given the same name. This, however, is an indication only of the memory of the social histories of families and clans. I also mentioned that this element, *juok*, in the naming sense, cannot be the material *chuny*, as the dead are never said to exercise the capacities related to having *chuny*. This ambiguity has led people in the postmissionary era to claim that what survives the corruption of the body is *tipo*, literally "the shadow." The motivation behind the suggestion of this term (*tipo*) seems to be an attempt to find a match for the Western Christian idea rendered by the term "soul," which, as we saw earlier, Thomas Aquinas described as the nonmaterial substance that survives corruption at death.[61] But a careful consideration reveals that this term is used only analogically and not in direct reference to an aspect or attribute of personhood. *Tipo* means shadow in the literal sense of the term, as in *tipo yath*, the shadow of a tree or of anything else when light does not penetrate it. Shadows are physical occurrences.

Because shadows are physical occurrences and have the general shape-image of the real object from which they are cast, the Luo talk of whatever survives the physical death of a person as their shadow, meaning that it bears the likeness of the real person. Hence the saying *tipo ng'ane neno e wang'a* (the image of so-and-so is present in my eyes, meaning that it appears to me vividly). Although visual imagery is used to express the idea of appearance, it is clearly understood in Dholuo that the appearance of the *tipo* of those who are no longer physically present does not involve direct sensory experience; it involves only memory. It is said that a dead person does not have a shadow, meaning that a dead person cannot stand on their own so that their shadow will be cast because of the obstruction of light. In terms reminiscent of the Humean idea of impressions, the Luo describe the vividness of memory by saying they "come to the eyes" (*biro e wang'*, or *neno e wang'*), that the images appear in the form of intense visual impressions. But in truth they are only being clear and distinct to the mind when the image has been imprinted by visual sensory experience. Christian converts have now been made to say that *tipo* (and sometimes *chuny*) rises to heaven, which does not make much sense in Dholuo.[62] Indeed, the Luo legends of Luanda Magere, the fabled indomitable hero from the Kano clan who could not be killed unless his shadow was speared, help underline the physical nature of the idea of *tipo*. The story shows that *tipo* is only a replicate of the body, not separate from it. It can conceal the ordinary and vulnerable nature of the body. The story of Luanda Magere describes him as *"ng'ato magalagala"* (a mysterious person), meaning that the concealment of his prowess in his *tipo* (shadow) could not have been an ordinary way of understanding personhood and its structure. Rather, his story teaches that virtue, particularly the virtue of courage in warfare, makes people stand out above ordinary folks and protects them from vulnerability. The association of the idea of *tipo* with his prowess, the diagnosis and treatment of his ailments, and the final slaying cannot have been intended to tell a metaphysical story about him. The description of him as having a body of granite (rock, *lwanda* in Dholuo) was not a literal characterization of the human body; rather, his prowess and courage were so "out of this world" that he became a legend. Today, many sons of Kano who are on their way to hunting expeditions or some other dangerous missions will pass by "The Rock" into which Magere turned in order to touch it as a source of the bravery and courage for which he is remembered.

How People Know

It appears inevitable, in pursuit of the nature of personhood by means of this analysis of language, to outline how consciousness and selfhood are related and what further light they may shed on the idea of the person.

Of the things we become aware of, the most intimate and immediate one is the reflexive awareness of being aware. The British philosopher Bertrand Russell called this experience acquaintance by introspection, saying that "we are not only aware of things, but we are often aware of being aware of them."[63] When we have a sensory experience, we are aware of having the experience, thus making the experience itself, like feeling warm or seeing a goat, an object with which we are acquainted. The Luo call such awareness by introspection *ng'eyo i chuny,* or *ng'eyo gi chuny,* "getting into the act of knowing itself." Thinking, or thought, is called *paro,* which is done in two different ways: *paro gi chuny* (thinking inside or to oneself) and *paro gi wich* (thinking in the head). *Aparo* (I am thinking, I think so) as a one-word sentence is usually taken to mean the latter—thought that has an object outside thought itself, as in the English sentence "I am thinking about or of something," where the "something" is the object outside thought and at which thought aims. This type of thinking is calculative and involves analysis. Solving mathematical and logical problems is done in the head (*goyo kwan e wich,* or *goyo kwan gi wich,* and *pimo wach gi wich*). The latter, *pimo wach gi wich,* translates literally as "determining the nature of speech" and focuses on truth (*adiera mar wach*), meaning (*ngech wach* or *tiend wach*), and sense (*donjo wach e wach moro*). People who are good (fast) at math and at solving logical problems are said to have "light heads" (*wich ma yot*), while people who are slow at these mental exercises are said to have "heavy heads" (*wich ma pek*). Thinking inside (*paro gi chuny*), on the other hand, is to turn inside into one's own conscience, to sort out one's awareness. When someone sorts their *chuny* (*nono chuny*), they are said to examine the seat, basis, or grounds of their believing as opposed to the nature of the belief they have. The latter would be the same as carrying out an epistemological or logical analysis (*nono tiend wach*). Thus, people are asked to probe their *chuny* if they are suspected of telling a lie. *Chuny* is said to be a person's best friend (*dhano osiep chunye*)—they can never lie to it. To examine one's *chuny* is thus to confront oneself to determine that what is inside is indeed what one is also projecting to the outside, what one is reporting or stating. It is obvious that examining *chuny,* becoming acquainted with one's own acquaintance, or knowing that one knows, reveals a self (*an awuon ei chunya*). But it is a gross error to take *chuny* as a substance that is independent of the act (of) *nono* (examining), because *chuny* does not become identical with the *an* (*-awuon*), which roughly translates into English as the "I-self." In fact, *an awuon ei chunya* translates as "I-self inside my *chuny* (self-awareness)," a rather cumbersome expression. Also, although it is said at death that someone's *chuny* is "disconnected" (*chunye chot*), this does not imply the heaving off of a thing or a part thereof from another thing. It simply means that life has stopped, as the flow of electric current stops when there is a break or disconnection in the wiring. The energy is not "separated" in the sense of being carried away toward an existence that is separate from the wires that carried it when it was present. Rather, its flow has been interrupted and, electrically speaking, the wires have "become dead," in contrast to their "live" status when connection allowed the flow of current.

At no time do the everyday uses of these concepts evoke or even remotely refer to the notion of *juok.* If the latter was indeed the basic metaphysical "stuff" of being human, one would expect some mention of it in reference to the inner operations of personhood that these latter terms address, as shown in the analyses above.

Conclusion

Juok is not about metaphysics, except in the sense that it is a concept about the character or nature of personhood. It has been pretty tempting, however, especially at the time Ogot and p'Bitek researched and completed their essays, to view such a complex concept in the metaphysical fashion because of the influence of Tempels's reading of African modes of thought. To Ogot, *jok,* or *juok* (pl. *jogi*) is a form of power, a capacity that humans and things are endowed with. Such capacity, he explains, enables them to interact at a quasi-physical level. To p'Bitek, *jok* are quasi-physical "things," or entities, and are apprehendable with the senses. He also claims that they have some biological characteristics, such as bleeding when pierced with spears and arrows.[64] Above all, says p'Bitek, they are deities and are objects of ritual among the Acholi. What both Ogot and p'Bitek fail to notice in their analyses is the emphasis they place on *juok* (*jok*) as the basis of a discourse on action and a relational order. It doesn't matter that the Acholi perform ritual to *jok.* The point is in the objective of the ritual. It is interesting, in fact, that the rituals performed to *jok* are usually in remembrance of an event that the community appears to want to come to terms with, for example in appeasing the *jok piny* or the "spirits" of those who died when they were buried under a mountain, probably by a mudslide. It makes sense to think that the Acholi, like most good people, feel some responsibility and bear a sense of guilt for a fate of their own kin that they were powerless to avert. Don't some good people among us, in our everyday lives, feel shame and guilt over their inability to help someone in distress? Don't such people say frequently, "I hope you (or they) don't think that I am just heartless and unconcerned"? Whether we can be held responsible for not helping someone in distress when it was in our power to (and we were able to) do so is a common ethical question. So, similarly, the Acholi continue to plead with their ancestors to continue to hold them in good stead despite what they fear might be perceived as an ethical shortfall on their part for not helping avert the calamity. The southern Luo deal with the burden of such guilt conscience by explaining that the person they did not help becomes *chien,* which returns to hound them. People so hounded often claim to "see" (meaning, I believe, to have nightmares about) the dead, who ask them why they took no action to help them when they were in distress. In other words, a good person, one who cares for others, will be disturbed by their own conscience when they have failed to do good to someone, especially if that person dies in the circumstances where they failed to help. Their failure to successfully help may not be directly responsible for the misfortune, but the deeply relational conscience does not easily absolve itself from the weight of possible guilt. Hence they seek the help of a diviner, an *ajuoga* or *jabilo,* to cleanse them of the guilt by partly appeasing the *chien* (the hounding dead) by means of a ritual performance.

What about counseling for people who are in distress as a result of witnessing a traumatizing event or happening? Indeed, trauma is a psychological experience that afflicts us through our memory of an unpleasant situation that we witnessed or were involved with. The Acholi, like most other humans, appear to be affected or traumatized by such events in their own histories. The rituals are their own counseling performances, a way of dealing with the burdens of historical awareness, namely of being aware of being historically responsible for the history of one's own lineage.

Although good people can be and frequently are found anywhere in the world, this sense of shame and guilt because of the distress of others is likely to occur where expectation of mutuality is high, as among the Acholi people described by p'Bitek. In such a "communalistic" society, individual and group security is fostered through a network of social relations ruled by a strong sense of unity and caring. Although it is not a rule of settlement, people in these networks are often related to each other as members of a clan or a large extended family, which makes affection another key factor in the closeness and sense of obligation toward other members of the network, regardless of the relative geographic proximity of their respective abodes or settlements. The key is in the morals that require people to recognize their place in the social network and to abide by the expectations that hold the network together rather than tear it apart. To this end, sharing and mutual dependency are central as the moral means by which the community is created, held together, and reproduced. Max Gluckman argued long ago that such social structures create a sense of expected parity between members of the community and that a sudden and isolated comparative advantage of a few members of the community spurs suspicion, conflict, and witchcraft accusations because it breaches the expectation of parity in a shared fate.[65] The rule of the game here, as Gluckman argues, is that there is no room for individual fate in such a community; successes and failures need to be experienced communally. Hence, it follows that in times of a calamity that consumes a section of the community, survivors, stricken by a lingering sense of guilt, feel the need to appease the assumed or possible jealousy of the dead (which in fact is their own conscience) and to clear themselves of any culpability for what befell those who perished. They carry the burden of a social conscience that reminds them that they have not shared the fate of their unfortunate kin, and they would transform their own existing history into guilt. To blunt this perceived social and moral guilt, the survivors, and their descendants for long after them, adopt self-blame and so enter a ritual pact with their unfortunate kin. The living appease the dead by making offerings to them so they don't become jealous and seek vengeance, so they don't become *chien.* According to p'Bitek, the dead became *jogi,* the *jok piny* for the Acholi. He says:

> The *jogi* are objects of ritual activities which they believe promote the well-being of a group or of an individual, or combat actual or threatened ill-health or misfortune. Once a year the entire chiefdom was mobilized around the chiefdom *jok,* and sacrifice and prayers were offered for the health and prosperity of the whole people. Clansmen would gather at the ancestral shrine and invoke the ghosts of their ancestors to protect the living members of the clan.[66]

At first glance, one gets the impression that p'Bitek's focus is the identity of the ghosts. The impression is made even stronger by his remark preceding this passage that "not only do the *jogi* have proper names, but they can also be, as it were, known through the senses."[67] On closer scrutiny, however, it becomes clear that the term *jok* used in this sense does not refer to the metaphysical substance of the dead but to their perceived ability to influence the mores of the living. They can make them happy (as when they are prosperous and in good health and have many children) or unhappy (as when they get sick, when they fail to get children, or when many of them die). Based on their conscience, the living view the outcomes of significant experiences as either rewards or retributions handed down by the dead. The focus is thus not on the nature of the ancestral ghosts per se but on the moral nature of the social order to which they still contribute through memory and imagination. By imagining their obligation to the departed, the living members of the community expand their moral world to include the historical community they share with the dead. This community may no longer be real in a corporeal sense, but it is an essential constituting part of a migrant community traversing time and facing other groups. To maintain their social identity through changing times and spaces and through their encounters with opposing groups along their migratory paths, community members are driven to "individualize and concretize" their connection with their past—with their historical community—by attributing events that affect them to the actions of the specific personalities of the past. Some moral theorists have argued that morality generally derives from just such an imaginative sensitivity toward others. By recognizing the moral agency of those who have participated in the making of their group and are now gone, the living Acholi, as p'Bitek described them, stipulate moral standards for themselves as measures that sustain an ideal social order. They want prosperity, and the dead should be happy with their desire; they want security and good health, and the dead should not be hostile. In other words, it is the capacity for vice that turns the dead into *jok,* just as a propensity for antisocial behavior turns the living into *jajok* (*jajuok*).

But just as not all living persons are *jajok* (*jajuok*), not every dead person becomes a community *jok* or *juok.* Through the mediation of the diviner, the *ajuoga,* the community selects who will become their *jok,* the person by whose name the family or clan will identify itself to future generations and distinguish itself from other families and clans. Such ancestral figures are not randomly selected at the whim of the diviner. Instead, the figure is usually of unquestionable public standing and character, a person of great charisma, generosity, wisdom, wealth, and leadership. In other words, personhood is not constituted of metaphysical parts that, as I described above, only make people human. Rather, in addition to human capacities, personhood is constituted by the various roles people play in making community real; individuals and community regulate and depend on each other for who and what they become. Personhood is constituted by the interplay between the culturally objectified perceptions of persons and the subjectively apprehended aspects of social life through which individuals express their subjectivity in opposition to or conformity to the conventionally defined roles, rules, and regulations of the habitus. As p'Bitek himself observed, the Luo appear to have placed focus on a world defined by the agency of persons and the impact of their actions on society, not by static ontological categories.[68] The self or personhood of the living is revealed partly through the cognitive and moral actions they perform and the emotions they express and partly by the perception of those affected by such actions and emotions. The dead too can be imagined only in behavioral terms, namely in terms of what it is assumed they would have liked or disliked as judged through a variety of actions attributed to them. The living imagine the moral choices they would have made and translate them into principles or guides for conduct. The "translation" and voicing of these imagined opinions of the dead is done by diviners. Ogot's idea of history suggests that people choose and commit to moral and social membership in particular ancestral genealogies—such as *jok'*Omolo or *jok'*Owiny, which are usually symbolized by the specific taboos that identify them—with whose practices and lineages they subsequently identify.[69] The claims that the *jogi* (or *juogi*)—the spirits of the dead—can be directly perceived or interacted with might be a reference to a complex way of dealing with moral and genealogical memories of the dead in the minds of the living. P'Bitek says that they "can . . . be . . . known through the senses," and G. E. M. Ogutu, another scholar of Luo religion, says that he himself has "heard the voices of people who died a long time ago as they spoke through the living, stating what they wanted the living to do."[70]

Ogutu did not encounter these dead directly; he heard them through a medium, a person who acts as the intermediary between the voices of the past and the will of the living. What he *actually* heard were the voices of the living (diviners) whose locutions were said to be the words of the dead. For the mediums to play this role, they speak in ways that must be seen to vary significantly from their own known tones and voices. The medium's change of voice (sometimes accompanied by incoherent statements) and abandonment of his or her usual posture (such as by falling in a trance) are widespread methods for transferring responsibility for what is said to the agency of the spirits. Such directives usually come at times of crisis in families or clans or in any other social unit that may see the need to search into their past for answers to their current problems. The fact that it is only during special moments that the authority and teachings of the dead are sought is a clear indication that such recall is never an ordinary matter. Indeed, it should never escape the attention of any observer, even a casual one, that the Luo regard anyone who claims to see or speak with the dead or any other form of invisible forces to be mentally sick or delusional. They say such a person is speaking with *jochiende,* or *jopiny,* meaning "people in their own heads," which is a phrase for delusional images. The methods and circumstances of mediumship have often led to the suggestion that it is a way for the voices of a community's past to reemerge for interpretation and translation for the living generations.

The medium's act of transmitting the messages of the dead builds on what is usual in our other mediatory practices—those that we consider the "normal" or "reasonable" requirements when we give importance and authority to our own claims. As Anthony Appiah says in the context of explaining the sustaining reason of ritual acts, "To understand these ritual acts what is necessary is what is necessary in the understanding of any acts; namely to understand what beliefs and intentions underlie them, so that we know what the actors think they are doing."[71] Isn't it the case that when we want to emphasize a point that originates with another person's thought we either report the relevant statements as that person actually gave them or is believed to have given them? We do this both in everyday casual talk that may remind us of the opinions of those we quote or when we are reporting what others have told us and when we cite our sources in the course of a formal presentation or analysis of an argument or view about the world. The practice of citing other people's works or statements plays the role of fortifying an idea or point of view that we agree with. Citing the speech or writing of people of high status lends credibility to our own voice or view. For this to work, the cited voice must be one that is publicly recognized and regarded by our audience as relevant relation to what we are saying. The citation of other people's words is part of how we socialize our knowledge claim; it is how we claim to some kind of validation for our words because they have already been accepted or approved of by our audience. Because such authorities usually are not directly available for questioning as authors of their own statements, their words can only be subjected to translation and interpretation. Similarly, the idea and practice of mediumship is a way of building a case for having a consensus over a formal communal property. So when a medium represents the voices of the *jogi* on a specific matter, the involvement of the entire community is invoked; it is not just his or her private interaction with the spirits in question. It is a public or social performance that many parties are called to participate in. As Heike Behrend observes in her study of Alice Lakwena's Holy Spirit movement in northern Uganda, "Spirits are not the projection of wishes. . . . Rather, they arise in a social process of interacting interpretation in which the spirit or its medium, the translator, and the audience all participate."[72] One can therefore appreciate the term "medium" in the quasi-literal sense of a "bridge" between the moral and customary ideals as asserted by the *jogi* and the living community of moral agents in need of guiding representations of the ideals. As the living intermediary, the medium delivers the prescriptive "statement" of past authorities for inclusion in the ongoing moral discourse among the living under the guidance of the diviner (*ajuoga* for the Anuak and Kenya Luo or *ajwaka* in Acholi). He or she becomes an expert and enjoys the privileges of the special relationship that ensues between him or her and the source.

It is important to note that the utterances of a medium are acceptable only during his or her ritual performance; similar behavior under different conditions would be harshly derided as psychotic. Any record of such utterances would show a pattern of poor use of language and reason, a feature that is quite distinctive of the speech of *juogi*. They are usually referred to as *dhum*, speech in an incomprehensible tongue. Precisely because they are given the context of "voices" from agents that are not "normal" like everyday persons are, poor use of language and reason is meant to draw a distinction between them (as the source of the voices and message) and the person of the medium. This is why the "speech" of the *juogi* requires translation and interpretation. This view implies two things: one, that the audience recognizes that the speech of the spirits is jumbled and senseless but refrains from trying to do anything about it (such as criticize it) because they know it is supposed to be "abnormal" or different; and two, that the attention of the audience is expected to focus on the lessons of the speech rather than on its form, especially after translation and interpretation when the medium regains or shifts back to his or her "normal" self (which allows him or her to sift grammar and sense from the gibberish utterances of the *juogi*). When, on the other hand, a person speaks to him or herself without a rationally justifiable cause (as when a person continues a verbal tirade because he or she has just been in a violent verbal exchange with another person), he or she is likely to draw curious attention aimed at determining his or her mental condition. To report that a person, *p*, has been seen speaking to him or herself on numerous occasions amounts to raising an alarm about the likelihood that his or her mental health is deteriorating. And when a sick and bedridden person exhibits locutionary hallucinations, he or she is said to "speak with *jochiende* (appearances of nonexistent people), usually a sign of a steep decline in his or her rational capacity. He or she is said to be really sick (*otuo*), a clear reference to a mental deviation from a known norm.[73]

What G. E. M. Ogutu observed cannot therefore be taken as literally as he claims, namely that he witnessed "people who had died a long time ago speak through the living." Apart from the apparent misuse of the concept of "witness" in the literal sense implied in the claim, the performance Ogutu referred to requires an understanding that moves from what is observed to what is intended or believed to be "really" taking place, as the participants in these rituals are pretty much aware of their respective roles in what to them too is not a literal act of everyday life.

**unitarianism:
son**

Although communitarianism has long been used by communities around the world as a pragmatic and spontaneous principle of social organization and guidance of moral conduct, it has fairly recently emerged as a doctrine or school of thought in social and moral philosophy. The difference is in the emphasis, which, at least in part, has been occasioned by the fading appeal of individualism and the many systems and values built on that principle. Some would probably put it slightly differently by saying that communitarianism is the result of the recession of one of the core values of modernism. It is the antithesis of individualism, but its manifestations in intellectual traditions around the world reveal important regional modifications. In the philosophical traditions of Europe and North America, communitarianism still lacks a uniform and normative expression that can be said to unite all of their exponents in sociopolitical or moral theory, but it has become there a fairly strong and important source of critique of the perceived excesses of the liberal ideology of individualism. It does not articulate a substantive theory of what a communitarian society ought to be or of which specific aspirations are to be expected of the inhabitants of a communitarian order, but its adherents ascribe to the general view that the status of the political and moral community have rights that are not just independent from those of the individual rights but are also more important in some crucial ways that warrant the freedoms of the individual for the goodness of the collective whole. Such a position may be considered to be largely a methodological rather than a substantive theory of communitarianism; its dominant image is that of a critique of individualism.

Deriving from Hegel, Western communitarianism maintains that the rights of individuals are not basic and that the collective can have rights that are independent of and even opposed to what individualists claim are the rights of individuals. Under this characterization,

222

communitarianism directly or indirectly follows in the path of a philosophical romanticism by which the state found a new definition and mystical meaning in the hands of the nineteenth-century German historical school of which Hegel was part. Inspired to some extent by the patriotic instinct to resist the French emperor who had conquered and trampled the disunited Germany, a new mood developed among German writers and poets, who turned their interests inward upon their own nation, their own people, their own race. For them, the people, the Volk, was endowed not merely with a history but with a sort of mystical essence and value that transcended both the merits of the nation's present members and the publically known facts of its past. To this depersonalized but emotionally powerful entity Rousseau's idea of the *volonté générale* as something different from the mere opinion of the majority, something that rather subsumed majority and minority in an irresistible higher element that defied numerical analysis, supplied a further dimension. Among German scholars of the time, this mystical sense of the nation awakened a sense of history and a passion to penetrate and understand the German past. A whole constellation of intellectuals inspired by national feeling appeared, leading to the formation of the Heidelberger Romantik, so called because of their nostalgic association of German cultural history with the destroyed streets of Heidelberg. Hegel was part of this historical school, as was Friedrich Carl von Savigny. The spirit of this generation of German intellectuals is instructive about the partial origins of Hegel's complex reliance on history—the dialectic—as the constitutive dynamic of reality. Indeed, this generation believed that what Germany needed was not a rationalistic corpus of legal mechanisms but a thorough insight into the history of her existing institutions. Only when this had been gained could a start be made on putting together the elements most suitable for a code of laws upon which the mystical essence of the state could rely.

The state, for Hegel, is not a simple, unitary concept but one with three separately conceived characters, all of which are interconnected; they all exist among the same population in the same territory but are still conceptually distinct. There is the state in the sense nearest to our own common usage, the "political" state that can be described by pointing to its institutions of government and lawmaking. Then there is the "civil" state, consisting of the mass of arrangements that individuals make with one another rather than having arrangements imposed upon them. These include contracts, marriages, and the establishment of corporations; things perhaps that might have spontaneously evolved even if the political state did not exist. And then there is the state in a far broader and less concrete sense, the state as the sum of all the ethical values, all the shared experiences and responses, the consciousness of belonging together through history, reinforced by religious and cultural homogeneity.

This "ethical" state is the one to which Hegel assigns supreme value and importance. It is in this alone that the individual achieves freedom and self-fulfillment through participation in its transcendent life. The expressions Hegel used to convey his ideas about the state, in this very special sense, can be found in his *Philosophy of Right:*

> The state in and by itself is the ethical whole, the actualisation of freedom; and it is an absolute end of reason that freedom should be actual. The state is Mind on earth and consciously realising itself there. . . . The march of God in the world, that is what the state is. The basis of the state is the power of reason actualising itself as will. In considering the Idea of the state, we must not have our eyes on particular states or on particular institutions. Instead we must consider the Idea, this actual God, by itself. . . .
>
> What the state demands from us as a duty is, *eo ipso,* our right as individuals, since the state is nothing but the articulation of the concept of freedom. The determinations of the individual will are given an objective embodiment through the state and thereby they attain their truth and their actualisation for the first time. The state is the one and only prerequisite of the attainment of particular ends and welfare.[1]

In the same book, *Philosophy of Right,* Hegel makes it clear that he genuinely believes in individual freedom and in the value of the individual and deplores evil or oppressive states. The state, he says, "is no ideal work of art; it stands on earth and so in the sphere of caprice, chance, and error, and bad behavior may disfigure it in many respects."[2] He disapproves of the state as Plato had ideally envisaged it because in it, "subjective freedom does not count"[3] and for Hegel subjective freedom must be respected, as for example by letting people choose their own calling in life.

Since Hegel, a thin layer of communitarianism has remained in Western thought. Contemporary Western communitarians, especially the Canadian philosopher Charles Taylor, claim to continue this Hegelian sense of the individual as part of a larger whole within which he or she attains her freedom by means of an incarnation of a historically creative mind. In Germany itself, Jürgen Habermas, the Frankfurt School critical theorist best known for his theory of communication, holds the general position that societies sustain themselves over time through a process of communication by which consensus on values, as manifested in individuals' conscious behavioral content, is kept alive through negotiations that lead to common understandings of and acceptance of cultural norms. For him, individuals are primarily participants in rational discourses aimed at producing the norms to direct their lives. Society, then, is the source of rationality by virtue of the discursive engagement between its members, who are driven by the search for a rational, consensual, and egalitarian basis of values. Other contemporary Western thinkers who are widely regarded to espouse communitarianism in their thought include American philosophers Alasdair MacIntyre, Michael Sandel, and Michael Walzer. Another American, the moral philosopher John Kekes, fits in this fold as well, but these individuals are by no means the only members of the club.[4] It appears that in the light of its Hegelian beginnings, Western communitarianism defines itself—at least so far—primarily as a critique and rejection of the images of the individual, which they identify with and in "western European"—by which they mean French and British—philosophy. In creating an opposition between "western European" and German philosophy, German thinkers' idea of community was akin to a Weltanschauung, or cosmology, a total view of the (natural and social) world that fundamentally conflicted with the essentially humanist and rationalist thought typical of the rest of Western civilization. Thus, in Steven Lukes's observation, "While the characteristically French sense of 'individualism' is negative, signifying individual isolation and social dissolution, the characteristically German sense is thus positive, signifying individual self-fulfilment and . . . the organic unity of individual and society."[5]

Georg Simmel, the nineteenth-century German sociologist and philosopher of culture, captures this new sense of the individual:

> The total organism which has grown out of the individuals engaged in the division of labor and which includes and mediates their interrelated effects and countereffects, shifts, so to speak, into a location high above them. The specificity of the individual thus requires a powerful political constitution which allocates his place to him, but in this fashion also becomes his master. It is for this reason that this individualism, which restricts freedom to a purely inward sense of the term, easily acquires an anti-liberal tendency. It thus is the complete antithesis of eighteenth-century individualism which, in full consistency with its notion of atomized and basically undifferentiated individuals, could not even conceive the idea of a collective as an organism that unifies heterogeneous elements.[6]

It appears, then, that from the nineteenth century, German social theorists were sharply opposed not only to the Kantian monadology but also to the contractarian view of the evolution of the state and the role of law in it. They were opposed to the view of the state as a mere watchdog to protect the freedoms of the individual against the hostilities of others. In its place they envisaged a society in which individuals were metaphysically connected through a principle that made each one a significant element of the whole. Thus, to attain freedom in this new sense of society, individuals were called upon to participate in a life of mutual dependency with others.

State and society were thus seen as forces that emerged out of the material of particular individuals and out of the intricacies of particular social and political institutions that embodied and incarnated the whole.

Commentators on the emergence of German Romanticism have observed that the sense of individualism implied in the passage from Hegel quoted above defined what became a German variation of the use of the term from its previous French use and sense. According to Steven Lukes, "There is, . . . quite distinct from [the] French use of the term, another use whose characteristic reference is German. This is the Romantic idea of 'individuality' (*individualität*), the notion of individual uniqueness, originality, self-realization—what the Romantics called *Eigentümlichkeit*—in contrast to the rational, universal and uniform standards of the Enlightenment, which they saw as 'quantitative', 'abstract' and therefore sterile."[7] Georg Simmel called it "the individualism of uniqueness [*Einzigkeit*] as against that of singleness [*Einzelheit*]."[8] Rival German expressions of individualism existed, some of which, like that of Max Stirner (1806–1856),[9] embraced the extremist side of the concept in the form of egoism.

Like their predecessors, contemporary Western communitarians strive to show that the individual has more interactive connections with the whole than libertarians recognize. While not denying the autonomy of the individual, they emphasize the significance of her participation in as well as dependence on the community for her sense of self, for her freedom, and for her moral development and agency. According to this view, individuals are constituted by the institutions and practices of which they are part and their rights and obligations derive from those same institutions. As Charles Taylor argues, there is "a connection between four terms: not just (a) our notions of the good and (b) our understandings of the self, but also (c) the kinds of narrative in which we make sense of our lives, and (d) conceptions of society, i.e., conceptions of what it is to be a human agent among human agents. . . . Our modern senses of the self not only are linked to and made possible by new understandings of good but also are accompanied by (i) new forms of narrativity and (ii) new understandings of social bonds and relations."[10]

Taylor's passages reflect MacIntyre's own view of the individual's construction of self-identity and agency as the result of participation in specific social bonds and the narratives of which they are part. In *After Virtue*, MacIntyre writes:

> I can only answer the question 'What am I to do?' if I can answer the prior question 'Of what story or stories do I find myself a part?' We enter human society, that is, with one or more imputed characters—roles into which we have been drafted—and we have to learn what they are in order to be able to understand how others respond to us and how our responses to them are apt to be construed. . . .

I am someone's son or daughter, someone else's cousin or uncle; I am a citizen of this or that city, a member of this or that guild or profession; I belong to this or that clan, that tribe, this nation. Hence what is good for me has to be the good for one who inhabits these roles. As such I inherit from the past of my family, my city, my tribe, my nation, a variety of debts, inheritances, rightful expectations, and obligations.[11]

These two passages from Taylor and McIntyre have prompted the charge by some liberals[12] that such social embeddedness of individuals gives them such irrevocable obligations that a person cannot rationally choose to reject obligations assigned to them by virtue of their situation within a whole. As we saw in chapter 3, an individual is always oppressed when he or she is constrained, either by a contract or by other conditionals, to follow the rules of a group only because of his or her membership in that group. I cannot choose to play by my own rules when I choose to be a member of a soccer team, for example, just like I cannot unilaterally choose to selectively modify some of the terms of my mortgage contract to suit my interests. It is not clear that the claim that we develop our sense of moral good based on our corresponding experiences with others implies that the rules that define our participation in such social bonds are irrevocable. At the center of this debate as it evolved in the West, especially in the United States, however, lies the idea of historical responsibility. According to MacIntyre, we inherit much that is good from our past, and when we do so we feel proud and stand up uninhibitedly to be counted as heirs of a tradition. We fight to justify our claims that we are connected with such a glorious past. The problem, he states, arises when the past brings a burden and a responsibility. In that case, it will usually appear convenient to many to invoke a separation from the past; we claim autonomy and disconnectedness with our inheritance. This, he argues, is common in societies whose pasts are burdened by the weight of historical atrocities. Modern individualism has made it possible for "those modern Americans who deny any responsibility for the effects of slavery upon black Americans, saying 'I never owned any slaves' . . . [and] the Englishman who says, 'I never did any wrong to Ireland; why bring up that old history as though it had something to do with *me*?' or the young German who believes that being born after 1945 means that what Nazis did to Jews has no moral relevance to his relationship to his Jewish contemporaries."[13] Many Africans can cite familiar variations of MacIntyre's point.

It is significant that both Taylor and MacIntyre return to Hegel; but even more significant, they too, like their German intellectual predecessors, take on and develop their social-moral theory against the brand of individualism that originated in the French and British traditions. This type of individualism derives, MacIntyre says, "from two distinct tendencies, one chiefly, though not only, domesticated in analytical philosophy and one at home in both sociological theory and in existentialism. The former is the tendency to think atomistically about human action and to analyze complex actions and transactions in terms of simple components. . . . [Thus] the unity of a human life becomes invisible to us when a sharp separation is made either between the individual and the roles that he or she plays."[14] This view compares well with Simmel's observation about "eighteenth-century individualism which, in full consistency with its notion of atomized and basically undifferentiated individuals, could not even conceive the idea of a collective as an organism that unifies heterogeneous elements."[15]

In political terms, the notion of the individual that these critiques envisaged is a fairly abstract one. It was born and developed between the middle of the seventeenth and the beginning of the nineteenth centuries and became the subject of the social contract arguments that begin with imagining humans in the state of nature. Even Rousseau, as both Hegel and Marx observed, at times speaks in terms of abstract individuals, as for example when, despite the social thrust of his thought, he writes in *The Social Contract* of the Legislator transforming "each individual, who is by himself a complete and independent [meaning 'solitary'] whole, into part of a greater whole from which he receives in some a manner his life and being."[16] Although Rousseau's epoch included Kant, the German philosopher's individual subject, who was quite distinct from that of the French, according to Simmel, was "abstract man, the individuality that is freed from all ties and specificities and is therefore always identical, the ultimate substance of personality and, thereby, the ultimate value of personality. However unholy man may be, Kant says, humanity in him is holy."[17] Thus, while for the French the sovereignty of the individual was the ultimate and only source of group authority and the community was only an aggregate—a mere union, whether tight or loose—of the wills and powers of individual persons, in Kantian philosophy, he says, "the ego has wrested its absolute sovereignty from all possible entanglements with nature, Thou, society."[18] All these thinkers appear to agree that all forms of social life were the creations of individuals and could only be regarded as means to individual goals. This is the individual John Rawls recently revived as the beneficiary of an equal right to the most extensive liberty that is compatible with a similar liberty for others. Against this view, those who conceive of the individual as essentially a social being claim that the real individual is one who is socially embedded, related to others in both history and tradition or, in Taylor's words, the one who lives and acts as an agent among agents. The interconnectedness of the social individual causes his idea of the moral and political good to extend beyond his or her own self. For him or her, the consequences of actions are right or wrong, just or unjust, based not on how they result in good or harm according to a law of nature applied to the social condition but on how they impact others in the community within which he or she is located. Simmel thinks that Kant's categorical imperative epitomized the attainment of the ideal ego that was quite distinct from that of Rousseau because he categorically states that "the 'true person' [that] is the same in every accidental man, has found its abstract perfection in Kant."[19]

According to MacIntyre, the goods individuals pursue cannot be comprehended outside the context of historical traditions. A living tradition, then, he says, "is an historically extended, socially embodied argument, and an argument precisely in part about the goods which constitute that tradition."[20] In other words, for MacIntyre, the rationale for justifying moral values, for accounting for what counts as justice, for example, is grounded in tradition. As a result, different types of practical rationales exist. A tradition, he contends,

> is such a movement in the course of which those engaging in that movement become aware of it and of its direction and in self-aware fashion attempt to engage in its debates and to carry its enquiries forward. The relationships which can hold between individuals and a tradition are very various, ranging from unproblematic allegiance through attempts to amend or redirect the tradition to large opposition to what have hitherto been its central contentions.[21]

In this respect, MacIntyre argues, liberalism is part of a discourse located in the heart of a search for solutions to practical problems, although its appeal to the greater part of society whose interests it supports is transforming it into an independent tradition. Its appearance in Western political and moral debate today marks a historical, literary, anthropological, and sociological moment in the evolution of specific problematics regarding how to understand, define, and set rules for the practical management of the specific societies that live in those circumstances. Those engaged together in these circumstances may agree or disagree about these rules (policies) and about the mechanisms (politics) for deriving or establishing them.[22] An acceptable concept of justice (such as that propounded by Robert Nozick,[23] for example, in opposition to that of Rawls) must be one that defines individual rights while correlating communal interests with individual rights and claims. Because it arises in a context where some groups are deprived and because of the perception that this condition is antagonistic to the achievement by all of the values liberalism articulates, Western communitarianism functions more as a watchdog for the common good than as a robust communitarian theory.

Communitarianism in African Systems of Thought

By contrast, Africa's recent intellectual trends have revealed a different, robust, and prescriptive idea of communitarianism, which they are only now articulating clearly and succinctly. However, there has also been a progression in these movements toward giving this doctrine a clear and succinct statement. Pronouncements that appeared to claim that the values of community override the freedoms and rights of the individual pervaded much of the rhetoric associated with nationalist movements for political and cultural independence in the sixties. While much of this rhetoric was brought to light in the language of nationalist politics, it was committed to writing by politicians who often doubled as Africa's pioneer intelligentsia. Among these were honorable individuals such as Léopold Sédar Senghor of Senegal, Kwame Nkrumah of Ghana, and Julius Nyerere of Tanzania. These people were not philosophers, and despite their obvious political and cultural significance, their pronouncements were not meant as philosophical claims. Their difference from Western communitarians, who *are* philosophers, lies in the fact that the African leaders could refer to traditional social and political orders in different specific cultural manifestations to support to their claims. In the case of Nyerere, these cultural expressions led to a bold but grossly unwise political decision to establish, in pursuit of the ideological aspirations of the ruling party at the time, Chama Cha Mapinduzi (CCM), *"jamaa* villages" modeled after traditional extended family homesteads or settlements. But sharp differences between culture and politics soon ran Nyerere's political villagization program aground. There can be no doubt that these politicians-turned-public-intellectuals influenced a whole tradition in African social theory. Committed to a new and radically different beginning for their respective countries and driven by the nationalist ambition to create out of Africa something that would be as radically different from the political system of her colonizers as it would be from the doctrinaire forms of government in the then-emerging socialist world, the African pioneers opted for a political program that would combine a recovery of values from Africa's living indigenous histories and social structures with an anti-capitalist ideology. While making allowance for practical variations based on national diversity, the general outline of the program was fairly common, precipitating what came to be popularly known in English as "African paths to socialism," or simply "African socialism." African socialism thus came to mean different things to different people, reflecting different configurations of Africa's indigenous traditions. While for some it meant a secular set of humane values based on altruism as the basis of social unity and cooperation among members, for others it built on the religious values of Islam, especially those that call for mutual respect among people and the practice of alms-giving. From the start, then, not only were African politicians proposing a variant brand of socialism, they were also making allowance for "many paths" to African socialism. In the context of Senghor's work, the former addressed the issue of economic alienation by uniting the members of the proletariat who were estranged from humanity while the latter addressed the additional yoke of colored peoples. In 1961 Senghor stated the following: "In both instances, revolt and struggle serve to 'abolish present conditions' and to 'transform the world' by re-establishing the natural equilibrium. Where colored peoples are concerned, it is accurate to speak of a 'revolt against the West.'"[24] Senghor had no doubt that cultural independence was a prerequisite for all other forms of independence because colonialism did not benefit the European bourgeoisie alone. Even the middle classes and the proletariat of Europe benefitted from colonialism. Furthermore, he argued, other than for economic reasons, colored peoples were colonized first and foremost because they were, in his words, "'primitive' and ugly to boot." It was therefore paramount that the socialist methodology be revisited because the struggles of the proletariat in Europe and of colonized Africans, as Sartre showed in *Orphée noir,* might have been "similar, perhaps, but not identical, for our situations are not the same."[25]

Also, and above all, Senghor argued,[26] the Marxist ethic did not stress the centrality of people and their freedom. Rather, it placed its materialist emphasis on the priority of the economic factor and the class struggle "to the detriment of man and his freedom. . . . It is a terribly inhuman metaphysics in which mind is sacrificed to matter, freedom to the determined, man to things." By contrast, he asserted,[27] West African "countries [are] built on the idea of community [Fr. *communautaires*] where the group holds priority over the individual; they are, especially, religious countries, unselfish countries, where money is not King." Although he did not give African socialism a clear definition, Senghor thought of the African varieties of socialism as indicators of what he saw as a deeply humanist mindset that he felt was the basis of and drive behind negritude. It is useful to note that his idea of Negro-Africans included the Berbers of the north. Negro-African society and what he called "the collectivist European society" were different:

> I would say that the latter is an *assembly of individuals.* The collectivist society inevitably places the emphasis on the individual, on his original activity and his needs. In this respect, the debate between "to each according to his labor" and "to each according to his needs" is significant. Negro-African society puts more stress on the group than on the individual, more on *solidarity* than on the activity and needs of the individual, more on the *communion* of persons than on their autonomy. Ours is a *community* society. This does not mean that it ignores the individual, or that collectivist society ignores solidarity, but the latter bases this solidarity on the activities of individuals, whereas the community society bases it on the general activity of the group.[28]

In the lines that follow this passage, Senghor attributes the African communitarian tendency to a way of life that is rooted in the individual's experience of the world: it is the way a person feels and thinks in union not only with all other people around him but "indeed with all other beings in the universe: God, animal, tree, or pebble."[29] Although Senghor is generally regarded to be among those who thought that the individual was subservient to the community, these statements do not support that impression. After all, the difference between civilizations lies in the ability of individual members of any society to learn, internalize, and successfully apply the cultural values of their group to beliefs, attitudes, and practices that integrate them with their group. Senghor made other statements that indicate his concession to some measure of autonomy for the individual in African societies. His earlier work, including his definition of negritude, addressed the "naturalness" with which Africans embrace and participate in nature instead of distancing themselves from it cognitively, but the idea of "naturalness" here probably refers to an inclination that is instilled over time through methods of enculturation until it becomes the unquestioned basis of thought, judgments, and practice. In other words, for him, African communitarian habits, just like the other axiomatic assumptions or "facts" of our basic judgments (including some judgments about right and wrong), are acquired, but in the context of the cognitive foundations of practice, they become part of Africans' expression of being.[30] Autonomy stops with the materiality of the individual body. Beyond their bodies, however, persons are socially conditioned; they are "herded," so to speak, toward specific civilizational worlds that are defined by whole sets of values, as manifested in the cognitive and practical behavior of their individual members that distinguish them from others. Whether as victims or as beneficiaries, people live their lives by the values instilled in them by the regimes of their social institutions. And when these institutions last long enough, the preferred values of those institutions begin to look "natural."

Together, these views have contributed to Senghor's now-well-known characterization of black peoples as distinguishable by their participative attitudes toward their cognitive and moral experiences. On this idea, he built what would later become a fashionable refrain for most essentialist black intellectuals: "Black people are communitarian by nature." Like most others who later espoused his idea, Senghor saw no need to make an analytical account of the claim that African societies were communitarian in their social-political ethic. Although this statement benefitted from the influence of well-known French critiques of the Cartesian tradition and became philosophically significant for what it claimed, its goal was not a philosophical one. Instead, Senghor and his admirers repeatedly simply asserted that having a communitarian stance toward the world was the basic and abiding truth about what it means to be an African.

Europe's constitutional retreat from African colonial states, which began with Ghana's independence in 1957, was, understandably, accompanied by aggressive nationalist campaigns for political independence and cultural difference from colonial Europe. For these campaigns, cultural difference, which was seen as bestowing, or restoring, a sense of authority to the native, was indeed expected to accompany the new political order and was to be seen not merely in objects but also, more importantly, in the processes by which such objects came to be known and applied to the regulation of life as formal icons of nativism. African nationalists frequently claimed that Western and African societies were defined by opposing sets of values—Western societies by capitalism and individualism and African societies by communitarianism "by nature,"[31] hence socialist at their core. Those who subscribed to Senghor's notion of negritude also claimed that African socialism was not godless but deeply religious. The idea of African socialism became both widespread and reasonable enough, despite variations of detail and strength of expression in the different official or national policy statements, to become the leading point in attempts to structurally and ideologically "Africanize" the public and social goals of new institutions.

The idea of African socialism as Senghor defined it under the rubric of participative experience was sharply criticized. In addition to the Stanislas Adotevi's and Marcien Towa's criticisms of negritude,[32] Frantz Fanon,[33] Ayi Kwei Armah,[34] and Samir Amin,[35] among others, were some of the sharpest critics of the idea that African socialism was attainable as defined under the dominant global political-economic conditions of the time. At the same time, and despite these influential critiques, the spirit of resistance in which the idea and movement were rooted was not lost and cannot be simply brushed away. Among those who embraced and became exponents of this view were African theologians who demanded that the mission churches be recognized as mature enough to integrate the traditions of their peoples into the expressive practices of the church, especially in conducting their liturgies. They expressed these views in the period immediately preceding and after the Second Vatican Council and the launch of the ecumenist movement. In a strategy quite similar to Senghor's distinction between doctrine and method, or his reconciliation of the universal (idea) and the particular (conditions) in the heart of the socialist system when he argued for "African roads to socialism," African ecclesiastical leaders set their eyes on revising—if not reversing—the process of acculturation by demanding dialogue on equal terms between the evangelizing churches and the emerging local hierarchies as the representatives of the local traditions of the mission world. In other words, the idea of "community" had come to refer to Africans' alteration of the discourse of conversion. In the Church, and in theology in particular, African cultures, religions, and sociopolitical situations were becoming forces for indigenizing secular and religious values and institutional structures as well as interpretations of Western origin.

African theologians have theorized that Africans' sense of community forms a strong foundation for the very ideas of communion, unity, and participation around which the Christian Church is structured as a community or family writ large. Their argument is that while the European Church was built on traditions that were long accustomed to thinking of the individual person as the pillar of society, the African Church already had a fertile ground upon which a Christian communitarianism could flourish.[36]

According to Vincent Mulago, a Franciscan theologian from the Democratic Republic of Congo (also known as the Belgian Congo and Zaire at different points in its past), participation with others in a common life forms the basis of an essentially African contribution to Christian theology. The principle of common participation, of oneness—*ubumwe*—refers to Bantu solidarity and the Bantu belief that a vital communion exists between the members of a family, a clan, or even an entire ethnic community or group. Each member of such a sociocultural group should strive toward the safety and preservation of the whole. As the real source of life, god communicated life to the first ancestors of the group, whose duty it is to perpetuate it in their own descendants. The ancestors and the other dead members of the group constitute an invisible but not inactive part of the total community. In present life, those who are alive reach their fullest potential when they live in ways that resemble the life of god and the lives of the ancestors. All those who participate in this common life are said to be *ntu*.[37]

François-Marie Lufuluabo, a Cameroonian theologian, offers a Bantu fable whose decoding unravels the Bantu expression of the spiritual and social unity of humans as the basis of their nature and destiny. According to the Bantu, he narrates, relational life is both the foundation and ideal of human existence. He writes:

> *Les Bantous ont un idéal plus profond, leur idéal fondamental. Mais il s'agit ici d'un idéal particulier, d'ordre secondaire. L'idéal humain, l'idéal tout court. Cet idéal, c'est ce qu'ils se représentent comme constituant la manière humaine d'être par excellence; celle vers la réalisation de laquelle l'homme tend de tout son être, par nature, celle pour la réalisation de laquelle il a été créé et existe.*

> The Bantu have their own profound and fundamental ideal by which they define the ideal for human existence and well-being. This ideal aims at the realization of what human nature demands, that for which humans were created and exist.[38]

For Lufuluabo, as it indeed was for many African ethnotheologians of his time, this ideal was the enrichment of life by ensuring the immortalization of persons through their offspring; everyone was regarded to have inescapable responsibility in this process. Thus, because Mutumba, the mythical ancestor of the Bantu, felt that his immortality was threatened by the death of his only son, he cursed god in anger, only to permanently bring his wrath upon humanity. And because death thus became an unavoidable evil, humans must live their lives with intensity in relation to others, the only ones through whom their lives can be made complete and can be enhanced so they can fulfill the specifically human nature. There is in this frame of mind an echo of Tempels's ethnophilosophical principles translated into ethnotheological principles that serve as a catechism for conversion. There is also an echo of the humanism of Pierre Teilhard de Chardin, which transmits to the African vision a universalizing Christology. In Africans' interpretation of Christianity, the principles of Christian teaching meet their need for a relational world at three crucial points: in its articulation and veneration of *life* as strong, abundant, intensive, and total; in the desire for *fertility* expressed in the form of abundant physical and moral parenthood; and in the pull toward a *vital union* that is lived as communion with kin, with other people, both living and dead. The latter, we saw earlier, are sometimes brought back through the scheme of moral memory by which they rejoin their living kin in the form of *juogi*. Most African theologians believed strongly that these principles would produce a new theological synthesis in which the Africanization of Christianity and the Christianization of African values would merge to form a new local Church built on an existing communitarian foundation.[39] The outcome, V. Y. Mudimbe would say,[40] is an institution *métisse*, a hybridized synthesis. It is no wonder, then, that African theologians thought that African religions are an important resource for today's civilizational values. After a Pan-African theologians' colloquium held in Cotonou (in the Republic of Benin) in August 1970, African theologians published an interesting document entitled *Les religions africaines comme source de valeurs de civilisation,* a fitting echo of Senghor's earlier dictum of 1960 that "we must extend this [African] solidarity vertically to Europe and to America, the daughter of Europe; horizontally to all Africa, even to Asia. This will be our positive contribution to the construction of the Civilization of the Universal."[41]

The Cultivation of the Person:
Culture as Education and Vice Versa

For Nyerere, as for Senghor, "African socialism was a deeply-seated attitude of mind"[42] that was carefully instilled into the belief and thinking modes of people by different informal methods of cultural education. In his view, however, the informally induced attitude was not a sufficient basis for building a scheme for a politically organized and predictable way of life in terms of economic production. Thus, from the national level down to the village, Nyerere saw leadership space for the political party, a space in which it would play the role of teacher and guide. Hence he felt that the party needed to be strong as well as visible at every level of public life. What Sékou Touré saw in the Leviathan of the PDG Nyerere incarnated in the party hierarchy, especially in its councils.

In Nyerere's view, attitudes of mind are taught. However, those who have adopted good attitudes need to be constantly protected from negative lures of superfluous attractions that can distract them from striving to cultivate fundamental human good. The view that consumer goods are identifiable with capitalist modes of production that flourish on inequality and strife became the pillar of Tanzania's Chama Cha Mapinduzi, and for Tanzanians an example of such a system was nearby—across the border to the north in Kenya. It is right, then, that these leaders stressed that the idea that "socialism was Africans' attitude of mind" did not imply that awareness of its basic principle (namely that "our actions should at all times be guided by regard for others' welfare") is a law of thought that comes wired into the African mind. If it were, then one would assume it to be a feature of the mind universally given to all Africans, and we wouldn't have to argue to convince anyone that it was morally better than other interests that guide people's conduct. Instinct pulls most of us toward favoring our own interests and believing that all is well only when we have it all. Tempering this instinct can come only as a result of convincing ourselves that the consequences of a life based on indulging the instinctive drive to fulfill one's own desires do not augur well for survival, as our own interests are likely to conflict with the interests of others. In other words, it is not enough merely to tell or teach people that it is good or virtuous to act with regard for others' welfare. We might do so diligently as a matter of obedience to a rule of life that has been taught to us (in other words, an order of life) but that by itself does not necessarily make us good. We know that nonhuman organisms follow the order of life even more diligently than we do. Ants fulfill their duties perfectly in a colony, but we don't say they are virtuous because they do so.

So, why is "acting with regard for others' welfare," which we have identified as the basic principle of "African socialism," a good thing to do? Nyerere called this conduct "the rational choice,"[43] implying by this, in my estimation, that a separate value made the principle good and that "acting with regard to others' welfare" depended upon the realization of the worth of this other value. In other words, there must be something else that, being greater in value, would be brought about or preserved when we act as required by the principle that he called "African socialism." Inversely, that something would be compromised or denied when we do the contrary. In his view, by adopting African socialism, "We are not aiming to replace our alien rulers by local privileged elites. But to create societies which ensure human dignity and self-respect for all. The concomitant of that is that every individual has the right to the maximum economic and political freedom which is compatible with equal freedom for all others; and that neither well-fed slavery nor the necessity to beg for subsistence are acceptable human conditions."[44]

The injection of a moral basis for "African socialism" was complex in its indication of and correction of the incompleteness of the virtue theory that often punctuates its rhetoric and in its response to the critics of the movement who said that it would not work in the modern Eurocentric world, which relegated the so-called Third World to the periphery of the global economic system. Its shout can be paraphrased thus: What about the moral argument? Here is what reads like Nyerere's justification for a different stance from what Wallerstein critically described as the Hobbesian (or Leviathanian) tendencies of absolutism that some African leaders have exhibited—Sékou Touré, for example, and Robert Mugabe most recently—under the guise of socialist protection of the interests of the people:

> I now propose to argue that there is no real choice. In practice Third World nations cannot become developed capitalist societies without surrendering the reality of their freedom and without accepting a degree of inequality between their citizens which would deny the moral validity of our independence struggle. I will argue that our present poverty and national weakness make socialism the only rational choice for us.[45]

In Nyerere's view, what cannot survive modern global and Eurocentric economic forces is not the moral value of people. Rather, it is what he called "Primitive communalism."[46] The point is clear, as it would be foolish to compare indigenous structures and the productive practices they supported with the structures and productive practices of industrialized societies. Similar unfair and unthoughtful comparisons have been criticized before.[47] At the same time, Nyerere's point is that what was timeless about the indigenous situation was the idea of the good that inspired and gave direction to the virtues and other moral aspirations of its practical organization.

Justification for "communalism," "communitarianism," or "African socialism," as it has alternatively been called in recent and contemporary discourse, is to be rationally sought in what it helps cultivate, promote, or preserve about the value of *"people."*[48] And such value, the basis of human rights, cannot be assessed merely by examining whether the world of material objects is successfully manipulated. Says Nyerere: "For the truth is that development means the development of people. Roads, buildings, the increases of crop output, and other things of this nature, are not development: they are only tools of development."[49] Working from a

"Frankfurtian" standpoint, Jean-Godefroy Bidima argues that even reason finds its sense only as a function of and in service to a social reality
as defined by the imposition of the jurisdiction of the word. The word,
as evinced by its appearance in palaver (*la palabre*), is the carrier and
imposer of rational controls over social relations and the self. When it is
used to establish relations and to reestablish them where there has been
conflict, Bidima explains, "the word (la parole)" in discourse is the normative ingredient of and means to an order in which participants enter into
mutual recognition. In this sense, he argues,[50] the language of practical
reason is superior to that of silent cognitive awareness (*ratio cognoscendi*),
which becomes its handmaiden. Reason has no impact on the world if it
does not make transformation of the world possible through action. In
the reconciliation of conflicts and the reestablishment of social harmony,
the goal of language becomes that of elevating the dignity of instead of
humbling the offender. "Pardon is not an activity aimed at humiliating
the pardoned person; rather, it is meant to reinstate him or her into a
dignified relationship with the other," says Bidima.[51] In other words, use
of language is assessed in accordance with the rational-purposive action
it is intended to achieve. Thus, in Bidima's analysis, discourse is not so
much about what one can know as it is about what it can permit one to
do. "It ensures justice in a way that transcends any other form of norma-
tivization, such as the letter of the law."[52] In order to be successful as its
own instrumental authority in establishing conflict-free relations between
people, discourse must be carried out truthfully and sincerely as people
express their intentions to others.

The ultimate good, or end value, that both socialism and *palabre* help
attain (or are in service of) must therefore be a good that is independent of them; it is that which confers value on them, thereby identifying
them as goods primarily in the sense of means. Because it cannot be
identified with anything or with any state in particular, the question that
we ought to ask is this: What, conceivably, can obtain when the arrangements described by socialism and *palabre* are the order by which people
live? In other words, what, if anything, would people, any people in the
form of a community or neighborhood, gain if they were in their conduct
of everyday life people who were always concerned about the well-being of
other people around them, for example by doing those things that reduce
the gaps in people's abilities to have reasonable levels of livelihood or by
doing things that uphold the rights of all people? In another sense, we may
also ask whether there is anything to be gained by establishing a social
atmosphere where people are at peace with each other because of actions
of actual mutual dependence but also, and perhaps more importantly, as
a matter of principle. Asked to expound on the nature of communalism
in the local setting among his Luo people in Kenya, the celebrated and
onetime paramount chief, Paul Mbuya Akoko, said the following:

Their idea of communalism is, I think, of a co-operative nature. For example, where one person had cattle [in an extended family or clan], everybody "ipso fact"[*sic*] had cattle. For the owner of the cattle would distribute his cattle among people who did not have cattle so that the less well-off people may take care of them. The result is that everybody had cows to look after and so milk to drink. . . . Where a person wants to get married but did not have such things as cows, etc. [to give as dowry for a bride], other people would "chip in." One person might contribute a calf whilst another a bull, and so forth. Thus, through the co-operative help of neighbours and relatives, a man who otherwise would have been in difficulty became able to cope with the expenses of getting married [and later] he too felt obliged to help others. . . . Help is thus spread throughout the community and everybody felt a sense of belonging.[53]

Mbuya forgets to mention two things about the example of lending of cattle to others. First, the poor man who receives such cattle on loan gets to keep as personal property every third offspring of each cow he receives. Such give-aways would in turn beget their own offspring. And if he was a good keeper, such a person often received cattle from several relatives and friends. This method often turned originally poor people into eventually rich owners of large herds. Second, the poor too could give cattle to the rich to take care of. For example, if a poor person had only one cow or bull that came to them, say, by way of dowry or another form of gift, he or she would give it to a relative who had more so the relative would help with the necessary care such as herding, and any benefits from the animal such as milk would go to the poor owner. Also, it is to be assumed that those who help the poor around them in this manner do not do so in their sleep—that is, in an unreflective way. In almost every village, there are always those whose lack of generosity acquire such infamy in their neighborhoods that they become known as the proverbial "unpollinated grain stalk" of the village. The value of the practice of enabling the poor by providing them some kind of stimulus for self-elevation lies solely in what it produces for others and almost never in self-gain. But those who endeavor to take advantage of others are very unpopular, for hard work is the very basis of and therefore a virtue by which the common good is significantly cultivated and sustained.

It would be accepted that the charitable acts Mzee Mbuya Akoko described produce some good things such as happiness for the beneficiaries of the act and sometimes also for the giver, whose good feeling about enabling someone else may bring him or her an experience of gratification. But the latter can hardly be counted among the things that qualify as self-interest, nor does it conform to any customary experience since it cannot be manifested. To be mindful of other people's welfare in this way and to be rationally guided by this awareness as the (general) norm or maxim of practice for all at all times is to act in cognizance of a good that transcends any known benefit for those who practice it. Its value lies in the general or common condition of relations that results from it, not just in this specific example but in all other cases and examples of good neighborliness. Let us call this state *ujirani, utubora,* or *ujamaa,*[54] a concept for which I use these Kiswahili terms to connote relational states that go beyond friendship or warm relations with a neighbor or kin. They describe the sociomoral states that every child is taught and that every right-thinking person is called upon to consider implementing as the objective of his or her everyday conduct.

We have seen that the basic ideas of African socialism and *palabre* as well as the idea of *juok* as a moral concept are strategies for forging a state of social cohesion. To achieve this state, people invest in cultivating and striving to live by forms of conduct that are deemed to help bring it about. In their general form, such conduct may include the following:

- Being a morally good person, which may mean, in general terms, a person who exhibits good will toward other people and their property. She wishes them good health and success in their endeavors and develops pride rather than jealousy in their achievements.

- Living a life of mutual concern for the welfare of others, such as in a cooperative creation and distribution of wealth as a way of ensuring that as many people as possible can meet the basic needs of a good life. This involves respect for other people's rights, not only negatively in the abstract, such as refraining from doing any harm to anyone, but also, and more importantly, positively by doing those things that help others achieve and enjoy those rights.

- Feeling integrated with as well as willing to integrate others into a web of relations free of friction and conflict. This is what people experience in a life of an integrated community, but people may extend it to strangers where its maturity is best manifested, and it is what is aimed at when people who have been in conflict are reconciled after they recant their adversarial will with truth and sincerity.

The saying that "a play is so only because there was some role division (with other people)" or that "a feast is so only if there are people to call it so" may apply to the reality of human life in general—namely, that a good life can be judged so only in a relational situation. A life of cohesion, or positive integration with others, becomes a goal, one that people design modalities for achieving. Let us call this goal communalism, or, as other people have called it, communitarianism. In light of this goal, the virtues listed above also become desirable.

Person and Community

It is no wonder, then, that the idea of our need to protect our interests and needs relates directly to our ability to recognize similar interests and needs in others. Wiredu has reminded us of the wisdom that underlies many principles of mutual recognition, that a life centered on self-interest is likely to be brutish, short, and unpleasant. It is upon recognition of the basic danger that lurks around the rejection of interdependence between people and between individuals and community that the Swahili people say, for example, that *"mkono mmoja haujikuni mgongoni"* (a hand does not scratch its own back). The dialectic of mutual dependence that this saying alludes to is most evident in how persons and societies constitute each other. While there can be no society without the individual persons who constitute it, only society confers the agentive roles and capacities by which persons are defined, identified, and judged. Many readers are likely to identify proverbs from their respective linguistic archives that express this basic idea of mutuality between humans or some variety of it.

Knowledge of communitarian values is passed on to individuals at crucial points in their growth and development from childhood to adulthood. This is done both systematically through well-defined procedures and randomly in the course of everyday life where people learn from the examples of others, from various modes of speech (such as orders, commendation and praise, criticism and rebuke, and proverbs and stories), and from a person's participative learning when he or she is asked to perform certain duties or is shown how to do normal things of life in some very specific ways. In African modes of thought, the concept of personhood is closely related to the defining capacities of humans. As we saw earlier, the seeds that determine it are acquired partly from the individual's socio-ontological past, but its ideal levels are attained through an individual's learning about and application of those capacities in ways that are considered to be socioculturally appropriate. In this sense, being a person is attained through an educational process that intensifies at every stage in a person's growth and development. Before their initiation, children are trained to carry messages across villages to kin and friends of the family. While it may appear simple, the act of sending children as messengers across villages has a very central benefit to their social development. Apart from training them to sharpen their ability to carefully listen, understand, remember, and precisely transmit verbal messages (Jack Goody has argued that such communicative precision is possible only in literate traditions where scripted texts are least likely to be altered or modified at the hands of every handler),[55] it teaches them other virtues as well. In addition to mental training, the practice of remembering and delivering verbal messages also trains children—and maybe adults as well—the virtues of obedience and service to others while also bringing them to the knowledge of close and distant relatives, an obvious attempt to fit the child into the larger social system of the extended family and beyond. It is in the extended family where one finds security and the best place to feel at home and to live a humane life. It should not escape anyone's notice that knowing the map of one's social belonging in the early stages of life may prove useful later when, as adults, people seek spouses who can be procured only from outside one's own matri- or-patriclan, as the case may be.

As they grow older, children go through more formalized processes of learning the ethics of communal virtues. Moral education and the acquisition of the values that sustain the social order are part of initiation rituals in most African societies. These rituals, which are an important aspect of the rites of passage, "create" a person out of the untamed and unmolded body of a child. Here, as recorded by Corinne A. Kratz, is an Ogiek elder's preparatory address to a young initiation candidate:

> Initiation is something that everyone has done. *ii*? But initiation—
> initiation—we must be completely brave for initiation. . . . It's some-
> thing you do bravely. And sit like a person. . . . Until you are finished.
> [At the end of it you will be transformed from] somebody's child who
> has become a person.[56]

Kratz explains that in Ogiek initiation ceremonies, individuals mature and learn through the rituals. Here is a record of Ogiek explanation of the changes brought to an individual who has gone through the ceremony:

> A child and an adult have the same heart, that doesn't change. It's
> the head that changes. Because they go and become clever. They're
> told to leave the playing of children and are shown secret things
> [*tuumwek*] so they are no longer the same as children. . . . They
> make the difference. They change someone into an adult. Then when
> they come out [from seclusion], they are just mature and still [not
> running about like children].[57]

It is during the period of seclusion during initiation ceremonies that young people are taught the values that sustain the social order. They are taught the knowledge that regulates their performance of adult roles, which inscribe the specific traditions and customs that define their community and distinguish it from others. From then on, in speech and in deed as well as in their body postures, their behavior is no longer excusable as children's behavior; they are now taken seriously and their speech and deeds are now considered to have consequences.

The secret knowledge of adulthood is not imparted to individuals in isolation from other members of their age-group because forging a group bond is one of the objectives of the learning that takes place during the ceremonies. Initiation is a communal ritual in which age-sets take an oath of collective responsibility to safeguard the deepest knowledge of society and its ways. They will learn more through the later stages of their growth and development and finally pass these secrets and new ones to the future generation they will oversee. Those outside these ranks can only guess at what the members of other ranks keep close to their hearts. But misbehavior of an initiated person is quickly condemned as indicative of that person's stupidity; bad conduct exposes one as ignorant of what he or she is expected to know by virtue of being an adult. That is, as an adult a person is expected to protect the customary ways through adherence to them. Hence the rebuke to a person who misbehaves or reasons poorly: "Why do you act (or reason) like you never went to the forest?" The period of seclusion in the forest gives society the space and time to cultivate and groom the person in the etiquette that embodies the fundamentally altruistic impulse underlying social being. It is when one acquires the art of culture that they are said to be cultured; that is, they are considered to be knowledgeable in the practices that define being human. From then on an initiate strictly observes the separations between public and private spaces and knows which things belong to either space. Circumcision and other cultural variables physically and permanently symbolize the attainment of this stage of growth and development in a person's life; these symbols mark the shedding of childhood and with the concomitant moral instruction at initiation mark the birth of the person as a moral agent. Lessons in endurance and self-control instill in the person the ability to subdue personal impulses and put before them the greater value of the common good. In societies with structures of age-set groups, every individual owes loyalty to the secrets of his or her age group first and then to their community as a whole. Due to this bond of secrecy, age-groups are often impenetrable by outsiders. But in appropriate company, people still enjoy their freedoms and idiosyncrasies with considerable elasticity, including the ability to make dirty jokes with age-mates of the same gender and other categories of individuals with whom one can have joking relations.

Communication and Communalism

While the origin of the contractarian theory of civil society is attributed to the eighteenth-century European philosophers, it does not take much common sense to realize that sheer survival would be rare and a matter of chance without some regulation of conduct in a way that calls on all to respect and honor the rights of all others. But the mechanics of contract alone would not suffice to make human life enjoyable and comforting without the values that, though not describable as ethical in the strictest sense, nevertheless account for much of what we appreciate about being with or related to other people. As we will see later in this section,

Kwasi Wiredu stresses the importance of humane values to human life. Moral and customary teachings at initiation put great emphasis on the consequences of each person's actions for the collective. No good society can come about without the efforts of every member of society. Similarly, no society can engender for its members a sense of safety and humane conditions of life unless everyone contributes to making those things possible. Through these moral premises, individuals grasp the significance of the idea that although every individual has, as the Luo say, "their own placenta," they would not be what they ought to be without the input of most of the others with whom they share a social space. Together with taboos, a subcategory of African moral systems, moral knowledge is closely monitored and tapped for the everyday management of social order and human welfare, a process that is considerably stronger among traditional than among modern Africans.[58] In this connection, everyone who desires social respectability aspires to comply with reasonable aspects of custom (the avoidance of social opprobrium) and taboos (the avoidance of spiritually sanctionable actions or inactions).

Wiredu alludes to another role of community in enhancing the mental development of the individual. This role, he argues, is played in the act of communication. Becoming truly and accomplished humans as members of specific communities is done through the communication that makes it possible for people to create coherent scenarios that articulate *shared* meanings. In *Cultural Universals and Particulars,* Wiredu has compellingly argued in defense of what he calls the quasi-physicalist position for the Akan, according to which the human mind, conceived as the functional *capacity* of the brain to formulate ideas and concepts, is formed in social settings through communication with others. It grows and matures with incremental changes in the span of an individual's communicative world. In other words, human nature is community-based. The cognitive and moral capacities of humans are developed by and in the context of their sociality. They are formed, he argues, through a learning process. He writes:

> To possess a specific concept, an idea, entails some linguistic ability, however slight. But such an ability is the result of training. Human life is a learning process, which begins almost immediately on arrival in the world. This learning has to be in the context of a society, starting with the narrow confines of mother or nurse and widening to larger and larger dimensions of community as time passes. This learning process, which at the start is nothing much more than a regime of conditioning, is, in fact, the making of mind. In this sense a new-born baby may be said to have a brain but no mind, a reflection that is in line with the traditional Akan view that a human creature is not a human person except as a member of a community.[59]

In all these examples, African scholars and ordinary African people appear to share the view that the individual is dependent on his or her social world to fulfill organic needs as well as for spiritual (moral and conceptual) growth. There is therefore an important difference between Wiredu's monistic (quasi-physicalist) view of the individual and the Dogon or Yoruba views that, at least in their appearance through ethnographic texts, are pluralist. Wiredu's position expresses only the narrow view that knowledge is gained and shared through sociality. One can also note that while the nationalist communitarians were wrong in attributing dependence on community to Africans as their ontological (that is, essentialist) character, they were right in their recognition of the role of community in the making of the human world. Wiredu's position is that the universal order conditions the nature of humans generally, not just Africans. He develops the experiential specific into a general and universal order and gives it a philosophical definition.

Communitarianism and Modern Society in Africa

Communitarianism is the political view or ethic that developmental and participatory rather than liberal democracy is the most effective means for checking and containing aberrant policy and polity. It is developmental because its major concern is to forge avenues for the recognition of new rights, and it is participatory because in order to win such recognition, it depends not only on rational argumentation but also on collective political action as an inseparable means of pressing for these new rights, which, in turn, are collectively shared with others. Communitarianism, then, is the collectivist vision of a polity in its struggle for moral and other group goals. Its strength lies in the ability of its chief defenders to convince the membership, both actual and potential, that the moral issues at hand are their right and are good for them as people and as members of a group and, more importantly, that such interests cannot be achieved unless all who accept them act together in solidarity as a group. In these senses of communitarianism, the idea includes some aspects of a way of life based on the acceptance of the strength of group morality at the cultural level. But because this level of communitarianism lacks a political institution at which its demands are directed, we shall call it a cultural morality. We can certainly recognize that it also becomes the basis for a political morality at that level, though. Communitarianism practiced by African societies fits this latter version.

Communitarianism represents the view that the attainment of human needs and interests is best served in union with others. This view may be as old as the idea of society itself. For that reason, there are aspects of it in every human society. The differences, in both practice and theory, lie in how people determine and justify the degree, and what specific respects, of indebtedness individuals ought to have toward each other and toward community. On one end of this spectrum lies absolute egoism, and on the other, as unimaginable as it may be, perhaps a form of absolute altruism, the sort that even Aristotle thought would be harmful to every person. As I explained above, determining these relations has very much been part of Western social thought as well, such as can be seen to set apart, for example, someone like the French Jean-Jacques Rousseau's individualism from the German Georg Simmel's communalism.[60] In Africa, its theoretical beginnings are linked to the emancipatory politics of independence from European colonialism. But as an ethic of everyday life and social order it precedes recent African political and intellectual movements. Its expression can be found in many local idioms in African communities. Among most Africans communitarianism is not a doctrine, although most would be able to clearly explain why the social order related to this ethic would be a better way of living for humans than any other mode. "It is humans who sacrifice for each other" (literally "it is among humans that one may decide to go hungry for a night so another person can eat"—*dhano ema nindo-niga wadgi kech*) is a common Luo saying used to exhort someone to help a needy relative. The saying points to the idea of interdependence as a characteristically human mode of life; it is urged as a moral good, not as a passive and mechanistic arrangement of the cosmic-social reality. Another example is the saying that *"dhier man k'owaduu ok moni nindo"* (a person's eyes do not miss sleep because his or her neighbor is poor). Although it appears to contradict the communitarian principle, this latter saying has its lesson, namely that one does not literally feel the pangs of hunger when it is his or her neighbor or sibling who is going hungry. Nor does one bleed because their companion has stubbed his or her own toe on a rock. However, knowing that someone in distress can be rescued only by someone who is better placed is the beginning of the consideration of the idea that a world where everyone is left to their own fate cannot be a world of happy people, at least not for everyone all the time. Hence, although one may not be literally rendered sleepless because their neighbor is in distress, the realization of reciprocity and interdependence is what breeds the ideal human condition. The saying teaches, in addition, that although communitarianism is not the death of individuality, its ideals are the reason we are called upon to be mindful and responsible individuals.

The first of these two sayings appears to suggest that the promotion of human well-being is a collaborative and reciprocal endeavor where those who are more able in some domains need to assist those who are less able. If not all Africans live within this humanistic ideal, at least they clearly define and long for it "in terms not only of human but also of humane values," as Wiredu says.[61] In its moral definition, communitarianism exemplifies belief in the principle of practical altruism as an important social virtue. It recognizes and encourages sharing with others as an important characteristic of human life. Like everywhere else in human societies, African communitarianism is a principle for guiding the practice of everyday life in ways that seek to create a humane world in which, to quote from Wiredu again, "individuals will have the chance of realizing their interests, conceived as being intrinsically bound up with the interests of others in society."[62] This belief system encourages everyone to carry out their share of responsibility in contributing to the creation of humane conditions of life for everyone. Africans tend to encourage people to fulfill this responsibility positively through good deeds toward others. African communitarianism has been cited as a significant economic factor in the regulation of the circulation of wealth.

People who are accustomed to regarding competitive access to the material goods of the modern economy as a significant way of expressing and celebrating variations in individual capacities are bound to find this social ethic very strange. They might even find it to be exploitative of those who work hard to build assets for themselves and their immediate families. The ethic of individualism as it has been well articulated in liberal social theory since Locke is that the individual has sole rights to the effects of his or her labor, which in turn is the effect of his or her individualized capacities. Thus, the pursuit of goods is primarily geared toward self-aggrandizement. Beyond this one has duties only toward one's spouse and children. Africans, on the other hand—and I mean here Africans whose productive lives are based in either or both the traditional and modern economic environments—appear to extend the boundary of their duty beyond spouse and offspring. The duty here is not translatable into a legal obligation, as the duty toward spouse and offspring would. It is guided by the ethic of communitarism, or the moral of altruism molded over time through the society's teachings on right and wrong, good and bad, noble and ignoble.

Some Africanist political economists[63] have called the economic practice of this distributive ethic "the economy of affection." The phrase has a critical side to it, but it also suggests a key difference between what is believed to be an organizing value of communitarianism and the organizing principles of liberalism. Such scholars of Africa's political economy have claimed that the African practice of the communalist ethic within the modern economy represents an anomaly. They suggest that adapting modern economic benefits to the communalist ethic contradicts one of the primary objectives of the modern liberal economy—its expected effects on the ability of individuals to increase and diversify their quality of life through access to modern consumer goods and benefits. Thus, while liberalism focuses on the definition and practice of values that promote and protect the right of the individual to justly pursue his or her interests (for example, the enactment of laws that protect the rights and freedoms of individuals and institutions), communitarianism builds on empathy and other such altruistic feelings. But while the benefits of such feelings can be taught, their practice can neither be determined nor enforced; it can only be encouraged.

It is true that the modern economy has brought several benefits to Africans at both the private and public levels. The Nigerian Nobel Prize–winning writer Wole Soyinka has suggested (I believe rightly) that the modern economy, together with its scientific and technological infrastructure and elements, has become so much part of Africa that it does not seem clever anymore to define a separate type of experience as truly African by virtue of its separation from the effects of the modern economy. In other words, one does not have to be "unmodern"—whatever that means—to be an "authentic" African. But Africans have appropriated the meaning and effects of the modern economy in their own ways. One of these ways is how Africans relate their access to modern economic benefits to the demands of their communalistic ethic. While many are pulled to either extremity of this ethic, several manage to keep some sort of balance, although not always on an equal basis. Those who are drawn to the extremity of communalism or to the balanced medium have to give up personally rewarding benefits or goods associated with the new economy, and there is little doubt that they experience the pain of sacrificing for others. But in doing this they are driven by a sense of culturally specific "obligation," the communitarian ethic. And somewhere among them, now and then, are those who have all the communitarian good will but do not have pockets deep enough to allow practical follow-ups.

Strictly speaking, the ethic of communalism is not a moral value like attending to a sick mother or going to war to protect one's own country would be. Failing to extend one's helping hand to a stranger in need is not a moral failure of similar degree to that of failing to help one's sick mother or refusing to enlist to fight for one's country at war. But consciously choosing not to help someone in need when we are in fact able to do so brings the realization that if we had acted differently, we could have improved the condition of life for one more person. Altruism requires that we do at least the minimum to help others when we can—what we ourselves would wish someone would do for us if we were in need of help. The Luo people of Kenya have a saying that only people "with hard eyes like those of a night-runner or witch" (wang' teko ka wang' jajuok, meaning individualistic boldness and an uncaring attitude toward others) have no feelings about others' needs. A person becomes a witch when he or she adopts animal-like characteristics in their behavior toward other people; they may want to strangle them or wish them other types of harmful fates. To behave in this way is to behave like a beast; that is why night-runners are proverbially said to transform themselves in the night and, with some wild animal they have tamed roam around and within other people's homes, often scaring people and destroying their property while they sleep. Thus, one becomes a witch by withdrawing from the known norms of human conduct; he or she becomes an *homme extraordinaire* in the negative sense.

At the base of communitarianism lies the transformation of the structures that relate the individual to the community to which he or she belongs into a moral resource. The sense of belonging, or the realization and acceptance that the self is located in the midst of others, becomes the basis of his or her moral outlook within the context of a common set of values. Within this mode of thought, no person is considered to be a self-sufficient entity in and for him or herself. Rather, it posits the existence of others as an essential part of the very structure of the self, from which emanates the communitarian exigency. The community is thus crucially differentiated from the "mass." It is not just a collectivity. Rather, it is built through deeds in which are inscribed a person's contribution to the building of the community. One assumes that this is the basis of the emphasis on moral education during initiation ceremonies, from which initiates emerge as full-fledged members of their community, agents of the moral and cognitive values on which the idea of their specific community is inscribed. Wiredu relates morals to custom in this way:

> In view here are such things as the prescriptions and proscriptions operative in a community regarding life and death, work and leisure, reward and retribution, aspirations and aversions, pleasure and pain, and the relationships between the sexes, the generations and other social categories and classes. The combined impact of such norms of life and thought in a society should give a distinctive impression of its morals.[64]

The recognition of common belonging should draw anyone toward the ethical principles that everyone is expected to take part in making it possible to realize the basic ideals of life. These aspirations do not flow out of Africans with a natural or metaphysical force. They are taught, and on different occasions people are reminded about the higher values of relational living. Like African theologians, African political leaders in the early days of independence (who often doubled as political visionaries) tried to lift this communitarian wisdom and way of life into a political morality—that is, into a rationalized and organizing ideology for modern political institutions. The different brands of "African socialism" fit this description. Like the theologians before them, these political leaders—and the intellectuals who stood by their side—believed that the values of individual worth and freedom were incompatible with those of communitarianism.

I believe differently. I believe that communitarianism has its value yet places burdens on individuals and that these burdens, if properly defined, do not oppress the individual as much as is often believed. But the values and expectations of the communitarian ethic can be misunderstood or even abused, just as the liberties of the individual under liberalism have been. I believe that because it calls for everyone to honor mutual and reciprocal responsibilities toward others, communitarianism is based on an inevitable fact of human life: that to exist within a social space—to occupy a point or to be an individual within a social space—is to differ, to be different. This is the point of the saying that one does not literally suffer sleeplessness because his or her neighbor is poor. But communitarianism goes further when it articulates the view that being inscribed in a social space requires everyone to realize that they cannot live in society and be indifferent. The ethic of active reciprocity means that everyone has a responsibility toward those with whom they share a social space. Everyone is called upon and is expected to make a difference by contributing to the creation of the humane conditions that, at least, enhance the community's ability to reduce unhappiness and suffering. Kwame Gyekye, another Ghanaian philosopher, has recently defended the African idea of communitarianism as one that does not oppose but in fact recognizes and upholds the status and rights of the individual.[65] While arguing that African communitarianism is not perfect, he believes that its shortcomings can be rectified and improvements can be made, especially in the area of integrating some aspects of individual rights with the values of communal good.

Kwasi Wiredu argues in *Cultural Universals and Particulars* that at least some of these rights, especially those that define and protect claims about basic human needs, are already clearly defined in the traditional thought systems and practices of some African societies, such as the Akan of Ghana. The very idea of a person in the Akan modes of thought suggests that the attainment of personhood is a function of the existence and utilization of certain social and material values; without these values, key aspects of being a person cannot emerge. Humans need family—and hence community—for their biological, cognitive, and moral growth and development before they are able to use these faculties for themselves and for others. According to Wiredu, such a network of kinship relations generates a system of rights and obligations.[66]

The Communitarian Ethic and Humane Society

Material well-being is probably good, especially if all people enjoy it, but is not by itself sufficient to create or generate a comprehensive sense of comfort in society. Well-being is complete when (apart from material prosperity) people feel that they are in an atmosphere of positive relations with other members of their society or neighborhood, when from other members of society come those gestures that reassure us that we are secure and in good rapport with those we interact with, whether or not we are personally acquainted with them. This kind of value may not be as obvious as what material prosperity or the lack of prosperity reveals. Yet without the feeling of safety and reassurance within society, even the most materially prosperous neighborhoods may not be desirable places to live. Thus, societies differ greatly with regard to just how their members feel that they are connected and bonded with other members. Those differences can be the result of either tough law enforcement or a matter of custom and social mores that are informally passed on to members of society about how to relate to others. They are generated and are upheld through adherence to a cultural morality such as communitarianism.

We saw when discussing the roles of initiation that in most African societies the passing down of such morality can be a serious matter that should not be left to the informal processes of inculcation. I call the content of such education social knowledge. In most traditional societies individuals were taught about the structure of their social environment and their place in that structure. This knowledge unveiled to them not only how they related to the whole but also how they were expected to behave toward everyone within it, social expectations that were determined by how the initiate was related to each member. These mores bind many an African whether they are traditional, modern, or a bit of both. But they are framed differently in different societies, and some of these modes of framing often present problems of theoretical interest to those who reflect upon them with deliberate sophistication. Here it might be easy to make some generalizations.

Respect for people of the other gender and for those in positions of gerontological and cultural seniority used to flow easily from most Africans who value indigenous traditions of society. Contrary to prevalent beliefs among people unversed in African traditions of decency, womenfolk are accorded utmost respect in most African societies that I know. Men strive to not be seen to be out of step by people of the female gender. There definitely are several community-specific ways of expressing this social ideal, but its basic aim is to require of all people of the male gender a strict observance of acceptable comportment before people of the opposite gender, including use of appropriate language. A person is morally good in this regard when he strictly observes the rules that separate gendered spaces in society and where such separation is made out of respect rather than to discriminate.

Charity and other virtues of altruism such as *politeness* and *benevolence* to others are perhaps the most celebrated aspects of African communitarian practices and ideals. Millions of Africans have been or are under threat of being victims of one or other type of calamity. Deliberate actions of other people, such as instigating wars or political instability, and other not-so-directly human-related happenings such as famine and floods have forced millions of Africans to flee their homes and countries for long periods of time. Although pictures of and from these situations already are disheartening beyond measure, one cannot imagine what it would be like without the charity and benevolence of all those others, Africans and non-Africans alike, who have taken refugees, pure strangers in most cases, into their homes and provided for them for no other reason than their concern for those who are experiencing hardship. One could cite an endless list of cases where this ethic has been a sustaining and reassuring value to millions of Africans in situations of near despair. Kwasi Wiredu rightly laments the serious threat posed to this ethic by industrialization and suggests that Africa's future might well lie in how wisely Africans learn to salvage their communalist ethic and balance it with the selectively acceptable aspects of modernization.[67] According to Gyekye, there should be no distinction between moral obligation in the strict sense and supererogation because the line between what does and what does not count as moral obligation appears to be arbitrary and difficult to determine. He writes:

> A harmonious cooperative social life requires that individuals demonstrate sensitivity to the needs and interests of others, if that society is to be a moral society. The reason is that the plight or distress of some individuals in the society is likely to affect others in some substantial ways. . . . Communitarian moral theory would see no real distinction between moral responsibility and moral ideals. . . . It considers the community as a fundamental human good, advocates a life lived in harmony and cooperation with others, a life of mutual consideration and aid and of interdependence, a life in which one shares in the fate of the other—bearing one another up—a life that provides a viable framework for the fulfillment of the individual's nature or potential.[68]

Not being charitable to others or sheer disregard of others especially in their times of need is condemned as antisocial in the sense of being contrary to the ideals that define and promote the ideal conditions of human life. A person who does not spend the full mourning period with the family of a deceased relative when they can and/or contribute to the funeral expenses in one of the several ways shared among relatives and friends is regarded and often loudly criticized as having the spirit of a witch. As most Africans know, being regarded as a witch, whether it is true or not and whatever the exact content of the accusation, can consume one's life through ostracization by one's neighbors and relatives. Its moral strength lies in its meaning that a witch is a person who lives spatially close to others yet is morally distant and indifferent to the values that define the social space that he or she shares with the community. Hence, selfish acts are likened to the practices of a witch. The Luo say that "the

eyes of a witch never back down from the confronting stare of others."
The meaning is obvious. Because a witch is antisocial, he or she will not
heed the prevailing moral conventions of his or her society. They will not
consider the opinions of others, for they are bent on following only their
very self-centered interests. Writing of the Kaguru moral system, Tom
Beidelman says:

> The idea of a witch is a "complex construction of the imagination,"
> one exerting a profound effect upon Kaguru. The character of a
> witch is physically and morally inverted from what the ideal, proper
> human being should be. Kaguru witches are not truly human at all,
> yet they appear in human form, living and interacting with others;
> otherwise they would not be dangerous.
>
> Kaguru beliefs in witches and witchcraft are attempts to imagine
> beings morally outside society, even as they are in some sense part of
> it. Witches are not fully accountable in a world where social beliefs
> and rules should provide a working order by which people secure
> their ends and needs in the company of others.[69]

As Beidelman rightly comments, "Belief in witchcraft is a mode of imagining evil, judged harmful, bad, and beyond any moral justification."[70] A
witch possesses supernatural powers that he or she uses to harm others.
Viewed in the context of communitarian ideals, the belief in witches
affirms the undesirability of the idea of individuality and the power of the
individual to negatively affect the course of things in the social order. But
even while such a belief affirms the power of individuality, it immediately
condemns its excesses. A witch harms others because he or she is jealous
of others' successes where he or she has failed. The condemnation of witchcraft, then, recognizes differences in individual endowments and abilities
to succeed. It recognizes healthy competition among people as well as the
deserved suffering that may result from one's failures, which might include
disobedience toward god and ancestral spirits. But it condemns a
witch's practices against others because it causes them unfair and unde-
served suffering.

As a matter of curiosity, the critiques of individual autonomy latent
in these passages from African texts compare well with those of Alisdair
MacIntyre, Charles Taylor, and John Kekes, all of whom critique the Western liberal idea of autonomy as a failure and as an escape from having to
address the prevalence of evil.[71]

Communitarianism expands the boundary of one's social space into a
moral entity with common concerns and one fate. How could it be otherwise? This moral imagination of the social order brings everyone into a
relationship of mutual responsibility toward the other. Toward children in
particular, African communities have different modes of expressing their

veneration. Ideally, like those of the ancestral dead, the innocent spirits of children have some supernatural power about them. They are beyond reproach and should not be harmed or be willed ill. While adults can bring calamities upon themselves through their own deeds or through what they have failed to do, misfortune to children can only come from a witch or from an ancestral spirit aiming to teach the living adult world a tough lesson for its failures and aberrations. Unfortunately, the worsening abuse cases against children in many parts of the continent are a call to all of us to rise to stop an eruption of infanticide, child labor, child rape, and other abuses against children.

One must admit that the moral teachings given during initiations and through the folktales that extend the lessons into the spheres of everyday life forever thereafter are not charters for social action. As Michael Jackson notes, "They are [only] explorations into the problems of right conduct."[72] What makes the difference is the constant making and remaking of the world through these narratives and other speech forms that help make moral inquiry and speculation present to all ages most of the time. As both Jackson and Beidelman observe about the Kuranko and Kaguru texts, respectively, the communitarian ethic teaches the worth of developing sympathetic awareness of other people in the context of a communal experience as the basis of awareness that the mutuality of respect and affection are worth keeping and cultivating. Because the stories are modeled on characters with close relations, they teach a cardinal lesson: that charity begins at home, among people with affinity for each other, then spreads out to the outside world based on the concept of equality, which, in turn, as we have seen, is built on the idea of each person's responsibility for the commonwealth of the extended family and society, and the human family at large.

In Lieu of a Conclusion: A Village Symposium on Experience

The setting is my rural Kenyan home in October 1991. At the center of this event was a dispute about whether, on what grounds, and when, a person should be obliged to observe *kwer* rituals (cleansing related to the death of a child). The background to the event was a crisis precipitated by what was envisioned by the convener, my father, as a threat to the well-being of a social group—in this specific case, his own family. What makes this symposium interesting to anyone with philosophical inclinations is the crucial issue it raises about the autonomy of morality when it is understood as the guide to action based on the dictates of the law of reason within each one of us. Following this law within guarantees not only the certainty but also the autonomy of morality as built firmly and solely on the principle of duty, or so it was argued.

As it turned out, the issue at hand was not opposition to moral duty, but *how* one determines what it is dutiful for us to do. In this sense, the symposium opened itself up to theoretical considerations of conflict between opposing moral perspectives in real-life situations. As it unfolded, the symposium ran into problems that are usually classified in moral discourse as problems of relevance; that is, it brought out considerations of whether, in the ensuing contestation between the opposing perspectives, there was really an argument instituted by applying the premises of one perspective to the deconstruction of the other. Because none of the disputants was an expert in ethics, the question of the origin and purpose of moral law—those principles to which we will commit to guide our understanding of and choices about what it is right for us to do—may not have been explicitly addressed, but, upon reflection, it certainly emerged from the practical concerns that were driving the dispute.

The Symposium[1]

F: I have called you here to listen to and help me resolve something which disturbs me deeply.

MO: What has gone wrong?

255

F: This child [reference to me] wrote to me recently from Nairobi. I read his letter and, in the end, I didn't want to believe that what I had read was true. At that time I thought that maybe it was the writing which had distorted what might have been a good idea. You know these young people cannot write Dholuo. So I kept the letter without responding to it. Today, I want all of you to help me understand it because the people involved are also all here.

UM: Some of them, in fact very many of them, cannot even speak correct Dholuo.

F: So I dropped the idea of responding to the letter, lest I too distort and therefore aggravate things further.

MO: Come to the point; tell us what has annoyed you so much.

F: This child wrote to me about an incident which took place in my home here, involving his sister-in-law from Mwer [clan]. You see, his younger brother and sister-in-law had a stillborn child in the month of May [1991]. Is stillbirth not considered as death of a person according to Luo customary belief and practice?

All: (in chorus): Yes [it is].

F: Which means that the incident must be treated with all the appropriate rites applicable thereto?

All: (in chorus): Yes.

MO: That is always so. Was there any dispute about it?

F: Now, you all know that later on [in early October] this same young lady had another misfortune. She lost her mother. Is it not in accordance with our [same] customary beliefs and practices that in such a situation, the young lady first completes all the rites applicable to her delivery and to the death of her child before she is made to perform the rites related to the death of her mother?

All: (in chorus): Yes.

F: Are these rites obligatory or according to choice?

UM: Those [kwer, or rites] are matters which should be obvious to them because they are adults now. Did they have any problems with any of these?

F: That is precisely the point. When Nyar Mwer [the young lady in question] came to the funeral of her late mother, she returned here, as per custom, on the third day of mourning, before going back for the final rite (kwero). So when she returned here, I told her that she was obliged to undergo the required rites for her child first before joining her sisters and brothers in the rites for their mother. But my daughter-in-law would not hear of what I had to say. She objected and said she would never follow those old practices, adding that she did not understand [read appreciate] what role they played in her life anyway. I was shocked, but I struggled to be calm. In the first place, no young person talks like that to an elder. Secondly, no woman talks like that to her in-laws. But I chose to address what I thought was the important issue. I said: if you do not understand what these things serve, then that is precisely the more reason why you should listen to and follow what I tell you, because I know and you don't. They have to do with the correct way of living. Living correctly is what makes homes what they are [as different from the wild]. It requires that people follow laid-down rules and perform laid-down practices. But my daughter-in-law responded by saying that in their home [of birth] they don't follow those things. This remark made me think that there was something wrong with my daughter-in-law or that it was me she didn't like to advise her. But even after her mother-in-law tried to talk to her, telling her that as a married woman she follows the practices of her home of marriage, the position remained unchanged. At which point I walked away to attend to my herds. But behind me, she packed her belongings and went to Nairobi. Apparently, when she reached Nairobi she went and told the whole story—from her side, because the letter I received contains many falsehoods—to her brother-in-law. The reason I have called you here is the content of the letter written to me by my son after he was briefed by his sister-in-law on the incident I have just described. The letter was annoying to me because it claimed I was unfair to Nyar Mwer. But what is important is that my son went ahead to tell me [in the letter] that they do not want to follow those customary rules. I felt estranged from and slighted by own children; I wondered whose customs they wanted to follow. Today I want them to explain, before you all here, why they think they cannot follow the ways by which we have lived for generations; why they think that today they are wiser than us and than our grandfathers who established the customs for us. They should tell you which these ways of theirs are and why they think it is me who must succumb to those ways of theirs. Do these children want to strip me of my patrimony? Do they want to turn my home into theirs? Who teaches who between me and them?

MO: You have talked too much. Let them too explain their side. My sister's son, are these things narrated by your father really true? I cannot believe what I have heard. Things like this [referring, I believe, to what was presented as rebellion of sons and their families to a father by refusing to practice *kwer* and, in the worse scenario, as an attempt to prevent the correct course of practice from taking place] never happen. They [omissions in the practice of vital *kwer* rituals] ruin and consume homes [defined in this case as a moral community]; they reduce humans [as individual members of the moral community] to nothingness. Explain to us what you had in mind.

D: My letter was not written in the mood that my father has given it here. If it had it, then I first want to be forgiven. My letter was based on the simple fact that here was a case where one person was saying "I do not believe in those things myself." So my question was: Why force someone into doing something she does not believe in the first place?

MO: You were talking for your sister-in-law. How about yourself? Do you or do you not believe in these *kweche*?

D: You see, things change from time to time. We people of the present generation see things differently . . .

F: Which are these new ways? That is what I want to hear you tell these elders seated here.

D: I was saying, we people see things differently. We have been brought up in new ways such as Christian ways . . .

F: And school, right? Is that what you want to tell us? According to who are they [new ways taught through the new epistemologies of Christianity and the school] better than what we are telling you?

M: Let him finish what he was saying. You like cutting people off.

F: You see, Nyar Oloo, I know how these young people think. There is not going to be anything new here. I joined the police force before these people were born. I became a Christian before they were born. These people who brought these things they are talking about I have known them for a long time.

MO: My sister's son, we too are Christians. As your father is saying, we became Christians a very long time ago. I became a Christian when I was a young girl, your mother here was not [yet] born. But that has not prevented me from practicing Luo [moral] customs. Where would I live if I did not? Or how would I relate to all those other people I share my big home [*dala*] with? So the way you are talking, my sister's son, is not the [right] way.

D: Despite the padre's teachings against them?

MO: Do you want to follow everything that the padre says? He is also a person like me . . . and like you. Have you ever seen any of them [meaning white missionaries] follow our customs? They follow theirs; and how would we know how and when they follow them?

F: These children ought to know (*nyaka ng'e*) that those things they call Christian are also other people's rules of correct living. Do you think they came from nowhere? They too are ways of other people. They have their owners. [I thought of this and the previous remark by MO as together making a very strong case against moral universalism.]

D: Are you people therefore saying that there should not ever be any change in these Luo ways? What about all those Christians who don't practice them anymore?

F: Then you tell us exactly why you think that these things of yours which you are talking about are better than what these people here are telling you.

MO: We have not said there is no change. Change there always is. But you are not saying it is for you to bring change in your father's home, are you? That is wrong, my sister's son.

M: Which homes are you talking about? How can you know how people live in their homes? Crucial *msengni* [pl. of *msango*, meaning "ritual"] have always been performed in the depth of night. How would you therefore know those who do from those who do not practice them? [This was a crucial suggestion that "true" Luo conversion to Christianity always remained suspect; that given the crucial importance of *kwer* in the definition of home, *dala*, there was likelihood that those who professed adherence to Christian ways by day probably practiced Luo ways, particularly *kwer*, by night, hidden away from public scrutiny by the deep privacy of the night. Indeed, the Luo traditionally advise against visits to other people's homes late in the night, lest one stumble into a private and secret practice of such deadly family rituals as *msango* and end up picking up the misfortunes being warded off thereby.]

F: This is my home [an expression of patriarchy over a specific moral community]. And these children together with their wives ought to realize that they do not live in this [space] alone [by themselves]. They share it with others, those who have died, those now present, and those still to be born. The uprightness of this home [defined in terms of social health instituted by the strict observance of *kwer* as well as by the absence of any breaches—by commission or omission—of any *kwer*] must be based on what is good for everybody. Whoever does not agree with me must with immediate effect establish his own home [as a separate moral space] where he can institute a tradition of new ways. But whoever wants to continue living in this my home must now, immediately, take stock of what is demanded of him [or her] and perform all the requirements. The deadline is tomorrow since today we have visitors. The elder Nyar Oloo (MO), I want you to conclude this meeting, or does anyone else have anything to say before that?

All (not really together, but unanimously): No.

MO: What else would there really be for me to add? I think we have agreed that these things are urgent and that they must perform them.

F: Just ask them. Maybe one or all of them would want to make their own homes where they can do things according to the changes they claim to believe in. In my view, only a *jajuok* does things according to their own pleasure. He [or she] is called *jajuok* precisely because he acts without caring about other people. Even when they kick someone else's door in the night and break their leg in the process, they will tell you they are fine with it because they have accomplished their own objective: to do as their compulsions push them to please themselves. Why can't a right-thinking person be mindful of how their action is likely to affect others?

MO: That is immaterial, for even if they wanted to, they would still be obligated to perform them [the *kweche* (rituals) in question] since the occurrences for which we are making demands belong here [to this moral space]. Did we not just bury a child at the back of this home the other day? And assuming that they decided [or were allowed] to move out, that would still leave all of you to face the consequences of our failure to satisfactorily resolve this matter. You would be torn apart, which is equal to extinction of this family; you who remain here and they who move out. Son of Otema, you and Nyar-Ugenya must buy a razorblade with which to get your heads shaven tomorrow morning. I am informed that your brother and his wife already performed their own cleansing ritual. The matter is closed and everyone must return to work as the visitors are about to arrive now.

D: I feel shut down.

MO: I know, but this does not have to be the end of this matter. There is nothing that cannot be resolved by discussion. We may not agree today, but we can sleep on the matter and then return to it, again and again, until we resolve it. But that is for another day.

Reflecting later, I thought, this whole event was a reminder to me of Shaaban Robert who said, in reference to the need for a defense of women's rights, that we should never be afraid or ashamed of pursuing what is good.[2] He thought that justice is such a good, and that the absence of justice was tantamount to one of the ten types of poverty. He puts it thus:

Kama mtu hana haki, chama chake maskini
Japo kuwa hana dhiki, lakini hana thamani
Laana za halaiki, zitamtoa maanani
Ukosefu wa haki, pia ni umaskini

Whoever lacks a sense of justice must be considered poor
Although such a person may not be in material distress, he/she will
    have no worth
The curse of abundance will exclude him from other people's
    thoughts
Lack of justice is a form of poverty.[3]

But what is the foundation of our knowledge of how we ought to act? Just think this: with exception of the Defendant (D) in the foregoing symposium, none of the disputants was aware that there once was someone far away in the land of Europeans, and quite famous by some accounts, who would have ridiculed them for exactly what their discursive efforts were aimed at: namely, seeking the basis for moral action in the content of experience. Yet in the instance of that early morning gathering, these villagers, armed only by what had always sustained their customs in consistency, the power of practical reason, were unknowingly holding their own against the person now held in the eyes of some of his contemporary admirers to be perhaps the greatest philosopher of recent times. That European man was Immanuel Kant. In his view, morality must be self-governing, free of any influences or interests of any kind, especially religious interests, or, as in this village case, customary interests as well. In his own circumstances, religion and custom did not have any distinction of significance, yet there can be occasions when what were once religions worldviews become part of inherited custom. In his view, we ought to be self-governing in our capacity as moral agents. How, then, do we, as humans, develop our moral knowledge if not by the strength of our reflection on good and evil, which are values that frequently emerge only from relational experiences? An answer is to be found in his view of moral law.

In the domain of moral judgments, Kant thought of reason as capable of extricating itself from the baggage of distractions that come with the corporeality of the subject. As with our knowledge of the external world of objects, Kant argued, it was possible to chart out the nature of thought to show how we can have certain knowledge of principles of moral conduct by following "the moral law within" us. In this moral domain, the objective would be determining or defining the cardinal principle on the basis of which a moral judgment must always be right for everyone by virtue of its rational status alone. Following such a self-regulating principle becomes a duty for the moral agent. For him, then, and in sharp contrast to the position suggested by the villagers, the crucial condition for being a moral agent is having autonomy of will. In this way, moral judgments too are guaranteed certainty and universality. In other words, moral judgments, like their counterparts in the sensory world, ought to have grounds upon which they are objectively true for all people at all times. For moral judgments to be so, they must be extricated from idiosyncratic interests of any kind and their rightness must be founded on the laws of moral judgment. Thus, the only valid ground for a moral act ought to be the product of this law, and that product should not only be right but also be the same for everyone in their "right mind," and to that principle they should strive to adhere. Such a law lies in the alliance between reason and good will. By the latter Kant meant the effort of rational beings to do what they ought to do instead of acting from inclination, for example by merely following a habit, custom, or self-interest.

The true function of reason, Kant argued, "must be to produce a will which is not merely good as a means to some further end, but is good in itself."[4] Thus, for Kant, doing our *duty*, following the demands of reason and doing as we *ought*, doing what is *right*, stands in direct opposition to the directions of desire or what pleases us and to the demands of our sensuous nature. Thus, to have *moral worth*, our actions must be the direct function of our sense of *duty* with regard to those acts. Inclination alone is not enough to bestow moral worth on our actions, not even when the inclination is to do what is our duty. Only the motive of duty bestows moral worth on an action. Moral worth has no specific object; rather, it depends, according to Kant, "merely on the principle of volition according to which, without regard to any objects of the faculty of desire, the action has been done."[5] It is not the purpose or goal of the action but the *principle* or *maxim* on the basis of which the action is performed that bestows moral worth on an action.

These Kantian propositions tally well with the standards of liberalism. According to the latter, for example, we should support an ordinance granting rights to a group of minorities against prevailing prejudices not because someone out there (and may be our own selves) stand to gain from (to be protected by) the consequences of such a law but purely on the ground that there is no rational ground to support its denial. In such a case, the act of supporting the rights of a minority group acquires a moral worth because it is based purely on the principle that individuals and groups should be granted all rationally defined freedoms and rights so long as they do not pose any threat to similar freedoms and rights of others. A moral person, according to Kant, is he or she who acts according to principle; he or she is a principled person. "Rather than act on the basis of the desires of the moment, the person of principle appeals to a general rule or rationally articulated reason in order to ascertain what to do."[6] Such a principle, as I mentioned a little earlier, must be one that transcends the moment.

All of the above appears well and good. But the question of any moral reasoning (and perhaps also hidden under the haystack of the villagers' discourse) is whether the principled person who says "I don't think that principle p would be right" does so in the absolute absence of any awareness of a situation, real or potential, in which the principle under consideration would be troublesome if acted upon. Of course one can think of any hypothetical situation to which the principle could apply. But one must also wonder whether there are any such things as perfect hypotheses that can fit every specific case. Take the villagers' case above. The convener, F, objects to such a suggestion on the ground that the situation at hand can only gain from a counterexample from a relevantly similar situation and says that he would not yield to abstract objections. His protest is not against the principle that people ought to act in a way that produces good for everyone beyond the interests of only one individual or a small section of society, which is a general principle. In fact, he insisted that this was precisely what he was protecting. He was objecting to the view, whether it was expressed openly or he only suspected that certain members of his family harbored it, that the worth of such principles is abstract and ought to be judged independently of any real situation. The appeal of assessing principles for moral action appears to emerge, as in the case of this village symposium, from those situations where a commonly agreed-upon principle points different people in a situation to different modus operandi, especially when these are in conflict with each other.

Village scenarios like the one narrated here do not reproduce the Platonic-type symposia, in that they are not the products of the imagination of a narrator who has a carefully designed plot. They arise from and often tend to only reaffirm and defend the familiar means by which the good ahead—such as the (communitarian) system of mutual dependence that adherence to custom produces—has always been produced and sustained. And so, as we saw in chapter 3 above, in the fervor of self-preservation, those ways, once unquestioned for a variety of reasons, escape scrutiny even when their usefulness is no longer obvious. Here is a newspaper report, just in, that exemplifies the need to scrutinize some of the "means" practiced in the traditional setting toward attaining a communal order.[7] The story features a Ms. Mercy Musomi, the executive director of Girl Child Network, whose mission, among other things, is to stop the physical and psychological violence against young women in the forms of female circumcision (also called female genital mutilation), early marriages, and other forms of exposure to humiliation. When visiting a group of about 300 girls who had run away from home to avoid forced circumcision, Ms. Musomi is reported to have said the following:

> The decision by the girls to run should not be misconstrued to mean that they defy their parents. These girls are aware of their rights and are saying no to violence meted against them. It does not matter that it is their parents leading them to such torture.[8]

A major question that arises from both the village symposium and the girls' escape is how one should regard the demands of tradition. How should one regard the moral status of traditional rules in relation to the Kantian idea of the origin of moral principles? Kant's idea of a true moral law can sound fuzzy for a person who is thinking about the nature and bases of the laws of custom, because he himself, as a historical subject, could not have been free of at least some form of customary law or belief. Also, it is indeed a long time since Kant wrote the *Grounding* (or *Groundwork*) *for the Metaphysics of Morals*. Therefore his theoretical forecast as well as what he believed to be the strength of the concepts he used may very well be different from our own. Consequently, our reading of this work may involve attributing to it different matters of importance as well as matters with different importance because of the kind of cases that concern us in our own time. Our discursive engagement with it stems from its possible effect on someone who observes in our own time competing opinions on cases beckoning for urgent resolution. There is no question that although some of the customs practiced by some of our communities as means for attaining the ultimate good as envisioned by them have become subject to skepticism, such ultimate goods may not have lost their status.

There must be another way of looking at how good lives are produced. In apparent concordance with Kant's separation of object or content of the moral principle (what he calls its goals or effects) from its form—that is, its universality and necessity—Kwasi Wiredu makes a distinction between custom and morality proper.[9] In other words, he draws a distinction between the relativity of fact and the objectivity or universality of value. The paradoxicality of the body allows for cultural variations in specific human beliefs and practices while fundamental basis of such beliefs and practices, which Wiredu considers to be the crucial point about being human, remains universally the same for all the members of the species. For him, as for Kant, such universality is grounded in the universality of the form—that is, rules of thought—in which human communication and human rules of survival are built. Wiredu agrees with Dewey that the foundation of logic lies in the biological complexity of humans. He would thus agree, I believe, with Schopenhauer too about the (evolutionary) flexibility of the human capacity not only to modify the content or object of morals but also to adapt to evolving conditions of survival more generally. He criticizes Hume's denial that induction has any value as inconsistent since Hume appeared to realize, despite his rejection of induction, that it was a crucial principle of how humans deal with matters of fact. On the other hand, he argues that he would agree with Kant's categorical imperative only if an "injection of a dose of compassion into [it] would convert it into a principle of *sympathetic* impartiality."[10] In other words, if its abstract normative form would be grounded in how people resolve real problems of life. According to Wiredu, it is not difficult to see the practical strength of such a principle, since "it takes little imagination to foresee that life in any society in which everyone openly avowed the contrary of this principle and acted accordingly inevitably would be 'solitary, poor, nasty, *brutish*,' and probably short."[11] According to this view, Kant's categorical imperative thus would have made more sense if it had been openly built on this human biological principle, which "is a human universal transcending cultures viewed as social forms and customary beliefs and practices. In being common to all human practice of morality, it is a universal of any non-brutish form of human life."[12] Here, Wiredu builds on what is well known to be a particularly underdeveloped aspect of Kant's enterprise. In other words, despite Kant's stress on the mind's discovery within itself of its own unity, that of the world, and the unity of the world and mind in experience, it still seemed as though Kant were moving from personal experience to suggestions of its supposed universality without adequate ontological grounds that transcended the individual psyche. Wiredu attempts to close that gap by suggesting that the unity between the particular and the universal does not reside in the abstract. Rather, it is in the biological unity of the species. For Wiredu, both cognitive and moral capacities of humans are the function of the organically specific type that humans are. Mind, the basis of cognitive and moral reason, is the function of this specific biological condition whose accomplishment depends on the social basis for being properly human. Reason resides in the social nature of humans, not in the unity of individual mind; it springs from and prospers by virtue of the act of communication. In fact, if a person were to be isolated from society and be deprived of communication with other humans from birth they would be confined to a "solitary, poor, nasty, and brutish" and no doubt also very short life.

The source of morality proper, Wiredu argues,[13] cannot be in the supernatural. He does not attribute the nonhuman powers to impose sanctions on those who have committed aberrations from the social order to the deities, the ancestors, or taboos. "Justification of behavior can [therefore] only take the form of relating it to rules. Obviously, the rules cannot be justified by reference to themselves but only by reference to higher order rules, where possible, and in other cases, to considerations more general than any specific rule of conduct."[14] In other words, justification of moral behavior must be sought in the discourses through and by which meanings and effects of behavior are examined and determined against specific and general motives of people in social settings. They are embedded in cultural practice.

Obviously, Wiredu presents a communitarian foundation of reason. While he is not ready to sacrifice the autonomy of the individual—because it is impossible to comprehend the nature of reason without the idea of the autonomy of the individual thinker (that is, the unified biological system that processes information)—he believes that it is not impossible to arrive at rational communal positions. In fact, he argues, there may be cases, for example in political organization, where a communitarian approach in the pursuit of common values and needs may be better than the democratic approach in its present-day renderings. He calls the communitarian approach polity by consensus rather than by a party system. In the former, official statements of leaders at various levels of the social stratum—that is, what was accepted as the governance of behavior—was the function, he writes, "not of any supposed divine inspiration but rather of whatever intrinsic persuasiveness [members'] ideas may have. . . . Now, this adherence to the principle of consensus was a premeditated option. It was based on the belief that *ultimately* the interests of all members of society are the same, although their immediate perceptions of those interests may be different."[15]

However, because much of contemporary African philosophy is comparative at core, it is important not only that philosophers carefully take into account the nature of philosophical discourses across cultural boundaries; they also need to take into account the social and historical circumstances that motivate and inspire a focus on specific value choices and the justifications for them. Belief in the ultimate universality of values eliminates the irrationality of conflict about them. But is there a chance that this can be so? According to Wiredu, "The Ashanti answer is 'Yes, human beings have the ability eventually to cut through their differences to the rock bottom identity of interests.' And, on this view, the means to that objective is simply rational discussion."[16] Communitarianism, then, anticipates potential conflict within itself, in contrast to the situation of a *"jadak-kende"*—the solitary person who lives like a "windowless monad"—which is why communitarianians believe that most problems of human relations can be resolved by dialogue, as in the Symposium à Cinq narrated above.

Notes

Introduction

1. See V. Y. Mudimbe and Kwame A. Appiah, "The Impact of African Studies on Philosophy," in *Africa and the Disciplines: The Contributions of Research in Africa to the Social Sciences and Humanities,* ed. Robert H. Bates, V. Y. Mudimbe, and J. O'Barr (Chicago: University of Chicago Press, 1993), 113–138.

2. Ibid., 114ff.

3. See Kwame A. Appiah, *Thinking It Through: An Introduction to Contemporary Philosophy* (New York: Oxford University Press, 2003). The first chapter is dedicated to "Mind." Wiredu's texts on the subject are discussed later in this book.

4. Irele's philosophical savvy has been demonstrated especially in his commentary on the work of contemporary French-speaking African writers. His most widely read piece in this regard was his substantive "Introduction" to Paulin J. Hountondji's *African Philosophy: Myth and Reality,* 2nd ed. (1983; Bloomington: Indiana University Press, 1996), but his essay "African Philosophy, Francophone," published in the *Routledge Encyclopedia of Philosophy,* vol. 1 (London, Routledge, 1998), which was rightly described by Kwasi Wiredu as "magisterial," best illustrates his acquaintance with the pivotal conceptual threads, debates, and developments of African philosophy in the French language.

5. Francis Abiola Irele, "Philosophy and the Postcolonial Condition in Africa," *Research in African Literatures* 35, no. 4 (2004): 160–170. This is a review essay on Hountondji's *The Struggle for Meaning.* Besides cautioning against preference for or dependence on European thinkers for theoretical leads, Irele also suggests that dismissing Senghor is tantamount to dismissing the entire corpus of thought embedded in African oral traditions. The question, however, is whether Senghor himself was original about the idea of intuition.

6. See Jean-Pierre Changeux and Paul Ricoeur, *What Makes Us Think? A Neuroscientist and a Philosopher Argue about Ethics, Human Nature, and the Brain,* trans. M. B. DeBevoise (Princeton, N.J.: Princeton University Press, 2000).

7. For representative examples, see Lidia Procesi and Martin Nkafu Nkemnkia, eds., in collaboration with Marco Massoni, *Prospettive di Filosofia Africana* (Roma: Editrice Internazionale, 2001); Filomeno Lopes, *Filosofia intorno al Fuoco* (Bologna: Editrice Missionaria Italiana, 2001); Filomeno Lopes, *Filosofia Senza Fetici* (Roma: Edizioni Associate, 2004); and Fabien Eboussi Boulaga, *Autenticità Africana e Filosofia: La crisi di Muntu: Intelligenza, responsabilita, liberazione,*

trans. Lidia Procesi (Milano: Christian Marinotti Edizioni, 2007). The latter is a translation of Fabien Eboussi Boulaga's French original *La crise du Muntu: Authenticité africaine et philosophie* (Présence Africaine, 1977). Of these authors, Lidia Procesi is kind of a rebel philosopher, given the rigidly and fiercely anti-African intellectual atmosphere in which she works, while Filomeno Lopes is a Rome-based native of Guinea Bissau with ecclesiastical affiliations.

8. V. Y. Mudimbe, *Les Corps glorieux des mots et des êtres. Esquisse d'un jardin africain à la bénédictine* (Paris and Montréal: Présence Africaine/Humanitas, 1994); V. Y. Mudimbe, *The Idea of Africa* (Bloomington: Indiana University Press, 1994); V. Y. Mudimbe, *Tales of Faith: Religion as Political Performance in Central Africa* (London: Athlone Press, 1997).

9. Praeg is a South African philosopher who believes that the key problem for African philosophy is not its search for identity but a moral one. He argues that Africa's quest for difference has left it wanting to be or to look like its assumed opposite instead of "just being" the Other. For him, the quest for autonomy is a failed project at best and a contradictory undertaking at worst. This view, to say the least, looks back to the sixties and is true of the ethnophilosophy of that time, and he correctly refers to my own evaluation of the humanizing role of philosophy in the eyes of ethnophilosophers then; see D. A. Masolo, *African Philosophy in Search of an Identity* (Bloomington: Indiana University Press, 1994), 158–193. Matters have changed since then, yet in light of the recent South African circumstance, the regeneration of the critique of ethnophilosophy might be understandable. To be sure, the significance of Africa's quest for autonomy in the various domains of its productive and expressive initiatives cannot be downplayed. It would be instructive for Praeg to show the unproductivity of the overplay of this authenticity discourse despite the likelihood that it will reemerge in the context of South Africa's search for a new ethical and political order. His point, however, does not come without irony: suddenly philosophers from the section in that nation that once appeared to condone and to enjoy the privileges bestowed upon them by a morally and politically perverse system now opportunistically want everyone to believe that they just stumbled on *ubuntu*—a Zulu variation of the Kiswahili and other Bantu forms of *utu,* the moral principle or epitome of recognizing and practicing universal humane values. (Many readers will recall this concept from Alexis Kagame's analysis of Bantu ontological categories.) Praeg appears to reckon that the search for the unconditional moral right, one that restores and distributes to all the normative principles of *ubuntu,* must be superior to exacting (or claiming) some form of sham equality by loading on to one's own head the cargo of Others. In a recent book, *Le Muntuïsme: L'Humanisme Intégral Africain* (Paris: Impr. ISI, 2006), Rudy Mbemba, a young Congolese scholar, revisits this concept by translating local poetic texts into ethnophilosophical and ethnotheological representations that are quite obviously influenced by both Tempels and the grand theologian Vincent Mulago. Osha, on the other hand, is a Nigerian philosopher who believes that no African text can be postcolonial enough if its author was educated in Europe or focuses on conceptual analysis.

10. See Raymond Aron, *Introduction to the Philosophy of History: An Essay on The Limits of Historical Objectivity* (Boston: Beacon Press, 1961), a translation by George J. Irwin of the French original, *Introduction à la philosophie de l'histoire: essai sur les limites de l'objectivité historique* (Paris: Librairie Gallimard, 1948).

11. Gregoire Biyogo, *Histoire de la philosophie africaine*, livre II: *Introduction à la philosophie moderne et contemporaine* (Paris: L'Harmattan, 2006), 95.

12. UNESCO and International Scientific Committee for the Drafting of a General History of Africa, *General History of Africa*, 8 vols. (London: Heinemann Educational Books, Ltd. and Berkeley: University of California Press, 1981–1993), different editors by volume.

13. J. D. Fage, and Roland Oliver, eds., *The Cambridge History of Africa*, 8 vols. (Cambridge, UK: Cambridge University Press, 1982–1984).

14. See, for example, Claude Sumner, *Ethiopian Philosophy*, vol. 2, *The Treatise of Zär'a Ya'eqob and of Wäldä Heywåt: Text and Authorship* (Addis Ababa: Commercial Printing Press, 1976); Claude Sumner, *Ethiopian Philosophy*, vol. 3, *The Treatise of Zär'a Ya'eqob and Wäldä Heywåt: An Analysis* (Addis Ababa: Commercial Printing Press, 1978); and Claude Sumner, *Classical Ethiopian Philosophy* (Los Angeles: Adey Publishing Company, 1994). See also Claude Sumner, "The Light and the Shadow: Zera Yacob and Walda Heywat, Two Ethiopian Philosophers of the Seventeenth Century," in *A Companion to African Philosophy*, ed. Kwasi Wiredu (Malden, Mass., and Oxford, UK: Blackwell Publishing, 2004), 172–182; and Teodros Kiros, "Zera Yacob and Traditional Ethiopian Philosophy," in *A Companion to African Philosophy*, 183–190. A final example of the general period is Souleymane Bachir Diagne, "Precolonial African Philosophy in Arabic," in *A Companion to African Philosophy*, 66–77.

15. E. William Abraham, "The Life and Times of Anton Wilhelm Amo," in *Transactions of the Historical Society of Ghana*, vol. 7 (Achimota: Historical Society of Ghana, 1964), 60–81. His most recent discussion of Amo appears in Wiredu, *A Companion to African Philosophy*, 191–199.

16. See Constance B. Hilliard, ed., *Intellectual Traditions of Pre-Colonial Africa* (Boston: McGraw-Hill, 1998). Although it has a misleading appearance, this text eludes the usual North American Afrocentric traps by merely presenting texts accompanied by brief commentary in a style similar to that of some of the work of renowned Congolese Egyptologist Théophile Obenga on classical Egyptian sources, especially Obenga's recent *La philosophie africaine de la période pharaonique* (Paris: L'Harmattan, 1990).

17. V. Y. Mudimbe, *The Invention of Africa: Gnosis, Philosophy, and the Order of Knowledge* (Bloomington: Indiana University Press, 1988), 35–43 and 153–186.

18. Ibid., 185.

19. Benetta Jules-Rosette, "Speaking about Hidden Times: The Anthropology of V. Y. Mudimbe," *Callaloo* 14, no. 4 (1991): 944–960.

20. Bertrand Russell, *The Problems of Philosophy* (New York: Oxford University Press, 1959), 16.

21. Mushete Ngindu and Kabe Mutuza, "Débat entre les professeurs [A. Mushete] Ngindu et [Kabe] Mutuza," in *La Philosophie Africaine: Actes de la 1ère Semaine Philosophique de Kinshasa* (Kinshasa: Faculté de Théologie Catholique, 1977), 167, my translation.

22. Paulin J. Hountondji, *The Struggle for Meaning: Reflections on Philosophy, Culture, and Democracy in Africa*, trans. John Conteh-Morgan (Athens: Ohio University Press, 2002). French original: *Combats pour le sens: Un itinéraire africaine* (1997).

23. Here I am invoking Franz Crahay's critique of the idea of a Bantu philosophy in his now-famous essay "Le Décollage conceptuel: conditions d'une

philosophie bantoue," *Diogène* 52 (1965): 61–84; and Hountondji's response a few years later in "Remarques sur la philosophie africaine contemporaine," *Diogène* 71 (1970): 120–140.

24. See Ngindu and Mutuza, "Débat," 169.

25. Kwasi Wiredu, *Philosophy and an African Culture* (Cambridge, UK: Cambridge University Press, 1980); Kwame A. Appiah, *In My Father's House: Africa in the Philosophy of Culture* (Oxford: Oxford University Press, 1992). Quote from "Safro Kwame, "Truth and the Akan Language: Kwasi Wiredu, Prologue," in *Readings in African Philosophy: An Akan Collection,* ed. Safro Kwame (Lanham, Md.: University Press of America, 1995), 186.

26. Sanya Osha, *Kwasi Wiredu and Beyond: The Text, Writing and Thought in Africa* (Dakar, Senegal: Council for the Development of Social Science Research in Africa, 2005).

27. D. A. Masolo, "Tradition, Communication, and Difference: Coming of Age in African Philosophy," *Research in African Literatures* 27, no. 1 (1996): 149–154.

28. Gayatri C. Spivak, *A Critique of Postcolonial Reason: Toward a History of the Vanishing Present* (Cambridge, Mass: Harvard University Press, 1999), 7.

29. What I refer to as "the social world" here could be comparable to what the Austrian philosopher Ludwig Wittgenstein called "the world" in the opening statement of the *Tractatus,* his widely discussed book. Ludwig Wittgenstein, *Tractatus Logico-Philosophicus,* trans. D. F. Pears and B. F. McGuinness, intro. Bertrand Russell (London: Routledge and Kegan Paul, 1961).

30. Sometimes rendered as *jok* (plural *jogi*) in some Luo dialects and, until now, generally understood to mean "spirits" of different origins that are capable of entering humans to possess them. Such people thus become the "mediums" through whom the "spirits" are believed to carry out a variety of performances. Humans perform rituals as procedures for acknowledging or responding to the demands of the *jogi.* M. G. Whisson, Henry Anyumba Owuor, Bethwell Allan Ogot, and Okot p'Bitek are the best-known scholars who have tried to analyze and explain this complex concept.

31. See Placide Tempels, *Bantu Philosophy,* trans. Colin King (Paris: Présence Africaine, 1959), 44.

32. Thomas Nagel, "Rawls and Liberalism," in *The Cambridge Companion to Rawls,* ed. Samuel Freeman (Cambridge, UK: Cambridge University Press, 2003), 82.

1. Philosophy and Indigenous Knowledge

1. See Appiah's *In My Father's House: Africa in the Philosophy of Culture* (Oxford: Oxford University Press, 1992) for critical discussions of the fate of African knowledge in the philosophies of other people, especially those whose views of Africa are driven by Western values and (mis)perceptions of Africa based on such values. Historically, the most obvious victims of Western misrepresentations have been African religious beliefs and practices. For example, as Appiah discusses in chapter 6 (pp. 107–136), Western scholars and missionaries alike were quick to brand African religious beliefs and practices as superstitions that failed to take account of the (scientific) causal laws of nature while ignoring similarities that lie at the heart of all religious beliefs, especially similar issues at the core of Christian faith. For a more detailed historical account and critique of Western scholarship on Africa, see V. Y. Mudimbe's well-known *The Invention of Africa: Gnosis,*

Philosophy, and the Order of Knowledge (Bloomington: Indiana University Press, 1988). On the fate of African religions more specifically, see Okot p'Bitek, *African Religions in Western Scholarship* (Nairobi: Kenya Literature Bureau, 1970).

2. Franz Crahay, "Le 'Décollage' conceptuel: conditions d'une philosophie bantoue," *Diogène* 52 (1965): 61–84.

3. Crahay's use of an aero-spatial metaphor (*décoller*; to lift off, as an astronaut would) to define the formalistic separation of philosophy from everyday knowledge can be read in different ways. One, as Hountondji read it, could be that philosophy is abstract while everyday knowledge is not. But it could also be read as suggesting that philosophy has nothing to do with the everyday pragmatic concerns that are evident in the different everyday forms of knowledge, both descriptive and prescriptive. Hountondji's critique of both Crahay and ethnophilosophy addresses the two senses of abstraction in relation to the structure of thought (mental representation).

4. Several titles signaled the increase in attention to indigenous knowledge systems. For examples, see Louise Grenier, *Working with Indigenous Knowledge: A Guide for Researchers* (Ottawa: International Development Research Centre, 1998); Linda T. Smith, *Decolonizing Methodologies: Research and Indigenous Peoples* (London: Zed Books, Ltd. and Dunedin: University of Otago Press, 1999).

5. Sandra Harding, "Is Modern Science an Ethnoscience? Rethinking Epistemological Assumptions," in *Postcolonial African Philosophy: A Critical Reader*, ed. Emmanuel C. Eze (Oxford, UK: Blackwell Publishers, 1997), 45–70. In this essay, in addition to restating several of the positions she has articulated and defended in her previous work, Harding provides wide and useful bibliographical data on recent social and cultural theorizations of science that spans gender, racial, political (North-South), and cultural perspectives. She is well known for *The Science Question in Feminism* (Ithaca, N.Y.: Cornell University Press, 1986); with Jean O'Barr, *Sex and Scientific Inquiry* (Chicago: University Of Chicago Press, 1987); and her edited work, *The "Racial" Economy of Science: Toward a Democratic Future* (Bloomington: Indiana University Press, 1993).

6. Carey-Francis Onyango, "A Critical Analysis of Constructive Realism: Towards a Theory of Scientific Theories and Their Relations to Physical Entities" (Ph.D. diss., University of Vienna, 1999).

7. Ibid., 2.

8. Among Bruno Latour's numerous works, the following are noteworthy: *Laboratory Life: The Social Construction of Scientific Facts* (London: Sage Publications, 1979); *Science in Action: How to Follow Scientists and Engineers through Society* (Cambridge, Mass.: Harvard University Press, 1987); and *We Have Never Been Modern* (Cambridge, Mass.: Harvard University Press, 1993).

9. See Paulus Gerdes, *Women, Art and Geometry in Southern Africa* (Trenton, N.J.: Africa World Press, 1998); Paulus Gerdes, *Geometry from Africa: Mathematical and Educational Explorations* (Washington, D.C.: The Mathematical Association of America, 1999); and Paulus Gerdes, *Awakening of Geometrical Thought in Early Culture* (Minneapolis, Minn.: Marxist Educational Press, 2003).

10. Onyango, "A Critical Analysis of Constructive Realism," 2.

11. Gayatri Chakravorty Spivak, *A Critique of Postcolonial Reason: Toward a History of the Vanishing Present* (Cambridge, Mass.: Harvard University Press, 1999), especially chapter 1.

12. Paulin J. Hountondji, "Producing Knowledge in Africa Today," *African Studies Review* 38, no. 3 (1995): 1–10.

13. Gayatri Chakravorty Spivak, "Questions of Multiculturalism," in *The Post-Colonial Critic: Interviews, Strategies, Dialogues,* ed. S. Harasym (New York: Routledge, 1990), 59–60.

14. The plural form of the Kiswahili word *mtumba,* which means a bale or load of cloth, is now widely used to refer to the huge bales of cheap, used, and (most of the time) unclean and unfit clothes that have found their way into and flooded the textile trade in East Africa and other regions of the continent from trash bins and consignment stores in Europe, the United States, and Canada. This clothing effectively drives local textile industries there out of existence. The trade, which manifests in a much worse form as what the British Guianese historian Walter Rodney pointed out nearly three decades ago (see *How Europe Underdeveloped Africa* [Washington, D.C.: Howard University Press, 1981]) is not only encouraged but is also dominated and controlled by the same African political leaders who are entrusted with making and overseeing the implementation of development policies and specific programs favorable to African economic growth and poverty reduction. Needless to say, a combination of this locally lucrative dumping-ground practice and ineffectual development programs make world trade agreements ineffective in reducing the poverty and dependency of societies with weaker economies.

15. Mudimbe, *The Invention of Africa*; Mudimbe, *The Idea of Africa* (Bloomington: Indiana University Press, 1994).

16. E. E. Evans-Pritchard, *Witchcraft, Oracles and Magic among the Azande* (Oxford: Oxford University Press, 1937).

17. See Peter Winch, "Understanding a Primitive Culture," *American Philosophical Quarterly* 1 (1964): 307–324. Publications on the debate engendered by the publication of this essay include the following: Robin Horton, "African Traditional Thought and Western Science," *Africa* 37, nos. 1–2 (1967): 50–71 and 155–187; Robin Horton, "Lévy-Bruhl, Durkheim and the Scientific Revolution," in *Modes of Thought,* ed. Robin Horton and Ruth Finnegan (London: Farber and Farber, 1973); Robin Horton, "Material-Object Language and Theoretical Language: Towards a Strawsian Sociology of Thought," in *Philosophical Disputes in the Social Sciences,* ed. S. C. Brown (Sussex: Harvester Press, 1979); Robin Horton, *Patterns of Thought in Africa and the West: Essays on Magic, Religion, and Science* (Cambridge: Cambridge University Press, 1993); Martin Hollis, "The Limits of Irrationality," in *Rationality,* ed. Brian Wilson (Oxford: Basil Blackwell, 1970); Martin Hollis, "The Social Destruction of Reality," in *Rationality and Relativism,* ed. Martin Hollis and Steven Lukes (Oxford: Basil Blackwell, 1982); Martin Hollis and Steven Lukes, eds., *Rationality and Relativism* (Cambridge, Mass.: MIT Press, 1982); S. C. Brown, ed., *Philosophical Disputes in the Social Sciences* (Sussex: Harvester Press, 1979); John Skorupski, *Symbol and Theory* (Cambridge: Cambridge University Press, 1976); Kwasi Wiredu, *Philosophy and an African Culture* (Cambridge, UK: Cambridge University Press, 1980); Barry Hallen, "Analytic Philosophy and Traditional Thought: A Critique of Robin Horton," in *African Philosophy: A Classical Approach,* ed. Parker English and K. M. Kalumba (Upper Saddle River, N.J.: Prentice Hall, 1996); and Barry Hallen, "Robin Horton on Critical Philosophy and Traditional Thought," *Social Order* 6, no. 1 (1977): 81–92. These authors and several others have opened up and broadened the debate to include general

philosophical inquiries into the nature of rationality, especially into the nature and limits of scientific claims and the limits of comparisons between different types of claims or knowledge, such as comparisons of the knowledge systems of science, magic, and religion. These concerns came to be called the "commensurability/incommensurability" debate. See for example Wiredu, *Philosophy and an African Culture*; and S. J. Tambiah, *Magic, Science, Religion, and the Scope of Rationality* (New York: Cambridge University Press, 1990).

18. Mudimbe, *The Invention of Africa*; and Mudimbe, *The Idea of Africa*.

19. Appiah, *In My Father's House*.

20. V. Y. Mudimbe and Kwame A. Appiah, "The Impact of African Studies on Philosophy," in *Africa and the Disciplines: The Contributions of Research in Africa to the Social Sciences and Humanities,* ed. Robert H. Bates, V. Y. Mudimbe, and Jean O'Barr (Chicago: University of Chicago Press, 1993), 113–138.

21. Paulin Hountondji, "Producing Knowledge in Africa Today," *African Studies Review* 38, no. 3 (1995): 1–10.

22. Jacques Derrida, *Positions,* trans. Alan Bass (Chicago: University of Chicago Press, 1981), 12.

23. I need to state at the outset that the goal here is not a substantive discussion of truth as expounded by Quine or Wiredu but rather a quick illustration of how philosophy gleans even its highly technical theories and ideas from everyday human practices, such as how we speak. As Bertrand Russell once observed, "In daily life, we assume as certain many things which, on a closer scrutiny, are found to be so full of apparent contradictions that only a great amount of thought enables us to know what it is that we really believe. . . . [Therefore] it is natural to begin with our present experiences, and in some sense, no doubt, knowledge is to be derived from them"; *The Problems of Philosophy* (New York, Oxford University Press, 1959), 7.

24. W. V. Quine, *From a Logical Point of View,* 2nd ed. (1953; Cambridge, Mass.: Harvard University Press, 1980), 22.

25. See Kwasi Wiredu, "Truth and the Akan Language," in *Readings in African Philosophy: An Akan Collection,* ed. Safro Kwame (Lanham, Md.: University Press of America, 1995), 185–186. Twi, I am informed, is one of several language groups that make up Akan.

26. Barry Hallen and J. O. Sodipo, *Knowledge, Belief, and Witchcraft: Analytic Experiments in African Philosophy,* 2nd ed. (Stanford, Calif.: Stanford University Press, 1997), 40–85.

27. Alexis Kagame, *La philosophie Bantu-Rwandaise de l'être,* Memoire no. 8 de l'Académie Royale des Sciences d'Outre-mer, Nouvelle série, tome xii (Bruxelles, 1956). The philosophical content of everyday or ordinary language is probably not as neatly laid out and structured as Kagame thought it was in Kinyarwanda, but at least it is recoverable from the samples of what is conceptually acceptable and unacceptable about its explicit expressions and implied beliefs.

28. *La Philosophie Bantu comparée* (Paris: Présence Africaine, 1975) was a good sequel to the earlier magnum opus.

29. See Edmund Husserl, *Idées directrices pour une phénoménologie,* trans. Paul Ricoeur (Paris: Gallimard, 1950), 35. See especially commentary (19).

30. Paul Ricoeur, *Husserl, An Analysis of His Phenomenology,* trans. Edward G. Ballard and Lester E. Embree (Evanston, Ill.: Northwestern University Press,

1967), 17. See also "Introduction à Ideen 1 de E. Husserl," in Edmund Husserl, *Idées directrices pour une phénoménologie,* trans. Paul Ricoeur, in ibid., xvi.

31. See Franz Crahay, "Le 'décollage' conceptuel: conditions d'une philosophie bantoue," *Diogène* 52 (1965): 61–84; and Paulin J. Hountondji, "Remarques sur la philosophie africaine contemporaine," *Diogène* 71 (1970): 120–140.

32. Sometimes Hountondji's emphasis on science, or the correlation of science and philosophy, appeared to embrace Marxist elements, especially via Althusser. Now he openly discusses how those roots embrace Husserl's legacy as well.

33. Edmund Husserl, "Phenomenology," in *Twentieth-Century Philosophy,* ed. Forrest E. Baird and Walter Kaufman, 2nd ed. (Upper Saddle River, N.J.: Prentice Hall, 1997), 5. Reprinted from *Encyclopaedia Britannica,* 14th ed. (London: The Encyclopaedia Britannica Company, 1932).

34. See Aimé Césaire, *Discourse on Colonialism,* trans Joan Pinkham (New York, Monthly Review Press, 1972).

35. Paulin J. Hountondji, "Producing Knowledge in Africa Today," *African Studies Review* 38, no. 3 (1995): 2.

36. The notion of the birth of consciousness from a shared world might evoke the memory of Wittgenstein's theory of culture-based pluralism in the *Investigations,* which was quite a shift from the universality of his previous work, the *Tractatus.* The former restored the philosophical significance of language to the indigenous circle in which it was spoken, so to speak, where use becomes a key factor in determining meaning. See Ludwig Wittgenstein, *Philosophical Investigations* (London: Basil Blackwell, 1968); and Wittgenstein, *Tractatus Logico-Philosophicus.*

37. See Okot p'Bitek, *Religion of the Central Luo* (Nairobi: East African Literature Bureau, 1971); and especially his *African Religions in Western Scholarship* (Nairobi: Kenya Literature Bureau, 1970).

38. Paulo Freire, *Pedagogy of the Oppressed,* rev. ed. (1970; New York, Continuum, 1993).

39. Ngũgĩ wa Thiong'o, *Decolonizing the Mind: The Politics of Language in African Literature* (London: James Currey, and Nairobi: Heinemann, 1986), 16.

40. See Kwasi Wiredu, *Cultural Universals and Particulars: An African Perspective* (Bloomington: Indiana University Press, 1996), 13–33, chapters 2 and 3.

41. K. Anthony Appiah, "Akan and Euro-American Concepts of the Person," in *African Philosophy: New and Traditional Perspectives,* ed. Lee M. Brown (New York: Oxford University Press, 2004), 21–34.

42. For a widely discussed representation of this practice, see the literature that begins in earnest with Peter Winch's 1964 critique of Evans-Pritchard's work on Azande explanations of witchcraft ("Understanding a Primitive Culture." *American Philosophical Quarterly* 1 [1964]: 307–324). However, Africans' response to the debate was provoked by Robin Horton's essay a few years later ("African Traditional Religion and Western Science," *Africa* 37, nos. 1 & 2 [1967]: 50–71 and 155–187) and the texts that constituted the so-called "rationality debate" that I mentioned earlier. See also other responses to that debate in general and to Horton in particular: Kwasi Wiredu, "How Not to Compare African Thought with Western Thought," *Ch'Indaba* 2 (1976): 4–8 (reprinted in Albert G. Mosley, ed., *African Philosophy: Selected Readings* [Englewood Cliffs, N.J.: Prentice Hall, 1995]); Barry Hallen, "Robin Horton on Critical Philosophy and Traditional Thought," *Second Order* 6,

no. 1 (1977): 81–92; and Kwame Gyekye, "Akan Language and the Materialism Thesis," *Studies in Language* 1, no. 2 (1977): 227–234.

43. See especially Jan Vansina, *Oral Tradition: A Study in Historical Methodology,* trans. H. M. Wright (Chicago: Aldine Publishing Co., 1965); Jan Vansina, *Oral Tradition as History* (Madison: University of Wisconsin Press, 1985); and Jan Vansina, *Paths in the Rainforests: Toward a History of Political Tradition in Equatorial Africa* (Madison: University of Wisconsin Press, 1990).

44. Chinua Achebe, *Morning Yet on Creation Day: Essays* (Garden City, N.Y.: Anchor Press, 1975), 159–175. See also Chinua Achebe, "'Chi' in Igbo Cosmology," in *African Philosophy: An Anthology,* ed. Emmanuel C. Eze (Malden, Mass. and Oxford, UK: Blackwell Publishers, 1998), 67–72.

45. Appiah, "Akan and Euro-American Concepts of the Person," 25–34.

46. B. Hallen and J. O. Sodipo, *Knowledge, Belief, and Witchcraft: Analytic Experiments in African Philosophy,* 2nd. ed. (Stanford, Calif.: Stanford University Press, 1997), 81. This new edition includes a new "Foreword" by W. V. O. Quine himself and a new "Afterword" by Hallen following the passing of Sodipo. The book was originally published in 1986 by Ethnographica Ltd. of London.

47. Ibid.

48. Godwin Sogolo, *The Foundations of African Philosophy: A Definitive Analysis of Conceptual Issues in African Thought* (Ibadan: Ibadan University Press, 1993), 31–32.

49. Hallen and Sodipo, *Knowledge, Belief, and Witchcraft,* 52.

50. Ibid., 63.

51. I take the Yoruba claim that "it is impossible [for a third party to err]" in a nonliteral sense to mean the ideal or objectivist case, if such a position were to be knowable. It is hard to imagine anyone holding on to the literal sense of the claim that whenever there are two discordant claims to truth, a third one must be right, especially where the third position merely confirms one of the disputing claims against the other. In other words, there could be cases where the third party was subject to the same or similar misleading conditions of perception, resulting in the position it confirms.

52. Ibid., 50 (emphasis theirs).

53. Ibid., 69 and 72.

54. Although their response appears to be addressed to a general attitude in Western scholarship toward Africa, Robin Horton's controversial and widely discussed essay, "African Traditional Thought and Western Science" (*Africa* 37, nos. 1 and 2 [1967]: 50–71 and 155–187) appears to be an exemplary case in their minds and a special target of their critique.

55. See Marcel Griaule, *Conversations with Ogotemmêli: An Introduction to Dogon Religious Ideas* (London: Oxford University Press for the International African Institute, 1965).

56. See Henry Odera Oruka, ed., *Sage Philosophy: Indigenous Thinkers and Modern Debate on African Philosophy* (Leiden: E. J. Brill Publishers, 1990), 141–143.

2. Philosophy and the Orders of Consciousness

1. Paulin Hountondji, "An Alienated Literature," in *African Philosophy: Myth and Reality,* 2nd ed. (1983; Bloomington: Indiana University Press, 1996), 33–46.

2. See "Introduction," in *African Philosophy as Cultural Inquiry*, ed. Ivan Karp and D. A. Masolo (Bloomington: Indiana University Press, 2000), 1–18.

3. For in-depth discussions of this cultural impasse, see V. Y. Mudimbe, *The Invention of Africa: Gnosis, Philosophy, and the Order of Knowledge* (Bloomington: Indiana University Press, 1988); V. Y. Mudimbe, *Tales of Faith: Religion as Political Performance in Central Africa* (London: The Athlone Press, 1997); D. A. Masolo, *African Philosophy in Search of Identity* (Bloomington: Indiana University Press, 1994); and Leonhard Praeg, *African Philosophy and the Quest for Autonomy: A Philosophical Investigation* (Amsterdam: The Rodopi Press, 2000).

4. See Paulin Hountondji, "Remarques sur la philosophie africaine contemporaine," *Diogène* 71 (1971): 120–121. See also Paulin J. Hountondji, *The Struggle for Meaning: Reflections on Philosophy, Culture, and Democracy in Africa*, trans. John Conteh-Morgan (Athens: Ohio University Press, 2002), 92 ff.

5. Chinua Achebe, *Morning Yet on Creation Day: Essays* (Garden City, N.Y.: Anchor Press, 1975), 161. See also Chinua Achebe, "'Chi' in Igbo Cosmology," in *African Philosophy: An Anthology*, ed. Emmanuel C. Eze (Malden, Mass., and Oxford, UK: Blackwell Publishers, 1998), 67–68.

6. Hountondji, *African Philosophy: Myth and Reality*, 2nd ed., 45.

7. Paulin J. Hountondji, "Occidentalism, Elitism: Answer to Two Critiques," *Quest: An African International Journal of Philosophy* 3, no. 2 (December 1989): 4; emphasis his.

8. See Olabiyi Balola Yaï, "Théorie et pratique en philosophie africaine: Misère de la philosophie spéculative (critique de P. Hountondji, M. Towa, et autres)," *Présence Africaine* 108 (1978): 65–89.

9. See Pathé Diagne, *L'Europhilosophie face à la pensée de négro-africaine; suivi de Problématique néo-pharaonique et épistemologie du réel* (Dakar: Sankore, 1981).

10. Karl Marx, *The Poverty of Philosophy*, in *The Collected Works of Karl Marx and Frederick Engels*, vol. 6, *Marx and Engels, 1845–48* (London: Lawrence & Wishart, 1975). Translation of Marx's *La Misère de la Philosophie* (1847).

11. Martin Heidegger, *What Is Philosophy?* trans. William Kluback and Jean T. Wilde (London: Vision Press, 1958), 31.

12. Kwasi Wiredu, *Cultural Universals and Particulars: An African Perspective* (Bloomington: Indiana University Press, 1996), 151.

13. Paulin Hountondji, "Occidentalism, Elitism: Answer to Two Critiques," *Quest: An African International Journal of Philosophy* 3, no. 2 (1989): 21.

14. Hountondji, *African Philosophy: Myth and Reality*, 2nd ed.

15. The original French edition of this book, *Sur la 'philosophie africaine': Critique de l'ethnophilosophie*, dates back to 1976 and was published by François Maspero, Paris. The first English edition was published in 1983.

16. The "Témoignages" were a collection of supportive statements by leading French and French-speaking African intellectuals published by *Présence Africaine* in 1948 as prelude to its edition of Tempels's book *La Philosophie bantoue*. "Témoignages sur la 'Philosophie bantoue' du P. Tempels," *Présence Africaine* 7 (1949): 252–278.

17. Dismas A. Masolo, "History of 'African Philosophy': A Critical Appraisal of the Development of Philosophical Discussion in Africa" (Ph.D. diss., Gregorian University, Rome, 1979), 101–106.

18. Hountondji, *African Philosophy: Myth and Reality,* 2nd. ed., ix. See also Hountondji, *The Struggle for Meaning,* 93.

19. See Hountondji's response to Kwame Gyekye's location of the origin of the term in Kwame Nkrumah's undefended doctoral dissertation at the University of Pennsylvania in 1943 in Hountondji, *Sur la 'philosophie africaine,'* xxi–xxii. It seems, however, that Hountondji used the term "ethnophilosophy" in a sense not quite identical with Nkrumah's, whose positive sense may have been driven by the nationalist ideology of the time. Ironically, however, Hountondji and others, especially Ezekiel Mphalele, Wole Soyinka, Kwasi Wiredu, Stanislas Adotevi, Marcien Towa, V. Y. Mudimbe, Mabika Kalanda, Okot p'Bitek, K. Anthony Appiah, and Ngũgĩwa Thiong'o, have suggested that the fervent ideological quest of the time may have contributed (at least in part and in the name of political and cultural autonomy, which are good ideas and goals or ideals in themselves) to the uncritical affirmations at the core of ethnophilosophy. While pursuing their own definitions and characterizations of cultural autonomy among Africans in a philosophical practice that is/was both indigenous and endogenous, Hountondji, Adotevi, Towa, Wiredu, Mudimbe, Kalanda, and Appiah, among others, did not think that ethnophilosophy—understood here only in the sense Hountondji gave it—did much to help achieve autonomy for African philosophical thought or traditions.

20. See, for example, Sandra Harding, "Is Modern Science an Ethnoscience? Rethinking Epistemological Assumptions," in *Postcolonial African Philosophy: A Critical Reader,* ed. Emmanuel C. Eze (Oxford, UK: Blackwell Publishers, 1997), 45–70; Sandra Harding, *The Science Question in Feminism* (Ithaca, N.Y.: Cornell University Press, 1986); Sandra Harding with Jean O'Barr, *Sex and Scientific Inquiry* (Chicago: University of Chicago Press, 1987); Sandra Harding, ed., *The "Racial" Economy of Science: Toward a Democratic Future* (Bloomington: Indiana University Press, 1987); Bruno Latour and Steve Woolgar, *Laboratory Life: The Social Construction of Scientific Facts* (London: Sage Publications, 1979); Bruno Latour, *Science in Action: How to Follow Scientists and Engineers through Society* (Cambridge, Mass.: Harvard University Press, 1987); and Paulus Gerdes, *Women, Art and Geometry in Southern Africa* (Trenton, N.J.: Africa World Press, 1998).

21. Hountondji, *African Philosophy: Myth and Reality,* 2nd. ed., viii.

22. Ibid., xiii.

23. Paulin Hountondji, "Recapturing," in *The Surreptitious Speech: "Présence Africaine" and the Politics of Otherness, 1947–1987,* ed. V. Y. Mudimbe (Chicago: University of Chicago Press, 1992), 238–248.

24. Hountondji, *African Philosophy: Myth and Reality,* 2nd ed., 89.

25. See Paulin J. Hountondji, "Remarques sur la philosophie africaine contemporaine," *Diogène* 71 (1970): 120–140; and Paulin J. Hountondji, "Le problème actuel de la philosophie africaine," in *La Philosophie contemporaine,* vol. 4, ed. Raymond Klibansky (Firenze: La Nuova Italia, 1971), 613–621.

26. See Kwasi Wiredu, *Philosophy and an African Culture* (Cambridge: Cambridge University Press, 1980), 12.

27. See Mudimbe, *The Invention of Africa.*

28. Wiredu, *Philosophy and an African Culture.*

29. See Paulin J. Hountondji, *The Struggle for Meaning: Reflections on Philosophy, Culture, and Democracy in Africa,* trans. John Conteh-Morgan (Athens:

Center for International Studies, Ohio University, 2002). Originally published as *Combats pour le sens* (Cotonou: Éditions du Flamboyant, 1997).

30. Ibid., Part I.

31. Ibid., 26.

32. Ibid., 28.

33. Ibid., 29.

34. Edmund Husserl, *The Crisis of European Sciences and Transcendental Phenomenology*, trans. and intro. David Carr (Evanston, Ill.: Northwestern University Press, 1970), 50.

35. Ibid., 157. The reader should recall my description of Bachelard in the introduction. Delineating between the a priori, which he described as pertaining to rationalism, and the a posteriori, or the domain of empiricism, Bachelard argued strongly that the a priori derives its legitimacy from being "the basis for a chain of reasoning," namely making sense of empirical data. See Gaston Bachelard, *The Philosophy of No: A Philosophy of the New Scientific Mind*, trans. G. C. Waterston (New York: Orion Press, 1968), 3–7.

36. It is this view that allows Hountondji to criticize Franz Crahay in the same essay, where he also blasts Tempels and his ethnophilosophical school. He argued, against Crahay's call for a *"décollage conceptuel"* as condition for African philosophy, that the contents of consciousness, whether they are cast in mythical representations (as Parmenides, Plato, Confucius, Hegel, Nietzsche, or Kagame did) or in fragile ideological foundations, are already abstract, since they are intentional contents of the mind—that is, a sort of conceptual representation of reality, claiming, ostensibly, that specific knowledge forms are not inimical to philosophy. Thus, they are not incompatible. See Hountondji, "Remarques sur la philosophie africaine contemporaine," 139–25.

37. F. Abiola Irele, "Philosophy and the Postcolonial Condition in Africa," *Research in African Literatures* 35, no. 4 (Winter 2004):164. This eloquent review of *The Struggle for Meaning* is one of the strongest and most constructive general critiques of Hountondji yet. I return to it later.

38. See Edmund Husserl, *Ideas: General Introduction to Pure Phenomenology*, trans. W. R. Boyce Gibson (London: George Allen & Unwin Ltd., 1931), 72–88, 112ff.

39. Ibid., 120. Italics in original.

40. Edmund Husserl, "Phenomenology," in *Twentieth-Century Philosophy*, ed. Forrest E. Baird and Walter Kaufman, 2nd ed. (Upper Saddle River, N.J.: Prentice Hall, 1997), 5. Reprinted from *Encyclopaedia Britannica*, 14th ed. (London: The Encyclopaedia Britannica Company, 1932).

41. Hountondji, "Remarques sur la philosophie africaine contemporaine."

42. In my review of the second edition of *African Philosophy: Myth and Reality*, I observed that it achieved at least one major thing: it gave Hountondji an opportunity to address his critics and explain the context of his earlier critique of ethnophilosophy without retracting any significant points from his original position; he only made his stand clearer and toned down the originally uncompromising language. See D. A. Masolo, "From Myth to Reality: African Philosophy at Century-End," *Research in African Literatures* 31, no. 1 (2000): 149–172. What I don't think is likely, however, is that he embraced the view that the content of pre- or unreflective consciousness is, in and of itself, a philosophy, the reason

being that pre-reflective consciousness (as explicated by Husserl and endorsed by Hountondji) is, contrary to what the ethnophilosophers tried to make of it, a mere state, a natural but passive disposition of consciousness as always "intending" something. The "naturally intending," as Husserl himself said and tried to justify as the task of the radical phenomenological method, needed analysis that, in his view, would bring philosophy and science into close collaboration. The same thing could be said, as I pointed out in 1980 and later in 1994, of what the authors of the famous "Témoignages" said of "the ontology of the Bantu" as Tempels described it, namely that by showing how deeply involved with the contemplation of Being primitive experience was, Tempels had illustrated that the contents of unreflective consciousness are philosophically significant but not necessarily significantly philosophical. (See Masolo, "History of 'African Philosophy,'" 101–106; and D. A. Masolo, *African Philosophy in Search of an Identity* [Bloomington: Indiana University Press, 1994], 65–66.) Thus, when all those leading French and French-speaking scholars gave their testimonials in praise of *Bantu Philosophy,* the precise object of their praise might have been very ambiguous at best; what was certain was that it was not the "philosophical mind" of the Bantu. In reality, they were praising the revelation of the metaphysical experience of the primitive, a view quite in vogue at the time among philosophers in search of the pristine and unpolluted experience of "Being" as the direct opposition to "Nothing." But Irele is certainly right that the debate on Husserl's significance to Africa might only be about to begin.

43. Husserl, "Phenomenology," 9.

44. Husserl, *Ideas,* 120.

45. Aimé Césaire, *Discourse on Colonialism,* trans. Joan Pinkham (New York: Monthly Review Press, 1972), 34–45.

46. Quentin Lauer, "Introduction," in Edmund Husserl, *La Philosophie comme Science Rigoureuse,* trans. and intro. Quentin Lauer (Paris: Presses Universitaires de France, 1955), 8 (my translation).

47. Ibid., 9.

48. This is not to be taken in the Anglo-American sense, which focuses on analyzing the nature or characteristics of science as knowledge and practice, but in the now largely defunct continental sense of the philosophical study of the natural world. Significant portions of this have now been incorporated into metaphysics and other portions have been incorporated into the philosophical study of the basic concepts of the natural sciences.

49. This view, which comes directly from Husserl's *La Philosophie comme Science Rigoureuse* (52 and 127n8), is contained in the first of the three factors that constitute the general idea of a rigorous science.

50. See Irele, "Philosophy and the Postcolonial Condition in Africa," 164–165.

51. Not only does the idea of agency lie at the center of conceptualizing action in epistemological, moral, and legal theories, it is also the ideal whose recognition, establishment, and respect drives and informs competing ideas of sociopolitical and cultural order, as can be seen in critical theories of freedom or analyses of such concepts as domination, both of which seek, at least partly (but ultimately) to identify situations or cases where agency has been denied to some subjects and argue for its restitution. For these and other reasons, the idea of agency as

a central component of the idea of selfhood occupies a special place in inter- and-intracultural analyses in postcolonial studies that focus on the state of subjectivity in conditions of varying levels of competition and conflict. Thus, although it clearly addresses issues regarding "states of mind" that are similarly addressed under analytic approaches, the focus on the socially generated psychological status of persons in conflictual relations often seeks to identify the location (in me or in the Other) of values as objects of desire or repulsion and therefore as grounds for observable behavior in the form of culture.

52. Jürgen Habermas, *Knowledge and Human Interests*, trans. Jeremy J. Shapiro (Boston: Beacon Press, 1971), 310.

53. Although it may not be obvious as a requirement for resolving this matter, determining whether a scheme of thought espouses a monistic or pluralist view of Self may depend primarily on the outcome of analyzing and determining the meaning and uses of different terminologies used in different languages to refer to the different and complex aspects of selfhood. Some discussion of this will come later in chapters 5 and 6. Also, it is on the reading of Senghor's statement on the Negro-African way of knowing as embracing or implying these critical questions that one may view it as straddling both the existentialist and analytic approaches to the understanding of the mind or consciousness.

54. See Ricoeur's translation of Husserl's *Ideen zu Einer Reinen Phaenomenologie und Phaenomenologischen Philosophie*: *Idées Directrices pour une Phénoménologie et une Philosophie Phénoménologique pures*, tome 1, *Introduction Générale à la Phénoménologie Pure* (Paris: Librairie Gallimard, 1950).

55. Paulin J. Hountondji, "Remarques sur la philosophie africaine contemporariane," *Diogène* 70 (1970): 120; Hountondji, *African Philosophy: Myth and Reality*, xxi, 33.

56. Bachelard, *The Philosophy of No*, 3.

57. Ibid., 6.

58. Ibid.

59. See "Introduction," in Hountondji, *African Philosophy: Myth and Reality*, 18.

60. Francis Abiola Irele, "Philosophy and the Postcolonial Condition in Africa," *Research in African Literatures* 35, no. 4 (2004): 165.

61. Pauline J. Hountondji, "Recapturing," in *The Surreptitious Speech: Présence Africaine and the Politics of Otherness, 1947–1987*, ed. V. Y. Mudimbe (Chicago: University of Chicago Press, 1992), 247.

62. Obviously, I am referring here to Senghor's classic dictum, viz., that African thinking was characterized by *sensibilité émotive*. See "Sensibilité émotive. L'émotion est nègre, comme la raison hellène," *Liberté*, vol. 1, *Négritude et Humanisme* (Paris: Éditions du Seuil, 1964), 24; emphasis in original.

63. See Jean-Godefroy Bidima, "Philosophy and Literature in Francophone Africa" (trans. Nicolas De Warren), in *A Companion to African Philosophy*, ed. Kwasi Wiredu (London and New York: Blackwell Publishers, 2004), 549–559.

64. Henri Bergson, *An Introduction to Metaphysics*, rev. ed., trans. T. E. Hulme, intro. Thomas A. Goudge (New York: The Liberal Arts Press, 1955).

65. Ibid., 21.

66. Ibid., 21–22.

67. Ibid., 22.

68. Ibid., 23–24; emphasis in the original.

69. Senghor, *Liberté,* tome 1, *Négritude et Humanisme* (Paris: Seuil, 1964), 22–25.

70. Léopold S. Senghor, *On African Socialism,* trans. Mercer Cook (New York, Frederick A. Praeger, 1964), 71.

71. For example, one could take the phrase "intuitive by participation" to mean not only what Bergson described as penetration of the object but also, in more recent English-language philosophy terms, as the erasure of the divide between mind and its content as separate realms or as separate substantive entities when contrasted with other specific objects. Yet the temptation to interpret his position as indicating mind to be a non-substance stream—of stimulations—by which objects come into consciousness needs to be resisted. It is not clear to me, for example, that Bergson and Senghor were not deeply Cartesian in their emphasis of the intuitive power of reason, its raison d'être.

72. For Hountondji's vehement opposition to this view of a thinking collectivity, see Hountondji, *The Struggle for Meaning,* 91.

73. Achebe, *Morning Yet on Creation Day,* 161; and Achebe, "'Chi' in Igbo Cosmology," 67.

74. Mudimbe, *The Invention of Africa,* 154.

75. Hountondji, *African Philosophy: Myth and Reality,* 2nd ed., 29.

76. Francis Abiola Irele, "Introduction," in Paulin J. Hountondji, *African Philosophy: Myth and Reality,* 2nd ed. (Bloomington: Indiana University Press, 1996), 29–30.

77. The fact that the debate rarely addressed the general and theoretical reasons that would make either individualism or communalism the better ethos is not entirely surprising, although the failure to do so adds to the unfortunate and continued lack of a systematic exposition of any view of our experience of the world. The political urgencies of the time appear to have dictated the course of the discourse, influencing more prominently some passing and unargued ideological statements about ethical divides between European and African worldviews than focused and systematic analyses of the ethical differences. Even for Hountondji himself, the point of reference was not, for example, Rousseau's passionate defense of the *liberté* of the individual but rather, as I have argued above, the subtle anthropology of Husserl's phenomenology, partly because it also provided the grounds for the notion of *la philosophie comme science rigoureuse.* Only a few African intellectuals, including Senghor (especially in *Pierre Teilhard de Chardin et la politique africaine, Liberté I,* and *Liberté III*), Nkrumah (in *Consciencism* and later), Julius Nyerere (in a 1979 essay entitled "The Rational Choice") attempted what appeared to be theoretical, metaphysical, and moral (respectively) groundings of the superiority of communalism or, as they called it, African socialism. An interesting debate on the meaning and sustainability of African socialism occurred in the mid-1960s between the late Kenyan politician Tom Mboya and the young and radical political scientist at Makerere University, Ahmed Mohiddin, also a Kenyan. See Ahmed Mohiddin, "Socialism or Capitalism? Sessional Paper No. 10 Revisited," *East Africa Journal* 4, no. 3 (March 1969): 7–16; and Tom Mboya, "Sessional Paper No. 10: It Is African and It Is Socialism," *East Africa Journal* 4, no. 5 (May 1969): 15–22. Throughout much of that decade, the idea of an indigenous socialist framework became a rallying point for different voices that did not always agree on the details of policy definitions or the structural modalities of

their implementation and real outcomes. Yet all of these voices were committed, at least ideologically, to some form of a universal political and cultural freedom from colonialist Europe as applicable to and demonstrable in different national configurations.

78. Hountondji, *Struggle for Meaning*, 174–175.

79. See Stanislas Adotevi, *Négritude et négrologues* (Paris: Union Générale d'Éditions, 1972); Marcien Towa, *Essai sur la problématique philosophique dans l'Afrique actuelle* (Yaoundé: Éditions Clé, 1971); and Marcien Towa, *L'Idée d'une philosophie négro-Africaine* (Yaoundé: Éditions Clé, 1979).

80. See Senghor, *On African Socialism*, 69–75.

81. Francis Abiola Irele, "Philosophy and the Postcolonial Condition in Africa," *Research in African Literatures* 35, no. 4 (2004): 164.

82. Ibid., 165.

83. The letter is published in Edmund Husserl, *Briefwechsel*, Band VII, *Wissenschaftlerkorrespondenz*, ed. Karl Schuhmann with Elisabeth Schuhmann (Dordrecht: Kluwer Academic Publishers, 1994).

84. Ibid., 161:15–18. Husserl tells Lévy-Bruhl that it is an unquestionable fact that his classic and groundbreaking work on the primitive people must be counted among the strong scientific works in general ethnology; see ibid., 161:30–32.

85. Called "Geisteswissenschaftlichen Anthropologie" in German, as contrasted with his description of Lévy-Bruhl's work as "wissenschaftlichen Ethnologie."

86. Husserl, *Briefwechsel*, Band VII, *Wissenschaftlerkorrespondenz*, 162: 1–12.

87. Ibid., 162:12–16.

88. Ibid., 162:16–24.

89. Pierre Keller, *Husserl and Heidegger on Human Experience* (Cambridge, UK: Cambridge University Press, 1999), 42.

90. Ibid.

91. Husserl, *Briefwechsel*, Band VII, *Wissenschaftlerkorrespondenz*, 162:27–38.

92. Keller, *Husserl and Heidegger on Human Experience*, 46.

93. See Edmund Husserl, *First Philosophy/Erste Philosophie*, in *Husserliana: Edmund Husserls Gesammlete Werke*, vols. 7–8 (The Hague: Martinus Nijhoff, 1956), 506.

94. Husserl, *Briefwechsel*, Band VII, *Wissenschaftlerkorrespondenz*, 162:39–163:15.

95. Ibid., 163:27–35.

96. Ibid., 163:39–164:12.

97. Edmund Husserl, "Philosophy and the Crisis of European Humanity," in Husserl, *The Crisis of European Sciences and Transcendental Phenomenology: An Introduction to Phenomenological Philosophy*, trans. and intro. David Carr (Evanston, Ill.: Northwestern University Press, 1970), Appendix 1, 269–299. This appendix is a lecture Husserl gave to the Vienna Cultural Society on May 7 and May 10, 1935 (exactly two months after the letter to Lévy-Bruhl, which is dated March 11, 1935).

98. See ibid., 276.

99. Ibid., 285.

100. Ibid., 288.

101. Ibid., 276–277.

102. Ibid., 278–279.

103. Husserl, *Briefwechsel,* Band VII, *Wissenschaftlerkorrespondenz,* 163: 15–19.

104. Husserl, *The Crisis of European Sciences and Transcendental Phenomenology,* 279. Brackets in original text.

105. Pierre Keller, *Husserl and Heidegger on Human Experience* (Cambridge, UK: Cambridge University Press, 1999), 41.

106. I have in mind here Hountondji's explanation for his selective application of an Althusserian reading of Marx's transformative view of philosophy to Africa's condition as a way of "forcing a reflection on the relation between science and politics, between positive knowledge of the real in general and society in particular, and the practical transformation of this society." As he says, he "acknowledged that in Africa as everywhere else, theory has meaning only if it is organized and subordinated to practice . . . [such as] 'political practice' and more precisely, 'liberating action' [so as to make] philosophy serve as a foundation to politics, and notably to the anti-imperialist struggle"; Hountondji, *Struggle for Meaning,* 85. This view of philosophy and its application to the appraisal of the African cultural and political condition of the time required, in Hountondji's view, a radical shift away from any absurd type of conformism. To achieve these objectives, Hountondji brought together aspects of Marxist and Husserlian perspectives because he believed them to be applicable to the African condition, an importation that he seems to feel was unquestionable. In addition to this assumption, Hountondji's claim that there is "positive knowledge of the real in general" that is applicable to "societies in their particularities" is an ambiguous and questionable idea.

107. Léopold Sédar Senghor, "The African Road to Socialism: Attempt at a Definition," in Senghor, *On African Socialism,* trans. Mercer Cook (New York: Frederick A. Praeger, 1964), 68. This essay was originally delivered as a speech at the first Young Seminar of the Party of African Federation (PFA in its French acronym) in May 1960.

108. Ibid.

109. Various forms of everyday discourse such as myths would in this sense appear to be already reflective because they are constituted of concepts and other abstract ideas. They are distinct from the pure intentionality of the pre-reflective stage of consciousness. Such a distinction underlies Hountondji's critique of Crahay's idea of the conditionality of a "*décollage*" from myths. For Hountondji, myths have already "*décollé*" from the pure intentionality of consciousness which, at least as Brentano saw it, is a mere relation between consciousness and an object.

110. Irele believed that because "the 'physio-psychology of the Negro' . . . intended to clarify those elements in an original organic constitution of the African, and of the black race in general, which make for a distinct manner in his perception of the world and, ultimately, in his mode of being . . . elements as constitutive of a particular quality of emotion [are tantamount to] a distinctive African mode of apprehension, one of the 'affective participation' of the black subject in the object of his experience." Francis Abiola Irele, "Introduction," in Paulin J. Hountondji, *African Philosophy: Myth and Reality,* 2nd ed. (1983; Bloomington, Indiana University Press, 1996), 18. Senghor first discussed this cognitive method in the famous 1961 essay "Nation et Voie Africaine du Socialisme," translated as

"Nationhood and the African Road to Socialism" in 1962. Both were reprinted in *On African Socialism*, trans. Mercer Cook (New York: Frederick A. Praeger, 1964).

111. Senghor, *On African Socialism*, 70.

112. Ibid. He refers to Gaëtan Picon, *Panorama des idées contemporaines* (Gallimard: Paris, 1957).

113. Senghor, *On African Socialism*, 71.

114. Ibid. (all italics in the original).

115. Ibid., 18. It can only be hoped that the undeniable importance of the theory does not derive solely from the fact that it was articulated by Senghor or that its articulation by Senghor signals its unassailability. On the other hand, it is indeed those matters that we regard to be important, partly because of how they have impacted our understanding of culture, that deserve our critical attention. No one will doubt, at least in our time, that negritude is one such matter. Recently, there has been an emergence of a physicalist theory of knowledge in the West, particularly in the United States, that derives partly from the growing tendency toward a physicalist view of mind in cognitive psychology and brain sciences. Some scholars have thought that this physicalist trend shares some affinity with some African concepts that they interpret as beliefs in "bodily ways of knowing." The works of George Lakoff and Mark Johnson, American professors of linguistics and philosophy, respectively, especially their *Metaphors We Live By* (New York: Basic Books, 1980) and *Philosophy in the Flesh* (New York: Basic Books, 1999), are two examples that embrace physicalist epistemology, although they echo elements of W. V. O. Quine's celebrated idea of "naturalized epistemology." A direct study of the poetics of "bodily cognition" in an African culture is that of Kathryn Linn Geurts, who, in her *Culture and the Senses: Bodily Ways of Knowing in an African Community* (Berkeley: University of California Press, 2002), uses Lakoff and Johnson's works as the basis of her analysis of southern Ghanaian Anlo-Ewe people's expanded realm of empirical sources of knowledge.

116. Francis Abiola Irele, *The African Imagination: Literature in Africa and the Black Diaspora* (New York: Oxford University Press, 2001), viii.

117. While Irele invokes Memmi's analysis of "the two answers of the colonized" to characterize Hountondji's confessions of his intellectual formation through the French educational system and French standards of thought as well as his dependency on Husserl as the foundation of his critique of ethnophilosophy (especially of Senghor's idea of negritude), Outlaw calls this relation with Europe and the pull away from it "the oedipal moments and maturation" in the journey of African philosophy. See Lucius T. Outlaw, Jr., *On Race and Philosophy* (New York: Routledge Publishers, 1996), 65ff.

118. Albert Memmi, *The Colonizer and the Colonized*, trans. Howard Greenfeld (Boston: Beacon Press, 1965), 119–120. As he explains the lifelong influence of Césaire, Fanon, and other architects of negritude on him, Hountondji explains that he had all along been aware of the inferiorizing effects of colonialism on the consciousness of the colonized; see *Struggle for Meaning*, 85–87.

119. Memmi, *The Colonizer and the Colonized*, 120.

120. Shaaban bin Robert, *Siku ya Watenzi Wote*. (Nairobi: Thomas Nelson and Sons, Publishers, 1968), 13. M. M. Mulokozi translates this title as "The Day of All Doers."

121. Robert, *Siku ya Watenzi Wote*, 111. My translation from Kiswahili. Notice that I have translated the phrase a little differently than Mulokozi did. He translates Shaaban's *"Jumuiya imekwisha jithibitisha yenyewe kuwa bora kwa kufuata mwendo wa ulimwengu na tabia ya watu wake"* as "The 'Jumuiya' has already proved its worth in accordance with the progress of the world and the nature of human beings." See Mugyabuso M. Mulokozi, "Two Utopias: A Comparative Examination of William Morris's *News from Nowhere* and Shaaban Robert's *Siku ya Watenzi Wote*," *Umma* 5, no. 2 (1975): 41. But Shaaban's emphasis is morality, the cultivation of the virtues, such as one finds in the habits of Adili, that make possible the creation of the *jumuiya* (republic)—community, or people united by and in their common goals as human beings. In that sense, then, Shaaban's point is that communities are created by the (moral) habits of people and that trusting that a perfect *jumuiya* is possible on that account—which is the theme of *Kusadikika*—will lead people and their representatives to press for their rights and to strive to protect them.

122. Robert, *Siku ya Watenzi Wote*, 111.

123. Ibid.

124. Mulokozi, "Two Utopias," 17.

125. Robert, *Siku ya Watenzi Wote*, 16.

126. Ibid., 139.

127. Ibid., 136.

128. Ibid., 5–12.

3. Revaluation of Values and the Demand for Liberties

1. There is no pretension here that what follows is *the* correct reading of this beautiful story, but it has all the threads that can be used to stitch together an image of it as a project in the reevaluation of values within a historical context.

2. Kwame A. Appiah, *In My Father's House: Africa in the Philosophy of Culture* (Oxford: Oxford University Press, 1992), 183.

3. Significantly, the completeness of the idea of a good life incorporates the notions that a feeling of self-fulfillment is the agent of a person's successes or achievements and that a person's agency for his or her own successes requires substantive freedom to deliberate, make choices, and take action.

4. Appiah, *In My Father's House*, 184.

5. Ibid., 184. Although not entirely viewed historically, as seemed to be the case in Mzee Appiah's quoted opinion on some aspects of Ashanti funerary practices, the "abominability" of a practice can be a function of time. That is, over time, some practices and beliefs are abandoned or replaced with others. This does not always imply that what is abandoned or replaced is deemed to have been "abominable." Sometimes it may only be that the objectives once served by an old practice have been abandoned. For example, people have built houses of prayer such as churches or mosques and have spent considerable amounts of time in these places. If the future generations of those worshippers become atheists or for some other reason cease to be like their ancestors in that particular regard, the buildings are abandoned and their value diminishes. But neither the structures nor the beliefs and practices they served become "abominable." However, the adherents of some extremes in cultural beliefs and practices around the world may later deem these beliefs and practices unaccept-

able because they have attained better knowledge of moral, cognitive, or political values. Who, for example, back in my own community in Western Kenya, would today send his friends to drag his bride home while she cries and wails across a whole country? The variables and complexities of the expanded social world have rendered the practice of dragging (*yuayo*) a bride impracticable because it is now vulnerable to many kinds of misunderstandings (such as falsely interpreting the crying of the bride to mean protest or interpreting the mock fight between her kin and the groom's friends to mean public disorder) from which it was protected in the past.

6. As we shall see later, these questions arose earlier in Kenya in a similar but geographically, culturally, and legally far removed context in the court case over the burial of Silvano Melea (S. M.) Otieno, like Appiah's father a renowned lawyer. Perhaps the fact that questions of such striking similarity could arise out of incidents that are so unrelated is an indication of how valid the interrogation of the force of communalism is.

7. This is not a condemnation of polygamy per se, either generally or in the form that prevails in the cultures of Sub-Saharan Africa, as polygyny is accorded various forms of protection in many African legal systems. As a result, many people engage in legal plural marriage arrangements. What is questioned here is the denial of the basic right of the individual to freely choose to enter the marriage arrangement of her preference.

8. A contrast between "consent" and "want" is intended here. While consenting to something implies "agreeing with" or "agreeing to go along with" someone or something that is separate and distant from a possibly divergent personal position, "wanting" something indicates a deeply personal desire or a self-initiated state of mind. One identifies with what he or she wants but sometimes only sympathizes with what they consent to, either for fear of blame and other repercussions or for purposes of remaining part of the group that is primarily benefitted by the consent. When we agree to something that we also want, the wanting gives us a personal stance and takes precedence with regard to how we value the wanted or desired thing or action. In this latter case we define ourselves as the primary agents in relation to our wants and desires.

9. V. Y. Mudimbe, *Parables and Fables: Exegesis, Textuality, and Politics in Central Africa* (Madison: University of Wisconsin Press, 1991), 139.

10. Ibid., 139–142; and Théodore Theuws, *Word and World: Luba Thought and Literature* (St. Augustin bei Bonn: Anthropos-Institut, 1983), 127–131.

11. A Luo charter, usually told to a young man either before or soon after he marries. The charter is delivered by a group of elders that may include his father, his paternal uncles, and on occasion, his mother or his paternal aunt.

12. T.O. Beidelman, *Moral Imagination in Kaguru Modes of Thought* (Washington, D.C. and London: Smithsonian Institution Press, 1993).

13. Ibid., 18–19.

14. T. O. Beidelman, *The Cool Knife: Imagery of Gender, Sexuality, and Moral Education in Kaguru Initiation Ritual* (Washington, D.C.: Smithsonian Institution Press, 1997), 80.

15. Corinne A. Kratz, *Affecting Performance: Meaning, Movement, and Experience in Okiek Women's Initiation* (Washington, D.C.: Smithsonian Institution Press, 1994), 30–34.

16. Ngũgĩ wa Thiong'o and Ngũgĩ wa Mĩriĩ, *I Will Marry When I Want,* trans. from Gĩkũyũ by the authors (Oxford and Portsmouth: Heinemann Educational Books, 1982), 16.

17. Gabriel Omolo, "Wach Nyombo" (Marriage Issues), musical recording, 1974.

18. Both objective and outcome are quite different for Gathoni of the Ngũgĩs, who falsely thinks that the enticements of the modern economy and social identity offer the freedom she craves. After being lured with the new materialism of the rich, she becomes a victim of the moral decadence of the new times and discovers that the freedom to marry when she wants is not guaranteed by the modern ways of deception, exploitation, betrayal, and hypocrisy that have come to define local rich people's morals. Modernity preaches a freedom that does not exist except for the few, who wrongly think of it as an opportunity to exploit and abuse the poor, regardless of whether they are their neighbors or kin. After making her pregnant, Mũhũũni—whose name, incidentally, means "crook" in Kiswahili—abandons Gathoni like a foot rug or dirt, knowing well, at least according to the authors' plot, that he had done and made of her what would have been unimaginable in the customary setting. The moral of the story is that there are no morals in capitalism. The rich, whether they are local or expatriate, are merely new implementers of the same old colonial ways in order to dispossess the poor of their only hope in life: their ancestral heritage in the form of land and cultural ways. In the eyes of the Ngũgĩs in *Ngaahika Ndenda,* freedom under present arrangements remains the property of the rich and only an illusion for the poor. (See Thiong'o Ngũgĩ and Ngũgĩ wa Mũriũ, *Ngaahika Ndenda* [Nairobi: Heinemann Educational Books, 1980]. The play was translated by the authors into English as *I Will Marry When I Want* [Nairobi: Heinemann Educational Publishers, 1982]). To regain or retain their freedom, the poor need to fiercely resist the ways of the modern economy and the institutions that breed and defend them. In the play, in Gĩcaamba's view, however, women did not have freedom even in the days prior to the white man's arrival.

19. Not that all Christians refrain from the use of, say, condoms, or would be opposed to abortion. As a matter of fact, in Africa, many Christians use condoms and support abortion, but those who do know well that they do so contrary to the official teachings or desires of their organizations.

20. In general legal and moral terms, individuals who lack the capacity to reason, to plan for the future, to detect causal and logical relations among events, or to control action according to principles applied more or less consistently from one occasion to the next are ascribed diminished responsibility for their actions, and their legal status as a person is diminished accordingly. Such individuals, such as children and the sick, retain and must continue to enjoy all their human rights, which must be respected under the protection of proxy agents such as appointed kin or an office of the state.

21. This does not mean opposition to tradition and custom. Rather, Appiah urges that tradition be made of good, carefully examined, and just ideas that would be acceptable and loved by most, even by the gods, for only such ideas can fulfill the ideal of tradition and custom—that is, to produce the ideal maxims by which those who live under them can abide.

22. For example, although contemporary liberalists are overwhelmingly secular in their arguments, the British philosopher John Locke, to whom many of liberal-

ists partly owe their position, based his belief in the fundamental equality of all men on the idea that they were all the workmanship and property of God, hence "made to last during his, not one another's Pleasure." John Locke, *The Second Treatise of Government*, in *Two Treatises of Government*, ed. Peter Laslett (1960; Cambridge, UK: Cambridge University Press, 2002), 271.

23. Martha Nussbaum et al., *For Love of Country: Debating the Limits of Patriotism* (Boston, Mass: Beacon Press, 1996), 3–17.

24. Ibid., 7.

25. Acts of cultural aggression and domination are not limited to situations of violence such as result from military and other forms of colonial occupation. They include acts in which foreign cultural beliefs and practices are introduced to recipients by means that earn their consent to participate for reasons other than a primary freedom and will to embrace the act. International child prostitution—which is part of the widespread and growing tourism-based commercial sex industry across the globe—is an example of preying on otherwise unwilling participants and of imposing foreign practices on indigenous populations in locations outside the imposer's home. Because of their age, education, and often also their socioeconomic circumstances, the victims are often people whose ability to choose is compromised, rendering them defenseless prey. Illicit drug trafficking and use is another example of preventable cultural hawking across national and cultural borders.

26. Kwame A. Appiah, "Cosmopolitan Patriots," in Nussbaum et al., *For Love of Country*, 22. While I agree with Appiah's position, I have added elsewhere that the international cosmopolitanism Nussbaum proposes opens up limitless opportunities for international aggression and oppression (in the name of global moral policing and oversight by dominant nations) of those deemed morally "dangerous" or threatening to the well-being of others. American president George Bush will be remembered, among other things, for openly declaring that he did not need an international consensus to carry out a preemptive military strike against any nation in order to defend the security of American people as part of a wider scheme to spread the American idea of freedom to other nations and cultures. See D. A. Masolo, "Raison et Culture: Les fondements de la morale dans un monde pluriel," *Diogène* 202, no. 2 (April–June 2003): 20–38; English version in *Diogenes* 51, no. 2 (2004): 19–31. Nussbaum herself has since softened her original position in order to embrace the inclusive strain that Appiah and others support, but it is obvious that despite this (re)consideration, her sympathies still lie with what she calls "the sterner thesis." See Martha Nussbaum, *Cultivating Humanity: A Classical Defense of Reform in Liberal Education* (Cambridge, Mass.: Harvard University Press, 1997), in which she still separates what is useful for immediate practical or policy-driven purposes from what is really ideal, as envisioned by Seneca in ancient Rome.

27. Appiah, "Cosmopolitan Patriots," 25. Appiah has since expanded this thesis, fleshed out into two separate but related themes, into two book-length defenses. One, *Cosmopolitanism: Ethics in a World of Strangers* (New York and London: W.W. Norton & Co., 2006), covers liberal cosmopolitanism on the strength of the view that at its very core, human history has been built upon the ability to recognize, accommodate, and respect the differences that define different ways of life. The other, *The Ethics of Identity* (Princeton, N.J.: Princeton University Press, 2005), covers rationally guided senses of identity.

28. As humans, some things distinguish us beyond our ability to preserve our species by biological reproduction. For example, we believe that a good human life is one that is not only biologically sound but also one that is humane, one that is not only free of harm but also one that cultivates and lets us enjoy happiness through self-appreciation of who we are and what we do or achieve, and, generally, one that provides us with most, if not all, of the values, primary and secondary, necessary for living a good human life. Most of the time, such perceptions, ideals, or goals and the modalities for appraising them are supplied by society.

29. Richard A. Wasserstrom, "Rights, Human Rights, and Racial Discrimination," in *Race and Racism,* ed. Bernard Boxill (Oxford, UK: Oxford University Press, 2001), 183. This essay was originally published in the *Journal of Philosophy* 61, no. 20 (1964).

30. It should be noted, however, that although Milingo's explanations of both his healing powers and their target are based on a claim to an African account of the world, the official opposition to his claims, including the Vatican's eventual intervention in the matter, sustain the Church's conservatism on doctrinal matters. His claims (and particularly his healing practices) appear to be more in sync with recent religious charismatic phenomena across the world. See Emmanuel Milingo, *Face to Face with the Devil* (Broadford, Victoria: Scripture Keys Ministries, 1991). This has not stopped some scholars of African Christianity from seeing elements of Africanness in Milingo's claims and from suggesting similarities with the social role of the witch doctor. See, for example, Aylward Shorter, *Jesus and the Witchdoctor: An Approach to Healing and Wholeness* (London: Geoffrey Chapman, 1985); and Adrian Hastings, "Emmanuel Milingo as Christian Healer," in Hastings, *African Catholicism: Essays in Discovery* (London: SCM, 1989), 138–155.

31. Fabien Eboussi Boulaga, *Christianity without Fetishes: An African Critique and Recapture of Christianity,* 2nd ed. (1984; Hamburg: LIT Verlag Münster, 2002), 2.

32. V. Y. Mudimbe, "Preface" to Boulaga, *Christianity without Fetishes,* i.

33. Ibid., ii. For a similar critique of Western views of African traditional beliefs see Appiah, *In My Father's House,* 107–136. The late Ugandan poet, critic, and dramatist Okot p'Bitek used to question, musingly, what was rationally superior about Christians' forced eloquence about a corpse dangling on a tree branch or about the so-called sacred anthropophagy (the eating and drinking of Christ's flesh and blood in holy communion) that provides the articles of universal faith for Christians. His questioning was, of course, not meant for intellectual entertainment; it was meant to point out the fundamental fetishism in Christianity at the same time that Christian missionaries were busy ridiculing the material objects in African traditional religions and dubbing them cannibalistic.

34. Boulaga, *Christianity without Fetishes,* 5.

35. Kenneth Good, *The Liberal Model and Africa: Elites against Democracy* (Houndsmill: Palgrave Publishers, 2002), 8.

36. Literally "people from the North," an expression used by a community in my country to refer to people from any other community whose ways are so far removed from their own that they can hardly stand them, thus thinking of them as the exact opposite of *wandu wa mucie* (those from home), whose ways are acceptably familiar.

37. The social repercussions of these practices are astounding. The girls are often widowed young and left with children of their own that they can hardly

care for or they are recycled in customary practices that virtually discard them into conditions of permanent destitution.

38. See Ivan Karp and D. A. Masolo, "Introduction: African Philosophy as Cultural Inquiry," in *African Philosophy as Cultural Inquiry*, ed. Ivan Karp and D. A. Masolo (Bloomington: Indiana University Press, 2000), 1–18.

39. It is worth noting that although the notion of rights has been subjected to gross abuse in Africa's recent political history, it has traditionally been the very foundation and heart of social order in African societies, both as the principle of distributive justice and as the basis of consensus-based democratic practices. Some minimal knowledge of distributive rights as applicable to one's social system was always a crucial part of knowledge required of all adults and was certainly mandatory for all seeking public office. Giving each person his or her due according to their position in society as regulated by specific maxims was an important element of justice and was therefore the anchor of order and peace.

40. The background to Auntie Akumu's observations is that an aunt was usually considered an ideal matchmaker or middleperson (*ja-gam*) for her brothers' children, who could rely on her counsel regarding the character of the potential mates she identified in the exercise of this role.

4. Understanding Personhood

1. Jean-Pierre Changeux and Paul Ricoeur, *What Makes Us Think? A Neuroscientist and a Philosopher Argue about Ethics, Human Nature, and the Brain*, trans. M. B. DeBevoise (Princeton, N.J.: Princeton University Press, 2000).

2. See, for example, the three-volume study in moral psychology edited by Walter Sinnot-Armstrong: *Moral Psychology*, vol. 1, *The Evolution of Morality: Adaptations and Innateness*; vol. 2, *The Cognitive Science of Morality: Intuition and Diversity*; and vol. 3, *The Neuroscience of Morality: Emotion, Brain Disorders, and Development* (Cambridge, Mass.: MIT Press, 2008).

3. Immanuel Kant, *Logic*, trans. and intro. Robert S. Hartman and Wolfgang Schwarz (New York: Bobbs-Merrill, 1974), 28–29.

4. Kwasi Wiredu, *Cultural Universals and Particulars: An African Perspective* (Bloomington: Indiana University Press, 1996), 13 (my emphasis). As the statement suggests, the idea of "human being" indicated here is a purely biological one, meaning the pre-conscious or pre-mental human, if we can imagine something like that; such an individual is not a person. The Luo would call this phantasmagoric being *"hono"* or *"mang'ong'o,"* that which, by lack of a piece in its making, did not attain its full development.

5. This assumption in Kant is made obvious in the opening paragraphs of his *Logic*:

Everything in nature, in the inanimate as well as the animate world, happens *according to rules*, although we do not always know these rules. Water falls according to the laws of gravity, and the locomotion of animals also takes place according to rules. . . .

The exercise of our own powers also takes place according to certain rules which we first follow without being conscious of them, until we gradually come to cognize them through experiments and long use of our powers, and finally make them so familiar to us that it costs us great effort to think them in abstraction. Thus, for example, general grammar is the form of a language as such. One also speaks, however, without knowing grammar, and he who speaks without knowing it actually does have a grammar and speaks according to rules, even though he is not conscious of them.

Like all our powers, *the understanding* in particular is bound in its acts to norms that we can investigate. Indeed, the understanding is to be regarded as the source and faculty of thinking rules generatim. For, just as sensibility is the faculty of intuitions, so the understanding is the faculty of thinking, that is, of bringing the presentations of the senses under rules.

Kant, *Logic*, 13. This view of mind, which Kant described as an aspect of "nature" that (like all other nature) is subject to rules of operation, is similar to that of later philosophers, such as Gilbert Ryle, who subscribe to the ideational sense of mind. Wiredu distinguished himself from Ryle's view in a 1987 essay: Kwasi Wiredu, "The Concept of Mind with Particular Reference to the Language and Thought of the Akans," in *Contemporary Philosophy, A New Survey*, vol. 5, *African Philosophy*, ed. Guttorm Fløidstad (Dordrecht: Martinus Nijhoff Publishers, 1987), 153–180, especially 155–157. Wiredu made a similarly clear distinction in the context of his explanation of Wilhelm Anton Amo's critique of Descartes' theory of mind. See Kwasi Wiredu, "Amo's Critique of Descartes' Philosophy of Mind," in *The Blackwell Companion to African Philosophy*, ed. Kwasi Wiredu (London and New York: Blackwell Publishers, 2004), 200–206.

6. By envisaging a process by which things develop from a state of potentiality to that of actuality, thus acquiring their essences.

7. Kwasi Wiredu, *Cultural Universals and Particulars: An African Perspective* (Bloomington: Indiana University Press, 1996), 13.

8. Some later German philosophers and sociologists have pointed out that Kant's philosophy, especially his moral theory, is built on the recognition of the equal dignity of the Other, as implied in the Golden Rule. Georg Simmel, for example, argued that Kant's ethics distinguished his idea of individual freedom radically from that of Rousseau and of other German philosophers who thought of freedom in terms of extreme egoism. A case can be made, however, that Kant's ethical recognition of the Other was merely a matter of principle and a function of his endeavor to lay down universal principles of objective moral judgments based on the contingent laws obtaining in the specific field of moral conduct. Simmel himself regarded Kant's philosophy to be monadological—that is, based on the perception of persons primarily as autonomous unities of understanding but nevertheless similar to each other because they all function on the basis of the same universal structures and laws of understanding. Kant's moral theory was a philosophical defense of Lutheranism against the encroachment of ecclesiastical authority on the freedom of individuals.

9. Kwasi Wiredu, "Metaphysics in Africa," in *A Companion to Metaphysics*, ed. Kim Jaegwon and Ernest Sosa (London and New York: Basil Blackwell Publishers, 1995), 313.

10. Kwasi Wiredu, "Akan Philosophical Psychology," in *Routledge Encyclopedia of Philosophy*, vol. 1 (London: Routledge, 1998), 138.

11. Kwasi Wiredu, *Philosophy and an African Culture* (Cambridge: Cambridge University Press, 1980).

12. Wiredu, *Cultural Universals and Particulars*.

13. Wiredu relied on Akan for reasons that go far beyond mere elegance and its capacity to expand the analytical possibilities of the field. Akan (as does any linguistic tool that is indigenous to a thinker) introduces a pluralistic base to philosophy by de-normativizing English (or any particular language, for that matter) as the ideal analytical tool. With this strategy, all languages are welcomed to a continuous and unending dialogue involving philosophical analyses across cultures, for philosophy is a discipline that stands to gain in both breadth and depth from comparative strategies. It should be stated clearly, however, that the notion of truth as opinion does not owe its strength to linguistic relativism. Rather, it is an analytical position grounded in the notion of the complex nature of the world as well as in our subjective relation to it. What the reader might want to pay attention to as this idea develops is how deeply Kantian it remains (because it defines our cognitive experience of the world as limited by and to what we can access as individual subjects while truth, defined as that which transcends these limitations toward an absolute realization, remains only an unreachable ideal) even as it critiques the individualist basis on which it is widely built.

14. As we shall see later, Sodipo and Hallen also illustrate this point in their book *Knowledge, Belief, and Witchcraft: Analytic Experiments in African Philosophy*, 2nd ed. (1986; Stanford, Calif.: Stanford University Press, 1997), specifically in their examination of the contrasting renditions of the concepts of "knowing" and "believing" through the English and Yoruba languages.

15. Edmund Husserl, *The Crisis of European Sciences and Transcendental Phenomenology*, trans. David Carr (Evanston, Ill.: Northwestern University Press, 1970), 277.

16. The same cannot be said of the body because we are able to think, realistically, of the human body without the capacity for thought, such as the body of a dead person. But Africans, and hopefully most people, would not and do not think of the lifeless human body as a person.

17. Placide Tempels, *Bantu Philosophy*, trans. Colin King (Paris: Présence Africaine, 1959). Other philosophers in the Western tradition whose names are often associated with vitalism include Leibniz (1646–1716) for his theory of monads; Henri Bergson (1859–1941), who coined the expression élan vital; and Alfred North Whitehead (1861–1947) for his notion of the category of actual occasion, developed within the wider scheme of the process philosophy he developed as a metaphysical critique of Cartesian substance dualism. Generally, the idea of the vital force has been key to the development of what has since come to be known as process theology, or neoclassical theology, which combines the theology of Aquinas with the metaphysics of Aristotle and can be summarized as the view that nature is a theater of interactions among ephemeral centers of creative activity, each of which becomes objectively immortal in the memory of God. In these senses, process theology, as advanced by one of Whitehead's best-known disciples, the American philosopher Charles Hartshorne, claims to rehabilitate St. Anselm's ontological argument. In *The Divine Relativity*, Hartshorne argued that God is supremely related to and responds to every actuality. Because the universe is God's body, the divine is both finite and infinite, temporal and eternal, contingent and necessary, and so on. Everything is a manifestation of the divine force, if you wish, that guides it on its own path to the realization or fulfillment of its intended goal, or

its actuality. See Charles Hartshorne, *The Divine Relativity: A Social Conception of God* (New Haven, Conn.: Yale University Press, 1948).

18. Particularly interesting are their two joint publications, George Lakoff and Mark Johnson, *Metaphors We Live By* (Chicago: University of Chicago Press, 1980); and George Lakoff and Mark Johnson, *Philosophy in the Flesh: The Embodied Mind and Its Challenge to Western Thought* (New York: Basic Books, 1999).

19. See Kathryn Linn Geurts, *Culture and the Senses: Bodily Ways of Knowing in an African Community* (Berkeley: University of California Press, 2002).

20. Lakoff and Johnson, *Metaphors We Live By,* 3.

21. Ibid., 4

22. By contrast, metaphors proper are characterized by ontological contrast between the two or more domains to which they are applied, but with the understanding that they are "ordinarily" applicable to only one or more of such cases, causing their application to other domains to require explanations based on the warranting analogies between the features of the relevant domains. In this sense, metaphors are either used to stand in for more appropriate terms or are indications of the lack of ordinary terms to apply to those analogous domains. For example, in English, we call the mouth of a river that geographical place where a river enters a larger body of water, either a lake or a larger river, because we have no "ordinary" term in English to identify such places. But it would be a head-jerking anomaly to call the same thing in Dholuo, my native language, a *"dhog aora,"* the direct translation of the English phrase "mouth of the river." In my mother tongue, we call such a place *sango,* because the term "mouth" is ordinarily reserved for the anatomical orifices that animal organisms use to ingest food and to make various kinds of noises. It is in this sense that "heavenly happiness" or "suffering in hell" are metaphors because the terms "being happy" and "suffering" are ordinarily used to describe mental states and sensations of people caused by certain experiences. Hence, "being in heaven" or "being in hell," as "places" that only dead people go to, cannot involve sensations (of which only living organisms are capable) that cause mental states associated with happiness or suffering. Also, because dead people do not go to either "heaven" or "hell" with their bodies, it must be only in metaphorical senses that we speak of them as "places." And if "heaven" and "hell" were actual physical locations, we would have no way of knowing what their characteristics are or would be except by extrapolating features of our known geographical reality.

23. Lakoff and Johnson, *Philosophy in the Flesh,* 47.

24. Ibid., 5–7.

25. Ibid., 4.

26. Ibid., 5.

27. Ibid., 12.

28. American anthropologist Kathryn L. Geurts has studied metaphors of the body and bodily control as part of the broader perceptual experience of reality among the Ewe of southeastern Ghana.

29. Geurts, *Culture and the Senses,* 10.

30. Yoruba folklore teaches, for example, that the body is the work of Obàtálá, while we get life from Elémi, our inner head from Àjàlá, free will and destiny from Ẹlẹ́gbá, and so on.

31. In his two wonderful books on Yoruba philosophical thought, namely *Knowledge, Belief and Witchcraft* (with S. O. Sodipo) and *The Good, the Bad,*

and the Beautiful, Barry Hallen gives very instructive analyses of *Ènìyàn* in which he reduces the deistic expressions of folklore to material (bodily) and nonmaterial (consciousness) aspects of personhood. Chapter 5 below aims at a similar demystification of the Luo concept of the person through a critical analysis of the idea of *juok* (*jok*).

32. See chapters 3 and 4 of Kwasi Wiredu, *Cultural Universals and Particulars: An African Perspective* (Bloomington: Indiana University Press, 1996).

33. Kwasi Wiredu, "African Philosophy, Anglophone," in *Routledge Encyclopedia of Philosophy,* vol. 1 (London and New York: Routledge, 1998), 102.

34. See Wiredu, "Akan Philosophical Psychology," 139.

35. See Anthony Ephirim-Donkor, *African Spirituality: On Becoming Ancestors* (Trenton, N.J. and Asmara: Africa World Press, Inc., 1997).

36. Ibid., 4.

37. See Aylward Shorter, *African Culture and the Christian Church: An Introduction to Social and Pastoral Anthropology* (Maryknoll, N.Y.: Orbis, 1974). His other study of African ethnotheology, *African Christian Theology: Adaptation, or Incarnations?* (Maryknoll, N.Y.: Orbis, 1977), is equally useful. As I have said elsewhere, this was the period that inspired such scholars as Vincent Mulago, Calvin Bahoken, François Lufuluabo, Bolaji Idowu, John Mbiti, Engelbert Mveng, and Tharcisse Tshibangu, who were all young members of the clergy at the time.

38. Ephirim-Donkor, *African Spirituality,* 4.

39. It is important to quickly dispel any confusion that may be associated with the notion of emergence. The idea here is not one that views mind as if it were a "new entity" that springs forth as a separate product of conscious experience. Rather, in play with other several factors, the brain is capable of organizing stimuli into states that are irreducibly mental.

40. Wiredu, *Cultural Universals and Particulars,* 16.

41. Ibid., 22.

42. Ibid., 16.

43. I use this colloquial and ambiguous or vague designation quite deliberately to indicate that part of this type of debate about the nature of mind involves descriptively identifying various ways that it may ontologically differ from or resemble other theories against which it is studied. Obviously, the onus of providing such a name or designation falls on the opponents of physicalists, since it is they who have to show precisely what thought or mind is if it is not physical. The difficulty of a more appropriate and positive term forces them to settle for the negative designation of "nonphysical."

44. Wiredu, *Cultural Universals and Particulars,* 16–18, but especially 17.

45. Ibid., 17.

46. Ibid., 16. Note how this statement comes after a brief but succinct critique of both realists and nominalists in the Western tradition.

47. Ibid., 21–22.

48. Michael Jackson and Ivan Karp, "Introduction," in *Personhood and Agency: The Experience of Self and Other in African Cultures,* ed. Michael Jackson and Ivan Karp (Uppsala: Acta Universitatis Upsaliensis, 1990), 17.

49. The grounds for Wiredu's theory of "truth as opinion" should begin unfolding with this strong view of mind as a capacity of the body, hence lacking the autonomy so strongly assumed of it in epistemological theories of the objectivity of

truth, as is claimed under the correspondence theory. The latter's pitfall appears to emerge from falsely considering the mind to be a transcendent organ or tool that enjoys an independent and privileged access to some inner realm of nature that is not experienced primarily on an empirical plane. For Wiredu, conscious states are subjective, and thus to fully understand them, one must understand what it is like to be in them, and one can do that only by taking up the experiential point of view as a subject in them.

50. Wiredu, *Cultural Universals and Particulars,* 49.

51. Despite its appearance of being merely metaphorically significant, the idea of the ex nihilo origin of things has been used toward different ends in the Western intellectual tradition. First, it is used to express the idea or belief that although God bears some similarities with humans in terms of being able to "make" things, he is also radically different from humans in that same respect because he does not need preexisting materials to make things; he can make them, even in their physical conditions, out of "nothing." In addition to this preeminently theological use, the idea of ex nihilo creation is also used in the Christian language to express the view that all creatures of God, especially humans, enjoy an equal autonomy because each owes their existence to God alone. This view was used widely even by theorists aiming to explain the basic civil and natural rights of all humans, such as the right to life. The idea of ex nihilo creation not only provides the basis of equal autonomy and the undeniability of such a right, it also acts as the objective basis of the argument itself.

52. Wiredu, *Cultural Universals and Particulars,* 49.

53. Kwame A. Appiah, *In My Father's House: Africa in the Philosophy of Culture* (Oxford: Oxford University Press, 1992), chapter 6, especially 112–113. Appiah's argument strongly subverts the idea, prevalent in Christian (especially Thomistic) philosophy, that it is the created world that "participates in"—that is, imitates— the exemplary divine maxims. For Appiah, the contrary is the case, for we accord certain forms of recognition to divinities and ancestors only because we deem these actions and gestures to be replicable to these nonsocial or no-longer-social beings only because the actions and gestures derive from and have their significance in the social realm. We then extend these relational values to the beings of the other world even with full knowledge that those beings will not make literal use of our material "gifts" to them the way our living relations do. Hence, it is they who are brought in to benefit from what we consider to be valuable in establishing a good relationship.

54. Inquiry into the essential and defining components of knowledge is a classic feature of epistemology. The traditional view referred to here was suggested long ago by Plato in the *Theaetetus* and later by Kant and identifies justification, truth, and belief as the three individually necessary and jointly sufficient components of propositional knowledge (that something is so). It claims that knowledge is justified true belief. Contemporary debate has challenged this view, with questions about justification attracting the largest share of attention, as can be found in the works of such influential epistemologists as Roderick M. Chisholm, William Alston, and Edmund Gettier. While the former two focus on the nature of justifications that either obligate or permit or are good enough for me to accept that p, Gettier became famous in the 1960s for challenging and giving examples to show the contrary of the view that if you have a justified true belief that p, then you know that p.

55. Hallen and Sodipo, *Knowledge, Belief, and Witchcraft*, 2nd ed., 60.

56. Wiredu, *Cultural Universals and Particulars*, 22.

57. The view of the person as a social being is not entirely absent from Euro-American thought, as the Frankfurt School has extended its influence across the Western world and beyond. Grounded especially in the philosophy of Kant and Hegel, social philosophy moved away from the old metaphysics significantly to focus on the nature of the dynamics that drive the confluence of social and personal life under the evolution of capitalism. Borrowing and departing from Marxist philosophy at the same time, for example, Jürgen Habermas has insisted that the present world condition no longer offers itself to the Marxist interpretation, which he believes has become largely obsolete and inapplicable in its original doctrinaire form. The rising standards of living in the West and the state's direct involvement with the economy all require a new look at the nature of oppression and a reconceptualization of the life situation of the working class and of alternative, more effective principles of reflection on the social condition and driving forces of emancipation. Based on this ambivalence toward Marxism alone, it is possible to see avenues of convergence between Habermas's theory of communication and Wiredu's dialogical framework with regard to the mechanisms for bringing about social change of a desired kind, as both strive to develop and clarify the conditions under which values and societal goals can become subject to self-conscious discussion rather than preestablished (objective) ends. Furthermore, Habermas's critique of Weber's atomistic and rational-purposive individual and his substitution of Weber's individual with one who is embedded in collective processes and guided by interactive relations for purposes of promoting cooperation and consensus sound closer to Wiredu's theory of truth as discursive and to the sociogenic models of human action prevalent in African thought than most other Western concepts of the person. I will say a little more about this later (in chapter 6).

58. It is usually assumed that any underlying attitudes of interests can either be reduced to objectively discernible psychological order or otherwise dismissible as an individualistic pathology. In this respect, Habermas's critique of Weber appears to have been aimed at Kant as well.

59. We shall see later, for example, that Wiredu's critique of Dewey's pragmatist theory of truth is based precisely on his understanding of "warranted assertibility" as an a priori definition of truth as opposed to one that is built on investigation.

60. The reader should note, however, that much of the essay "Metaphysics in Africa," in which Wiredu asserts that African variety in metaphysical conceptions is radically un-Kantian, is dedicated to the discussion of the concept of God, the ontological implications of the semantics of existence, and the concepts of free will and immortality. See Kwasi Wiredu, "Metaphysics in Africa," in *A Companion to Metaphysics*, ed. Jaegwon Kim and E. Sosa (London: Basil Blackwell Publishers, 1995), 312–315.

61. On this subject the work of the British social theorist Steven Lukes has been helpful; see Steven Lukes, *Individualism* (New York: Harper & Row, 1973); and Michael Carrithers, Steven Collins, and Steven Lukes, eds., *The Category of the Person: Anthropology, Philosophy, and History* (Cambridge, UK: Cambridge University Press, 1985). The latter's comparisons of the ideas of self within different cultural expressions is particularly interesting.

62. Inalienably linked to the various Western notions of what ideas or meanings are is the view that if it can be determined that ideas or meanings are "entities" out there somewhere, then each knower has or can achieve a direct and independent knowledge of them. Indeed, the Socratic practice was based on the belief that much confusion in our uneducated everyday lives notwithstanding, everyone had this autonomous access to ideas, only because ideas were the very basis of a person's ability to discern different things in experience. Other people could help an individual remember the different ideas or meanings reflected by objects in the world, but knowledge of them was ultimately an individual enterprise. On the basis of his theory of mind and of meanings, Wiredu presents a view that is sharply different from this atomistic or monadological view, not only of ideas but also of the epistemological enterprise.

63. My concern here is not so much with the different aspects or "types" of meaning as it is with the general metaphysical status of meaning or meanings, even as I accept the view that understanding the nature, or similarities and differences, of the "types" adds immensely to having and appreciating a full view of the metaphysical status (the sort of things) of meanings.

64. For example, an utterance can mean different things: it can have various combinations of literal or figurative meanings; it can have meanings intended by the speaker; or it can have descriptive meanings, prescriptive meanings, emotive meanings, or cognitive meanings.

65. As we shall see in the next chapter, this idea of meaning points in the direction popularly attributed to the American philosopher W. V. O. Quine's critique of the analytical claims about the necessary relations between certain meanings.

66. In his work *Intentionality: An Essay in the Philosophy of Mind* (Cambridge, UK: Cambridge University Press, 1983), American philosopher John Searle explains that the semantics of a natural language are the result of the mind, which imposes conditions of satisfaction or aboutness on objects. Despite some similarity between these two positions, it would appear that Searle's focus is the formal relationship between the expressions in a language and the meanings that are derived from them while Wiredu's focus is a search for the sequence in the occurrence of the two despite their functional relationship in the (successful) completion of communication. His focus seeks to settle an anthropological problem—the social basis of the making of persons as the goal of human-beingness—first before tackling the formal one.

67. Note that although they are not identical, mind and meaning appear simultaneously as the defining constituents of thought; mind is the capacity, embedded in the physical nature of humans, to think, or to form meanings, while meaning, or thought, is both the constituting content of mind as well as the object on account of which we talk of mind. Thus, while we say that "meanings exist in the mind," it also appears, as far as we can gather from Wiredu's interpretation, that the Akan use of the same term for both mind and thought (*adwene*) is not merely rhetorical. In fact, we are likely to appreciate the analytical implications of the Akan single expression for both mind and thought when we consider it in relation to the judgments we make of soundness of thought as causally related to the associated soundness of mind and, in most such cases, to the physical soundness (that is, proper "wiring" and functioning) of the brain itself. If we can allow ourselves some extension of this view, one could infer from it that mind

and meaning are not only logically but ontologically interrelated; not only can one not think of one without the other but one (mind) is the ontological function of the other (thought).

68. Wiredu, *Cultural Universals and Particulars,* 22. In respect to their functional role within, or service to, the specific human biological constitution, these laws of thought-formation are not different from nor are they privileged over, say, the laws that we learn in physics to make our visual perception of objects possible, with the obvious difference that our sharing of the latter with other animals is more evident.

69. It is this view that separates Wiredu from Dewey's idea of truth as the "warranted assertibility" of propositions. Wiredu explains that he would accept Dewey's view if "warranted assertibility" and truth were related not only in logical terms but also by inquiry.

70. Arguments around the highly publicized case of Mrs. Terry Schiavo, the U.S. woman from Florida who had been declared brain dead but was kept hooked to a life-support system for over one decade (ending in late March 2005), centered on whether she was capable of the basic actions of a person such as recognizing other people and responding to their communicative signs or lacked them despite exhibiting such bodily behaviors as turning her eyes or processing the liquid foods she was fed. Together with these arguments, but much less emphasized, was the recognition that a person's communicative capacities regulate not just their performances but also their feelings about being connected with others, their interaction and enjoyment of others. The feeling of being with others, and, even more, the ability to interact with them, translates a purely mechanical ability into one in which social self-recognition is generated through an interactive exchange of signs and meanings, one that turns mere human life into a humane experience. Partly because they often lack appropriate mechanical equipment to make things better and easier and partly because they believe deeply in what makes people feel and enjoy their humanity, children in my village will play soccer with their crippled siblings on their backs or the latter will themselves request to play goal-keeping positions, just so they too can play their part in being with others.

71. The first dualism is the substance dualism that starts with Plato and culminates in the classic arguments of Descartes, while the second one describes the binary (physicalist-mentalist) approach that has become the feature of the post-Cartesian debate on the subject.

72. Richard Taylor, *Metaphysics,* 4th ed. (Englewood Cliffs, N.J.: Prentice Hall, 1992). See also Richard Taylor, "Reality Consists of Matter," in *Classic Philosophical Questions,* 9th ed., ed. James A. Gould (Upper Saddle River, N.J.: Prentice Hall, 1998), 421–436. The latter essay was originally published as "How to Bury the Mind-Body Problem," *American Philosophical Quarterly* 6 (April 1969): 136–143.

73. Among the many titles, see Daniel Dennett, *Content and Consciousness,* 2nd ed. (1969; London: Routledge and Kegan Paul 1986); Daniel Dennett, *Brainstorms: Philosophical Essays on Mind and Psychology,* 3rd. ed. (1978; New York: Penguin, 1999); Daniel Dennett, *The Intentional Stance* (Cambridge, Mass.: MIT Press, 1987); and Daniel Dennett, *Consciousness Explained* (Boston: Little Brown, 1991).

74. Kwasi Wiredu, "The Concept of Mind with Particular Reference to the Language and Thought of the Akans," in *Contemporary Philosophy: A New Survey,*

vol. 5, *African Philosophy*, ed. G. Fløistad (Dordrecht: Martinus Nijhoff Publishers, 1987), 157.

75. Kwasi Wiredu, "Death and the Afterlife in African Culture," in *Person and Community: Ghanaian Philosophical Studies, I,* ed. Kwasi Wiredu and Kwame Gyekye (Washington, D.C.: Council for Research in Values and Philosophy, 1992), 139. It is not clear, to me at least, if Wiredu has introduced a third constituent of personhood at this point. We saw that the non-Cartesian mind is not a substance but a function of thought, which in turn is a stimulative reaction proper to the biology of humans "triggered" into existence by communication and by means of which they become communicatively (i.e., sociocognitively) connected to the world around them. What we see as the subject of the essay on immortality or the afterlife is, in his own words, "a kind of being that is conceived in the image of a person . . . [and] can appear at, or disappear from, places without regard to speed limits for matter in motion or to the laws of impenetrability . . . [and is also] capable of action at a distance in which a living person may be severely affected without perceptible contact" (139). If indeed this substance is independent of both the material body and the communico-cognitive function that we have called mind, then it introduces an interesting aspect of ambiguity into Wiredu's ontological scheme, which is usually regarded to be monistic. I will reconsider the issue later when I examine Okot p'Bitek's analysis of the idea of *juok.*

76. Kwasi Wiredu, "The Concept of Spirit in an African Philosophy, with an Application to the Philosophy of Mind," in *Metaphysics, An Introduction to Unity and Diversity*, ed. Avery Kolers and D. A. Masolo (Peterborough, Ont.: Broadview Press, forthcoming).

77. Aristotle, *On the Soul,* Book II, 413a, in *The Complete Works of Aristotle,* vol. 1, ed. Jonathan Barnes (Princeton, N.J.: Princeton University Press, 1984), 657.

78. Aristotle, *On the Soul,* Book I, 403a, 5–9, in ibid., 462.

79. Saint Thomas Aquinas, *Summa Contra Gentiles,* Book Two, *Creation*, trans. with intro. and notes by James F. Anderson (Notre Dame, Ind.: University of Notre Dame Press, 1956), 158.

80. Ibid., 254–259.

81. John S. Mbiti, *African Religions and Philosophy* (London: Heinemann, 1969), 25.

82. The fictional story told by Grace Ogot in her novel *The Promised Land* or the legend of Nyamgondho in the myth of Simbi Nyaima tell of these rival human ideals, the images of good and evil.

83. See Wiredu, *Cultural Universals and Particulars,* 29.

84. Ibid.

85. Ibid.

86. Ibid.

87. Historians reckon that the concept of *person,* or *persona,* as individual, was never part of classical Greek thought, which was overly preoccupied with the universal, the ideal, and the abstract. Instead, it is a Latin word that, at least until the advent of Christianity, designated the mask worn by actors and that allowed them to amplify their voices (*personare*) to communicate with the audience or assembly. It was also used to denote specific roles in theatrical action.

88. A robust and technical discussion of "truth as opinion" is to be found in Kwasi Wiredu, *Philosophy and an African Culture* (Cambridge, UK: Cambridge

University Press, 1980), especially in chapters 8 and 12, but there are significant clarifications to the original version of the theory, in the form of a rejoinder to critics in the "Postscript" to Wiredu, *Cultural Universals and Particulars.*

89. Wiredu, *Cultural Universals and Particulars,* 22.

90. See for example Henry O. Oruka, "Truth and Belief," *Universitas* (Ghana) 5, no. 1 (1975); and Henry O. Oruka, "For the Sake of Truth: A Response to Wiredu's Critique of 'Truth and Belief,'" *Quest* 11, no. 2 (1988): 3–22. Another discussion of Wiredu's theory of truth can be found in Peter Boduntin, ed. *Philosophy in Africa: Trends and Perspectives* (Ife, Nigeria: University of Ife Press, 1985), 43–102.

91. D. A. Masolo, *African Philosophy in Search of an Identity* (Bloomington: Indiana University Press, 1994).

92. Wiredu, *Philosophy and an African Culture,* chapter 12.

93. Ibid., 196.

94. Ibid., 176–177. According to this scheme, belief, or opinion (as the two terms are interchangeably used), is a matter of rational inquiry, not of will or an arbitrary view held for its own sake.

95. In Wiredu, *Philosophy and an African Culture,* 197 ff., Wiredu refers to Alfred Tarski's famous article, "The Semantic Conception of Truth and the Foundations of Semantics," in *Readings in Philosophical Analysis,* ed. Herbert Feigl and W. Sellars (New York, Appleton-Century-Crofts, Inc., 1949), 52–84.

96. See Kwasi Wiredu, "Truth: A Dialogue," chapter 12 of Wiredu, *Philosophy and an African Culture.* Wiredu's discussion of Tarski's substitution takes place on 197–201. In "The Semantic Conception of Truth and the Foundations of Semantics," Tarski explains that we can form the name of the sentence "snow is white" by replacing it with the letter p. Then, "We form the name of this sentence and we replace it by another letter, say 'X'. We ask now what is the logical relation between the two sentences 'X *is true*' and 'p.' It is clear that from the point of view of our basic conception of truth these sentences are equivalent. In other words, according to this equivalence schema (T), the following equivalence holds: X *is true if, and only if, p.*" Tarski, "The Semantic Conception of Truth and the Foundations of Semantics," 55. This is the replacement result of the equivalence formulated as "The sentence 'snow is white' is true if, and only if, snow is white." Ibid., 54.

97. Wiredu, *Philosophy and an African Culture,* 200.

98. Ibid., 196.

99. Ibid., 210.

100. Ibid., 177.

101. Ibid., 211.

102. Ibid., 232.

103. "There are inter-personally specifiable criteria of rationally warranted assertibility. The existence of such criteria is made possible by the fact that human beings have certain similarities of basic physiological and mental make-up. This is what lies at the back of the possibility of human community—the possibility, that is, of the use of language and logic among men, the possibility of agreement as also of disagreement, the possibility of moral relations, and so on. The purpose of arguing when there is disagreement among persons is to bring it about by non-arbitrary means that they are of one opinion, that is to say, one rationally warranted opinion." Ibid., 210–211.

104. Wiredu's idea of truth is not that it is the result of a convention. If truth could be attained in the sense implied by the correspondence theory, it would indeed be what the objectivists claim. The difference, however, is that truth is not attainable through the objectivist scheme, hence it remains the ideal objective of any serious epistemological inquiry. Thus, no amount of mere agreement among persons can constitute truth; but when we say, for example, that we agree with the statement that "*p* (Omolo is in Siaya)" is true, all we mean is that our opinion coincides with the opinion that "*p* (Omolo is in Siaya)" is a true statement. In other words, we agree with the statement. Thus, Wiredu's view of truth is vastly different from that of the constructivist position.

105. Wiredu, *Philosophy and an African Culture*, 113.

106. Kwasi Wiredu, "The Concept of Truth in the Akan Language," in *Philosophy in Africa: Trends and Perspectives*, ed. P. Bodunrin (Ife: University of Ife Press, 1985), 43–54.

5. *Juok* as the Moral Foundation of Personhood

1. Although no disagreement with any specific idea in Yoruba thought is implied here, the possibility of such divergence in philosophical understanding or explanation of reality is always very much at the heart of the philosophical enterprise. What is important to note, however, is that such expository work, including that of Barry Hallen and J. O. Sodipo, already referenced above, opens doors to much knowledge and debate. Other works include Barry Hallen's other volume, *The Good, the Bad, and the Beautiful: Discourse about Values in Yoruba Culture* (Bloomington: Indiana University Press, 2000); and Segun Gbadegesin, *African Philosophy: Traditional Yoruba Philosophy and Contemporary African Realities* (New York: Peter Lang Publishers, 1991). In addition, they contain ample bibliographical listings of other scholarly works.

2. See Marcel Griaule, "Rôle du silure *Clarias Senegalensis* dans la procréation au Soudan Français," in Johannes Lukas, *Afrikanistiche Studien* (Berlin: Akademie-Verlag, 1955), 299–311; Marcel Griaule, *Conversations with Ogotemmêli: An Introduction to Dogon Religious Ideas* (London and Oxford: Oxford University Press, 1965); Marcel Griaule and G. Dieterlen, *Le Renard Pâle*, tome I, *Le mythe cosmogonique. Fascicule I: La création du monde* (Paris: Institut d'Ethnologie, 1965), lxxii; S. De Ganay, *Les Devises des Dogon* (Paris: Institut d' Ethnologie, 1941), xli; Germaine Dieterlen, *Les âmes des Dogon* (Paris: Institut d'Ethnologie, 1941), xl; and Germaine Dieterlen, "L'image du corps et les composantes de la personne chez les Dogon," in *La notion de personne en Afrique noire*, ed. Germaine Diterlen (Paris: Éditions du Centre National de la Recherche Scientifique, 1973), 206–229.

3. Dieterlen, "L'image du corps et les composantes de la personne chez les Dogon," 206.

4. Marcel Griaule, "Philosophie et religion des noirs," *Présence Africaine* 8–9 (1950): 307–321.

5. Maurice Mauss, *Sociologie et Anthropologie* (Paris: Presses Universitaires de France, 1960).

6. See Bethwell A. Ogot, "The Concept of Jok," *African Studies* 20, no. 2 (1961): 123–130; Okot p'Bitek, "The Concept of Jok among the Acholi and Lango," *Uganda Journal* 27 (1963): 15–30; Okot p'Bitek, *Religion of the Central Luo* (Nairobi: East African Literature Bureau, 1971); and Okot p'Bitek, *African Religions in*

Western Scholarship (Nairobi: Kenya Literature Bureau, 1970). Ogot and p'Bitek are influenced in their analyses by other interpretations (mostly those of missionaries) of *"juok"* as the term is used in the different Lwoo languages (mostly Shilluk, Acholi, Langi, and Dholuo).

7. Kwasi Wiredu, *Cultural Universals and Particulars: An African Perspective* (Bloomington: Indiana University Press, 1996), 136.

8. p'Bitek, *African Religions in Western Scholarship*, 6.

9. Ibid., viii.

10. Clifford Geertz, *The Interpretation of Cultures* (New York: Basic Books, 1973); James Clifford, *The Predicament of Culture: Twentieth-Century Ethnography, Literature, and Art* (Cambridge, Mass.: Harvard University Press, 1988); George Marcus and James Clifford, eds., *Writing Culture: The Poetics and Politics of Ethnography* (Berkeley: University of California Press, 1986); George Marcus and Michael M. J. Fischer, *Anthropology as Cultural Critique* (Chicago: University of Chicago Press, 1986); and Johannes Fabian, *Time and the Other: How Anthropology Makes Its Object* (New York: Columbia University Press, 1983).

11. See V. Y. Mudimbe, *The Invention of Africa: Gnosis, Philosophy, and the Order of Knowledge* (Bloomington: Indiana University Press, 1988); and Kwame A. Appiah, *In My Father's House: Africa in the Philosophy of Culture* (Oxford: Oxford University Press, 1992)·

12. See Wiredu, *Cultural Universals and Particulars: An African Perspective*; and Ngũgĩ wa Thiong'o, *Decolonizing the Mind: The Politics of Language in African Literature* (London: James Currey; Nairobi: Heinemann, 1986).

13. Rosalind Shaw, "The Invention of 'African Traditional Religion,'" *Religion* 20 (1990): 339.

14. Ibid., 340.

15. See also V. Y. Mudimbe, *Tales of Faith: Religion as Political Performance in Central Africa* (London: Athlone Press, 1997).

16. Ogot, "The Concept of Jok," 123.

17. Ibid.

18 Ibid.

19. G. R. Lienhardt, "The Shilluk of the Upper Nile," in *African Worlds,* ed. G. R. Lienhardt (Oxford: Oxford University Press, 1954); P. P. Howell and W. P. G. Thomson, "The Death of the Reth of the Shilluk and Installation of His Successor," *Sudan Notes and Records* 27 (1946); E. E. Evans-Pritchard, *Nuer Religion* (Oxford: Oxford University Press, 1956).

20. Lienhardt, "The Shilluk of the Upper Nile," 155.

21. Luo folklore still portrays the universe pretty much in pre-Copernican terms, in that it speaks of the sun as a sort of mysterious thing because it is capable of traversing the earth from east (Ugwe) to west (Yimbo) within a short time. Because of its role in the dialectic of time, the sun is regarded as part of the dominance of transcendental time whose secrets are yet to be discovered. So when people say, *"Iru-na maber"* (let each of your appearances bring me luck), there is no indication that they are addressing the physical sun as a divinely powered entity. The utterance is no more religious than wishing onself or someone else a "happy journey" or a "happy new year."

22. Duration is always of something while nothing that exists is thinkable outside duration or time. Sometimes the Luo say *"Oru wuod Aming'a,"* a tautological

phrase that combines two different expressions of the same meaning, *"ru piny"* and *"aming'a piny"*—both of which mean "the (relative) eternity of the universe"—by separating and converting the prefixes *"ru"* (which means long duration in terms of days and nights—many days and nights) and *"aming'a"* (which also means long duration in terms of a temporal stretch—a very long stretch of time) into personal nouns related by descent in which *"Oru"* becomes the "son of" *"Aming'a."* The Luo use this tautology to claim that "forever" (or eternity; *aming'a*) and the countable duration of days and nights are closely related. This *piny* is the center of the universe and of human experience, there is no rival other. For references to other ideas associated with the concept of *"piny"* see Atieno-Odhiambo's essay "A World-View for the Nilotes? The Luo Concept of Piny," in *African Historians and African Voices,* ed. E. S. Atieno Odhiambo (Basel: P. Schlettwein, 2001).

23. Mudimbe, *Tales of Faith,* 151.

24. See J. H. Driberg, *The Lango: A Nilotic Tribe of Uganda* (London: T. F. Unwin, 1923); G. R. Lienhardt, "The Shilluk of the Upper Nile," in *African Worlds,* ed. G. Lienhardt (Oxford: Oxford University Press, 1954); T. T. S. Hayley, "The Power Concept in Lango Religion," *Uganda Journal* 7 (1940): 98–122; and T. T. S. Hayley, *Anatomy of Lango Religion and Groups* (Cambridge: Cambridge University Press, 1947). p'Bitek's critique of these early and christocentric studies of the concept of *jok* is in his 1963 essay "The Concept of Jok among the Acholi and Lango," while his critique of Tempels and Ogot is in a brief 1964 review of Tempels's book. See Okot p'Bitek, "Fr. Tempels' Bantu Philosophy," *Transition* 13 (1963): 15–17.

25. p'Bitek, *African Religions in Western Scholarship,* 59.

26. The Mill Hill missionaries would later introduce "Nyasae" or "Were" from the Luhya language into the Dholuo lexicon for this new metaphysical entity.

27. p'Bitek, *African Religions in Western Scholarship,* 65, emphasis in the original.

28. See p'Bitek, *Religion of the Central Luo,* 40–43.

29. Ibid., 50.

30. H. Owuor Anyumba, "Spirit Possession among the Luo of Central Nyanza, Kenya," Occasional Papers in East African Traditional Religion, Department of Religious Studies and Philosophy, Makerere University, Kampala, 1954, 1–46. See also H. Owuor Anyumba, "The Historical Dimensions of Life-Crisis Rituals: Some Factors in the Dissemination of Juogi Beliefs among the Luo of Kenya up to 1962," unpublished conference paper, June 1974.

31. See B. A. Ogot, *History of the Southern Luo* (Nairobi: East African Publishing House, 1967). This excellent text remains the most detailed and authoritative history of the Padhola and Kenya Luo to date.

32. p'Bitek, *Religion of the Central Luo,* 59–120; and p'Bitek, *African Religions in Western Scholarship,* 70–79.

33. p'Bitek, *African Religions in Western Scholarship,* 70.

34. Ibid., 71

35. Ibid.

36. Fabien Eboussi-Boulaga, *Christianity without Fetishes: An African Critique and Recapture of Christianity* (Hamburg: LIT Verlag Münster, 2002), 4.

37. It is important to note that the evocation of the authority of either of the sources usually arises in contexts where they are being disputed. Because people

are already critical agents within their social settings, no laws are considered infallible, regardless of their origin. The evocation of such laws, then, is not meant to override possible transgressions but to bring them to scrutiny in the face of specific situations. The Luo say that *"chik ok mak gi kor"* (laws are not held [meant to be applied] with the thorax); they have goals, and so are constantly and critically revised and negotiated alongside those goals.

38. Ogot, "The Concept of Jok," 124.

39. John S. Mbiti, *African Religions and Philosophy* (London: Heinemann Educational Books, 1969).

40. Oginga Odinga, *Not Yet Uhuru: An Autobiography* (New York: Hill and Wang, 1967), 42.

41. Ibid., 55.

42. Anyumba, "Spirit Possession among the Luo of Central Nyanza, Kenya."

43. The Luo refer to the various Kalenjin groups collectively as "Lango," as distinct from their own kin, the Langi of Eastern Uganda, of whom p'Bitek and Ogot write in their studies of the Luo.

44. p'Bitek, *African Religions in Western Scholarship*, 73.

45. An observation can be made that even the apparently morally neutral role of mediumship is not easily accepted by those who are informed by diviners that *juogi* are seeking them out to be their mediums. The hesitance and resistance on the part of the mediums-to-be are due to the expectations that define the public manifestation of being a medium. The distinctive qualities, capacities, and roles with which society endows such a person and the behavioral restrictions the public expects of them can be overwhelming and contrary to how the person herself might wish to view herself and play her role in society. For example, mediumship has the capacity to limit the medium's freedom by prescribing what he or she can and cannot do for successful participation in the role of a medium. What one observes in the public life of a medium is their struggle to balance the demands of another agent (such as the spirit) that "resides" in them with the daily obligations of their own lives so they can exercise their freedoms, capacities, and other roles. It is a struggle between self-knowledge and identity, on the one hand, and knowledge and identity of self as imposed by society, on the other.

46. Anyumba, "The Historical Dimensions of Life-Crisis Rituals."

47. D. A. Masolo, "From Village to Global Contexts: Ideas, Types, and the Making of Communities," in *Diversity and Community: An Interdisciplinary Reader*, ed. Philip Alperson (Malden, Mass. and Oxford, UK: Blackwell Publishers, 2002), 89.

48. Kwasi Wiredu, *Cultural Universals and Particulars: An African Perspective* (Bloomington, Indiana University Press, 1996), 29.

49. Eboussi-Boulaga, *Christianity without Fetishes*, 4.

50. There are no known material interests or gains associated with the actions of a *jajuok*; usually they don't take or damage other people's property. It is therefore assumed that they derive pleasure from causing fear and panic in others. Sadism, the inclination and practice of meting different sorts of pain or suffering to others as source of pleasure, does indeed fit the classic notion of *juok* as social mischief.

51. There are several tales of people who have been killed in the act, but they are only whispered in gossip and are told as big community secrets that will

surely vary from the accounts of the immediate relatives of the victim. Without any regard for whatever other story is circulating in the community, the relatives present their own account as the "official" and public version, fully aware that it will not be publicly countered. Occasionally someone daring will publicly charge another with *juok*, which the accused will usually either not respond to or will vehemently deny, thus leaving their accuser looking like it is they who are ill motivated due to their unprovable charges.

52. Meyer Fortes, "On the Concept of the Person among the Tallensi," in *La Notion de Personne en Afrique Noire*, ed. G. Dieterlen (Paris: Éditions du Centre National de la Recherche Scientifique, 1973), 287.

53. Ibid.

54. See, for example, Michael Carrithers, S. Collins, and S. Lukes, eds., *The Category of the Person: Anthropology, Philosophy, History* (Cambridge: Cambridge University Press, 1985).

55. Charles Taylor, *Human Agency and Language: Philosophical Papers 1* (Cambridge, Cambridge University Press, 1985), 80.

56. Charles Taylor, *Sources of the Self: The Making of the Modern Identity* (Cambridge, Mass.: Harvard University Press).

57. T. O. Beidelman, *Moral Imagination in Kaguru Modes of Thought* (Washington, D.C.: Smithsonian Institution Press, 1993), 139.

58. Hayley, "The Power Concept in Lango Religion." See also Hayley, *Anatomy of Lango Religion and Groups.*

59. In his 1964 review of Tempels's *Bantu Philosophy*, p'Bitek was very critical of those who attempt to follow Tempels by trying to explain *juok* as the most general attribute of all things (Being). See p'Bitek, "Fr. Tempels' Bantu Philosophy," 15–17.

60. There is no passiveness in the Luo moral system. A person who remains passive or turns away from a situation that requires their action in order to be righted commits *juok* because such passiveness is equated with a (deliberate) decision to not do good; it is equivalent to wishing that the harmful outcome may come to pass and thus not helping to avert it. Only a *jajuok* remains mum or refrains from action in instances where they could help.

61. See Aquinas, *Summa Contra Gentiles*, Book Two, *Creation*, trans. with intro. and notes by James F. Anderson (Notre Dame, Ind.: University of Notre Dame Press, 1956), especially chapters 65 and 79.

62. Incidentally, the Luo have great stories about Tanzanian medicine men and women who are said to be capable of calling the shadows of absent people to appear in a basin of water so they can "slaughter" them by imitating the act on their shadows. Commentaries falsely assume that the Luos' belief in the mechanism of the calling is the reason they fear Tanzanian witchcraft. But actually the reason for their fear is their awe for the absurdity of the claim that someone's *tipo* can actually appear at a place where they themselves are not. For that to happen, the responsible medicine woman or man must be an extraordinary or unusual human, and it is this imagination that causes fear in many Luo people who encounter such awe-causing stories. Anyone would feel a little funny if they heard that someone they thought was ordinary was actually not.

63. B. Russell, *The Problems of Philosophy* (1912; Indianapolis: Hackett Publishing Co., 1990), 49.

64. The idea here is very similar to that found in the legend of Luanda Mage-re among the Southern Luo and, like the latter, does not appear to refer to any substantive metaphysical entity.

65. Max Gluckman, *Custom and Conflict in Africa* (New York: Barnes and Noble, 1969).

66. p'Bitek, *African Religions in Western Scholarship*, 73.

67. Ibid., 74.

68. Ibid., 72–73.

69. The picture of the Luo and neighboring communities given in B. A. Ogot, *History of the Southern Luo*, vol. 1, *Migration and Settlement* (Nairobi: East African Publishing House, 1967) is one that constantly lays to rest the idea of purity as the basis of ethnic, clan, or other types of unit identities. Ogot argues repeatedly in this excellent book that as we know them today, the groups are pretty much made up of clusters with diverse origins and their names have either been modified by the dominant constituent groups or have disappeared altogether over the years. In other words, he says, "as was common in those days [of migrations], unrelated peoples migrating together, sharing common experiences and settling together in one area, often regarded themselves, after several generations, as relatives" (164).

70. G. E. M. Ogutu, "The African Perception," in *Immortality and Human Destiny: A Variety of Views*, ed. Geddes McGregor (New York: Paragon House, 1985), 106.

71. Appiah, *In My Father's House*, 109.

72. Heike Behrend, *Alice Lakwena and the Holy Spirits: War in Northern Uganda 1985–97*, trans. Mitch Cohen (Oxford: James Currey, 1999), 137.

73. People can be either only physically sick or only mentally sick. But when someone starts by being physically sick first, any signs of lapses in their speech or reasoning capacity are taken seriously as indications of total degeneration of their personhood. As a result, more than one type of expertise is usually required in the efforts to restore their health. In addition to the herbalist, perhaps the help of a diviner (*ajuoga*) would be sought to deal with the manifestations of psychological sickness as well.

6. Two Forms of Communitarianism

1. G. W. F. Hegel, *Philosophy of Right*, trans. T. M. Knox (London: Oxford University Press, 1967), 279–280.

2. Ibid.

3. Ibid.

4. In the bibliography below I have listed the titles of works that express the views of philosophers that are commonly regarded to be communitarian. It is, however, important to note that communitarianism, like liberalism, the idea or view that communitarians are generally critical of, does not always stand for a single and homogeneous notion shared by all its adherents.

5. Steven Lukes, *Individualism* (New York: Harper & Row, 1973), 22.

6. Georg Simmel, *The Sociology of Georg Simmel*, trans., ed., and intro. Kurt H. Wolff (New York: The Free Press, 1964), 82.

7. Lukes, *Individualism*, 17–18.

8. Simmel, *The Sociology of Georg Simmel*, 51.

9. Max Stirner, *The Ego and Its Own,* trans. S. T. Byington, ed. D. Leopold (Cambridge: Cambridge University Press, 1994); original German published in 1844 as *Einzige und Sein Eigentum.* For a critical discussion of this work, see J. P. Clark, *Max Stirner's Egoism* (London: Freedom Press, 1976).

10. Charles Taylor, *Sources of the Self: The Making of the Modern Identity* (Cambridge, Mass.: Harvard University Press), 105.

11. Alasdair MacIntyre, *After Virtue: A Study in Moral Theory,* 2nd ed. (1981; Notre Dame, Ind.: University of Notre Dame Press, 1984), 216–220.

12. A good example of which can be found in A. Buchanan, "Assessing the Communitarian Critique of Liberalism," *Ethics* 99, no. 4 (1988): 852–882; and A. Buchanan, "Liberalism and Group Rights," in *In Harm's Way,* ed. J. Coleman and A. Buchanan (Cambridge: Cambridge University Press, 1994).

13. MacIntyre, *After Virtue,* 220.

14. Ibid., 204.

15. Simmel, *The Sociology of Georg Simmel,* 82.

16. Jean-Jacques Rousseau, *The Social Contract and Discourse on the Origin of Inequality,* ed. and intro. Lester G. Crocker (1762; New York: Washington Square Press, 1967), 43.

17. Simmel, *The Sociology of Georg Simmel,* 70.

18. Ibid., 70.

19. Ibid., 72–73.

20. MacIntyre, *After Virtue,* 222.

21. Alasdair MacIntyre, *Whose Justice? Which Rationality?* (Notre Dame, Ind.: University of Notre Dame Press, 1988), 326.

22. See MacIntyre, *After Virtue,* 244–255.

23. See Robert Nozick, *Anarchy, State, and Utopia* (New York: Basic Books, 1974).

24. Léopold S. Senghor, *On African Socialism,* trans. and intro. Mercer Cook (New York: Frederick A. Praeger, 1964), 10. Earlier, in *L'Expérience Guinéenne et l'Unité Africaine* (Paris: Présence Africaine, 1959) and *L'Action du Parti Démocratique de Guinée et Lutte pour l'Emancipation Africaine* (Paris: Présence Africaine, 1959), Sékou Touré had expressed similar sentiments regarding a partial overlap between the Marxist doctrine and African social reality and needs. Specifically, Sékou Touré declared, the rejection of some of the principles identified with Marxism "was less by philosophical conviction than because of a desire to preserve at any price African solidarity, which alone is capable of leading us to realize our destiny and which alone may enable us to preserve our originality and to impose upon the world respect of the African man and his deeds" (*L'Expérience Guinéenne et l'Unité Africaine,* 394). According to Immanuel Wallerstein (in "The Political Ideology of the P.D.G.," *Présence Africaine* 40 [1962]: 30–41), the rhetoric of the African leader, in its articulation of the (creation and) integration of the new nationhood as the primary political goals, bore more affinities with Hobbesianism than with Marxism, a recipe for and prelude to autocracy and, as would happen with Sékou Touré himself later, a push toward unstoppable despotic depersonalization and suppression of the people. By proclaiming himself the embodiment and protector of the people's interests, the leader effectively made himself the absolute authority beyond reproach.

25. Senghor, *On African Socialism,* 67–69.

26. Ibid., 76–77.

27. Ibid., 77.

28. Ibid., 93–94.

29. Ibid., 94.

30. There is an indication here of similarity between Senghor's structuralist view of the socially determined individual and Pierre Bourdieu's idea of the logic of practice. See, for example, Pierre Bourdieu, *Outline of a Theory of Practice,* trans. Richard Nice (Cambridge: Cambridge University Press, 1977); and Pierre Bourdieu, *The Logic of Practice,* trans. Richard Nice (Stanford, Calif.: Stanford University Press, 1990).

31. As in Nyerere's sense of the same phrase—"by nature"—Senghor could not have meant that Africans developed this ethical attitude as a type of genetically acquired condition, hence a passive inclination, as this would have had problematic metaphysical implications for the differences in the psychological makeup of people. We do know, however, that his idea of negritude was a sociohistorical one, one that indicated a civilization; hence "by nature," as applied to an ethical value, could only have been a cultural reference to the values by which African and African-descended people evaluate the moral quality of their actions.

32. Stanislas Adotevi, *Négritude et négrologues* (Paris: Union Générale d'Éditions, 1972); Marcien Towa, *Essai sur la problématique philosophique dans l'Afrique actuelle* (Yaoundé: Éditions Clé, 1971); and Marcien Towa, *L'Idée d'une philosophie négro-Africaine* (Yaoundé: Éditions Clé, 1979).

33. Frantz Fanon, *The Wretched of the Earth,* trans. Constance Farrington (New York: Grove Press, 1968).

34. Ayi Kwei Armah, "African Socialism: Utopian or Scientific?" *Présence Africaine* 64, no. 4 (1967): 6–30.

35. Samir Amin, *Capitalism in the Age of Globalization: The Management of Contemporary Society* (London and Atlantic Highlands, N.J.: Zed Books, 1997); Samir Amin, *Eurocentrism,* trans. Russell Moore (New York: Monthly Review Press, 1989); and Samir Amin, "The Social Movements in the Periphery: An End to National Liberation?" in Samir Amin, Giovanni Arrighi, Andre Gunder Frank, and Immanuel Wallerstein, *Transforming the Revolution: Social Movements and the World System* (New York: Monthly Review Press, 1990), 96–138.

36. See Vincent Mulago, "Dialectique existentielle des Bantu et sacramentalisme," in *Aspects de la culture noire* (Paris: Librairie Arthème Fayard, 1958), 146–171; Vincent Mulago, "Christianisme et culture africaine: Apport africaine à la Théologie," in *Christianity in Tropical Africa—Studies Presented and Discussed at the Seventh International African Seminar at the University of Ghana, April 1965,* ed. C. G. Baeta (London: Oxford University Press, 1968), 308–317; and Vincent Mulago, "La religion traditionelle, élément central de la culture Bantu," in *Les religions africaines comme source des valeurs de civilisation, Colloque de Cotonou 16–22 August, 1970* (Paris: Présence Africaine, 1972).

37. Mulago, "La religion traditionelle, élément central de la culture Bantu," 116.

38. Francois-Marie Lufuluabo, "La conception bantoue face au Christianisme," in *Personnalité Africaine et Catholicisme* (Paris: Présence Africaine, 1962), 58 (my translation).

39. Meinrad Hebga, *Émancipation d'Églises sous tutelle: essai sur l'ère post-missionaire* (Paris: Présence Africaine, 1976), 76–78.

40. See V. Y. Mudimbe, *Tales of Faith: Religion as Political Performance in Central Africa* (London, The Athlone Press, 1997), especially chapter IV.

41. Société africaine de culture, *Les religions africaines comme source de valeurs de civilization: Colloque organisé par la Société africaine de culture* (Paris: Présence Africaine, 1972); Senghor, *On African Socialism*, 90.

42. Julius K. Nyerere, *Ujamaa: Essays on Socialism* (Dar es Salaam: Oxford University Press, 1968), 1.

43. Julius Nyerere, "The Rational Choice," in *African Socialism in Practice: The Tanzanian Experience*, ed. Andrew Coulson (1979; Nottingham, UK: Spokesman, 1982), 19–26.

44. Ibid., 19.

45. Ibid., 20.

46. Ibid.

47. See the critical literature that responds to Robin Horton's widely debated essay that compared the purported theoretical principles around which beliefs in African traditional religions are organized with the theoretical premises of Western science. Horton's original essay was "African Traditional Thought and Western Science," *Africa* 37, nos. 1–2 (1967): 50–71 and 155–187, reprinted in his *Patterns of Thought in Africa and the West: Essays on Magic, Religion and Science* (Cambridge: Cambridge University Press, 1993), 19–49. Critical essays include Barry Hallen, "Robin Horton on Critical Philosophy and Traditional Thought," in *Second Order* 6, no. 1 (1977): 81–92, revised as "Analytic Philosophy and Traditional Thought: A Critique of Robin Horton," in *African Philosophy: A Classical Approach*, ed. P. English and K. M. Kalumba (Upper River Saddle River, N.J.: Prentice Hall, 1996); Kwasi Wiredu, "How Not to Compare African Thought with Western Science," *Ch'Indaba* no. 2 (July–December 1976): 4–8, reprinted in *African Philosophy: An Introduction*, ed. Richard Wright (Washington, D.C.: University Press of America, 1977) and in *African Philosophy: Selected Readings*, ed. Albert G. Mosley (Englewood Cliffs, N.J.: Prentice Hall, 1995); K. Anthony Appiah, *In My Father's House: Africa in the Philosophy of Culture* (New York: Oxford University Press, 1992); and V. Y. Mudimbe and K. Anthony Appiah, "The Impact of African Studies on Philosophy," in *Africa and the Disciplines: The Contributions of Research in Africa to the Social Sciences and Humanities*, ed. Robert H. Bates, V. Y. Mudimbe, and Jean O'Barr (Chicago: University of Chicago Press, 1993). The philosophical publications and debates that became the corpus of the so-called rationality debate, of which Horton's essay was a pertinent part, are part of the practice of false comparison of traditional thought to knowledge that is organized and systematically researched and controlled by experts. It grew out of E. E. Evans-Pritchard's now-classic work on Zande conceptions of oracles, magic, and witchcraft, *Witchcraft, Oracles, and Magic among the Azande* (London: Oxford University Press, 1937), but by genealogy goes back to the work of such people as Lèvy-Bruhl earlier in the twentieth century.

48. Julius Nyerere, "Freedom and Development," in *African Socialism in Practice: The Tanzanian Experience*, ed. Andrew Coulson (1979; Nottingham, UK: Spokesman, 1982), 27–35 (emphasis in original).

49. Ibid., 27.

50. Jean-Godefroy Bidima, *La Palabre: Une juridiction de la parole* (Paris: Éditions Michalon, 1997), 11–21.

51. Ibid., 21.

52. B. Atangana, "Actualité de la palabre," *Études* 324 (1966): 462, quoted in Bidima, *La Palabre*, 20.

53. Henry O. Oruka, ed., *Sage Philosophy: Indigenous Thinkers and Modern Debate on African Philosophy* (Leiden and New York, E. J. Brill Publishers 1990), 141.

54. These are relational terms with moral connotations (*ujirani* means neighborliness; *utubora* means ideal or perfect humaneness; and *ujamaa* means interdependence). Two of them have been used before and are popular concepts in sociopolitical literature from East Africa. *Ujamaa* was popularized by the work of the late Julius Nyerere of Tanzania and *utubora* by Shaaban Robert. This specific use of *ujirani*, on the other hand, although a correct Kiswahili word as used here, is my own invention.

55. Jack Goody, *The Domestication of the Savage Mind* (London: Cambridge University Press, 1997).

56. Corinne A. Kratz, *Affecting Performance: Meaning, Movement, and Experience in Okiek Women's Initiation* (Washington, D.C.: Smithsonian Institution Press, 1994), 3.

57. Ibid., 97.

58. See Kwasi Wiredu, "Morality and Religion in Akan Thought," in *Philosophy and Cultures*, ed. Henry O. Oruka and D. A. Masolo (Nairobi: Bookwise Publishers, 1983), 6–13.

59. Kwasi Wiredu, *Cultural Universals and Particulars: An African Perspective* (Bloomington, Indiana University Press, 1996), 19.

60. Again, as I already said earlier, recent theoretical proposals and defenses of communitarianism as a significant aspect of political and moral thinking in Western intellectual tradition can be found in the works of such influential scholars as Charles Taylor, Alasdair MacIntyre, Michael Sandel, Jürgen Habermas, and John Kekes, among others. See Michael L. Gross, *Ethics and Activism: The Theory and Practice of Political Morality* (Cambridge: Cambridge University Press, 1997).

61. Kwasi Wiredu, "Our Problem of Knowledge: Brief Reflections on Knowledge and Development in Africa," in *African Philosophy as Cultural Inquiry*, ed. Ivan Karp and D. A. Masolo (Bloomington: Indiana University Press, 2000), 182.

62. Ibid.

63. See, for example, Goran Hyden, *No Shortcuts to Progress: African Development Management in Perspective* (Berkeley: University of California Press, 1983).

64. Kwasi Wiredu, "The Moral Foundations of an African Culture," in *Person and Community: Ghanaian Philosophical Studies I*, ed. Kwasi Wiredu and Kwame Gyekye (Washington, D.C.: Council for Research in Values and Philosophy, 1992), 193.

65. Kwame Gyekye, *Tradition and Modernity: Philosophical Reflections on the African Experience* (New York and London, Oxford University Press, 1997), 35–76.

66. Wiredu, *Cultural Universals and Particulars*, Chapter 12.

67. Wiredu, "Our Problem of Knowledge."

68. Gyekye, *Tradition and Modernity*, 72–76.

69. Tom O. Beidelman, *Moral Imagination in Kaguru Modes of Thought* (Washington, D.C. and London: Smithsonian Institution Press, 1993), 138.

70. Ibid., 138.

71. Alisdair MacIntyre, *After Virtue: A Study in Moral Theory*, 2nd ed. (1981; Notre Dame, Ind.: University of Notre Dame Press, 1984); Charles Taylor, *Sources of the Self: The Making of the Modern Identity* (Cambridge, Mass.: Harvard Uni-

versity Press, 1989); and John Kekes, *Against Liberalism* (Ithaca, N.Y.: Cornell University Press, 1997).

72. Michael Jackson, *Allegories of the Wilderness* (Bloomington, Indiana University Press, 1982), 31.

In Lieu of a Conclusion

1. In the dialogue, F = Father, the convener of the event; MO = Min Omondi, village elder and oldest sister of M; M = Mother; UM = Uncle Moi, older brother of F; All = the group of the rest of village elders summoned as a kind of jury; D = Defendant.

2. Shaaban Robert, *Koja la Lugha* (Nairobi: Oxford University Press, 1945), 13.

3. Ibid., 18.

4. Immanuel Kant, *Grounding for the Metaphysics of Morals,* trans. James W. Ellington (Indianapolis and Cambridge, UK: Hackett Publishing Company, 1981), 9, 396.

5. Ibid., 13, 400.

6. Robert L. Arrington, *Western Ethics: An Historical Introduction* (Malden, Mass., and Oxford, UK: Blackwell Publishers, 1998), 266.

7. *The Standard* (Nairobi, Kenya), April 14, 2009.

8. Winsley Masese, "Seeking Equality for the Girl-Child," *The Standard* (Nairobi, Kenya), March 7, 2009. In the same edition of the newspaper, there is another story entitled "Girl Bleeds to Death after Undergoing FGM."

9. Kwasi Wiredu, *Cultural Universals and Particulars: An African Perspective* (Bloomington: Indiana University Press, 1996).

10. Ibid., 29.

11. Ibid.

12. Ibid.

13. Kwasi Wiredu, "Morality and Religion in Akan Thought," in *Philosophy and Cultures,* ed. H. O. Oruka and D. A. Masolo (Nairobi: Bookwise Publishers, 1983), 5–13.

14. Ibid., 7.

15. Ibid., 185.

16. Ibid.

References

Abímbolá, Kolá. *Yorùbá Culture: A Philosophical Account*. Birmingham, UK: Iroko Academic Publishers, 2006.

Abímbolá, Wandé. *Ifá Will Mend Our Broken World: Thoughts on Yoruba Religion and Culture in Africa and the Diaspora*. Roxbury, Mass.: Aim Books, 1997.

———. "The Yoruba Concept of Human Personality." In *La Notion de personne en Afrique noire*, ed. Germaine Dieterlen, 73–89. Paris: Éditions du Centre National de la Recherche Scientifique, 1973.

Achebe, Chinua. *Morning Yet On Creation Day*. Garden City, N.Y.: Anchor Books, 1975.

———. *Things Fall Apart*. London: Heinemann Educational Books, 1958.

Adotevi, Stanislas. *Négritude et négrologues*. Paris: Union Générale d'Éditions, 1972.

Amin, Samir. *Capitalism in the Age of Globalization: The Management of Contemporary Society*. London and Atlantic Highlands, N.J.: Zed Books, 1997.

———. *Eurocentrism*. English trans. Russell Moore. New York: Monthly Review Press, 1989.

———. "The Social Movements in the Periphery: An End to National Liberation?" In Samir Amin, Giovanni Arrighi, Andre Gunder Frank, and Immanuel Wallerstein, *Transforming the Revolution: Social Movements and the World System*, 96–138. New York: Monthly Review Press, 1990.

Anyumba, H. Owuor. "The Historical Dimensions of Life-Crisis Rituals; Some factors in the Dissemination of Juogi Beliefs among the Luo of Kenya up to 1962." Paper presented at the Limuru Conference on the Historical Study of East African Religions, 1974.

———. "Spirit Possession among the Luo of Central Nyanza, Kenya." Occasional Papers in African Traditional Religion, Department of Religious Studies and Philosophy, Makerere University, 1954.

Appiah, Kwame A. "Cosmopolitan Patriots." In *For Love of Country: Debating the Limits of Patriotism*, ed. Joshua Cohen. Boston: Beacon Press, 1996.

———. *Cosmopolitanism: Ethics in a World of Strangers*. New York and London: W.W. Norton & Co., 2006.

———. *The Ethics of Identity*. Princeton, N.J.: Princeton University Press, 2005.

———. *Experiments in Ethics*. Cambridge, Mass.: Harvard University Press, 2008.

——. *In My Father's House: Africa in the Philosophy of Culture.* Oxford: Oxford University Press, 1992.

——. *Thinking It Through: An Introduction to Contemporary Philosophy.* Oxford: Oxford University Press, 2003.

Aristotle. *On the Soul (De Anima).* In *The Complete Works of Aristotle,* ed. Jonathan Barnes. Revised Oxford translation, vol. 1. Princeton, N.J.: Princeton University Press, 1984.

——. *The Politics.* Trans. T. A. Sinclair, revised and re-presented by Trevor J. Saunders. 1962; London: Penguin Books, 1981.

Armah, Ayi Kwei. "African Socialism: Utopian or Scientific?" *Présence Africaine* 64, no. 4 (1967): 6–30.

Aron, Raymond. *Introduction à la philosophie de l'histoire: essai sur les limites de l'objectivité historique.* Paris: Librairie Gallimard, 1948.

Arrington, Robert L. *Western Ethics: An Historical Introduction.* Malden, Mass., and Oxford, UK: Blackwell, 1998.

Atangana, B. "Actualité de la palabre." *Études* 324 (1966): 453–469.

Atieno-Odhiambo, E. S. "A World-View of the Nilotes? The Luo Concept of Piny." In *African Historians and African Voices,* ed. E. S. Atieno Odhiambo, 57–67. Basel: Schlettwein Publishing, 2001.

——, ed. *African Historians and African Voices: Essays Presented to Professor Bethwell Allan Ogot.* Basel, Switzerland: P. Schlettwein Publishing, 2001.

Aquinas, St. Thomas. *Summa Contra Gentiles.* Book 2, *Creation.* Trans. with intro. by James F. Anderson. Notre Dame, Ind.: University of Notre Dame Press, 1975.

Bachelard, Gaston. *The Philosophy of No: A Philosophy of the New Scientific Mind.* New York: Orion Press, 1968.

Bates, Robert H., V. Y. Mudimbe, and Jean O'Barr, eds. *Africa and the Disciplines: The Contributions of Research in Africa to the Social Sciences and Humanities.* Chicago: University of Chicago Press, 1993.

Behrend, Heike. *Alice Lakwena & the Holy Spirits: War in Northern Uganda 1986–97.* Oxford: James Currey, 1999.

Beidelman, T. O. *The Cool Knife: Imagery of Gender, Sexuality, and Moral Education in Kaguru Initiation Ritual.* Washington, D.C.: Smithsonian Institution Press, 1997.

——. *Moral Imagination in Kaguru Modes of Thought.* Washington, D.C. and London: Smithsonian Institution Press, 1993.

Berlin, Isaiah. *The Proper Study of Mankind: An Anthology of Essays.* New York: Farrar, Strauss, and Giroux, 1998.

Bidima, Jean-Godefroy. *L'Art Négro-Africain.* Paris: Presses Universitaires de France, 1997.

——. "Introduction. De la traversée: raconter des expériences, partager le sens." *Rue Descartes* 36 (2002): 7–18. Special edition: Philosophies africaines: traversées des expériences.

——. *La Palabre: Une juridiction de la parole.* Paris: Éditions Michalon, 1997.

——. *La philosophie Négro-Africaine.* Paris: Presses Universitaires de France, 1995.

——. "Philosophy and Literature in Francophone Africa." English trans. Nicolas De Warren. In *A Companion to African Philosophy,* ed. Kwasi Wiredu, 549–559. London and New York: Blackwell, 2004.

———. *Théorie critique et modernité négro-africaine. De l'École de Francfort à la "Docta Spes africana."* Paris: Publications de la Sorbonne, 1993.

Biyogo, Grégoire. *Histoire de la philosophie africaine. Livre II, Introduction à la philosophie moderne et contemporaine.* Paris: L'Harmattan, 2006.

Boxill, Bernard, ed. *Race and Racism.* Oxford: Oxford University Press, 2001.

Brown, S. C., ed. *Philosophical Disputes in the Social Sciences.* Sussex: Harvester Press, 1979.

Changeux, Jean-Pierre, and Paul Ricoeur. *What Makes Us Think? A Neuroscientist and a Philosopher Argue about Ethics, Human Nature, and the Brain.* Trans. M. B. DeBevoise. Princeton, N.J.: Princeton University Press, 2000.

Clark, J. Desmond, J. D. Fage, Roland Oliver, Richard Gray, John E. Flint, G. N. Sanderson, A. D. Roberts, and Michael Crowder, eds. *The Cambridge History of Africa.* 8 vols. Cambridge: Cambridge University Press, 1982–1984.

Clark, J. P. *Max Stirner's Egoism.* London: Free Press, 1976.

Clifford, James. *The Predicament of Culture: Twentieth-Century Ethnography, Literature, and Art.* Cambridge, Mass.: Harvard University Press, 1988.

Clinton, Hillary R. *It Takes a Village and Other Lessons Children Teach Us.* New York: Simon and Schuster, 1995.

Coulson, Andrew, ed. *African Socialism in Practice: The Tanzanian Experience.* Nottingham, UK: Spokesman Publishers, 1979.

Crahay, Franz. "Le 'décollage' conceptuel: conditions d'une philosophie bantoue." *Diogène* 52 (1965): 61–84.

Derrida, Jacques. *Positions.* Trans. Alan Bass. Chicago: University of Chicago Press, 1981.

Devisch, René. "The Cosmology of Life Transmission." In *Things as They Are: New Directions in Phenomenological Anthropology,* ed. Michael Jackson, 94–114. Bloomington: Indiana University Press, 1996.

Diagne, Pathé. *L'Europhilosophie face à la pensée de négro-africaine; suivi de Problématique néo-pharaonique et épistemologie du reel.* Dakar: Sankore, 1981.

Diagne, Suleymane Bachir. Precolonial African Philosophy in Arabic." In *A Companion to African Philosophy,* ed. Kwasi Wiredu, 66–77. New York and Oxford: Blackwell, 2004.

Dieterlen, Germaine. *Les âmes des Dogon.* Paris: Institut d'Ethnologie, XL, 1941.

———. "L'image du corps et les composantes de la personne chez les Dogon." In *La Notion de Personne en Afrique Noire,* ed. Germaine Dieterlen. Paris: Éditions du Centre National de la Recherche Scientifique, 1973.

———, ed. *La Notion de Personne en Afrique Noire.* Paris: Éditions du Centre National de la Recherche Scientifique, 1973.

Driberg, J. H. *The Lango: A Nilotic Tribe of Uganda.* London: T. F. Unwin, 1923.

Eboussi-Boulaga, Fabien. *Christianity without Fetishes: An African Critique and Recapture of Christianity.* 1984; repr., Hamburg: LIT Verlag Münster, 2002.

English, Parker, and Kibujjo M. Kalumba, eds. *African Philosophy: A Classical Approach.* Englewood Cliffs, N.J.: Prentice Hall, 1996.

Ephirim-Donkor, Anthony. *African Spirituality: On Becoming Ancestors.* Trenton, N.J.: Africa World Press, 1997.

Evans-Pritchard, E. E. *Nuer Religion.* Oxford: Oxford University Press, 1956.

———. *Witchcraft, Oracles and Magic among the Azande.* Oxford: Oxford University Press, 1937.

Eze, Emmanuel C. *Achieving Our Humanity: The Idea of the Postracial Future.* New York and London: Routledge, 2001.

———, ed. *Postcolonial African Philosophy: A Critical Reader.* Oxford: Blackwell, 1997.

Fabian, Johannes. *Time and the Other: How Anthropology Makes Its Object.* New York: Columbia University Press, 1983.

Fanon, Frantz. *The Wretched of the Earth.* Trans. Constance Farrington. New York: Grove Press, 1968.

Fortes, Meyer. "On the Concept of the Person among the Tallensi." In *La Notion de Personne en Afrique Noire,* ed. G. Dieterlen, 283–319. Paris: Centre National de la Recherche Scientifique, 1973.

Fløistad, Guttorm, ed. *Contemporary Philosophy, A New Survey.* Vol. 5, *African Philosophy.* Dordrecht: Martinus Nijhoff Publishers, 1986.

Freire, Paulo. *Pedagogy of the Oppressed.* Rev. ed. New York: Continuum, 1993.

Ganay, S. De. *Les Devises des Dogon.* Paris: Institut d'Ethnologie, XLI, 1941.

Gbadegesin, Segun. *African Philosophy: Traditional Yoruba Philosophy and Contemporary African Realities.* New York: Peter Lang, 1991.

Geertz, Clifford. *The Interpretation of Cultures.* New York: Basic Books, 1973.

Gerdes, Paulus. *Awakening of Geometrical Thought in Early Culture.* Minneapolis: Marxist Educational Press, 2003.

———. *Geometry from Africa: Mathematical and Educational Explorations.* Washington, D.C.: The Mathematical Association of America, 1999.

———. *Women, Art and Geometry in Southern Africa.* Trenton, N.J.: Africa World Press, 1998.

Geurts, Kathryn Linn. *Culture and the Senses: Bodily Ways of Knowing in an African Community.* Berkeley: University of California Press, 2002.

Goody, Jack. *The Domestication of the Savage Mind.* London: Cambridge University Press, 1977.

Gordon, Lewis. *An Introduction to Africana Philosophy.* Cambridge: Cambridge University Press, 2008.

Graness, Anke, and Kai Kresse, eds. *Sagacious Reasoning: Henry Odera Oruka in Memoriam.* Frankfurt am Main: Peter Lang, 1997.

Grenier, Louise. *Working with Indigenous Knowledge: A Guide for Researchers.* Ottawa: International Development Research Center, 1998.

Griaule, Marcel. *Conversations with Ogotemmeli: An Introduction to Dogon Religious Ideas.* London: Oxford University Press for the International African Institute, 1965.

———. "Philosophie et religion des noirs." *Présence Africaine,* nos. 8–9 (1950): 307–321.

———. "Rôle du silure *Clarias Senegalensis* dans la procréation au Soudan Français." In Johannes Lukas, *Afrikantische Studien,* 299–311. Berlin: Akademie-Verlag, 1955.

Griaule, Marcel, and G. Dieterlen. *Le Renard Pâle.* Tome I, *Le mythe cosmogonique.* Paris: Institut d'Ethnologie, LXXII, 1965.

Gross, Michael L. *Ethics and Activism: The Theory and Practice of Political Morality.* Cambridge: Cambridge University Press, 1997.

Gyekye, Kwame. *An Essay on African Philosophical Thought: The Akan Conceptual Scheme.* Rev. 2nd ed. Philadelphia: Temple University Press, 1995.

———. "Person and Community in Akan Thought." In *Person and Community: Ghanaian Philosophical Studies I,* ed. Kwasi Wiredu and Kwame Gyekye, 101–122. Washington, D.C.: Council for Research in Values and Philosophy, 1992.

———. *Tradition and Modernity: Philosophical Reflections on the African Experience.* New York: Oxford University Press, 1997.

Habermas, Jürgen. *Knowledge and Human Interests.* Trans. Jeremy J. Shapiro. Boston: Beacon Press, 1971.

———. *Moral Consciousness and Communicative Action.* Trans. Christian Lenhardt and Shierry Weber Nicholsen. Cambridge, Mass.: MIT Press, 1990.

———. *Time of Transitions.* Ed. and trans. Ciaran Cronin and Max Pensky. Cambridge, UK: Polity Press, 2006.

Hallen, Barry. *African Philosophy: The Analytic Approach.* Trenton, N.J., and Asmara: Africa World Press, 2006.

———. "Analytic Philosophy and Traditional Thought: A Critique of Robin Horton." In *African Philosophy: A Classical Approach,* ed. Parker English and K. M. Kalumba. Upper Saddle River, N.J.: Prentice Hall, 1996.

———. *The Good, the Bad, and the Beautiful: Discourse about Values in Yoruba Culture.* Bloomington: Indiana University Press, 2000.

———. *A Short History of African Philosophy.* Bloomington: Indiana University Press, 2002.

Hallen, Barry, and J. O. Sodipo. *Knowledge, Belief, and Witchcraft: Analytic Experiments in African Philosophy.* 2nd ed. 1986; Stanford, Calif.: Stanford University Press, 1997.

Harasayam, S., ed. *The Post-Colonial Critic: Interviews, Strategies, Dialogues.* New York: Routledge, 1990.

Harding, Sandra. "Is Modern Science and Ethnoscience? Rethinking Epistemological Assumptions." In *Postcolonial African Philosophy: A Critical Reader,* ed. Emmanuel C. Eze, 45–70. Oxford, UK: Blackwell, 1997.

———. *The Science Question in Feminism.* Ithaca, N.Y.: Cornell University Press, 1986.

———, ed. *The "Racial" Economy of Science: Toward a Democratic Future.* Bloomington: Indiana University Press, 1993.

Harding, Sandra, and Jean O'Barr. *Sex and Scientific Inquiry.* Chicago: University of Chicago Press, 1987.

Hayley, T. T. S. *Anatomy of Lango Religion and Groups.* Cambridge: Cambridge University Press, 1947.

Hebga, Meinrad. *Émancipation d'Églises sous tutelle: essai sur l'ère post-missionaire.* Paris: Présence Africaine, 1976.

Hegel, G. W. F. *Philosophy of Right.* Trans. T. M. Knox. 1942; Oxford: Clarendon Press, 1967.

Hilliard, Constance B., ed. *Intellectual Traditions of Pre-Colonial Africa.* Boston: McGraw-Hill, 1998.

Hollis, Martin. "The Limits of Irrationality." In *Rationality,* ed. Brian Wilson. Oxford: Basil Blackwell, 1970.

———. "The Social Destruction of Reality." In *Rationality and Relativism,* ed. Martin Hollis and Steven Lukes. Oxford: Basil Blackwell, 1982.

Hollis, Martin, and Steven Lukes, eds. *Rationality and Relativism.* Cambridge, Mass.: MIT Press, 1982.

Horton, Robin. "African Traditional Thought and Western Science." *Africa* 37, nos. 1–2 (1967): 50–71 and 155–187.

———. *Patterns of Thought in Africa and the West: Essays on Magic, Religion, and Science.* Cambridge: Cambridge University Press, 1993.

Hountondji, Paulin J. *African Philosophy: Myth and Reality.* 2nd ed. 1983; Bloomington: Indiana University Press, 1996.

———. *Combats pour le sens: un itineraire africain.* Cotonou: Les Éditions du Flamboyant, 1997.

———. "Occidentalism, Elitism: Answer to Two Critiques." *Quest: An African International Journal of Philosophy* 3, no. 2 (1989): 3–30.

———. "Producing Knowledge in Africa Today." *African Studies Review* 38, no. 3 (1995): 1–10.

———. "Le problème actuel de la philosophie africaine." In *La philosophie contemporaine,* vol. 4, ed. Raymond Klibanski, 613–621. Firenze: La Nuova Italia Editrice, 1971.

———. "Recapturing." In *The Surreptitious Speech: "Présence Africaine" and the Politics of Otherness 1947–1987,* ed. V. Y. Mudimbe, 238–248. Chicago: University of Chicago Press, 1992.

———. "Remarques sur la philosophie africaine contemporaine." *Diogène* 71 (1970): 120–140.

———. *The Struggle for Meaning: Reflections on Philosophy, Culture, and Democracy in Africa.* Trans. John Conteh-Morgan. Athens: Center for International Studies, Ohio University, 2002.

Howell, P. P., and W. P. G. Thomson. "The Death of the Reth of the Shilluk and Installation of His Successor." *Sudan Notes and Records* 27 (1946): 4–85.

Husserl, Edmund. *Briefwechsel.* Band VII, *Wissenschaftslerkorrespondenz.* Dordrecht: Kluwer Academic Publishers, 1994.

———. *The Crisis of European Sciences and Transcendental Phenomenology.* Trans. David Carr. Evanston, Ill.: Northwestern University Press, 1970.

———. *Ideas: General Introduction to Pure Phenomenology.* Trans. W. R. Boyce Gibson. London: George Allen and Unwin, 1931.

———. *Idées Directrices pour une Phénoménologie et une Philosophie Phénoménologique pures.* Tome 1, *Introduction Générale à la Phénoménologie Pure.* Trans. from German by Paul Ricoeur. Paris: Librairie Gallimard, 1950.

———. *La Philosophie comme Science Rigoureuse.* Trans. with intro. by Quentin Laurer. Paris: Presses Universitaires de France, 1955.

Hyden, Goran. *No Shortcuts to Progress: African Development Management in Perspective.* Berkeley: University of California Press, 1983.

Idowu, Bolaji E. *African Traditional Religion: A Definition.* London: SCM Press Ltd., 1973.

Irele, Francis Abiola. *The African Imagination: Literature in Africa and the Black Diaspora.* New York and Oxford: Oxford University Press, 2001.

———. "Introduction." In Paulin J. Hountondji, *African Philosophy: Myth and Reality.* 2nd ed. Bloomington: Indiana University Press, 1996.

———. "Philosophy and the Postcolonial Condition in Africa." *Research in African Literatures* 35, no. 4 (Winter 2004): 160–170.

Jackson, Michael, Charles S. Bird, Luc De Heusch, James Fernandez, Ivan Karp, John Middleton, Victor Turner, and Roy Willis. *Allegories of the Wilderness:*

Ethics and Ambiguity in Kuranko Narratives. Bloomington: Indiana University Press, 1982.

Jackson, Michael, and I. Karp. "Introduction." In *Personhood and Agency: The Experience of Self and Other in African Cultures*, ed. Michael Jackson and I. Karp, 15–30. Uppsala, Sweden: Uppsala University, 1990.

Jackson, Michael, ed. *Things as They Are: New Directions in Phenomenological Anthropology*. Bloomington: Indiana University Press, 1996.

Kant, Immanuel. *Anthropology from a Pragmatic Point of View*. Trans. with intro. and notes by Mary J. Gregor. The Hague: Martinus Nijhoff, 1974.

———. *Grounding for the Metaphysics of Morals*. Trans. James W. Ellington. Indianapolis and Cambridge, UK: Hackett, 1981.

———. *Logic*. Trans. with intro. Robert S. Hartman and Wolfgang Schwarz. Indianapolis and New York: Bobbs-Merrill Co., 1974.

Kaphagawani, Didier. "Some African Conceptions of Person." In *African Philosophy as Cultural Inquiry*, ed. Ivan Karp and D. A. Masolo, 66–79. Bloomington: Indiana University Press, 2000.

Karp, Ivan, and D. A. Masolo, eds. *African Philosophy as Cultural Inquiry*. Bloomington: Indiana University Press, 2000.

Kekes, John. *Against Liberalism*. Ithaca, N.Y.: Cornell University Press, 1997.

Keller, Pierre. *Husserl and Heidegger on Human Experience*. Cambridge, UK: Cambridge University Press, 1999.

Kigunga, Raphael. *Anthropology of Self: Person, Myth in Africa: A Basic Indigenous Education on Human Responsible Behaviour Communication*. Frankfurt am Main and New York: Peter Lang, 1996.

Kiros, Teodros. "Zera Yacob and Traditional Ethiopian Philosophy." In *A Companion to African Philosophy*, ed. Kwasi Wiredu, 183–190. New York and Oxford: Blackwell, 2004.

Kratz, Corinne A. *Affecting Performance: Meaning, Movement, and Experience in Okiek Women's Initiation*. Washington, D.C.: Smithsonian Institution Press, 1994.

Kuhn, Thomas S. *The Structure of Scientific Revolutions*. Chicago: University of Chicago Press, 1962.

Küng, Hans. *Does God Exist? An Answer for Today*. Trans. Edward Quinn. Garden City, N.Y.: Doubleday, 1980.

———. *Infallible? An Inquiry*. Trans. Edward Quinn. Garden City, N.Y.: Doubleday, 1971.

Kwame, Safro, ed. *Readings in African Philosophy: An Akan Collection*. Lanham, Md.: University Press of America, 1995.

Lakoff, George, and Mark Johnson. *Metaphors We Live By*. New York: Basic Books, 1980.

———. *Philosophy in the Flesh: The Embodied Mind and Its Challenge to Western Thought*. Chicago: University of Chicago Press, 1999.

Latour, Bruno. *Laboratory Life: The Social Construction of Scientific Facts*. London: Sage, 1979.

———. *Science in Action: How to Follow Scientists and Engineers through Society*. Cambridge, Mass.: Harvard University Press, 1987.

———. *We Have Never Been Modern*. Cambridge, Mass.: Harvard University Press, 1993.

Lauer, Quentin. "Introduction." In Edmund Husserl, *La Philosophie comme Science Rigoureuse.* Trans. with intro. by Quentin Lauer. Paris: Presses Universitaires de France, 1955.

Lienhardt, Godfrey R. *Divinity and Experience: The Religion of the Dinka.* Oxford: Clarendon Press, 1961.

———. "The Shilluk of the Upper Nile." In *African Worlds,* ed. G. R. Lienhardt. Oxford: Oxford University Press, 1954.

———, ed. *African Worlds.* Oxford: Oxford University Press, 1954.

Lufuluabo, François-Marie. "La conception bantoue face au Christianisme." In *Personnalité Africaine et Catholicisme,* 57–72. Paris: Présence Africaine, 1962.

Lukes, Steven. *Individualism.* New York: Harper & Row, 1973.

MacGregor, Geddes, ed. *Immortality and Human Destiny: A Variety of Views.* New York: Paragon House, 1985.

MacIntyre, Alasdair. *After Virtue: A Study in Moral Theory.* 2nd ed. 1981; Notre Dame, Ind.: University of Notre Dame Press, 1984.

———. *Whose Justice? Which Rationality?* Notre Dame, Ind.: University of Notre Dame Press, 1988.

———, ed. *Hegel: A Collection of Critical Essays.* Garden City, N.Y.: Doubleday & Company Anchor Books, 1972.

Marcus, George, and James Clifford, eds. *Writing Culture: The Poetics and Politics of Ethnography.* Berkeley: University of California Press, 1986.

Marcus, George, and Michael M. J. Fischer. *Anthropology as Cultural Critique.* Chicago: University of Chicago Press, 1986.

Masolo, D. A. "African Philosophy: A Historical Overview." In *A Companion to World Philosophies,* ed. Eliot Deutsch and Ron Bontekoe, 63–77. Malden, Mass.: Blackwell, 1997.

———. *African Philosophy in Search of Identity.* Bloomington: Indiana University Press, 1994.

Maurier, Henri. *Philosophie de l'Afrique noire.* St. Augustin bei Bonn: Anthropos-Institut, 1976.

Marx, Karl. *The Poverty of Philosophy.* In *The Collected Works of Karl Marx and Frederick Engels.* Vol. 6, *Marx and Engels, 1845–48,* 105–212. London: Lawrence and Wishart, 1975. English translation of *La Misère de la philosophie* (1847).

Mbembe, Achille. *On the Postcolony.* Berkeley: University of California Press, 2001.

Mbiti, John S. *African Religions and Philosophy.* London: Heinemann Educational Books, 1969.

Mboya, Tom. "Sessional Paper No. 10--It Is African and It Is Socialism." *East Africa Journal* 6, no. 5 (May 1969): 15–22.

Memmi, Albert. *The Colonizer and the Colonized.* Trans. Howard Greenfeld. Boston: Beacon Press, 1967.

Modood, Tariq. "'Difference,' Cultural Racism, and Anti-Racism." In *Race and Racism,* ed. Bernard Boxill, 238–256. Oxford: Oxford University Press, 2001.

Mohiddin, Ahmed. "Sessional Paper No. 10 Revisited." *East Africa Journal* 6, no. 3 (March 1969): 7–16.

Mudimbe, V. Y. *Les Corps glorieux des mots et des êtres. Esquisse d'un jardin africain à la bénédictine.* Paris/Montréal: Présence Africaine/Humanitas, 1994.

————. *The Idea of Africa.* Bloomington: Indiana University Press, 1994.

————. *The Invention of Africa: Gnosis, Philosophy, and the Order of Knowledge.* Bloomington: Indiana University Press, 1988.

————. *Parables and Fables: Exegesis, Textuality, and Politics in Central Africa.* Madison: University of Wisconsin Press, 1991.

————. *Tales of Faith: Religion as Political Performance in Central Africa.* London: Athlone Press, 1997.

————, ed. *The Surreptitious Speech: Présence Africaine and the Politics of Otherness, 1947–1987.* Chicago and London: University of Chicago Press, 1992.

Mudimbe, V. Y., and Anthony K. Appiah. "The Impact of African Studies on Philosophy." In *Africa and the Disciplines: The Contributions of Research in Africa to the Social Sciences and Humanities,* ed. Robert H. Bates, V. Y. Mudimbe, and Jean O'Barr, 113–138. Chicago: University of Chicago Press, 1993.

Mulago, Vincent. "Christianisme et culture africaine: Apport africain à la Théologie." In *Christianity in Tropical Africa--Studies Presented and Discussed at the Seventh International African Seminar at the University of Ghana, April 1965,* ed. C. G. Baeta, 308–317. London: Oxford University Press, 1968.

————. "Dialectique existentielle des Bantu et sacramentalisme." In *Aspects de la culture noire,* 146–171. Paris: Librairie Arthème Fayard, 1958.

————. "La religion traditionelle, élément central de la culture Bantu." In *Les religions africaines comme source des valeurs de civilisation, Colloque de Cotonou 16–22 August 1970.* Paris: Présence Africaine, 1972.

Mulokozi, Mugyabuso M. "Two Utopias: A Comparative Examination of William Morris's *News from Nowhere* and Shaaban Robert's *Siku ya Watenzi Wote.*" *Umma* 5, no. 2 (1975).

Nietzsche, Friedrich. *Genealogy of Morals.* Trans. Walter Kaufmann and R. J. Hollingdale. New York: Vintage Books, 1967.

Nkrumah, Kwame. *Consciencism: Philosophy and Ideology for Decolonisation and Development with Particular Reference to the African Revolution.* London: Panaf Books, 1970.

Nozick, Robert. *Anarchy, State, and Utopia.* New York: Basic Books, 1974.

Nussbaum, Martha C. "Patriotism and Cosmopolitanism." In *For Love of Country: Debating the Limits of Patriotism,* ed. Joshua Cohen. Boston: Beacon Press, 1996.

Nyerere, Julius K. "Freedom and Development." In *African Socialism in Practice: The Tanzanian Experience,* ed. Andrew Coulson, 27–35. Nottingham, UK: Spokesman Publishers, 1979.

————. "The Rational Choice." In *African Socialism in Practice: The Tanzanian Experience,* ed. Andrew Coulson, 19–26. Nottingham, UK: Spokesman Publishers, 1979.

————. *Ujamaa: The Basis of African Socialism.* London: Oxford University Press, 1968.

————. *Ujamaa: Essays on Socialism.* Dar es Salaam: Oxford University Press, 1968.

Nzegwu, Nkiru U. *Family Matters: Feminist Concepts in African Philosophy of Culture.* Albany: State University of New York Press, 2006.

Obenga, Théophile. "Egypt: Ancient History of African Philosophy." In *A Companion to African Philosophy,* Kwasi Wiredu, 31–49. New York and Oxford: Blackwell, 2004.

————. *La philosophie africaine de la période pharaonique, 2780–330 avant notre ère.* Paris: l'Harmattan, 1990.

Odinga, Oginga. *Not Yet Uhuru: An Autobiography.* New York: Hill and Wang, 1967.

Ogot, Bethwell A. "The Concept of Jok." *African Studies* 20, no. 2 (1961): 123–130.

————. *History of the Southern Luo.* Vol. 1, *Migration and Settlement.* Nairobi: East African Publishing House, 1967.

Ogutu, G. E. M. "The African Perception." In *Immortality and Human Destiny: A Variety of Views,* ed. Geddes MacGregor. New York: Paragon House, 1985.

Onyango-Abuje, John C. *Fire and Vengeance.* Nairobi: East African Publishing House, 1975.

Onyango, Carey-Francis. "A Critical Analysis of Constructive Realism: Towards a Theory of Scientific Theories and their Relations to Physical Entities." Ph.D. diss., University of Vienna, 1999.

Oruka, Henry O. *Sage Philosophy: Indigenous Thinkers and Modern Debate on African Philosophy.* Leiden: J. Brill, 1990.

————. "Sagacity in African Philosophy." *The International Philosophical Quarterly* 23, no. 4 (1983): 383–393.

Parkin, David. "Islam among the Humors: Destiny and Agency among the Swahili." In *African Philosophy as Cultural Inquiry,* ed. Ivan Karp and D. A. Masolo, 50–65. Bloomington: Indiana University Press, 2000.

p'Bitek, Okot. *African Religions in Western Scholarship.* Nairobi: Kenya Literature Bureau, 1970.

————. "The Concept of Jok among the Acholi and Lango." *Uganda Journal* 27, no. 1 (1963): 15–29.

————. "Fr. Tempels' Bantu Philosophy." *Transition* 13 (1964): 15–17.

————. *Religion of the Central Luo.* Nairobi: East African Literature Bureau, 1971.

Quine, W. V. O. *From a Logical Point of View.* 2nd ed. Cambridge, Mass.: Harvard University Press, 1980.

Rettová, Alena. *Afrophone Philosophies: Reality and Challenge.* Zdenek Susa: Středokluky, 2007.

Robert, Shaaban bin. *Koja la Lugha.* Nairobi: Oxford University Press, 1945.

————. *Kusadikika: Nchi Iliyo Angani.* 1951; Nairobi: Evans Brothers Limited, 1966.

————. *Siku ya Watenzi Wote.* Nairobi: Thomas Nelson and Sons, 1968.

————. *Utubora Mkulima.* Nairobi: Evans Brothers Limited, 1968.

Robinson, John A. T. *Honest to God.* Philadelphia, Pa.: Westminster Press, 1963.

Rodney, Walter. *How Europe Underdeveloped Africa.* Washington, D.C.: Howard University Press, 1981.

Rorty, Amelie O. *The Identities of Persons.* Berkeley: University of California Press, 1976.

Russell, Bertrand. *The Problems of Philosophy.* 1912; Indianapolis: Hackett, 1990.

Ryle, Gilbert. *The Concept of Mind.* London: Hutchinson, 1949.

Sandel, Michael J. *Liberalism and the Limits of Justice.* 2nd ed. 1982; Cambridge, UK: Cambridge University Press, 1998.

Senghor, Léopold S. *Liberté.* Tome II, *Nation et voie africaine du socialisme.* Paris: Seuil, 1971.

————. *Liberté*. Tome I, *Négritude et humanisme*. Paris: Seuil, 1964.
————. *On African Socialism*. Trans. with intro. by Mercer Cook. New York: Frederick A. Praeger, 1964.
Serequeberhan, Tsenay. *African Philosophy: The Essential Readings*. New York: Paragon House, 1991.
Shaw, Rosalind. "'Tok Af, Lef Af': A Political Economy of Temne Techniques of Secrecy and Self." In *African Philosophy as Cultural Inquiry,* ed. Ivan Karp and D. A. Masolo, 25–49. Bloomington: Indiana University Press, 2000.
————. "The Invention of 'African Traditional Religion.'" *Religion* 20 (1990): 339–353.
Simmel, Georg. *The Sociology of Georg Simmel*. Trans., ed., and with an intro. by Kurt H. Wolff. New York: Free Press, 1950.
Sinnott-Armstrong, Walter, ed. *Moral Psychology*. Vol. 1, *The Evolution of Morality: Adaptations and Innateness*. Cambridge, Mass., and London: MIT Press, 2008.
————. *Moral Psychology*. Vol. 2, *The Cognitive Science of Morality: Intuition and Diversity*. Cambridge, Mass., and London: MIT Press, 2008.
————. *Moral Psychology*. Vol. 3, *The Neuroscience of Morality: Emotion, Brain Disorders, and Development*. Cambridge, Mass., and London: MIT Press, 2008.
Smith, Linda Tuhiwai. *Decolonizing Methodologies: Research and Indigenous Peoples*. London: Zed Books; Dunedin (New Zealand): University of Otago Press, 1999.
Sogolo, Godwin. *Foundations of African Philosophy: A Definitive Analysis of Conceptual Issues in African Thought*. Ibadan: Ibadan University Press, 1993.
Spivak, Gyatri Chakravorty. *A Critique of Postcolonial Reason: Toward a History of the Vanishing Present*. Cambridge, Mass.: Harvard University Press, 1999.
————. "Questions of Multiculturalism." In *The Post-Colonial Critic: Interviews, Strategies, Dialogues,* ed. S. Harasayam. New York: Routledge, 1990.
Stirner, Max. *The Ego and Its Own*. Trans. S. T. Byington, ed. D. Leopold. Cambridge: Cambridge University Press, 1994.
Sumner, Claude. *Classical Ethiopian Philosophy*. Los Angeles: Adey Publishing Company, 1994.
————. *Ethiopian Philosophy*. Vol. 2, *The Treatise of Zär'a Yæqob and Wäldä Heywât: Text and Authorship*. Addis Ababa: Commercial Printing Press, 1976.
————. *Ethiopian Philosophy*. Vol. 3, *The Treatise of Zär'anYæqob and Wäldä Heywât: An Analysis*. Addis Ababa: Commercial Printing Press, 1978.
————. "The Light and the Shadow: Zera Yacob and Walda Heywat." In *A Companion to African Philosophy,* ed. Kwasi Wiredu, 172–182. New York and Oxford: Blackwell, 2004.
Taiwo, Olufemi. *Legal Naturalism: A Marxist Theory of Law*. Ithaca, N.Y., and London: Cornell University Press, 1996.
Taylor, Charles. *Hegel and Modern Society*. Cambridge: Cambridge University Press, 1979.
————. *Human Agency and Language: Philosophical Papers 1*. Cambridge: Cambridge University Press, 1985.
————. *Philosophy and the Human Sciences: Philosophical Papers 2*. Cambridge, UK: Cambridge University Press, 1985.
————. *Sources of the Self: The Making of the Modern Identity*. Cambridge, Mass.: Harvard University Press, 1989.

Taylor, Richard. *Metaphysics*. 4th ed. Englewood Cliffs, N.J.: Prentice Hall, 1992.
———. "Reality Consists of Matter." In *Classic Philosophical Questions*, 9th ed., ed. James A. Gould, 421–436. Upper Saddle River, N.J.: Prentice Hall, 1998. Originally published as "How to Bury the Mind-Body Problem." *American Philosophical Quarterly* 6 (April 1969): 136–143.

Tempels, Placide. *Bantu Philosophy*. Trans. Colin King. Paris: Présence Africaine, 1959.

Theron, Stephen. *Africa, Philosophy and the Western Tradition: An Essay in Self-Understanding*. Frankfurt am Main: Peter Lang, 1995.

Theuws, Théodore. *Word and World: Luba Thought and Literature*. St. Augustin bei Bonn: Anthropos-Institut, 1983.

Touré, Sékou. *L'Action du Parti Démocratique de Guinée et Lutte pour l'Émanicipation Africaine*. Paris: Présence Africaine, 1959.

———. *L'Expérience Guinéenne et l'Unité Africaine*. Paris: Présence Africaine, 1959.

Towa, Marcien. *Essai sur la problématique philosophique dans l'Afrique actuelle*. Yaoundé: Éditions Clé, 1971.

UNESCO. *General History of Africa*. 8 vols. Paris and London: Heinemann Educational Books, Ltd., 1981–1993.

Verran, Helen. *Science and an African Logic*. Chicago: University of Chicago Press, 2001.

Wallerstein, Immanuel. "The Political Ideology of the P. D. G." *Présence Africaine* 40 (1962): 30–41.

Walzer, Michael. *Spheres of Justice*. New York: Basic Books, 1983.

wa Thiong'o, Ngũgĩ. *Decolonizing the Mind: The Politics of Language in African Literature*. London: James Currey; Nairobi: Heinemann, 1986.

Watson-Verran, Helen, and David Turnbull. "Science and Other Indigenous Knowledge Systems." In *Handbook of Science and Technology Studies*, ed. S. Jasanoff, G. Markle, T. Pinch, and J. Petersen. Thousand Oaks, Calif.: Sage, 1995.

Welbourn, Frederick B., and Bethwell A. Ogot. *A Place to Feel at Home: A Study of Two Independent Churches in Western Kenya*. Nairobi and Oxford: Oxford University Press, 1966.

Wilson, Brian, ed. *Rationality*. Oxford: Basil Blackwell, 1970.

Winch, Peter. "Understanding a Primitive Culture." *American Philosophical Quarterly* 1 (1964): 307–324.

Wingo. *Veil Politics in Liberal Democratic States*. Cambridge: Cambridge University Press, 2003.

Wiredu, Kwasi. "Akan Philosophical Psychology." In *Routledge Encyclopedia of Philosophy*. Vol. 1. London: Routledge, 1998.

———. "Amo's Critique of Descartes' Philosophy of Mind." In *Companion to African Philosophy*, ed. Kwasi Wiredu, 200–206. London and New York: Blackwell, 2004.

———. "The Concept of Mind with Particular Reference to the Language and Thought of the Akans." In *Contemporary Philosophy: A New Survey*. Vol. 5, *African Philosophy*, ed. Fløistad Guttorm, 153–179. Dordrecht: Martinus Nijhoff, 1987.

———. *Cultural Universals and Particulars: An African Perspective*. Bloomington: Indiana University Press, 1996.

————. "Death and the Afterlife in African Culture." In *Person and Community: Ghanaian Philosophical Studies I,* ed. Kwasi Wiredu and Kwame Gyekye, 137–152. Washington, D.C.: The Council for Research in Values and Philosophy, 1992.

————. "Metaphysics in Africa." In *Companion to Metaphysics,* ed. Kim Jaegwon and Ernest Sosa, 312–315. London: Blackwell, 1995.

————. "The Moral Foundations of an African Culture." In *Person and Community: Ghanaian Philosophical Studies I,* ed. Kwasi Wiredu and Kwame Gyekye, 193–206. Washington, D.C.: The Council for Research in Values and Philosophy, 1992.

————. "Morality and Religion in Akan Thought." In *Philosophy and Cultures,* ed. Henry O. Oruka and D. A. Masolo, 6–13. Nairobi: Bookwise Publishers, 1983.

————. "Our Problem of Knowledge: Brief Reflections on Knowledge and Development in Africa." In *African Philosophy as Cultural Inquiry,* ed. Ivan Karp and D. A. Masolo, 181–186. Bloomington: Indiana University Press, 2000.

————. *Philosophy and an African Culture.* Cambridge, UK: Cambridge University Press, 1980.

————. "Truth and the Akan Language." In *Readings in African Philosophy: An Akan Collection,* ed. Safro Kwame. Lanham, Md.: University Press of America, 1995.

Wiredu, Kwasi, and K. Gyekye, eds. *Person and Community: Ghanaian Philosophical Studies I.* Washington, D.C.: The Council for Research in Values and Philosophy, 1992.

Wittgenstein, Ludwig. *Philosophical Investigations.* Ed. G. E. M. Anscombe and R. Rhees, trans. G. E. M. Anscombe. Oxford: Blackwell, 1953.

————. *Tractatus Logico-Philosophicus.* Trans. D. F. Pears and B. F. McGuinness. 1922; Atlantic Highlands, N.J.: Humanities Press International, 1962.

Wright, Richard. *African Philosophy: An Introduction.* 3rd ed. Lanham, Md.: University Press of America, 1984.

Yaï, Olabiyi Babalola. "Théorie et pratique en philosophie africaine: Misère de la philosophie spéculative (critique de P. Hountondji, M. Towa, et autres)." *Présence Africaine* no. 108 (1978): 65–89.

Index

abortion, 119, 287n19
absolutism, 237
abstraction: and consciousness,
   278n36; and ethnophilosophy, 18,
   26, 33, 271n3
academic marketplace, and African
   philosophy, 1, 4, 5–6, 15
Achebe, Chinua, 40, 41, 55, 83, 96–97,
   100, 102, 154
Acholi cosmology, 37, 38, 40, 190–93,
   198, 215–18
adili (righteousness), 97, 98, 285n121
Adotevi, Stanislas, 84–85, 233, 277n19
aesthetics, and indigenous languages, 37
Africa: independence and autonomy
   of, 4, 7, 22, 230, 232, 246, 268n9;
   perceptions of, 270n1; postindependence political governance of,
   10, 83; representations of, 24, 185,
   186; Western domination of, 7
African knowledge: critical discussions
   of, 270n1; and cultural inquiry,
   131; as dependent, 3, 60; and emotion, 78, 95; European conceptions
   of, 18, 83; Hountondji on, 53,
   56–57, 79; as indigenous knowledge, 51–52; in integration with
   other knowledge systems, 79, 80;
   misrepresentation of, 36; philosophy distinguished from, 54–55;
   production of, 23, 56, 78, 83; and
   rationality debate, 272–73n17,
   274n42; and science, 78. *See also*
   indigenous knowledge

African nations: boundaries of, 39–40;
   and communitarianism, 230, 233;
   and Marxism, 231, 307n24; political
   model for, 105, 233; poverty in, 63
African oral traditions: ambiguity in,
   182; Hountondji on, 59, 74, 79, 81;
   Irele on, 267n5; oral versus scribed
   knowledge, 27, 60; and personhood,
   182–83; and Senghor, 78–79; styles
   of, 28. *See also* orality
African philosophy: autonomy of,
   277n19; and Catholicism, 3–4; collective cultural beliefs as, 54–55;
   and colonialism, 185; and communalism, 140; and communitarianism, ❧
   229–35; contribution to changing
   world, 60, 76; cultural integration
   of, 3; and differentiated schools of
   thought, 21–22; and dualism, 141,
   150, 151; in French language, 2,
   6, 7–8, 58, 267n4, 276n16; history
   of, 4–6, 7, 14–15; and immortality,
   171; and indigeneity, 21–22; and
   indigenous languages, 39, 44–49;
   and indigenous sages, 49–50; and
   individual rights, 118, 119; and
   knowledge, 157; and meaning, 164;
   and mind, 144, 161; and personhood, 135, 139, 141–43, 149, 150,
   155, 158, 159–60, 169; themes of,
   1, 4–5, 6, 7, 140; translation of, 44;
   and truth, 174; and universality of
   disciplines, 20; and Western philosophy, 1–2, 6–7, 9, 134, 275n54

327

African religious beliefs and practices: and African ethnotheology, 151, 186, 234–35; and African socialism, 233; B. A. Ogot on, 187–88; and colonialism, 186, 187; and communitarianism, 234–35, 249; lack of proselytizing in, 40; and liberalism, 124–25; and missionaries, 36–37, 38, 53, 127, 187, 190, 191–92, 193, 196, 197–98, 212, 270n1, 289n33, 303n26; Western misrepresentations of, 36–37, 187, 190, 270n1; and Yoruba deities, 183

African socialism, 84, 85, 230, 231, 233, 235–40, 249, 281–82n77

African way of knowing, 2

African-American philosophy, 3

Africanism, 78

Afrocentrism, 56

agency: and African philosophy, 155; and ceremonial events, 116–17; and communitarianism, 226–27, 228; and consent versus want, 108, 117, 118, 286n8; and Dholuo language, 202–203; and good life, 285n3; and individual rights, 106; and mind, 74; and postcolonial discourse, 84, 279–80n51; and selfhood, 279–80n51

agriculture, 64–65, 78

ajuoga, 206, 207, 209–10, 216, 218, 220

Akan language: and African philosophy, 44, 292n13; and immortality, 169, 170; and mind, 152, 162, 165–66, 167, 170, 244, 297n67; and personhood, 141, 150–51, 156, 164, 168, 170, 250; and truth, 161, 181

Akoko, Paul Mbuya, 238–39

Allen, Brian, 19–20

Alston, William, 295n54

Althusser, Louis, 60, 61, 77, 283n106

altruism, 246, 247, 248, 251

ambitions, 62–63

Amin, Samir, 25, 60, 65, 233

Amo, Anton Wilhelm, 5, 291n5

Anglo-American tradition: and African philosophy, 1–2; and epistemology, 45–46; and everyday beliefs, 31;

and exegesis, 141; and individualism, 227–28; and knowledge, 48, 49, 157; and meaning, 162; and mind, 76, 281n71; and science, 279n48

Anlo-Ewe people, 149, 284n115

Annan, Kofi, 102

Anselm, Saint, 292n17

anthropological scholarship: and balance of power, 113; and colonialism, 186, 187; and Husserl, 85–86, 88, 90, 282n84; and indigenous knowledge, 18, 24, 26; and *juok*, 188, 191; and perceptions of Africa, 185; and personhood, 135, 182, 184, 208; and philosophy, 136, 137–38; and schemes and regulations, 116

antirealism, and realism, 23–24

Anyumba, Owuor, 192, 193, 198

Appiah, Joe, 106, 285n5

Appiah, Kwame A.: and African philosophy, 1, 2; on African religious beliefs, 270n1; and changes in moral wisdom, 102; and conflicts between communal demands and individual choices, 35; on contrasting African thought to Western thought, 40; and cosmopolitanism, 123, 288nn26,27; and custom, 10; and ethnophilosophy, 277n19; and everyday beliefs, 50; and historical consciousness, 103; and impact of tradition, 102–103, 104; and individual rights, 104, 118, 119, 123; and liberalism, 123; and mind, 3; on personhood, 41; and rationality debate, 26; and relationality, 295n53; on rituals, 219–20; on translation, 42

Aquinas, Thomas, 169, 213, 292n17

Aristotle: on altruism, 246; and communitarianism, 14; on immortality, 169; and metaphysics, 54, 292n17; and personhood, 151, 155; and potentiality to actuality, 138, 291n6

Armah, Ayi Kwei, 233

Aron, Raymond, 5

149, 150, 183–84, 280n53; and philosophy, 140–41, 292n13; and Wiredu, 157, 169; and Wittgenstein, 274n36

politics: and anonymous community, 83; changes in, 131; and colonial domination, 38; and communitarianism, 230, 236, 245, 247, 249, 266; and custom, 130; and independent African nations, 105, 233; and indigeneity, 22; and indigenous knowledge, 62; and individual rights, 132, 290n39; and individualism, 228; and liberalism, 108; and missionaries, 125; and oppression, 118; and perceptions of Africa, 185; and *piny*, 194; and populism, 57, 84; and socialism, 62, 84, 85, 230, 231, 233, 235–40, 249, 281–82n77

polygamy, 108, 115, 133, 286n7
polygyny, 82, 286n7

postcolonial discourse: and agency, 84, 279–80n51; and Appiah, 103; and decolonized mind, 38, 185; and forced dependency syndrome, 25; and indigeneity in African philosophy, 21–22; and indigenous knowledge, 36; and knowledge construction, 24; and language, 40; and mind, 74–75, 279–80n51; and traditional versus modern, 27

postmodernity, 103
Praeg, Leonhard, 4–5, 268n9
primitive mentality, 56, 85–87, 90, 91, 96
primitivism, 18, 58, 187, 196
Procesi, Lidia, 3, 268n7
process theology, 292n17
Protagoras, 159
Proudhon, Pierre-Joseph, 56
psychologism, 67
psychology, 86, 90, 93, 136, 138–39, 144
public health, 133

Quine, W. V. O.: and indigenous knowledge, 44, 49; and meaning, 28–29, 297n65; and naturalized epistemology, 284n115; and translation, 30–31, 37, 45, 46; and truth, 273n23

racism, 91, 123–24
rationalism, 77, 78, 85
rationality debate, 26, 272–73n17, 274n42, 309n47
Rawls, John, 14, 228, 229
realism: and antirealism, 23–24; of everyday beliefs, 33
reality: conceptual representation of, 69, 278n36; and Hountondji, 66–67, 69; Husserl on, 69–70; and theory, 17–20; Wiredu on, 141–42
reason: and communalism, 50; and communitarianism, 238, 265–66; and disputation, 128; and Heidegger, 58; and Husserl, 72; and individual rights, 134; and liberalism, 105, 119, 120–21; and moral judgments, 12, 35, 106, 255, 261, 262, 263, 265; and physicalism, 147, 148; and Robert, 98, 101; and science, 77–78; and Senghor, 92; and values, 82, 84; and Western philosophy, 147
reductionism, 147, 155
reference, theory of, 28–29
relativism, 24, 165, 177, 178, 179, 180
Ricoeur, Paul, 2–3, 32, 76, 136
rituals: Appiah on, 219–20; and children, 108, 130; and gender, 108–109; pain associated with, 108, 130, 154; participants in, 221; and personhood, 242–43; and values, 244, 249, 251, 256–60
Robert, Shaaban bin, 97–101, 102, 104, 162, 261, 285n121, 310n54
Rodney, Walter, 272n14
Rome Conference of the European Society of Culture and the African Society of Culture, 91
Rousseau, Jean-Jacques, 223, 228, 229, 246, 281n77, 291n8
Russell, Bertrand, 7, 8, 214, 273n23
Ryle, Gilbert, 167–68, 291n5

D. A. Masolo is Professor of Philosophy and Justus Bier Professor of Humanities at the University of Louisville. He is author of *African Philosophy in Search of Identity* (Indiana University Press, 1994) and editor (with Ivan Karp) of *African Philosophy as Cultural Inquiry* (Indiana University Press, 2000).